THE PASSOVER HAGGADAH

הגדה של פסח

THE PASSOVER
HAGGADAH
הגדה של פסח

With Commentary from the Classic Commentators,
Midrash, Kabbalah, the Chasidic Masters and the
Haggadah of the Lubavitcher Rebbe

Compiled by
Rabbi Yosef Marcus

KEHOT PUBLICATION SOCIETY
770 Eastern Parkway, Brooklyn, New York 11213

THE PASSOVER
HAGGADAH

Published and Copyrighted © 2011

Third Printing 2020

by

KEHOT PUBLICATION SOCIETY

770 Eastern Parkway / Brooklyn, New York 11213

(718) 774-4000 / Fax (718) 774-2718

editor@kehot.com

Orders:

291 Kingston Avenue / Brooklyn, New York 11213

(718) 778-0226 / Fax (718) 778-4148

www.kehot.com

3 5 7 9 11 12 10 8 6 4

Design and Layout: Spotlight - Brooklyn, NY

Library of Congress Record available at:
https://lccn.loc.gov/2012550958

ISBN: 978-0-8266-0139-1

Printed in China

～ CONTENTS ～

PREFACE

With gratitude to the Almighty we present this new edition of *Haggadah shel Pesach*—The Passover Haggadah—with a new commentary anthologized from the works of the classic commentators, Midrash, and the Chabad Rebbes.

The anthology was compiled by Rabbi Yosef Marcus. The translation of the Haggadah in this edition is based on Rabbi Jacob Immanuel Schochet's translation (published in *Haggadah for Pesach with An Anthology of Reasons and Customs* (Kehot, 1984; revised ed. 2003)), and was in some instances modified by Rabbi Marcus.

The project was initiated and directed by Rabbi Yosef B. Friedman. Special thanks are due to Rabbis Dovid Olidort, Avraham D. Vaisfiche, Yirmiya Berkowitz and Mendel Laine.

Kehot Publication Society
10 Shevat, 5771

IMPORTANT NOTE:

As this book is a translation of the Haggadah's Hebrew text, it generally flows right to left, in the direction of Hebrew writing. In consideration of the English reader, however, the Haggadah's commentary, in any given two-page spread, runs from the left-side page to the right-side page. To make this more obvious, we have added "a" and "b" to the page numbers: the left side of the spread is 24a, for example, and the right side is 24b.

The introduction and appendices to the Haggadah, however, flow right to left and are numbered accordingly.

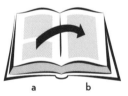

a   b

Haggadah Spreads

INTRODUCTION

The Haggadah, like all of Torah, is comprised of both body and soul. Every mitzvah or Torah verse contains multiple levels of meaning. For example, the significance of eating matzah on Pesach can be explained in various ways. From the perspective of the "body" of Torah, eating matzah is a psychological exercise that causes us to remember and internalize the faith lessons of the Exodus. But the "soul" of Torah offers a deeper perspective; namely, that the very ingestion of matzah as a mitzvah has the mystical effect of strengthening our faith in God.[1]

Like *mitzvot*, the Torah text also comprises multiple layers. For example, the Haggadah cites a verse regarding Abraham's having resided on "the other side of the river." Read simply, on what is known as the *peshat* (plain or simple) level of interpretation, this refers to Abraham's geographic origins. Delving deeper, however, we learn from the Midrash that the verse is also alluding to Abraham's *aloneness* in serving God—the rest of civilization was on one side serving idols, while Abraham was on "the other side," serving God. Delving even deeper, the *Zohar* reveals that the phrase alludes to the spiritual origins of Abraham's *soul* in the heavenly realms.[2]

The present commentary explores the body and soul of the Haggadah, the *peshat* and the *remez*, the "legal" and the "mystical."

৪ THE SIMPLE CHILD ৪

Like the four types of children mentioned in the Haggadah, there are several types of Haggadah readers. In composing the present translation and commentary, we had in mind a broad spectrum of readers. There is the "simple" child, for example, who may lack the knowledge to ask detailed and complex questions but is blessed with the gift of curiosity.[3]

When the simple child reads in the Haggadah that firstborn *animals* died during the last plague, he or she wonders why. When reading that the king of Egypt died and the Jewish people called out to God, the curious child wants to know how one event led to the other. When a verse is cited in the Haggadah, the curious reader wonders about the original context of the verse. What is

---

1. See below, p. 74b.
2. See below, p. 44b.
3. See below, p. 42b, "Too Smart for Questions."

the context and background, for example, of the verse *blood, fire and pillars of smoke*, or *his sword outstretched over Jerusalem*? A phrase like "Covenant between the Parts" may not intrigue the "wise" child; the curious child wants to know what the covenant was and what "between the parts" means.

Our approach, therefore, was not only to provide a collection of interesting commentaries. ***We sought first and foremost to read the Haggadah through the eyes of a curious reader, and to consistently anticipate and answer questions that may arise.*** The rituals of the Seder are also addressed first and foremost from the curious child's point of view. Why do we eat less than an ounce of the *karpas*? Why do we move the Seder Plate aside before reciting the Mah Nishtanah? Why do we eat two portions of matzah instead of one? Such questions are addressed consistently throughout the Haggadah.

The first goal of the commentary, then, is to provide a firm grounding in the *basic meaning* of the Haggadah and its rituals, the *body* of the Haggadah, to enable the reader to answer the simple question: "What is this?"

Yet, as mentioned, the Haggadah contains an inner dimension as well, which speaks, perhaps more loudly, to our inner dimension, to our souls. The commentary therefore includes teachings from the *soul* of Torah, providing insight into the inner significance of the exile and the Exodus as well as the mystical implications of the rituals and the customs.

The commentary is divided into several general sections:

❧ TRANSLATION AND INTERPOLATION ❧

Following, to some degree, the style of the Kehot commentary employed in the Kehot edition of *The Torah*, the translation itself includes parenthetical insertions, in a smaller font size, that help provide context as well as explain obscure or puzzling phrases.[4] This style enables one to read through and understand the Haggadah without having to look back and forth from the text to the commentary to decipher the simple meaning of the text.

The translation itself is a modified version of Rabbi Jacob Immanuel Schochet's original translation.

❧ NOTES & INSIGHTS ❧

The shaded area, called *Notes & Insights*, provides greater elaboration at times on the abovementioned interpolations, as well as providing additional commentary from the classic commentators on issues in the text about which one may "not know to ask."

Notes & Insights also includes halachic analysis of the *mitzvot* and customs

---

4. Unless otherwise noted by a note, these interpolations are based on the commentary in the *The Rebbe's Haggadah*, which include the Rebbe's original insights as well as earlier commentaries that the Rebbe cites. Where the Rebbe does not address a particular issue, we have cited from the classic commentators. Where feasible, we have inserted the Rebbe's commentary even where no particular question seems apparent.

of the Seder, particularly Chabad custom, as well as the history and structure of the Haggadah and its rituals, as explained below.[5]

In addition, *Notes & Insights* provides additional laws, primarily drawn from *Shulchan Aruch HaRav*, the Code of Jewish Law compiled by the founder of the Chabad Movement, Rabbi Schneur Zalman of Liadi. For example, in the case of matzah, the central item of the Seder, the commentary includes several pages of laws regarding such issues as the type of matzah which can be used for the Seder, the definition of "*shemurah*" matzah, and so on.

It should be noted that the sources provided are not always the *original* source for the given teaching. For example, we have at times referred to the *Shulchan Aruch HaRav* as the source for a given teaching—even when the teaching can be found in earlier sources—because of the authoritative and decisive status of the *Shulchan Aruch HaRav*, especially among Chabad Chasidim.

৪ HISTORY AND SOURCES ৪৪

While matzah and *maror* are commanded in the Torah (though the *maror* obligation today is Rabbinic), other rituals are first cited in the Mishnah, while others, such as setting out a cup of Elijah, are of much later origin. The reader is provided a review of these issues in the *Notes & Insights*.

Notes & Insights also provides the "history" or sources of the various sections of the Haggadah, whether a given section is referred to in the Mishnah or is a later addition of the Talmud, or of a later period. *Notes & Insights* also includes explanations and sources for the unique version of the Chabad Haggadah, such as the order of the Four Questions or the insertion of an entire verse that does not appear in most other *Haggadot*.[6]

The non-shaded area comprises three types of commentary, identified by three icons:

৪ MIDRASH ৪৪

As its name suggests, this section contains "Midrashic" or "Aggadaic" material, which in contrast to *peshat* commentary, reveals deeper layers within Torah, a reading between the lines of sorts. This material also includes stories about the exile and the Exodus, which provide a "behind the scenes" look and greater insight into the experience of our ancestors and their relationship with God.

While much of this section is derived from the books known as Midrash (such as *Midrash Rabbah* and *Midrash Tanchuma*), it also includes commentary from later commentators, such as *Ritva*, or *Abarbanel*, when the latter appear to be giving a Midrashic interpretation.

---

5. In these contexts, *Notes & Insights*, which is generally *peshat*-oriented, also provides non-*peshat* commentary.

6. See page 51a.

Studying the Aggadaic portion of Torah has a particularly profound spiritual effect on a person, as our Sages taught on the verse (Deuteronomy 10:20) *You shall fear God…and* cleave *to Him*:

> *If you wish to know the One who spoke and the world came into being—study Aggadah. You will thereby come to know the Holy One blessed is He and cleave to His ways.* —SIFREI, EIKEV §49
>
> *Most secrets of the Torah, i.e., the wisdom of Kabbalah and knowledge of God, are hidden in the Aggadot.*[7] —RABBI SCHNEUR ZALMAN OF LIADI, CITING ARIZAL

☙ CHASIDUS ❧

The goal of the Seder is not merely to *remember* the past but to *relive* it and thereby influence our *present*. The Seder experience should change us, influencing our behavior long after the Seder night. Hence the Chasidus section. Chasidus, like Midrash, is part of the inner dimension of Torah, the *soul* of Torah. The Chasidic teachings on the Haggadah illuminate the inner, spiritual dynamics of the Exodus and its eternal relevance. They help us derive practical lessons from the Haggadah text that can be applied to our daily lives, in bettering our character, becoming more aware of our Godly soul, and drawing closer to God through study of Torah and performance of *mitzvot*.

This section, which makes up the bulk of the commentary, contains the teachings of Chabad Chasidus. Most of the material is derived from the teachings of the Lubavitcher Rebbe, Rabbi Menachem M. Schneerson, of blessed memory, but includes teachings of all the Chabad Rebbes, as well as Rabbi Yisrael Baal Shem Tov and Rabbi DovBer of Mezritch. Special thanks are due to Rabbi Avraham D. Vaisfiche of Kehot for providing an anthology of Rabbi Yosef Yitzchak's commentaries on the Haggadah.

☙ KABBALAH ❧

This section derives primarily from Chabad Chasidus as well; however, it includes material that is more abstract. This section also includes teachings from Kabbalistic works, such as the *Zohar*, the writings of the *Arizal*, and *Shaloh*.

While perhaps most suitable for a reader with some background in Jewish mysticism, the "Kabbalah" section provides all readers a glimpse into the more esoteric dimension of Torah. **Most of this material, as well as much of the Chasidus section, appear here in English for the first time.**

---

7. *Igeret Hakodesh*, ch. 23. See also Rabbi Schneur Zalman's *Hilchot Talmud Torah* 2:2.

❧ THE REBBE'S HAGGADAH ☙

The *Notes & Insights* section is derived primarily from the the Rebbe's commentary on the Haggadah, entitled *Likkutei Taamim U'Minhagim* (Anthology of Reasons and Customs), which we refer to as *The Rebbe's Haggadah*. This relatively concise Haggadah was first published in 5706 (1946), during the lifetime of the Rebbe's predecessor and father-in-law, Rabbi Yosef Yitzchak Schneersohn, and was hailed by the Torah scholars of the time for its brilliance, originality and ability to say much in few words.[8]

We have sought to convey and preserve the flavor of the Rebbe's meticulous analysis and his methodical review of the major opinions on a given subject. We did so by citing whole pieces of the commentary, including the exhaustive sources the Rebbe provides. **Many of these passages appear here in English for the first time.**

The Rebbe's commentary deals primarily with halachic issues, customs, and *peshat*. The Rebbe cites the primary sources and reasons for each of the rituals and customs, at times providing his own original explanation for a given custom.

The Rebbe addresses *peshat* issues by citing various earlier commentators, including *Shibolei Haleket*, *Abarbanel*, *Maharal*, *Chida*, *Chatam Sofer*, and others. At times the Rebbe provides his own original interpretation. The Rebbe also cites several Chasidic teachings, primarily from the talks of Rabbi Yosef Yitzchak.

❧ FOLLOWING THE LEADS ☙

The Rebbe paints a "full picture" in his review of a given subject, and provides sources for further study, both in halachic matters as well as mystical subjects. For example, in discussing the poem *Kadesh Urechatz*, the Rebbe first provides a review of the various opinions of where this poem originates and sources for several alternative poems, then points out that the Kabbalistic works follow what is now the standard version of the poem, then concludes the review by providing two sources for homiletic readings of the poem, namely in the commentaries of *Alshich* and *Chida*.

In the present commentary, we have taken some of these leads provided by the Rebbe and cited the relevant sources either in full or in brief. Thus, the entire *Kadesh Urechatz* is explained according to the interpretations of *Alshich* and *Chida*.

Similarly, in the passage "This is the Bread of Affliction," the Rebbe mentions that the *Shaloh* explains why the passage was composed in Aramaic according to Kabbalah. Taking this lead, we have provided the *Shaloh*'s explanation.

❧ ADDITIONAL PESHAT COMMENTARY ☙

As mentioned above, our first concern was to anticipate and address questions that would occur to the curious reader. Many such questions are

---

8. See, for example, Rabbi Shlomo Yosef Zevin (editor of the *Encyclopedia Talmudit*) in his *Sofrim U'Sefarim*.

addressed in the Rebbe's commentary and we have cited the Rebbe's explanations or those of the commentators he cites.

Where the Rebbe does not address such questions, we have provided commentary from the classic sources, including at times from the Rebbe's own works, such as *Likkutei Sichot*. In addition, we have added other *peshat* commentary from the classic commentators.

❧ EQUALITY ☙

A unique feature of the present edition is the attempt to address each passage individually and equally. Graphically, each passage, with few exceptions, is given its own two-page spread. The passage begins and ends on the same spread. Similarly, the commentary on any given spread addresses the Haggadah text of that spread. There is no commentary "overflow" from one spread to another.

The reader can thus read a passage in its entirety, have a read or glance at the commentary, then move on to a new spread, a new passage, and new commentary.

∾ ℃

❧ DEED, NOT MIDRASH, IS PRIMARY ☙

The night of the Seder is one of great opportunity. The great Divine revelation that occurred in Egypt and enabled our Exodus reoccurs each year. By adhering to the sacred rituals of the Seder and reading the Haggadah we make ourselves receptive to absorbing that revelation.

The importance of deed in Judaism is well known. One who meditates all night on the concept of matzah but fails to actually *eat* matzah has of course failed to perform the mitzvah.[9] The reader is therefore strongly encouraged to read the section "Terms and Measurements for the Seder" on page 11, which provide the technical yet essential details of how to perform the *mitzvot* of the Seder night in the proper way (see "Every Detail," page 24b below).

While study and understanding is of course important, the latter pale in comparison to the importance of the deed and the proper performance thereof (see beginning of the story on page 79a below.).

It is our hope that this edition of the Haggadah will enhance the Seder experience of its readers and help them internalize the message of Pesach so that its impact is felt throughout the year. And may we very soon open the door to welcome Elijah the Prophet, who will herald the future redemption, when the process that was begun with our Exodus from Egypt over 3300 years ago will finally come to its ultimate fruition.

Rabbi Yosef Marcus
S. Mateo, CA

---

9. See *Chida* on "What does the wicked one say."

ELEMENTS OF THE SEDER

The basic elements of the Seder, such as the matzah, *maror, afikoman*, and so on, are addressed at length in the commentary on the Haggadah. Two salient aspects of the Seder that could not be elaborated upon in the Haggadah because of space restrictions are presented here: the significance of the Four Cups and the halachic aspects of *Maggid*, the mitzvah of retelling the story of the Exodus on the night of the Seder.

❧ THE MITZVAH TO REMEMBER THE EXODUS ❧

What is the difference between our obligation tonight and our *daily* obligation to remember the Exodus? The Rebbe cites the following differences:

REMEMBERING THE EXODUS DAILY	THE UNIQUE PESACH OBLIGATION
Biblically, mental remembrance is sufficient	Must be verbalized as in the verse, **Tell** your child
Brief mention is sufficient	Must be told as a story (according to some)
Can be fulfilled alone	Must be told as an answer to another's question (according to some)
Not counted as one of the 248 positive *Mitzvot*	Counted as one of the 248 positive *Mitzvot* (according to most authorities)
Not applicable in the Messianic Age according to Ben Zoma	Applicable in the Messianic Age
Once mentioned, there is no mitzvah to repeat it.	The Mitzvah extends throughout the night (or until midnight according to R. Elazar ben Azariah), even after one has already told the story.

❧ THE FOUR CUPS ❧

The mitzvah to drink Four Cups during the Seder was mandated by the Sages. Usually, we recite a blessing over Rabbinic *mitzvot*—such as *Blessed are you God…who has…commanded us to kindle the Chanukah light.* One of the reasons why we do not recite a blessing thanking God for the mitzvah of the Four Cups is that we only recite a blessing over a mitzvah that is completed without interruption (*Kol Bo; Rokeach*).

The four cups commemorate many things. The following are cited in *The Rebbe's Haggadah*:

Four Expressions of Redemption:

In His promise to redeem Israel, God used "four expressions of redemption" (Exodus 6:6-7), corresponding to the four decrees Pharaoh imposed upon Israel (*Shemot Rabbah* 6:4):

First decree: Pharaoh instructed his taskmasters to overwhelm the Israelites with work and make them sleep at the work sites. He hoped to thereby prevent them from procreating.

Second decree: When Pharaoh saw that his plan had failed and that the Israelites were multiplying in even greater number (the women came out to the fields to be with their husbands), he commanded the midwives to kill the newborn males.

Third decree: When this plan failed, Pharaoh commanded his servants to drown the newborn males in the Nile.

Fourth decree: He increased their workload by making them collect their own straw.

Four Stages of Redemption:

The four expressions also allude to the four stages of redemption, each of which is worthy of celebration over a cup of wine. The following are the four expressions and the stages they represent (*Kol Bo*):

"Therefore say to the children of Israel, 'I am G-d, and—

1. I **will take you out** *from under the burdens of Egypt [i.e., from the* **harsh labor]**

2. I **will save you** *from their labor [i.e.,* **any** *labor or subjugation at all]*

3. I **will redeem you** *with an outstretched arm and with great judgments [i.e., your taskmasters will be punished]....*

4. I **will take you** *to Me as a people [at Sinai]...."*

Kabbalistically, the four expressions correspond to the four aspects of *kelipah*—Divine concealment—that Israel had been subservient to in Egypt. In the process of redeeming Israel, God shattered these "four *kelipot*"[10] (*Tola'at Yaakov*).

In addition to its connection to the four *expressions*, the four cups also correspond to the following:

---

10. *Kelipah* literally means a "shell" and refers to anything that conceals Divinity, as a shell conceals a fruit. The four *kelipot* are comprised of: 1) the irredeemable "three impure *kelipot*," which give energy to forbidden things, and 2) *kelipat nogah*, which gives energy to permitted things that can either be elevated or degraded. These four realms of evil are all alluded to in the vision of Ezekiel: *I saw, and behold, there was* (1) *a* **stormy wind** *coming from the north*, (2) *a* **great cloud**, (3) *a* **flashing fire**, *and* (4) *a* **luminescence** *surrounding it..."* (Ezekiel 1:4).

Four Cups of the Dream

The four references to the cup of Pharaoh in the dream of the butler (Genesis 40:11-13), a dream that, as our sages tell us, alludes to the redemption of Israel (see *Bereishit Rabbah* 88:5).

The Four Empires that Subjugated Israel

1. Babylon   2. Media   3. Greece   4. Rome

Cups of Retribution

The four cups of retribution that God will one day give to the nations who persecuted Israel. At that time, He will also give Israel four cups of comfort:

Four Cups of Comfort

1. *G-d is my…portion and my **cup**…* (Psalms 16:5)

2. *…you anointed my head with oil, my **cup** overflows* (Psalms 23:5)

3. 4. *I shall raise a **cup** of salvations…* (Psalms 116:13). Since "salvations" is stated in the plural it alludes to *two* cups (Jerusalem Talmud, *Pesachim* 10:1).

Kabbalistically, the four cups represent the four letters of God's Name Y-H-V-H (*Siddur Shaloh*):

1. **Yud** — י   2. **Hey** — ה   3. **Vav** — ו   4. **Hey** — ה

৪৪ WOMEN AND THE FOUR CUPS ৪৪

Women are generally exempt from time-related obligations, such as *tefillin* and *tzitzit*. This qualification applies only to active obligations, not to prohibitions. The prohibition of *chametz* thus applies equally to men and women.

In some cases, the Torah does obligate women in time-related obligations, such as in the *mitzvot* of matzah and Kiddush.

What about the Four Cups? The Talmud teaches that women are obligated to drink the Four Cups, since "they also were a part of the miracle" of the Exodus (*Pesachim* 108a-b).

"They Also"

The Talmud uses the same expression—"they also were a part of the miracle"—to explain why women are obligated to observe the *mitzvot* of Purim and Chanukah. According to *Rashbam*, this phrase means that women *played a primary role* in the miracle. During Purim and Chanukah the miracle came about through women (Esther and Yehudit); likewise during Pesach, "it was in the merit of the righteous women of that generation that our ancestors were redeemed from Egypt" (*Sotah* 11b).[11]

Tosfot, however, question *Rashbam's* interpretation, stating that the expression "they *also*" implies a *secondary* position. *Tosfot* therefore reject *Rashbam's*

---

11. See below, p. 53b.

reading, which implies a *primary* role. *Tosfot* interpret the phrase to mean that women also experienced the miracle, since they too were enslaved to and redeemed from Egypt.

Tosfot, however, must contend with the fact that women are not obligated to dwell in a Sukkah—which commemorates the miraculous shelter God provided us in the desert—even though women surely experienced that shelter as well!

Biblical vs. Rabbinic

Tosfot explain that the "they also" argument only applies to Rabbinic *mitzvot*. In the case of Biblical *mitzvot*, unless the Torah itself obligates women, usually implicitly (such as in the case of Kiddush and matzah), they are exempt.

Maharal explains this difference as follows: Regarding Biblical *mitzvot*, such as Sukkah, the essential and primary reason for the mitzvah is beyond our understanding. Although the Torah offers a reason—to recall the shelter God provided us in the desert—this is not the primary reason.

The Rabbinic mitzvah of the Four Cups, by contrast, was established by the Rabbis to commemorate our liberation from Egypt. It therefore follows that women are included in the mitzvah as well.

Rabbi Levi Yitzchak's View

The Kabbalist Rabbi Levi Yitzchak Schneerson, following the view of *Rashbam*, suggests that the special role of women in the Pesach story relates also to Yocheved and Miriam, who defied Pharaoh's decree to kill the newborn males.[12]

In regard to *Tosfot*'s argument—that "they *also*" seems to imply not a greater role, but a secondary role—Rabbi Levi Yitzchak explains that this "secondariness" does not refer to the role of women in the redemption or to their obligation to drink the Four Cups, but to their experience of the exile, since the decree of Pharaoh to kill the newborns did not apply to females. In fact, says Rabbi Levi Yitzchak, from a Kabbalistic perspective, the Four Cups relate *primarily* to women (*Likkutei Levi Yitzchak, Igrot*, p. 273).[13] This coincides with the teaching that the Four Cups correspond to our four Matriarchs: Sarah, Rivkah, Rachel, and Leah (*Maharal; Shaloh*).

---

12. See below, p. 68a.

13. From a lengthy letter to his son, Rabbi Menachem Mendel (future Lubavitcher Rebbe) and daughter-in-law, Rebbetzin Chaya Mushka, before Pesach of 5692 (1932).

Terms & Measurements for the Seder

By Rabbi Jacob Immanuel Schochet

Specific instructions for the proceedings of the Seder are offered in the appropriate places of the Haggadah. It is important, though, to be aware of the proper measures for the various requirements.

🙚 Four Cups of Wine 🙘

Four cups of wine are to be drunk during the Seder, by both men and women. The minimum size for each cup is a *revi'it* (lit., one fourth [of a *log*]), which is about 3.5 fluid ounces (nearly 105 milliliters).[14] Ideally one should drink the *whole cup* each time; if this is not possible, one is to drink at least a little more than half of the cup. It is better to use a smaller cup (with minimum size) and to drink the whole cup than using a larger one and not drinking all of it.

🙚 Karpas 🙘

One should eat *less* than a *kezayit* (a fraction less than an ounce, nearly 26 grams) of the Karpas, that is, not more than half an ounce.

🙚 Matzah 🙘

Matzah must be eaten three times during the Seder:

1. The first time at the beginning of the meal, after reciting the Motzi and the special blessing for the matzah. This initial consumption of matzah is a Biblical precept (*de'orayta*), and thus more stringent. For this initial consumption one is to use two *kezeitim*: one *kezayit* of the top matzah, and one *kezayit* of the middle (broken) matzah. However, by Biblical precept only one *kezayit* need be consumed, while the other *kezayit* is a Rabbinic precept (*derabanan*). Practically speaking this means:

    One *kezayit* matzah is a fraction less than one ounce (25.6 grams). It is to be remembered, though, that in chewing the matzah, some particles

---

14. Actually the precise amount (Rabbi Avraham Chaim Noeh's calculation in his authoritative *Shiurei Torah*) is 86 milliliters (2.9 fluid oz.), which one may rely on. In view of more common practice I rounded it off upward to the size mentioned.

will crumble, and some remain between the teeth, and are not swallowed; thus one should take a little bit more than the size stated to assure the swallowing of a whole *kezayit*.

In terms of spatial dimensions:

Machine-baked *matzot* are generally of uniform size and weight (approximately 1.2 ounces, or 36 grams). Hand-baked *matzot* vary in both size and density. Nonetheless, the *average* hand-baked matzah has a diameter of 10-10 1/2 inches, and weighs 2.3 ounces (66 grams). One *kezayit* of matzah (slightly less than one ounce) is then a piece 5 by 7 inches in area.

If someone should find it difficult to consume two *kezeitim* of this size, one may use a smaller amount for the second *kezayit* (which, as stated, is *derabanan*), namely about two-thirds of an ounce (17.3 grams), thus a third less than the first *kezayit* (or roughly 4 by 6 inches).

2. The second time is the matzah used for *Korech*—the sandwich of matzah and *maror*. This, too, is a Rabbinic precept (*derabanan*). Thus here, too, if it is *difficult* to follow the stricter measure of approximately one ounce, one may suffice with just two-thirds of an ounce (17.3 grams) of matzah.

3. The third time one is to eat matzah is the *afikoman*, of which one should ideally consume two *kezeitim*. If this is difficult, one *kezayit* is enough. Eating the *afikoman* is also *derabanan*, thus if unable to consume the full size for a *kezayit*, one may suffice with the smaller size of two-thirds of an ounce (17.3 grams) per *kezayit*.

Note: In each of these three cases one should complete the consumption of the required amount in *four to seven minutes*.

৪ MAROR ৪

Since the destruction of the *Beit Hamikdash* and the consequent absence of the Pesach offering, the precept of eating bitter herbs is *derabanan*. Thus one may suffice with the smaller measure of a *kezayit*, namely two-thirds of an ounce (17.3 grams).

This applies to the original consumption of *maror* by itself, as well as for the *maror* used for *Korech*.

For both *Maror* and *Korech* it is our custom to use a mixture of horseradish and *chazeret* (lettuce) to make up the required amount of a *kezayit*. When using the stems of romaine lettuce, however, the amount for a *kezayit* is slightly higher—namely a little *more* than 2/3 of an ounce (19.2 grams).

Note: For both *Maror* and *Korech* one should complete the consumption of the required amount in *four to seven minutes*.

SUGGESTIONS FOR THE SEDER

✢ MATZAH ✢

Only three *matzot* are placed on the Seder plate, and generally not every-one has his/her own Seder plate. This means that the leader of the Seder has to distribute the required amounts for all participants from his *matzot*. The three *matzot*, thus, will obviously not be sufficient for everyone, and certainly not for the *afikoman*, which is itself just more than half a matzah. However, when it comes to distributing matzah for *Motzi*, *Korech* and *afikoman*, one can supplement the original *matzot* with others which should be prepared beforehand.

It is advisable to prepare with care pieces of matzah in the proper sizes before the Seder, and to keep them near the leader, so that they can then be distrib-uted with smaller pieces from the Seder plate at the appropriate times.

✢ ZEROA ✢

It is customary to take a section of a fowl's neck bone. We are particular not to eat of the *zeroa*, so as to avoid any similarity to the Pesach offering. It is therefore preferable to remove almost all the flesh from the *zeroa* (but not all of it).

✢ CHAZERET ✢

The prevalent custom is to use romaine lettuce for *chazeret*. Some use endives or iceberg lettuce. When using such leaves, especially romaine lettuce, one must be *careful to check them for insects* before the Seder. Many insects are very small, the same color as the leaves, and thus difficult to detect. It is advisable, therefore, to use only the center ribs, as they can be examined and cleaned much more easily, rather than whole leaves.

✢ ADDITIONAL NOTE ✢

On the eve of Pesach one is not allowed to eat any matzah (and on the first day of Pesach one should limit the eating of matzah), so that when eating mat-zah at the Seder (to fulfill the mitzvah) it will be a conspicuous event and one will do so with proper appetite. For the same reason one should not eat *maror* on the eve of Pesach and on the first day. Moreover, it is our custom not to eat matzah during the 30 days preceding Pesach.

It is also our custom that from the morning of the eve of Pesach, until after the *Korech* of the second Seder, one does not eat any of the ingredients of the *charoset* and *maror*.

The Passover HAGGADAH
הגדה של פסח

סדר בדיקת חמץ
~ SEARCHING FOR CHAMETZ ~

- In the weeks and days leading up to Pesach, we thoroughly cleanse our properties and belongings of any vestige of *chametz*. On the night preceding the night of the Seder, we perform a search by candlelight for *chametz*.

- When Pesach occurs on Saturday night, we search for the *chametz* on Thursday night and burn it on Friday morning.

- The evening prayers in the synagogue should precede the search. One who typically prays the evening prayers in the synagogue should pray prior to the search, even if praying at home. One who typically prays at home should perform the search immediately upon nightfall before praying.

- It is customary to put ten well-wrapped pieces of hard *chametz* around the home some time before the search that will then be found during the search and burnt the next morning.

- The search should begin after nightfall and be performed by candlelight. One should search even in obscure places, such as in cracks in the floor.

- It is customary to use a wooden spoon, a feather, a beeswax candle, and a paper bag, all of which is later burned with the *chametz*.

- One should refrain from speaking between the blessing and the beginning of the search, even concerning the search itself. Throughout the search one should not speak about anything that is not relevant to the search.

- It is best if all adult males in the home participate in the search. They should stand near the head of the household to hear and recite *amen* to the blessing. Each of them then searches one section of the home. They should all begin the search in the room nearest the place where the blessing is said and only then go on to search other parts of the house.

- After burning the *chametz* in the morning, one should clean out one's pockets to empty any *chametz* crumbs that may have settled there.

---

service of Shavuot. For our ultimate goal is not merely to subdue our inner "animal" but to gradually transform it so that it too can stand before God, face to face (*Rabbi Schneur Zalman of Liadi*).[2]

❧ WHY BOTHER? ❧

The mitzvah is to *search* for *chametz*, not to *find chametz*. One therefore fulfills the mitzvah regardless of whether *chametz* is found (*Shibolei Haleket*).[3]

At times, we retreat from a positive endeavor for fear of failure. "Why bother reaching out to another," one might say, "if I may be rebuffed? Why try to educate a seemingly difficult student, if my efforts will probably fail?"

The dynamic of the *chametz* search—that it is a mitzvah to *search* not *find*—invalidates that excuse. For even if we were to fail, theoretically, our good deed remains a good deed. Furthermore, even if we do not see immediate results, we must know that ultimately our efforts will have a positive impact. Such is the nature of a genuine effort (*The Rebbe*).[4]

∽ THE INNER CHAMETZ ∾

Chametz is a metaphor for the human being's inclination toward selfish and spiritually harmful behavior. Hence the Talmudic teaching: "Israel desires to fulfill God's will. Who is stopping them? The leavening that is in the dough" (*Berachot* 17a)—referring to the evil inclination.

This explains the extraordinary degree of the *chametz* prohibition, particularly the fact that we must banish every last *chametz* crumb from our ownership.

As *Radvaz* writes—after suggesting and then eliminating all possible legal/rational explanations for the severity of the prohibition—only a mystical interpretation can explain the *chametz* prohibition:

"…I therefore rely on what our Sages stated in the Midrash, that *chametz* on Pesach alludes to the evil inclination…we must therefore chase it away entirely from upon us and search ourselves in all the pathways and hidden places of our thoughts—even a miniscule amount must be destroyed…" (*Responsa of Radvaz* §576; cf. *Sefer Hachinuch* §15 and §16).

As *Chida* points out: Usually, the mystical reason for a mitzvah constitutes a deeper dimension that goes beyond the obvious, "straightforward" reason (*peshat*). In the case of *chametz*, however, the straightforward interpretation *is* the mystical interpretation (*Simchat Haregel* 12).[1]

❈ THE CHAMETZ MYSTERY ❈

Chametz and matzah are opposites. Matzah is unpretentiously flat and plain tasting; *chametz* is inflated and tasty.

Matzah therefore parallels humility and self-restraint, while *chametz* parallels the self-importance of ego and the superficial satisfaction of self-indulgence.

The Torah therefore forbids *chametz* to the extreme during Pesach, since one must eradicate all vestige of the evil inclination and the ego. By eradicating its dietary manifestation, we weaken its spiritual manifestation as well.

This, however, begs the question: Why is *chametz* permitted during the *rest* of the year? Furthermore, how is it that *chametz* is *required* during the Shavuot Temple service?

The Seven-Week Spiritual Transformation

Every year, beginning with the first day of Pesach, we enter a "spiritual program" designed to help us leave "Egypt" and condition us to encounter God at Sinai, seven weeks later, on the holiday of Shavuot. During the Exodus, our spiritual lowliness was such that it was as if our backs were to God. Our goal for Shavuot is to align ourselves with God, to stand "face to face."

Our Divine sensibility needs no preparation for this encounter. It is our animalistic consciousness that is in need of transformation. Once transformed, it too can stand before God and receive the Torah. We can then love God with all our heart, with both our Godly and selfish inclinations.

Why seven weeks? Kabbalah teaches that the animalistic consciousness possesses *seven* primary impulses. Left to their own devices, these impulses lead us away from our true selves. Our task is to transform these impulses and harness their passion for goodness. For example, passionate desire for material pleasures can be transformed into passionate desire to cleave to God, the source of all existence. Egotistical pride can be transformed into a healthy pride borne of an awareness of one's Godly potential.

The Spiritual Novice

Hence the seven weeks between Pesach and Shavuot: Each week we work on transforming one of the seven impulses.

But in order to *transform* the animal soul's impulses (*it'hapcha*), we must first *subdue* them (*itkafya*).

During Pesach, the ego must be completely and unconditionally humbled. This enables us to begin the process of transforming the ego and harnessing its power for holiness.

Chametz is therefore permitted after Pesach and becomes a mitzvah during the Temple

סדר בדיקת חמץ

Before starting the search, recite the following blessing while holding the lit candle:

בָּרוּךְ אַתָּה יְיָ אֱלֹהֵינוּ מֶלֶךְ הָעוֹלָם, אֲשֶׁר קִדְּשָׁנוּ
בְּמִצְוֹתָיו, וְצִוָּנוּ עַל בִּעוּר חָמֵץ. (Listeners — אָמֵן)

After the search, place the candle, feather, and spoon in the paper bag. Tie it well, with the spoon handle protruding. Nullify the *chametz* that may have been overlooked by saying the following (in a language that you understand):

כָּל חֲמִירָא וַחֲמִיעָא דְּאִכָּא בִרְשׁוּתִי, דְּלָא חֲמִיתֵיהּ וּדְלָא
בְעַרְתֵּיהּ וּדְלָא יְדַעְנָא לֵיהּ, לִבָּטֵל וְלֶהֱוֵי הֶפְקֵר
כְּעַפְרָא דְאַרְעָא.

Store the bag of *chametz* (as well as any *chametz* that will be consumed in the morning) out of the reach of children or animals, who may scatter it.

סדר ביעור חמץ

On the fourteenth of Nissan, *chametz* may only be eaten until the end of the fourth "hour" (check your local Jewish calendar for exact times). In the fifth "hour," burn any remaining *chametz*, including the ten pieces. Once again, nullify any possibly overlooked *chametz* with the following statement (in a language that you understand):

כָּל חֲמִירָא וַחֲמִיעָא דְּאִכָּא בִרְשׁוּתִי, דַּחֲזִיתֵיהּ וּדְלָא
חֲזִיתֵיהּ, דַּחֲמִיתֵיהּ וּדְלָא חֲמִיתֵיהּ, דְּבַעַרְתֵּיהּ וּדְלָא
בְעַרְתֵּיהּ, לִבָּטֵל וְלֶהֱוֵי הֶפְקֵר כְּעַפְרָא דְאַרְעָא.

Continue with the following prayer:

יְהִי רָצוֹן מִלְּפָנֶיךָ יְיָ אֱלֹהֵינוּ וֵאלֹהֵי אֲבוֹתֵינוּ, כְּשֵׁם שֶׁאֲנִי מְבַעֵר חָמֵץ
מִבֵּיתִי וּמֵרְשׁוּתִי, כָּךְ תְּבַעֵר אֶת כָּל הַחִיצוֹנִים, וְאֶת רוּחַ
הַטֻּמְאָה תַּעֲבִיר מִן הָאָרֶץ, וְאֶת יִצְרֵנוּ הָרָע תַּעֲבִירֵהוּ מֵאִתָּנוּ, וְתִתֶּן
לָנוּ לֵב בָּשָׂר לְעָבְדְּךָ בֶּאֱמֶת, וְכָל סִטְרָא אַחֲרָא וְכָל הַקְּלִפּוֹת וְכָל
הָרִשְׁעָה בֶּעָשָׁן תִּכְלֶה, וְתַעֲבִיר מֶמְשֶׁלֶת זָדוֹן מִן הָאָרֶץ, וְכָל הַמְּעִיקִים
לַשְּׁכִינָה תְּבַעֲרֵם בְּרוּחַ בָּעֵר וּבְרוּחַ מִשְׁפָּט כְּשֵׁם שֶׁבִּעַרְתָּ אֶת מִצְרַיִם
וְאֶת אֱלֹהֵיהֶם בַּיָּמִים הָהֵם בִּזְמַן הַזֶּה, אָמֵן סֶלָה.

17b

∾ SEARCHING FOR CHAMETZ ∾

Before starting the search, recite the following blessing while holding the lit candle:

Blessed are You, GOD, our God, King of the universe, who has sanctified us with His commandments and commanded us concerning the removal of *chametz*.

After the search, place the candle, feather, and spoon in the paper bag. Tie it well, with the spoon handle protruding. Nullify the *chametz* that may have been over-looked by saying the following (in a language that you understand):

All leaven and anything leavened that is in my possession, which I have neither seen nor removed, and about which I am unaware, shall be considered nullified and ownerless as the dust of the earth.

Store the bag of *chametz* (as well as any *chametz* that will be consumed in the morning) out of the reach of children or animals, who may scatter it.

∾ BURNING THE CHAMETZ ∾

On the fourteenth of Nissan, *chametz* may only be eaten until the end of the fourth "hour" (check your local Jewish calendar for exact times). In the fifth "hour," burn any remaining *chametz*, including the ten pieces. Once again, nullify any possibly overlooked *chametz* with the following statement:

All leaven and anything leavened that is in my possession, whether I have seen it or not, whether I have observed it or not, whether I have removed it or not, shall be considered nullified and ownerless as the dust of the earth.

Continue with the following prayer:

May it be Your will, God, our God and God of our fathers, that just as I remove the *chametz* from my house and from my possession, so shall You remove all the "extraneous forces." Remove the spirit of impurity from the earth, remove our evil inclination from us, and grant us a heart of flesh to serve You in truth. Make all the *sitra achara,** all the *kelipot,** and all wickedness be consumed in smoke, and remove the dominion of evil from the earth. Remove with a spirit of destruction and a spirit of judgment all that distress the *Shechinah,* just as You destroyed Egypt and its idols in those days, at this time. *Amen, Selah.*

Kabbalistic terms for forces of impurity.

סדר קרבן פסח

ונשלמה פרים שפתינו ותפלת מנחה היא במקום תמיד של בין הערבים ובזמן שבית המקדש היה קיים הפסח היה נשחט
אחר תמיד של בין הערבים כן ראוי לעסוק בסדר קרבן פסח אחר תפלת המנחה ויאמר זה:

קָרְבָּן פֶּסַח מֵבִיא מִן הַכְּבָשִׂים אוֹ מִן הָעִזִּים זָכָר בֶּן שָׁנָה, וְשׁוֹחֲטוֹ בָּעֲזָרָה בְּכָל מָקוֹם, אַחַר חֲצוֹת אַרְבָּעָה עָשָׂר דַּוְקָא, וְאַחַר שְׁחִיטַת תָּמִיד שֶׁל בֵּין הָעַרְבַּיִם, וְאַחַר הֲטָבַת נֵרוֹת שֶׁל בֵּין הָעַרְבַּיִם. וְאֵין שׁוֹחֲטִין אֶת הַפֶּסַח עַל הֶחָמֵץ. וְאִם שָׁחַט קוֹדֶם לַתָּמִיד, כָּשֵׁר, וּבִלְבַד שֶׁיְּהֵא אַחַר מְמָרֵס בְּדַם הַפֶּסַח כְּדֵי שֶׁלֹּא יִקְרַשׁ עַד שֶׁיִּזְרְקוּ דַּם הַתָּמִיד, וְאַחַר כָּךְ יִזְרְקוּ דַּם הַפֶּסַח זְרִיקָה אַחַת כְּנֶגֶד הַיְסוֹד. וְכֵיצַד עוֹשִׂין? שָׁחַט הַשּׁוֹחֵט, וְקִבֵּל הַכֹּהֵן הָרִאשׁוֹן שֶׁבְּרֹאשׁ הַשּׁוּרָה וְנָתַן לַחֲבֵרוֹ, וַחֲבֵרוֹ לַחֲבֵרוֹ, וְהַכֹּהֵן הַקָּרוֹב אֵצֶל הַמִּזְבֵּחַ זוֹרְקוֹ זְרִיקָה אַחַת כְּנֶגֶד הַיְסוֹד, וְחוֹזֵר הַכְּלִי רֵיקָן לַחֲבֵרוֹ, וַחֲבֵרוֹ לַחֲבֵרוֹ, וּמְקַבֵּל כְּלִי הַמָּלֵא תְּחִלָּה וְאַחַר כָּךְ מַחֲזִיר הָרֵיקָן. וְהָיוּ שׁוּרוֹת שֶׁל בָּזִיכֵי כֶסֶף וְשׁוּרוֹת שֶׁל בָּזִיכֵי זָהָב. וְלֹא הָיוּ לַבָּזִיכִין שׁוּלַיִם, שֶׁמָּא יַנִּיחֵם וְיִקְרַשׁ הַדָּם. אַחַר כָּךְ תּוֹלִין אֶת הַפֶּסַח וּמַפְשִׁיטִין אוֹתוֹ כֻּלּוֹ, וְקוֹרְעִין אוֹתוֹ, וּמְמַחִין אֶת קְרָבָיו עַד שֶׁיֵּצֵא הַפֶּרֶשׁ, וּמוֹצִיאִין אֶת הָאֵמוּרִים, וְהֵם: הַחֵלֶב שֶׁעַל הַקֶּרֶב, וְיוֹתֶרֶת הַכָּבֵד, וּשְׁתֵּי כְלָיוֹת וְהַחֵלֶב שֶׁעֲלֵיהֶן, וְהָאַלְיָה לְעֻמַּת הֶעָצֶה, וְנוֹתְנָם בִּכְלִי שָׁרֵת, וּמוֹלְחָם וּמַקְטִירָם הַכֹּהֵן עַל גַּבֵּי הַמִּזְבֵּחַ כָּל אֶחָד לְבַדּוֹ. וְהַשְּׁחִיטָה וְהַזְּרִיקָה וּמִחוּי קְרָבָיו וְהֶקְטֵר חֲלָבָיו דּוֹחִין אֶת הַשַּׁבָּת, וּשְׁאָר עִנְיָנָיו אֵינָם דּוֹחִין אֶת הַשַּׁבָּת. וְכֵן אֵין מוֹלִיכִין אֶת הַפֶּסַח לַבַּיִת כְּשֶׁחָל בְּשַׁבָּת, אֶלָּא כַּת הָאַחַת הֵם מִתְעַכְּבִים עִם פִּסְחֵיהֶם בְּהַר הַבַּיִת, וְהַכַּת הַשְּׁנִיָּה יוֹשֶׁבֶת לָהּ בַּחֵיל, וְהַשְּׁלִישִׁית בִּמְקוֹמָהּ

◦◦ THE PESACH OFFERING ◦◦

"We offer the words of our lips in place of the sacrifice of bullocks." The Minchah prayer takes the place of the daily afternoon offering; and in the time of the *Beit Hamikdash,* the Pesach offering was sacrificed after the daily afternoon offering. Thus it is appropriate to study the order of the Pesach offering after Minchah, by saying the following:

The Pesach offering is brought from yearling male lambs or goats, and slaughtered anywhere in the Temple court only after midday of the fourteenth of Nissan, after the slaughtering of the daily afternoon offering and after the afternoon cleaning of the cups of the menorah. One should not slaughter the Pesach offering while *chametz* is in his possession. If he slaughtered it before the daily afternoon offering, it is acceptable, provided that someone stir the blood of the Pesach offering so that it will not congeal until the blood of the daily afternoon offering will have been sprinkled, and then the blood of the Pesach offering is sprinkled once toward the base of the altar. How is it done? The *shochet* slaughters it, and the first Kohen at the head of the line receives it and hands it over to his colleague, and his colleague to his colleague, and the Kohen nearest the altar sprinkles it once toward the base of the altar. He returns the empty vessel to his colleague, and his colleague to his colleague, receiving first the full vessel and then returning the empty one. There were rows of silver vessels and rows of golden vessels, and the vessels did not have flat bottoms lest they set them down and the blood become congealed. Afterwards they hung the Pesach offering, flayed it completely, tore it open, and cleansed its bowels until the wastes were removed. They took out the parts offered on the altar, namely, the fat that is on the entrails, the lobe of the liver, the two kidneys with the fat on them, and the tail up to the backbone, and placed them in a ritual vessel. The Kohen then salted them and burned them upon the altar, each one individually. The slaughtering, the sprinkling of its blood, the cleansing of its bowels and the burning of its fat override the Shabbat, but other things pertaining to it do not override the Shabbat. Likewise, if [the fourteenth of Nissan] occurs on Shabbat, the Pesach offerings are not carried home, but one group remains with their Pesach offerings on the Temple mount,

עוֹמֶדֶת. חָשְׁכָה, יָצְאוּ וְצָלוּ פְּסְחֵיהֶם. בִּשְׁלֹשָׁה כִּתּוֹת
הַפֶּסַח נִשְׁחָט, וְאֵין כַּת פְּחוּתָה מִשְּׁלֹשִׁים אֲנָשִׁים. נִכְנְסָה
כַּת הָרִאשׁוֹנָה, נִתְמַלְּאָה הָעֲזָרָה, נוֹעֲלִין אוֹתָהּ. וּבְעוֹד
שֶׁהֵם שׁוֹחֲטִין וּמַקְרִיבִין אֶת הָאֵמוּרִים, קוֹרְאִין אֶת הַהַלֵּל.
אִם גָּמְרוּ אוֹתוֹ קוֹדֶם שֶׁיַּקְרִיבוּ כֻלָּם, שׁוֹנִים אוֹתוֹ, וְאִם
שָׁנוּ יְשַׁלֵּשׁוּ. עַל כָּל קְרִיאָה תּוֹקְעִין שָׁלֹשׁ תְּקִיעוֹת: תְּקִיעָה
תְּרוּעָה תְּקִיעָה. גָּמְרוּ לְהַקְרִיב, פּוֹתְחִין הָעֲזָרָה. יָצְאָה כַּת
רִאשׁוֹנָה, נִכְנְסָה כַּת שְׁנִיָּה, נוֹעֲלִין דַּלְתוֹת הָעֲזָרָה. גָּמְרוּ,
פּוֹתְחִין, יָצְאָה כַּת שְׁנִיָּה, נִכְנְסָה כַּת שְׁלִישִׁית, וּמַעֲשֶׂה
כֻלָּן שָׁוִין. וְאַחַר שֶׁיָּצְאוּ כֻלָּן רוֹחֲצִין הָעֲזָרָה, וַאֲפִילוּ בְּשַׁבָּת,
מִפְּנֵי לִכְלוּךְ הַדָּם שֶׁהָיָה בָהּ. וְכֵיצַד הָיְתָה הָרְחִיצָה? אַמַּת
הַמַּיִם הָיְתָה עוֹבֶרֶת בָּעֲזָרָה, וְהָיָה לָהּ מָקוֹם לָצֵאת מִמֶּנָּה,
וּכְשֶׁרוֹצִין לְהָדִיחַ אֶת הָרִצְפָּה, סוֹתְמִין מָקוֹם יְצִיאָתָהּ,
וְהִיא מִתְמַלֵּאת עַל כָּל גְּדוֹתֶיהָ מִפֹּה וּמִפֹּה, עַד שֶׁהַמַּיִם
עוֹלִים וְצָפִים מִכָּאן וּמִכָּאן, וּמִקַּבֵּץ אֵלֶיהָ כָּל דָּם וְכָל
לִכְלוּךְ שֶׁהָיָה בָּעֲזָרָה. וְאַחַר כָּךְ פּוֹתְחִין מָקוֹם יְצִיאָתָהּ,
וְהַכֹּל יוֹצֵא עַד שֶׁנִּשְׁאַר הָרִצְפָּה מְנֻקָּה וּמְשֻׁפָּה. זֶהוּ כְּבוֹד
הַבַּיִת. וְאִם הַפֶּסַח נִמְצָא טְרֵפָה, לֹא עָלָה לוֹ עַד שֶׁמֵּבִיא
אַחֵר.

זהו הענין בקיצור גדול. וצריך האדם הירא וחרד על דבר ה' לקרות אותו בזמנו שתעלה קריאתו במקום הקרבתו וידאג על
חורבן הבית ויתחנן לפני ה' בורא עולם שיבנה אותו במהרה בימנו אמן.

the second group sits in the *chel* [an area just outside the Temple court], and the third stands in its place [in the courtyard]. After nightfall they go to their places and roast their Pesach offering. The Pesach offering was slaughtered in three groups, each group consisting of no less than thirty men. The first group entered, filling the Temple court. They closed [its doors], and while they were slaughtering it and offering its parts on the altar, they [the Levi'im] recited the Hallel. If they finished [Hallel] before all had sacrificed, they repeated it, and if they repeated it [and were not finished yet], they recited it a third time. Each time Hallel was recited, [the Kohanim] sounded three blasts of the trumpet: *tekiah, teruah, tekiah*. When the offering was ended, they opened the doors of the Temple court, the first group went out and the second entered, and they closed the doors of the Temple court. When they finished, they opened the doors, the second group went out and the third entered. The procedure of each group was the same. After they all had left, they washed the Temple court, even on Shabbat, of the dirt of the blood. How was the washing done? A water duct passed through the Temple court and had an outlet from the court. When they wished to wash the floor, they shut the outlet and the stream overflowed its sides until the water rose and flooded the [floor] all around and all the blood and dirt of the court were gathered to it. Then they opened the outlet, everything flowed out and the floor was completely clean; this is the honor of the Temple. If the Pesach offering was found to be unfit, one did not fulfill his obligation until he brings another one.

This is a very brief description of the order of the Pesach offering. The God-fearing person should recite it in its proper time, so that its recital should be regarded in place of its offering. One should be troubled about the destruction of the *Beit Hamikdash*, and plead before God, the Creator of the universe, that He rebuild it speedily in our days, Amen.

עֵרוּב תַּבְשִׁילִין

When the first two days of Pesach occur on Thursday and Friday, one should make an *"eruv tavshilin"* on Wednesday. The *eruv tavshilin* ritual permits one to prepare food on the festival for Shabbat, which is otherwise forbidden. (Generally, one cannot cook on a festival for a meal that will be eaten after the festival.) The *eruv* acts as a reminder for the general prohibition of cooking for after the festival and that a special dispensation for Shabbat has been made. It also reminds us to prepare for Shabbat. The *eruv* consists of taking a matzah and a significant cooked food designated for Shabbat (such as meat, fish, or an egg) and reciting the blessing and statement below.

It is customary, if possible, to appoint an adult male to act as an "agent" through whom one grants a share in one's *eruv* to the entire community. One who does not have an "agent" skips the following section:

Hand the matzah and cooked food to the "agent" and say:

אֲנִי מְזַכֶּה לְכָל מִי שֶׁרוֹצֶה לִזְכּוֹת וְלִסְמוֹךְ עַל עֵרוּב זֶה.

The "agent" raises the food items a *tefach* (approximately 3 inches) and then returns them to the one making the *eruv*.

Hold the matzah and other food item and recite the following:

בָּרוּךְ אַתָּה יְיָ, אֱלֹהֵינוּ מֶלֶךְ הָעוֹלָם, אֲשֶׁר קִדְּשָׁנוּ בְּמִצְוֹתָיו, וְצִוָּנוּ עַל מִצְוַת עֵרוּב.

The following must be recited in a language that one understands:

בְּדֵין יְהֵא שָׁרֵא לָנָא לַאֲפוּיֵי וּלְבַשּׁוּלֵי וּלְאַטְמוּנֵי וּלְאַדְלוּקֵי שְׁרָגָא וּלְתַקָּנָא וּלְמֶעֱבַד כָּל צָרְכָנָא מִיּוֹמָא טָבָא לְשַׁבַּתָּא, לָנָא וּלְכָל יִשְׂרָאֵל הַדָּרִים בָּעִיר הַזֹּאת.

Put aside the food items to be eaten on Shabbat.

- After an *eruv* has been made, it is permissible to cook food on Friday for Shabbat (but not on Thursday for Friday). One must, however, cook this food well before nightfall, so that it would be possible for one to theoretically benefit from the food on the Friday of the festival, and one is not cooking exclusively for Shabbat. One must save the food designated for the *eruv* until all the tasks necessary for Shabbat have been completed.

- It is customary to use an entire matzah for the *eruv*, which is then used on Shabbat as one of the two *lechem mishneh* on Friday night and Shabbat day and is eaten at the third Shabbat meal. Although each household should have its own *eruv*, one who forgot to make one can rely on the rabbi's *eruv*, which is done on behalf of the entire community.

∽ ᴇʀᴜᴠ Tᴀᴠsʜɪʟɪɴ ᴄ

When the first two days of Pesach occur on Thursday and Friday, one should make an "*eruv tavshilin*" on Wednesday. The *eruv tavshilin* ritual permits one to prepare food on the festival for Shabbat, which is otherwise forbidden. (Generally, one cannot cook on a festival for a meal that will be eaten after the festival.) The *eruv* acts as a reminder for the general prohibition of cooking for after the festival and that a special dispensation for Shabbat has been made. It also reminds us to prepare for Shabbat. The *eruv* consists of taking a matzah and a significant cooked food designated for Shabbat (such as meat, fish, or an egg) and reciting the blessing and statement below.

It is customary, if possible, to appoint an adult male to act as an "agent" through whom one grants a share in one's *eruv* to the entire community. One who does not have an "agent" skips the following section:

Hand the matzah and cooked food to the "agent" and say:

I hereby grant a share in this *eruv* to anyone who wishes to participate in it and to rely upon it.

The "agent" raises the food items a *tefach* (approximately 3 inches) and then returns them to the one making the *eruv*.

Hold the matzah and other food item and recite the following:

Blessed are You, GOD our God, King of the universe, who has sanctified us with His commandments, and commanded us concerning the mitzvah of *eruv*.

Through this it shall be permissible for us to bake, to cook, to put away [a dish to preserve its heat], to kindle a light, and to prepare and do on the Festival all that is necessary for the Shabbat—for us and for all Israelites who dwell in this city.

Put aside the food items to be eaten on Shabbat.

- After an *eruv* has been made, it is permissible to cook food on Friday for Shabbat (but not on Thursday for Friday). One must, however, cook this food well before nightfall, so that it would be possible for one to theoretically benefit from the food on the Friday of the festival, and one is not cooking exclusively for Shabbat. One must save the food designated for the *eruv* until all the tasks necessary for Shabbat have been completed.

- It is customary to use an entire matzah for the *eruv*, which is then used on Shabbat as one of the two *lechem mishneh* on Friday night and Shabbat day and is eaten at the third Shabbat meal. Although each household should have its own *eruv*, one who forgot to make one can rely on the rabbi's *eruv*, which is done on behalf of the entire community.

הדלקת נרות

- It is customary to give charity before lighting the festival candles. The festival lights are kindled at least eighteen minutes before sunset. Girls from the age of three should light their own candle. Married women customarily light two candles. Many families add an additional candle for each of their children. Where there are no women, a man should light the candles.

- After lighting the candle(s), draw your hands three times around the lights and towards your face, then place them over your eyes and recite the appropriate blessings.

- If the first night of Pesach occurs on Friday night and one forgot to light the candles before sunset, no candles should be lit at all.

- On the second night of Pesach, or when the first night occurs on Saturday night, the lights are kindled after nightfall from a pre-existing flame. Nightfall is approximately 45–60 minutes after sunset (consult a Jewish calendar for the exact time in your area).

On Friday evening, add the words in shaded parentheses.

בָּרוּךְ אַתָּה יְיָ, אֱלֹהֵינוּ מֶלֶךְ הָעוֹלָם, אֲשֶׁר קִדְּשָׁנוּ בְּמִצְוֹתָיו, וְצִוָּנוּ לְהַדְלִיק נֵר שֶׁל (שַׁבָּת וְשֶׁל) יוֹם טוֹב.

בָּרוּךְ אַתָּה יְיָ, אֱלֹהֵינוּ מֶלֶךְ הָעוֹלָם, שֶׁהֶחֱיָנוּ וְקִיְּמָנוּ וְהִגִּיעָנוּ לִזְמַן הַזֶּה.

תקוני שבת

When the first night of Pesach occurs on Friday night, recite the following quietly upon returning home from the synagogue:

שָׁלוֹם עֲלֵיכֶם מַלְאֲכֵי הַשָּׁרֵת מַלְאֲכֵי עֶלְיוֹן מִמֶּלֶךְ —Say three times
מַלְכֵי הַמְּלָכִים הַקָּדוֹשׁ בָּרוּךְ הוּא:

בּוֹאֲכֶם לְשָׁלוֹם מַלְאֲכֵי הַשָּׁלוֹם מַלְאֲכֵי עֶלְיוֹן מִמֶּלֶךְ —Say three times
מַלְכֵי הַמְּלָכִים הַקָּדוֹשׁ בָּרוּךְ הוּא:

בָּרְכוּנִי לְשָׁלוֹם מַלְאֲכֵי הַשָּׁלוֹם מַלְאֲכֵי עֶלְיוֹן מִמֶּלֶךְ —Say three times
מַלְכֵי הַמְּלָכִים הַקָּדוֹשׁ בָּרוּךְ הוּא:

צֵאתְכֶם לְשָׁלוֹם מַלְאֲכֵי הַשָּׁלוֹם מַלְאֲכֵי עֶלְיוֹן מִמֶּלֶךְ —Say three times
מַלְכֵי הַמְּלָכִים הַקָּדוֹשׁ בָּרוּךְ הוּא:

꙳ CANDLE LIGHTING ꙳

- It is customary to give charity before lighting the festival candles. The festival lights are kindled at least eighteen minutes before sunset. Girls from the age of three should light their own candle. Married women light two candles. Many families add an additional candle for each of their children. Where there are no women, a man should light the candles.

- After lighting the candle(s), draw your hands three times around the lights and towards your face, then place them over your eyes and recite the appropriate blessings.

- If the first night of Pesach occurs on Friday night and one forgot to light the candles before sunset, no candles should be lit at all.

- On the second night of Pesach, or when the first night occurs on Saturday night, the lights are kindled after nightfall from a pre-existing flame. Nightfall is approximately 45–60 minutes after sunset (consult a Jewish calendar for the exact time in your area).

On Friday evening, add the words in shaded parentheses.

Blessed are You, GOD our God, King of the universe, who has sanctified us with His commandments, and commanded us to kindle the (Shabbat and) Yom Tov light.

Blessed are You, GOD our God, King of the universe, who has granted us life, sustained us and enabled us to reach this occasion.

꙳ HYMNS FOR FRIDAY NIGHT ꙳

When the first night of Pesach occurs on Friday night, recite the following quietly upon returning home from the synagogue:

Say three times—**Peace unto you**, ministering angels, messengers of the Most High, of the supreme King of kings, the Holy One, blessed be He.

Say three times—**May your coming** be in peace, angels of peace, messengers of the Most High, of the supreme King of kings, the Holy One, blessed be He.

Say three times—**Bless me with peace**, angels of peace, messengers of the Most High, of the supreme King of kings, the Holy One, blessed be He.

Say three times—**May your departure** be in peace, angels of peace, messengers of the Most High, of the supreme King of kings, the Holy One, blessed be He.

כִּי מַלְאָכָיו יְצַוֶּה לָּךְ, לִשְׁמָרְךָ בְּכָל דְּרָכֶיךָ: יְיָ יִשְׁמָר צֵאתְךָ וּבוֹאֶךָ, מֵעַתָּה וְעַד עוֹלָם:

אֵשֶׁת חַיִל מִי יִמְצָא, וְרָחֹק מִפְּנִינִים מִכְרָהּ. בָּטַח בָּהּ לֵב בַּעְלָהּ, וְשָׁלָל לֹא יֶחְסָר. גְּמָלַתְהוּ טוֹב וְלֹא רָע, כֹּל יְמֵי חַיֶּיהָ. דָּרְשָׁה צֶמֶר וּפִשְׁתִּים, וַתַּעַשׂ בְּחֵפֶץ כַּפֶּיהָ. הָיְתָה כָּאֳנִיּוֹת סוֹחֵר, מִמֶּרְחָק תָּבִיא לַחְמָהּ. וַתָּקָם בְּעוֹד לַיְלָה, וַתִּתֵּן טֶרֶף לְבֵיתָהּ, וְחֹק לְנַעֲרֹתֶיהָ. זָמְמָה שָׂדֶה וַתִּקָּחֵהוּ, מִפְּרִי כַפֶּיהָ נָטְעָה כָּרֶם. חָגְרָה בְעוֹז מָתְנֶיהָ, וַתְּאַמֵּץ זְרוֹעֹתֶיהָ. טָעֲמָה כִּי טוֹב סַחְרָהּ, לֹא יִכְבֶּה בַלַּיְלָה נֵרָהּ. יָדֶיהָ שִׁלְּחָה בַכִּישׁוֹר, וְכַפֶּיהָ תָּמְכוּ פָלֶךְ. כַּפָּהּ פָּרְשָׂה לֶעָנִי, וְיָדֶיהָ שִׁלְּחָה לָאֶבְיוֹן. לֹא תִירָא לְבֵיתָהּ מִשָּׁלֶג, כִּי כָל בֵּיתָהּ לָבֻשׁ שָׁנִים. מַרְבַדִּים עָשְׂתָה לָּהּ, שֵׁשׁ וְאַרְגָּמָן לְבוּשָׁהּ. נוֹדָע בַּשְּׁעָרִים בַּעְלָהּ, בְּשִׁבְתּוֹ עִם זִקְנֵי אָרֶץ. סָדִין עָשְׂתָה וַתִּמְכֹּר, וַחֲגוֹר נָתְנָה לַכְּנַעֲנִי. עֹז וְהָדָר לְבוּשָׁהּ, וַתִּשְׂחַק לְיוֹם אַחֲרוֹן. פִּיהָ פָּתְחָה בְחָכְמָה, וְתוֹרַת חֶסֶד עַל לְשׁוֹנָהּ. צוֹפִיָּה הֲלִיכוֹת בֵּיתָהּ, וְלֶחֶם עַצְלוּת לֹא תֹאכֵל. קָמוּ בָנֶיהָ וַיְאַשְּׁרוּהָ, בַּעְלָהּ וַיְהַלְלָהּ. רַבּוֹת בָּנוֹת עָשׂוּ חָיִל, וְאַתְּ עָלִית עַל כֻּלָּנָה. שֶׁקֶר הַחֵן וְהֶבֶל הַיֹּפִי, אִשָּׁה יִרְאַת יְיָ הִיא תִתְהַלָּל. תְּנוּ לָהּ מִפְּרִי יָדֶיהָ, וִיהַלְלוּהָ בַשְּׁעָרִים מַעֲשֶׂיהָ:

מִזְמוֹר לְדָוִד, יְיָ רֹעִי לֹא אֶחְסָר. בִּנְאוֹת דֶּשֶׁא יַרְבִּיצֵנִי, עַל מֵי מְנֻחוֹת יְנַהֲלֵנִי. נַפְשִׁי יְשׁוֹבֵב, יַנְחֵנִי בְמַעְגְּלֵי צֶדֶק לְמַעַן שְׁמוֹ. גַּם כִּי אֵלֵךְ בְּגֵיא צַלְמָוֶת לֹא אִירָא רָע, כִּי אַתָּה עִמָּדִי, שִׁבְטְךָ וּמִשְׁעַנְתֶּךָ הֵמָּה יְנַחֲמֻנִי. תַּעֲרֹךְ לְפָנַי שֻׁלְחָן נֶגֶד צֹרְרָי, דִּשַּׁנְתָּ בַשֶּׁמֶן רֹאשִׁי, כּוֹסִי רְוָיָה. אַךְ טוֹב וָחֶסֶד יִרְדְּפוּנִי כָּל יְמֵי חַיָּי, וְשַׁבְתִּי בְּבֵית יְיָ לְאֹרֶךְ יָמִים:

דָּא הִיא סְעוּדָתָא דַּחֲקַל תַּפּוּחִין קַדִּישִׁין:

אַתְקִינוּ סְעוּדָתָא דִּמְהֵימְנוּתָא שְׁלֵמָתָא חֶדְוָתָא דְמַלְכָּא קַדִּישָׁא. אַתְקִינוּ סְעוּדָתָא דְמַלְכָּא, דָּא הִיא סְעוּדָתָא דַּחֲקַל תַּפּוּחִין קַדִּישִׁין, וּזְעֵיר אַנְפִּין וְעַתִּיקָא קַדִּישָׁא אַתְיָן לְסַעֲדָא בַּהֲדַהּ:

For He will instruct His angels on your behalf, to guard you in all your ways. GOD will guard your going and your coming from now and for all time.

Who can find a wife of excellence? Her value far exceeds that of gems. The heart of her husband trusts in her, he lacks no gain. She treats him with goodness, never with evil, all the days of her life. She seeks out wool and flax, and works willingly with her hands. She is like the merchant ships; she brings her food from afar. She rises while it is still night, gives food to her household, and sets out the tasks for her maids. She considers a field and buys it; from her earnings she plants a vineyard. She girds her loins with strength, and flexes her arms. She realizes that her enterprise is profitable; her lamp does not go out at night. She puts her hands on the spindle, and her palms grasp the distaff. She holds out her hand to the poor, and extends her hands to the destitute. She does not fear for her household in the frost, for her entire household is clothed [warmly] in scarlet. She makes her own tapestries; her garments are of fine linen and purple. Her husband is well-known at the gates, as he sits with the elders of the land. She makes linens and sells [them]; she provides the merchants with girdles. Strength and dignity are her garb, she looks smilingly toward the future. She opens her mouth with wisdom, and the teaching of kindness is on her tongue. She watches the conduct of her household, and does not eat the bread of idleness. Her children rise and acclaim her, her husband—and he praises her: Many daughters have done worthily, but you surpass them all. Charm is deceptive and beauty is naught; a God-fearing woman is the one to be praised. Give her praise for her accomplishments, and let her deeds laud her at the gates.

A Psalm by David. GOD is my shepherd, I shall lack nothing. He makes me lie down in green pastures; He leads me beside still waters. He revives my soul; He directs me in paths of righteousness for the sake of His Name. Even if I will walk in the valley of the shadow of death, I will fear no evil, for You are with me; Your rod and Your staff—they will comfort me. You will prepare a table for me before my enemies; You have anointed my head with oil; my cup is full. Only goodness and kindness shall follow me all the days of my life, and I shall dwell in the House of GOD for many long years.

This is the meal of the holy Chakal Tapuchin.

Prepare the meal of perfect faith, which is the delight of the holy King; prepare the meal of the King. This is the meal of the holy *Chakal Tapuchin*, and *Z'eir Anpin* and the holy Ancient One come to join her in the meal.

סדר הגדה
ORDER OF THE HAGGADAH

Notes & Insights

❧ EVERY DETAIL ❧

The famed Maharil, Rabbi Yaakov ben Moshe HaLevi Mollin, writes:

"Every person should tremble with awe to follow the instructions of the Sages who instituted the order of the Seder and the Haggadah. Do not take the matter lightly. Even if there are some things at the Seder that do not seem critical to you, act prudently to observe them, for there is nothing trivial among them."

❧ THE CONVERT ❧

It would seem that converts ought to be exempt from celebrating Pesach, since neither they nor their ancestors were in Egypt.[5] The Torah therefore tells us (Numbers 9:14): *If a convert will dwell with you, he shall prepare a Pesach offering....* The words *with you* mean **as one of you**. For within our Exodus lies an eternal redemption for the soul of the convert as well.

The Exodus was not merely a *physical* migration, but a spiritual redemption that affected all of Israel, including those souls whose connection to Israel was not yet revealed (see *Or Hachaim* on Numbers, ibid.).

❧ HAGGADAH HISTORY ❧

The order of the Haggadah and the Seder is discussed in the *Mishnah* (compiled 2nd century CE), tractate *Pesachim*, chapter 10; *Mechilta* on *parshat Bo*, as well as in the Babylonian and Jerusalem Talmuds in the above tractate.

The order of the Haggadah in a structured format can be found in the Siddur of Rav Amram Gaon (9th century CE), as well as in the Siddur of Rav Saadiah Gaon, Rambam's *Mishneh Torah*, *Machzor Vitri*, et al.

The mystical interpretation of the Haggadah can be found in the work *Pri Etz Chaim* (16th

century) and in the Siddur of the Arizal (*The Rebbe's Haggadah*).

❧ HAGGADAH: THE NAME ❧

The title "Haggadah" appears in the Talmud (*Pesachim* 115b). It means "telling" and is derived from the phrase (Exodus 13:8): *And you shall tell—v'higadeta—your child [the story of the Exodus].*

Some understand "Haggadah" to mean "thanksgiving and praise," i.e., it is a book of praise to God for taking us out of Egypt. *Targum Yerushalmi* likewise interprets a similar word in the verse (Deuteronomy 26:3) *higadeti hayom la'Hashem Elokecha*—as "I *praise* [God] this day." Rav Saadiah Gaon likewise translates the verse into Arabic in this way (*Avudraham*).

The Rebbe adds: "Some have *Aggadah* with the letter *Alef*. (See *Dikdukei Sofrim* on *Pesachim* 115-116 [who revises all occurrences of *Haggadah* to *HaAggadah*]; *Tosfot* on *Avodah Zarah* 45a, s.v. *Amar* [where he refers to *Aggadat HaPesach*]; several other *Rishonim* likewise have *Aggadah* [see, e.g., *Mordechai* on *Pesachim* 117a])."

❧ RECLINING ❧

The Midrash relates that God afforded the Israelites royal treatment in the desert, having them lie down to recline in the manner of kings upon their couches (*Bamidbar Rabbah* 1:2). Our Sages derived from this that even the most poverty-stricken Jew should not eat on Pesach night without reclining (*Shemot Rabbah* 20:18).[6]

One should recline to the left, since any other sort of reclining—to the right,[7] on one's stomach, or on one's back—is not the proper form of reclining (*Pesachim* 108a; *Rambam, Hilchot Chametz u'Matzah* 7:8).

❧ A FATHER'S ADVICE ❧

"My father once told me: 'Yosef Yitzchak! During the Seder, one must think about becoming a mensch—and God will help. This is especially true when opening the door for Elijah. Don't pray for material things; pray for spiritual blessings."[8]

—RABBI YOSEF YITZCHAK OF LUBAVITCH

~ SETTING UP THE SEDER PLATE ~

יסדר על שולחנו קערה בג׳ מצות מונחים זה על זה, הישראל ועליו הלוי ועליו הכהן. ועליו לימין הזרוע, וכנגדו לשמאל הביצה, תחתיהם באמצע המרור, ותחת הזרוע החרוסת, וכנגדו תחת הביצה הכרפס, ותחת המרור החזרת שעושין כורך.

BEITZAH
ביצה

KARPAS
כרפס

CHAZERET
חזרת

ZEROA
זרוע

MAROR
מרור

CHAROSET
חרוסת

KOHEN | כהן
LEVI | לוי
YISRAEL | ישראל

The Seder should begin soon after returning home from the synagogue, but not before nightfall. It is customary to prepare the *Ka'arah* (Seder Plate) after nightfall. On the second night, the table should not be set before nightfall.

Organize the Seder Plate in the following order:

MATZAH | מצה	**1.** Three whole *matzot* are placed on a tray or large plate. Each indvidual matzah should be surrounded top and bottom by cloth (or napkins). Place the first matzah in the lowest "compartment." This will be the "**Yisrael**" matzah. Place another (the "**Levi**" matzah) above it, and another matzah above these (the "**Kohen**" matzah).
ZEROA | זרוע	**2.** Place a roasted fowl's neck bone on top of the *matzot*, on the upper right side. One should not eat from the *zeroa*. It is Chabad custom to remove most of the meat from the bone.
BEITZAH | ביצה	**3.** Place a hard-boiled egg on the upper left side.
MAROR | מרור	**4.** Place a *kezayit* (approx. an ounce) of bitter herbs in the center. It is customary to use romaine lettuce and horseradish for *maror*.
CHAROSET | חרוסת	**5.** Place a mixture of apples, nuts, pears on the lower right side, under the *zeroa*. (Add wine before eating the *maror*.)
KARPAS | כרפס	**6.** Place a raw onion (or a boiled potato) on the lower left side, under the egg.
CHAZERET | חזרת	**7.** Place a *kezayit* of bitter herbs in the center, under the *maror*. It is customary to use romaine lettuce and horseradish for *chazeret*.

24a

description of Bezalel (great-grandson of Miriam, sister of Moses), one of the two men chosen by God to lead the construction of the Tabernacle. God imbued Bezalel with an innate talent for all sorts of craftsmanship, including (Exodus 31:5) "stone craft (**charoshet** *even*) and wood craft (**charoshet** *etz*)." The Hebrew words for stone and wood respectively, **even** and **etz**, can be seen as acronyms for the Yiddish names of the *charoset* ingredients: *epel* (apple), **bahren** (pear), **nissen** (nuts), **engber** (ginger), and *tzimerind* (cinnamon). However, the custom is not to use the latter two ingredients for fear they may contain some *chametz* (*The Rebbe's Haggadah*).

৪ KARPAS—VEGETABLE ৪

When reversed, the consonants of the word **karpas** can be read as: *s-p-r-kh*. "S" in Hebrew is represented by the letter *samech*, which stands for the number 60. "P-r-kh" or *perekh*, means crushing labor. *Karpas* thus alludes to the *60* myriad (600,000) Israelites who were subjected to *crushing labor* (*Avudraham*). See below on *Karpas*.

Any non-*maror* vegetable can techinally be used (*Shulchan Aruch HaRav, Orach Chaim* 473:16). Chabad custom is to use an onion (or a potato) for *karpas* (*The Rebbe's Haggadah*).

৪ CHAZERET—ROMAINE LETTUCE ৪

Although we use romaine lettuce and horseradish for both "*maror*" and "*chazeret*," they are called by different names, since the mystical implications of the name "*maror*" relate more to the spiritual dimension of the *maror* of the Seder Plate, whereas the mystical implications of the name "*chazeret*" relate to *Korech,* when the *chazeret* is used (*The Rebbe's Haggadah*).

Romaine lettuce is sweet and soft at the outset, but when left in the ground, its stem hardens and becomes "bitter as wormwood."[14] It is therefore best to use this lettuce, since it reflects the manner in which we were seduced into slavery. The Egyptians manipulated us with sweet words and rewards, but eventually embittered our lives (*Pesachim* 39a; *Levush; Chacham Tzvi* §119; *Shulchan Aruch HaRav* 473:30).

৪ KABBALISTIC PERSPECTIVE ৪

The Arizal teaches that the Seder Plate encompasses the ten *sefirot* (Godly attributes):

Seder Plate Item	Corresponding Sefirah
Three Matzot	*Chochmah, Binah* and *Daat* (Wisdom, Understanding, Knowledge)
Zeroa	*Chesed* (Kindness)
Beitzah	*Gevurah* (Strength)
Maror	*Tiferet* (Beauty/Harmony/Mercy)
Charoset	*Netzach* (Victory/Determination)
Karpas	*Hod* (Glory/Humility)
Chazeret	*Yesod* (Foundation/Attachment)
The Tray	*Malchut* (Kingship)

⤳ THE SEDER PLATE ⤦

❧ THREE MATZOT ❧

The Jewish community of Kairouan [eastern Tunisia] once asked Rav Sherira Gaon: "Why do we take three *matzot* on the night of Pesach, no less and no more?"

Rav Sherira pointed to an allusion to this custom in the story of the angels' visit to Abraham and Sarah, which occurred during Pesach (*Bereishit Rabbah* 48:13). Abraham asked Sarah to prepare *three* measures of flour for baking cakes (Genesis 18:6).[9]

The three *matzot* also evoke the three "mountains" of the world, our Patriarchs: Abraham, Isaac, and Jacob (*Maaseh Rokeach* 16:58).

❧ ZEROA & THE EGG ❧

The Sages instituted that we have two cooked foods before us during the recitation of the Haggadah. These commemorate the two sacrifices that our ancestors partook of during the Seder in Temple times:

1) the Paschal lamb,[10] and

2) the Chagigah offering, a sacrifice brought to celebrate the festivals (*Pesachim* 114b).[11]

The custom arose to use part of the *zeroa* (foreleg) of an animal and an egg to signify the following:

The animal's foreleg, or arm, represents G-d's arm (*zeroa*, in Hebrew). The Aramaic word for egg (*be'a*) can also mean *desire*. Together, the two words allude to the following:

"The Merciful One *desired* to redeem us with an 'outstretched *arm*'[12] (*Kol Bo* citing the Jerusalem Talmud).[13]

❧ MAROR—BITTER HERBS ❧

The bitter herbs remind us of the bitter times we had in Egypt. In a personal sense, we experience "*maror*" when we contemplate our distance from Godliness and cry bitter tears over our spiritual inadequacy. This sort of honest self-appraisal, which evokes our yearning to be close to God, awakens God's great mercy upon us.

Kabbalistically, the *zeroa* is associated with kindness and the egg with strength. The *zeroa* is therefore placed on the right side, which is associated with kindness, while the egg is placed on the left side, the side of strength.

Maror is placed in the middle, since mercy is the synthesis of kindness and strength (*Likkutei Torah, Shir Hashirim* 14d; see *Kabbalistic Perspective* below).

❧ CHAROSET—THE DIP ❧

The clay-like *charoset* reminds us of the clay with which our ancestors were forced to work. [Even the word *charoset*, a generic term referring to any type of dip (*Machzor Vitri*), approximates *charsit*, which means clay (*Mordechai* citing Jerusalem Talmud).] We add an acrid substance to the mix (*Pesachim* 116a) to remind us of how the teeth of Israel were set on edge by the harshness of their bondage (*Bach*).

The *charoset* is made from fruits to which the people of Israel have been compared in the Torah (*Teshuvot HaGeonim*). This mixture is then softened with a red liquid to commemorate the blood of the first plague (Jerusalem Talmud, *Pesachim* 10:3).

Pri Etz Chaim points to a mnemonic for the ingredients of *charoset* in the Torah's

סִימָן סֵדֶר שֶׁל פֶּסַח

קַדֵּשׁ. וּרְחַץ. כַּרְפַּס. יַחַץ. מַגִּיד. רָחְצָה. מוֹצִיא. מַצָּה. מָרוֹר. כּוֹרֵךְ. שֻׁלְחָן עוֹרֵךְ. צָפוּן. בָּרֵךְ. הַלֵּל. נִרְצָה.

soothing words.[15] Perhaps you will say, "From where shall I have what to give to the poor?" The answer is: *Yachatz*—divide your bread, and give a portion to the less fortunate.

Sanctify and purify your behavior (*kadesh-urechatz*) and you will merit *karpas-yachatz*: The "harsh labor" of life (*karpas*), the yoke of financial worries, and other anxieties will be broken (*yachatz*) and removed from you (*Alshich; Chatam Sofer*).

מַגִּיד רָחְצָה **Maggid Rachtzah:** Don't be satisfied with your own spiritual work; reach out to others and teach them (*maggid*).

[Your efforts will be enhanced if you] consistently seek out and *cleanse* yourself (*rachtzah*) of character flaws (see *Alshich; Chida*).

מוֹצִיא מַצָּה **Motzi Matzah:** *Matzah*, which is unbloated and simple, represents humility. It thus alludes to the good inclination, the opposite of *chametz*, which alludes to the evil inclination (see above, Searching for *Chametz*).

Motzi means to extract (as in *hamotzi lechem min ha'aretz*: "Blessed are You, God…who *extracts* bread from the earth").

Through your spiritual work, charity, and reaching out to others, you will extract (*motzi*) your good inclination (*matzah*) from its dormancy and give it dominion over your life (*Alshich*).[16]

מָרוֹר כּוֹרֵךְ **Maror Korech:** Now that you have allowed your good inclination to emerge, wrap the *matzah* and *maror* together: Educate and elevate your evil inclination—symbolized by

the maror—so that you may serve God with both of your inclinations (*Alshich*).

Additionally, in reaching out to others, incline your shoulder to help carry their burdens—wrap together (*korech*) their bitter woes (*maror*) and carry it for them (*Chatam Sofer*).

שֻׁלְחָן עוֹרֵךְ **Shulchan Orech:** Remember that God's table is always set; it is within His capacity to sustain those who trust in Him (*Ben Ish Chai*).

By fulfilling all the above, you will merit a "set table" in this world and to the *hidden blessings* (*tzafun-beirach*) of the World to Come (*Chatam Sofer; Alshich*).

צָפוּן בָּרֵךְ **Tzafun Beirach:** Recognize that there are two types of blessings in life: those we can clearly see and those we remain unaware of. Remember to thank God not only for the revealed blessings and miracles but for the *tzafun-beirach*, the hidden blessings as well. Your praise of God (*hallel*) is then complete and accepted (*nirtzah*) (*Ben Ish Chai*).

הַלֵּל נִרְצָה **Hallel Nirtzah:** Some hidden blessings appear to us as troubles. *Hallel* means to praise God for the good as well as what appears to us as negative. In the words of Rabbi Akiva (*Berachot* 60b): "All that the Merciful one does is for the good."

[Internalize the above, and you will] always be in a state of *nirtzah*, conditioned to *accept favorably* whatever challenges you may face. Anger and disappointment, even momentary, should become foreign and unknown (*Chida*).

∽ MNEMONIC FOR THE PESACH SEDER ∾

Kadesh	Recite Kiddush
Urechatz	And Wash hands
Karpas	Eating the Vegetable
Yachatz	Breaking/Dividing the middle matzah
Maggid	Relating the Pesach story
Rachtzah	Washing the hands
Motzi	Blessing of Hamotzi over matzah
Matzah	Blessing over and eating of Matzah
Maror	Eating the Bitter Herb
Korech	Wrapping Together of matzah and maror
Shulchan Orech	A Set Table (eating the festive meal)
Tzafun	Eating the Hidden afikoman
Beirach	Blessing after the meal
Hallel	Recitation of Hallel
Nirtzah	Our Seder is Accepted Favorably by God

 Notes & Insights

✡ SEDER MNEMONIC ✡

In *Machzor Vitri* this mnemonic/poem is cited in the name of *Rashi*. Some attribute it to one of the *Tosfot*, Rabbi Shmuel of Falaise.

Other versions of the poem are cited in *Sefer HaPardes* (*Rashi*), *Hagahot Maimoniot*, and *Avudraham*. However, in the Kabbalistic works *Pri Etz Chaim, Mishnat Chasidim*, and *Siddur HaArizal*, the currently standard *Kadesh Urechatz* is used.

Alshich, Chida and others provide interpretations of the mnemonic as spiritual instruction (*The Rebbe's Haggadah*; see below).

✡ THE FIFTEEN STEPS OF SPIRITUAL INSTRUCTION ✡

קַדֵּשׁ וּרְחַץ **Kadesh Urechatz:** *Sanctify* (or *separate*) yourself from unhealthy behaviors and *cleanse* yourself from them (*Chida, Alshich*).

Additionally, through the fulfillment of *mitzvot*, you *sanctify* yourself for the future and *wash* yourself of the spiritual maladies of the past. Torah is like an elixir that not only strengthens its patients for the future, it cures them of every previous illness and pain (*Ben Ish Chai*).

כַּרְפַּס יַחַץ **Karpas Yachatz:** The humble vegetable teaches us to be modest and yielding by remembering that we are not perfect—our character is *divided* between good qualities and those that can be improved (*Chida; Ben Ish Chai*).

Be satisfied with a simple vegetable dipped in salt water—*karpas*. But reserve this austerity for yourself. For the other, for the poor, fill their palm with plenty, and encourage them with

קדש
Kadesh

English translation of Kiddush is on page 28

All present fill their cups for Kiddush. Fill to the top and overflow a little. Say:

אַתְקִינוּ סְעוּדָתָא דְמַלְכָּא עִלָּאָה, דָּא הִיא סְעוּדָתָא דְקוּדְשָׁא בְּרִיךְ הוּא וּשְׁכִנְתֵּיהּ.

• Stand for Kiddush. Take the cup of wine in the right hand, pass it to the left hand, and lower it onto the palm of the right hand. The cup should be held three *tefachim* (approximately 9 in.) above the table throughout the Kiddush. (Note that this procedure is followed every time the cup is held throughout the Seder.)

Look at the festival candles (as on Shabbat and other festivals), then say:

On Friday night, begin here.

יוֹם הַשִּׁשִּׁי. וַיְכֻלּוּ הַשָּׁמַיִם וְהָאָרֶץ וְכָל צְבָאָם. וַיְכַל אֱלֹהִים בַּיּוֹם הַשְּׁבִיעִי מְלַאכְתּוֹ אֲשֶׁר עָשָׂה, וַיִּשְׁבֹּת בַּיּוֹם הַשְּׁבִיעִי מִכָּל מְלַאכְתּוֹ אֲשֶׁר עָשָׂה. וַיְבָרֶךְ אֱלֹהִים אֶת יוֹם הַשְּׁבִיעִי וַיְקַדֵּשׁ אֹתוֹ, כִּי בוֹ שָׁבַת מִכָּל מְלַאכְתּוֹ אֲשֶׁר בָּרָא אֱלֹהִים לַעֲשׂוֹת.

 Notes & Insights

Many have the custom that the leader of the household does not pour the wine but rather has someone else fill his cup in the manner of a king. This is not the Chabad custom (*The Rebbe's Haggadah*).

✥ A HALACHICALLY UNIQUE KIDDUSH ✥

In addition to the general Rabbinic mandate to recite Kiddush on *any* festival,[17] tonight's Kiddush gains an additional element: it is one of the Four Cups. This latter element sets it apart in the following ways:

• Kiddush can be recited over bread (or matzah). Tonight, it must be recited over wine.

• Only one person must drink the wine (though it is best for everyone to have a sip). Tonight, all must drink their cup of wine.

• One who cannot afford or does not react well to wine need not use wine for Kiddush. The Sages, however, deemed the obligation to drink the Four Cups so essential that they required everyone to do so, even one who reacts unfavorably to wine or who may have to "sell his garments" to afford it (*Nedarim* 49b; *Pesachim* 99b).

• One can recite Kiddush before nightfall and usher in Shabbat or a festival early.[18] The Four Cups, however, must be drunk during the time that one can fulfill the mitzvah of matzah, namely, after nightfall. Tonight, therefore, Kiddush must be recited after nightfall.

• One is only obligated to drink approximately two ounces of the Kiddush wine. Tonight, one must drink the entire cup, or at least most of it (*The Rebbe's Haggadah*).

On a weeknight, begin here. Glance at the wine and say:

סַבְרִי מָרָנָן

בָּרוּךְ אַתָּה יְיָ, אֱלֹהֵינוּ מֶלֶךְ הָעוֹלָם, בּוֹרֵא פְּרִי הַגָּפֶן.

On Friday night, add the words in shaded parentheses.

בָּרוּךְ אַתָּה יְיָ, אֱלֹהֵינוּ מֶלֶךְ הָעוֹלָם, אֲשֶׁר בָּחַר בָּנוּ מִכָּל עָם, וְרוֹמְמָנוּ מִכָּל לָשׁוֹן, וְקִדְּשָׁנוּ בְּמִצְוֹתָיו. וַתִּתֶּן לָנוּ יְיָ אֱלֹהֵינוּ בְּאַהֲבָה (שַׁבָּתוֹת לִמְנוּחָה וּ)מוֹעֲדִים לְשִׂמְחָה, חַגִּים וּזְמַנִּים לְשָׂשׂוֹן, אֶת יוֹם (הַשַּׁבָּת הַזֶּה וְאֶת יוֹם) חַג הַמַּצּוֹת הַזֶּה, וְאֶת יוֹם טוֹב מִקְרָא קֹדֶשׁ הַזֶּה, זְמַן חֵרוּתֵנוּ, (בְּאַהֲבָה) מִקְרָא קֹדֶשׁ, זֵכֶר לִיצִיאַת מִצְרָיִם. כִּי בָנוּ בָחַרְתָּ וְאוֹתָנוּ קִדַּשְׁתָּ מִכָּל הָעַמִּים, (וְשַׁבָּת) וּמוֹעֲדֵי קָדְשֶׁךָ (בְּאַהֲבָה וּבְרָצוֹן) בְּשִׂמְחָה וּבְשָׂשׂוֹן הִנְחַלְתָּנוּ: בָּרוּךְ אַתָּה יְיָ, מְקַדֵּשׁ (הַשַּׁבָּת וְ)יִשְׂרָאֵל וְהַזְּמַנִּים.

On Saturday night, add the following:

במוצאי שבת מקדשים יקנה"ז. יין, קידוש, נר, הבדלה, זמן:

Glance at the festival candles while reciting the following blessing:

בָּרוּךְ אַתָּה יְיָ, אֱלֹהֵינוּ מֶלֶךְ הָעוֹלָם, בּוֹרֵא מְאוֹרֵי הָאֵשׁ.

בָּרוּךְ אַתָּה יְיָ, אֱלֹהֵינוּ מֶלֶךְ הָעוֹלָם, הַמַּבְדִּיל בֵּין קֹדֶשׁ לְחוֹל, בֵּין אוֹר לְחֹשֶׁךְ, בֵּין יִשְׂרָאֵל לָעַמִּים, בֵּין יוֹם הַשְּׁבִיעִי לְשֵׁשֶׁת יְמֵי הַמַּעֲשֶׂה. בֵּין קְדֻשַּׁת שַׁבָּת לִקְדֻשַּׁת יוֹם טוֹב הִבְדַּלְתָּ, וְאֶת יוֹם הַשְּׁבִיעִי מִשֵּׁשֶׁת יְמֵי הַמַּעֲשֶׂה קִדַּשְׁתָּ, הִבְדַּלְתָּ וְקִדַּשְׁתָּ אֶת עַמְּךָ יִשְׂרָאֵל בִּקְדֻשָּׁתֶךָ: בָּרוּךְ אַתָּה יְיָ, הַמַּבְדִּיל בֵּין קֹדֶשׁ לְקֹדֶשׁ.

One who recited the שֶׁהֶחֱיָנוּ blessing during candle lighting should not recite it here.

בָּרוּךְ אַתָּה יְיָ, אֱלֹהֵינוּ מֶלֶךְ הָעוֹלָם, שֶׁהֶחֱיָנוּ וְקִיְּמָנוּ וְהִגִּיעָנוּ לִזְמַן הַזֶּה.

שותה הכוס בישיבה בהסיבת שמאל דרך חרות

Drink the entire cup without interruption, seated and reclining to the left as a sign of freedom. One who cannot drink the entire cup should drink at least most of it.

Festivals, (in love and favor,) in happiness and joy. Blessed are You, God, who sanctifies (the Shabbat and) Israel and the festive seasons.

On Saturday night, add the following:

Glance at the festival candles while reciting the following blessing:

Blessed are You, God, our God, King of the universe, who creates the lights of the fire.

Blessed are You, God, our God, King of the universe, who makes a distinction between sacred and profane, between light and darkness, between Israel and the nations, between the seventh day and the six workdays. You have made a distinction between the holiness of the Shabbat and the holiness of the festival, and You have sanctified the seventh day above the six workdays. You have set apart and made holy Your people Israel with Your holiness. Blessed are You, God, who makes a distinction between holy and holy.

One who recited the following during candle lighting should not recite it here.

Blessed are You, God, our God, King of the universe, who has granted us life, sustained us, and enabled us to reach this occasion.

Drink the entire cup without interruption, seated and reclining to the left as a sign of freedom. One who cannot drink the entire cup should drink at least most of it.

 Notes & Insights

יוֹם הַשִּׁשִּׁי **The sixth day.** The Kiddush for Shabbat should seemingly begin with the paragraph *And the heavens and the earth...were completed.* Why does it begin with the words *Yom Hashisi, The Sixth Day*—which are the last two words of the preceding verse?

The reason *Yom Hashisi* is added is to spell out God's Name, Y-H-V-H in the first letters of the first four words of the Friday night Kiddush: *Yom Hashishi Vayechulu Hashamaim* (Rema, *Shulchan Aruch, Orach Chaim* 271:10).

Why then do we not begin from the beginning of the verse that ends with *Yom Hashishi?*

We want to avoid the beginning of the verse—*G-d saw all that He had made and behold it was very good*—since our Sages interpret "very good" as an allusion to death (see below

on p. 68b, "Holy Harshness"; *Responsa Chatam Sofer, Orach Chaim* §10).

חַג הַמַּצּוֹת **Festival of Matzot.** This is how Passover is called throughout the Torah. Why, then, do Jews generally call it "Pesach"?

In the Torah, God calls the festival by a name that praises the Jewish People: Even though we did not know what awaited us in the desert, we immediately and unhesitatingly followed the instruction to leave Egypt, without even waiting for our dough to rise.

We, in turn, refer to the festival in a way that praises God: Pesach means to skip, referring to God's skipping over our homes during the plague of the firstborn (*Kedushat Levi, Parshat Bo*).[19]

28b

～ KADESH—RECITING THE KIDDUSH ～

All present fill their cups for Kiddush. Fill to the top and overflow a little. Say:

Prepare the meal of the supernal King. This is the meal of the Holy One, blessed be He, and His Shechinah.

Stand for Kiddush. Take the cup of wine in the right hand, pass it to the left hand, and lower it onto the palm of the right hand. The cup should be held three *tefachim* (approximately 9 in.) above the table throughout the Kiddush. (Note that this procedure is followed every time the cup is held throughout the Seder.)

Look at the festival candles (as on Shabbat and other festivals), then say:

> **On Friday night, begin here.**
>
> **The sixth day.** And the heavens and the earth and all their hosts were completed. And on the seventh day God finished His work which He had made, and He rested on the seventh day from all His work which He had made. And God blessed the seventh day and made it holy, for on it He rested from all His work which God created to make.

On a weeknight begin here. Glance at the wine and say:

Attention, Gentlemen!

Blessed are You, God, our God, King of the universe, who creates the fruit of the vine.

On Friday night, add the words in shaded parentheses.

Blessed are You, God, our God, King of the universe, who has chosen us from among all people, and raised us above all tongues, and made us holy through His commandments.

And You, God, our God, have given us in love (Shabbats for rest and) festivals for happiness, feasts and festive seasons for rejoicing, (this Shabbat day and) the day of this Feast of Matzot, and this Festival of holy convocation, the Season of our Freedom, (in love), a holy convocation, commemorating the departure from Egypt.

For You have chosen us and sanctified us from all the nations, and You have given us as a heritage Your holy (Shabbat and)

∾ Urechatz—Washing the Hands ∾

ורחץ   ונוטל ידיו ואינו מברך.

All present now wash their hands in the following manner:

- Pick up the cup containing the water in your right hand. Pass it to your left hand, and pour three times on your right hand. Then pass the cup to your right hand and pour three times on your left hand. (It is customary to hold the cup with a towel when pouring on the left hand.)

- A little water from the final pouring should remain in the left hand, which is then rubbed over both hands together.

- Dry your hands.

- The blessing *al netilat yadaim* is not said.

environment, nothing but the king is meant to be acknowledged (see *Chagigah* 5b).

Similarly, after attaining holiness and standing, as it were, in God's palace, one reexamines the self and purifies it of anything that is not completely permeated with Divine awareness.

This is the *urechatz*, the washing, that follows the sanctification of *kadesh* (*The Rebbe*).[21]

੪ THE KABBALISTIC "AND" ੪

 Kabbalistically, *kadesh* and *urechatz* represent *chochmah* and *binah*—the first two steps in the intellectual process. *Chochmah* is the flash of insight, the kernel of an idea. *Binah* is where the seminal point is fleshed out and articulated.

Whereas the rest of the fifteen steps represent the emotions—each of which exists independent of the others—*chochmah* and *binah* are interdependent. In the words of the *Zohar* (III:4a), they are "like two friends that never part":

The seminal point of *chochmah* depends upon *binah* for its articulation; the articulation that occurs in *binah* must constantly be imbued

with the seminal point of *chochmah*, so that it remains loyal to the original idea.

Back and Forth

Although we generally think of *chochmah* as preceding and feeding *binah*, the truth is that the relationship is bi-directional:

When the point of *chochmah* is expanded in *binah*, *chochmah* itself is enhanced by the experience. This is because *binah* possesses certain properties that stem from a source that transcends *chochmah*. This enables *binah* to extend "lower" than *chochmah*, since that which is higher has the ability to extend lower. (For example, the brilliant teacher can explain a profound concept even to those with poor intelligence, whereas a lesser teacher can only explain the idea to the wise.)

Through its interaction with *binah*, *chochmah* gains from *binah's* superior qualities.

This is the mystical explanation for why *Kadesh* and *Urechatz*—*chochmah* and *binah*—are connected with an "and"—reflecting the symbiotic relationship of *chochmah* and *binah*.[22]

Notes & Insights

❧ WASHING THE HANDS ❧

Most are familiar with the obligation to wash one's hands prior to eating bread. There is also an obligation to do so prior to eating wet foods (see *Pesachim* 115a). Since we are about to eat a wet vegetable, we wash our hands in accordance with the above law.

Why do we omit the blessing?

According to some authorities, we are not required to wash for wet foods nowadays. We therefore do not recite a blessing over this washing, in accordance with the rule that we do not recite a blessing over a mitzvah whose requirement is not certain.

For if we are indeed not required to perform the mitzvah, our blessing (e.g., "Blessed are You, God...who...*commanded* us concerning the washing of the hands") will have been meaningless. We would thus have uttered God's name improperly.

Why are we particularly careful to wash for a wet vegetable on this night?

Even those who are generally not careful about washing for wet foods throughout the year, do so during the Seder, thus adding another unusual ritual to intrigue the children (*Chok Yaakov*).

❧ ADDITIONAL LAWS ❧

Many Jews do not generally observe the obligation to wash before eating wet foods. This behavior need not be protested, since one can find support for it amongst some halachic authorities. Nevertheless, the prevailing opinion is that washing is required.

Washing is required even if one dips the tip of a food into liquid and holds the food without touching the liquid. Furthermore, if it is the sort of food that is usually eaten without a utensil, such as a wet apple, washing is required even when eating the food with a utensil. Wet food that is normally eaten with a utensil, such as soup, does not require washing (see *Shulchan Aruch HaRav, Orach Chaim* 158:3).

❧ SANCTIFY AND WASH ❧

In the poem *Kadesh-Urechatz*, the first two steps are unique in that they are conjugated with an "and"—Sanctify *and* Wash.

Chida offers a halachic explanation: The "and" tells us that washing must be done *after* the Kiddush, even for those who normally wash *before* Kiddush. Or, even one who washed prior to Kiddush would have to wash again at this point.

❧ AN UNUSUAL SEQUENCE ❧

Urechatz alludes to "washing our hands" of the idolatry of Egypt. We did so by offering the Paschal lamb and thus slaughtering and defying the idol of Egypt. More broadly, then, *Urechatz* alludes to cleansing ourselves of the impurity caused by misdeeds.

(*Urechatz,* which can connote bathing, also evokes Egypt's refusal to allow the Israelite women to use the river as a *mikveh* of purification. The first plague, which turned the river to blood, came as a punishment for this crime (*Chida*).)

It would seem that washing, purification, should be the *first* step of the Seder, *followed*

by *Kadesh*, sanctification.[20] The reversal on this night alludes to a loftier type of purity, one that follows and *transcends* sanctity. This is not the purification from dirt or blemishes, but purification from all sense of self:

In the King's Presence

One who achieves a state of holiness and closeness to God is as if standing before God. When standing before a king, even a mortal one, one stands with absolute and undivided attention to the king. Behavior that is no crime at all outside the king's presence could be a capital offense in the palace. Drawing attention to the self is completely out of place, since, in that

כרפס
Karpas

∽ DIPPING & EATING THE KARPAS ∾

כרפס   נוטל פחות מכזית כרפס ויטבול במי מלח או חומץ ויברך:

- Take less than an ounce (*kezayit*) of the *karpas*, dip it into salt water, and recite the following blessing. Bear in mind that this blessing also applies to the bitter herbs of *Maror* and *Korech*.

בָּרוּךְ אַתָּה יְיָ, אֱלֹהֵינוּ מֶלֶךְ הָעוֹלָם, בּוֹרֵא פְּרִי הָאֲדָמָה.

Blessed are You, God, our God, King of the universe, who creates the fruit of the earth.

יכוין להוציא גם המרור בברכה זו:

Eat the *karpas* without reclining.

Keep the *maror* in mind. Some authorities maintain that the *maror* requires the blessing *borei pri ha'adamah*. Others maintain that the latter is covered by the blessing on the matzah. It is therefore best to keep the *maror* in mind when reciting the blessing on *karpas*, to satisfy the former view (see *Shulchan Aruch HaRav*

473:17-18). [One who forgot to do so should not recite *borei pri ha'adamah* on the *maror*.][29]

Leftovers. "I have not seen that leftover *karpas* is replaced on the Seder Plate. Consequently, from this point on there are only five foods on the Seder Plate" (*The Rebbe's Haggadah*).

❧ ELEMENTS OF KARPAS ❧

In addition to intriguing the children and reminding us of the crushing labor, the *karpas* ritual evokes many other ideas, including the following:

Freedom: In celebration of our freedom, we eat in luxury, enjoying an appetizer prior to the meal in the manner of the free (*Bach*).

Joseph's Robe: There is one event that one can point to as the very *first* in a long sequence of events that led to our enslavement: Jacob giving Joseph a beautiful robe. This ignited the jealously of his brothers and ultimately led them to sell Joseph as a slave. This led to Jacob's descent to Egypt, which led to the enslavement of all of Israel to Pharaoh (see *Shabbat* 10a).

This robe was called *ketonet pasim*, a fine woolen robe (Genesis 37:3). Commenting on the word ***pasim***, Rashi relates it to the word ***karpas***: "This is an expression referring to fine

woolen garments, as in Esther (1:6): *Carpets of karpas (green wool)....* The *karpas* at the Seder thus evokes Joseph's coat, the object that led to the exile (*Rabbenu Manoach*).

Medicinal Properties: *Karpas* was eaten and topically applied by our ancestors in Egypt to soothe their wounds and bruises, especially to reduce swelling (*Orchot Chaim*).

Two Dippings: The first dipping (*karpas*) alludes to the events that led to our descent into Egypt. The second dipping (*maror*) alludes to the mitzvah for which we merited to ascend.

Descent: The first dipping alludes to the brothers dipping Joseph's coat into animal blood to fool Jacob into thinking that Joseph had been devoured by a wild animal.

Ascent: The second dipping alludes to when God commanded us to dip a hyssop into blood and place the blood on our doorposts prior to the plague of the firstborn (*Maasei Hashem*).

৪৪ KARPAS ৪৪

Throughout the year, traditionally, a meal begins with breaking bread. Tonight, we veer from tradition and taste a vegetable prior to the meal (Mishnah, *Pesachim* 114a). This is done to intrigue the children (*Rashi, Rashbam, Rambam* ad loc.).[23]

The Mishnah does not require any particular vegetable to be used. However, the custom is to use a vegetable called *karpas* because the word **karp**as, spelled backward, alludes to the crushing labor—**perek**h—we suffered in Egypt (*Maharil*; see above, commentary on the Seder Plate and below, pp. 51a-b on "*They embittered their lives*").

When Did the Custom to Use Karpas Arise? In the *Siddur Rav Amram Gaon* (9th century CE), *karpas* is mentioned as one of a *few* options among other vegetables. *Rambam* and *Tur* refer only to vegetables and make no mention of *karpas per se*.

The *Shulchan Aruch* calls for "*karpas* or a different vegetable." Rabbi Schneur Zalman of Liadi, in his *Shulchan Aruch*, initially outlines the obligation and refers only to "vegetables." In a later paragraph, he writes that it is customary to seek out a vegetable called *karpas*, which he translates as *Apiaceae*.

So Which Vegetable is Karpas? *Chatam Sofer* writes: *My teacher, Rabbi Nattan Adler, labored and toiled to determine which vegetable is called* karpas. *He did so because it 'emerged from the mouth' of that great rabbi, Maharil, that* karpas *should be used. My teacher found that it is called apia [Apium],*[24] *which in German is sellerie (celery).*[25] The author of *Machatzit Hashekel* comes to the same conclusion. Others have identified it with parsley and other vegetables. Some suggest that *karpas* is a general term that refers to several types of vegetables.[26] Chabad custom is to use onions (or potatoes).[27]

The Dip. We dip the vegetable prior to saying the blessing so that we can eat the vegetable without interruption, immediately after reciting the blessing (*Chok Yaakov*). When eating bread, however, we say the blessing *before* dipping the bread in salt. This is done because we recite the blessing before cutting the bread (so that the blessing is said over a whole or larger loaf) (*The Rebbe's Haggadah*).

The Mishnah does not specify what the vegetable should be dipped into. Some dip the *karpas* into *charoset*, others dip it into wine. The custom to use salt water or vinegar follows the opinion of *Tosfot* on *Pesachim* 114a (cf. *Rashbam*; *Rosh*; *Pri Chadash*).

When Pesach occurs on Shabbat, it is best to prepare the salt water prior to Shabbat. One who forgets to do so may prepare the salt water on Shabbat but only in the amount that is absolutely necessary for this dipping (*Shulchan Aruch Harav, Orach Chaim* 473:19).

Less Than a Kezayit. Normally, whenever we are required to eat something in fulfilling a mitzvah, such as eating matzah or *maror*, we must eat at least a *kezayit*—nearly twenty-six grams or a fraction less than an ounce. Eating anything less than a *kezayit* is not defined as "eating."

Yet we do *not* need to eat a *kezayit* of the *karpas* vegetable. For the primary objective is not to eat the *karpas* per se, but to intrigue the children, which can be accomplished even with less than a *kezayit* (*Hagahot Maimoniot*).

One should in fact *avoid* eating more than a *kezayit*, since doing so creates the halachic dilemma of whether an after-blessing should be recited (*Maharil*).[28]

One who did eat a *kezayit* should not recite an after-blessing, since there is an opinion that the latter is covered by the after-blessing following the meal. And whenever there is a dispute over whether a blessing is required, we err on the side of not saying the blessing, lest we unjustifiably recite God's name in a possibly unnecessary blessing (*Magen Avraham; Shulchan Aruch HaRav* 473:17-18).

~ BREAKING THE MATZAH ~

יחץ ויקח מצה האמצעית ופורסה לשנים חלק אחד גדול מחבירו והלק הגדול יניח לאפיקומן והקטן מניח בין הב' מצות:

- Break the middle matzah into two pieces (while still covered by the cloth), one larger than the other.

- Break the larger piece into five pieces, then wrap it in cloth and set aside to serve as *afikoman*.

- The smaller piece remains between the two whole *matzot*.

perceive, there is an undercurrent of goodness and Divine awareness that is permeating the world. We have studied the smaller piece for long enough; it is time for the *afikoman* of history to make its appearance (*The Rebbe*).[33]

✥ THE FIVE PIECES ✥

Kabbalah
Rabbi Yosef Yitzchak of Lubavitch did not know if his father, Rabbi Shalom DovBer, was deliberately breaking the *afikoman* into five pieces. Once, the *afikoman* broke into six pieces and Rabbi Shalom DovBer set the sixth piece aside. His son then asked him what the significance of the five pieces was. Rabbi Shalom DovBer replied: "*Az men vil altz vissen, vert men gech alt*—one who wants to know everything becomes old quickly."

Later, during a walk, the Rebbe heard his son sigh and realized that he was upset that he did not merit to hear the reason for the five pieces. He said to his son, "I see that it is very important to you," and then proceeded to explain: The middle matzah corresponds to Isaac, whose primary attribute is *Gevurah*, strength or severity. The word *yachatz* thus contains three of the letters of *Yitzchak*. *Afikoman* is related to the "Kindness of Abraham." *Afiko-man*, which means "bring out food," corresponds to Abraham, who provided nourishment to all, and whose primary attribute was Kindness. Kabbalah teaches that *Gevurah* is made up of five elements.

By breaking the middle matzah, we "break" the severity and "sweeten" its five elements with the "Kindness of Abraham" (*Sefer Hasichot 5698*, p. 261).

✥ YACHATZ IN YEMEN ✥

Rabbi Yaakov Sapir HaLevi (1822-1885) writes in his travelogue of a Pesach spent in Yemen, in the city of Sana'a:

"*They bake fresh matzah each day of Pesach in the custom of their forefathers, since their women are very quick and conscientious in the baking of the matzot....*

"*At the Seder, one participant takes a matzah, ties it in a napkin, places it on his shoulders and walks around the house. The others ask him: 'Why are you doing this?' To which he responds: 'So did our ancestors do when they left Egypt in haste.'*"

✿ YACHATZ ✿

We break the matzah prior to beginning the story of the Exodus (*Ran* citing *Rav Hai Gaon*), so that the story is told over matzah fit for the mitzvah—"poor man's bread"—i.e., a broken piece (see *Pesachim* 115b). The larger piece is set aside for the *afikoman*, since it is a significant mitzvah, one through which we commemorate the Pesach offering (*Maharil*; *Bach*).

We wrap the *afikoman* in a cloth (see *Zohar* II:158b; *Tur* and *Shulchan Aruch* §473). This commemorates the way we left Egypt with the leftover matzah (and *maror*) wrapped in our garments (Exodus 12:34, and *Rashi* ad loc.; see *Rokeach* and *Beit Yosef*). We place it among the pillows (*Hamanhig*) so that it is not inadvertently eaten during the meal (*Siddur Yaavetz*).

✿ STEALING THE AFIKOMAN ✿

Some have the custom that children "steal" the *afikoman* and redeem it for a prize (see *Chok Yaakov*). This is not the Chabad custom (see *The Rebbe's Haggadah*).[30] Indeed several authorities have questioned the prudence of this custom (see *Otzar Minhagei Chabad*).

Some Jews have the custom to place the *afikoman* on their shoulders prior to hiding it, since this was how the Israelites left Egypt, with the leftover matzah (and *maror*) bundled on their shoulders (*Magen Avraham* 473:22; *Yaavetz*). Although they had many animals that could have carried these bundles, they insisted on carrying them themselves because they cherished these items used for a mitzvah (*Rashi* on Exodus 12:34 from *Mechilta*).

✿ TWO REDEMPTIONS ✿

Midrash The two halves of the matzah correspond to the two redemptions we are celebrating tonight.[31] The first half of the Seder focuses on the redemption from Egypt. This was an incomplete redemption, since it was followed by exile later in our history. It is therefore represented by the smaller piece of matzah, which remains in front of us as we recount the Exodus from Egypt.

The second half of the Seder focuses on the future, eternal redemption. This future redemption is represented by the *afikoman*, which remains hidden, just as the day of our future redemption remains hidden from us (*Chatam Sofer*[32]; see *Chida*).

✿ UNITY OF OPPOSITES ✿

Chasidus The two pieces of the matzah embody two starkly different realities. The small piece is "**poor** man's bread"; the larger piece is the *afikoman*, which must be eaten at the end of the meal, like a dessert, in the manner of the **rich** who continue eating even after having eaten their fill.

This duality of the middle matzah is an example of the duality that runs throughout the

Seder: On the one hand we are celebrating freedom—drinking wine, reclining, and so on—yet at the same time reliving the bitterness of the slavery. The matzah itself is both the bread of slaves and the poor, and at the same time "the bread of faith" and "bread of healing." But it is in the middle matzah that this contrast is most stark, since the very same matzah contains two seemingly contradictory elements.

How is it that these very different elements—poverty and wealth—should find a home in the same matzah?

The answer is that the two are interconnected: the small and broken pieces of life—the challenges and the struggle—bring "the larger piece," the richness of life, to the fore.

When we look around the world today, we may see spiritual poverty and brokenness. We may find it hard to imagine that there is another piece to this very "matzah"—a hidden piece ready to emerge. The story of the Exodus, however, tells us to be optimistic: From the depths of darkness in which we had become immersed in Egypt, we were, in a matter of moments, transported into the historic and unparalleled spiritual revelations of the Exodus.

In truth, despite the darkness that we

מגיד
Maggid

Uncover the *matzot* partially and say:

הָא לַחְמָא עַנְיָא דִּי אֲכָלוּ אַבְהָתָנָא בְּאַרְעָא דְמִצְרַיִם. כָּל דִּכְפִין יֵיתֵי וְיֵכוֹל, כָּל דִּצְרִיךְ יֵיתֵי וְיִפְסַח. הָשַּׁתָּא הָכָא, לְשָׁנָה הַבָּאָה בְּאַרְעָא דְיִשְׂרָאֵל. הָשַּׁתָּא עַבְדִּין, לְשָׁנָה הַבָּאָה בְּנֵי חוֹרִין.

The *matzot* are covered.

✒ BREAD OF AFFLICTION ✒

The term Bread of Affliction or Bread of Poverty (*lechem oni* in Hebrew or *lachma anya* in Aramaic), derives from Deuteronomy 16:3: *you shall eat…matzot, bread of affliction, for in haste you went out of the land of Egypt.* The following are some of the connotations contained in this term:

Bread of Affliction: Matzah recalls the affliction we suffered in Egypt (*Sifrei* cited by *Rashi*).

Bread of Recitation: The Talmud points out that the letters that form the word *oni*, affliction/poverty, can also connote recitation (*oneh*).

Matzah is thus "the bread over which many things are recited"—i.e., the Haggadah and the Hallel.

Pauper's Bread: This has two interpretations.

1) Just as a poor man does not have a complete loaf, so too the mitzvah of matzah is performed with a broken piece of matzah, as mentioned above regarding *Yachatz*.

2) "Just as when a poor couple bakes bread—he heats up the oven and she bakes, so too with matzah: he heats up the oven and she bakes." I.e., because they are so hungry, the woman prepares the dough while her husband is heating the oven so that it can be placed in the oven as soon as the oven gets hot. Similarly, matzah is baked as expeditiously as possible to ensure that it does not become *chametz* (*Pesachim* 116b and *Rashbam* and *Ran* ad loc.).

✒ UNDER THE WHIP ✒

Some commentators maintain that the Israelites ate matzah as slaves in Egypt because their taskmasters, whips in hand, did not give them enough time to allow their dough to rise (*Sforno*).[35]

Today, too, the "whip" of everyday life rushes us along from one material concern to another, leaving us little time to focus on our Creator and our spiritual lives.[36] Our material worries and ambitions consume our minds, dulling our spiritual sense.

By referring to this aspect of the matzah at the start of the Seder, we appeal to the one who feels spiritually distant, the one who says: "What connection do I have to the Seder, to freedom and joy? I know well my spiritual poverty."

To this the Haggadah responds: "Do not despair. In Egypt, too, we ate the bread of poverty, materially and spiritually, and there appeared to be no escape from Pharaoh's crushing whip. Yet, God freed us, elevating us to the highest heights. So too, now, though *this year we are 'here,'* and *this year we are 'slaves,'* very soon we will go from slavery to freedom and from darkness to great light…" (*The Rebbe*).[37]

Next year we will be free. "*We should not have to wait until next year Erev Pesach to be free. It can happen now. Then automatically, 'next year we will be free'….*"[38]
—RABBI YOSEF YITZCHAK OF LUBAVITCH

～ GENERAL INTRODUCTION ～

Uncover the *matzot* partially and say:

This is the bread of affliction that our ancestors ate in the land of Egypt. Whoever is hungry, let him come and eat; whoever is in need, let him come and conduct the Pesach [Seder]. This year we are here; next year in the Land of Israel. This year we are slaves; next year we will be free.

The *matzot* are covered.

 Notes & Insights

❧ MATZAH IN EGYPT? ❧

We eat matzah to commemorate our ancestors' baking of matzah out of *the dough that they had taken* out *of Egypt...* (Exodus 12:39). Yet the phrase "this is the bread of affliction that our ancestors ate *in* Egypt" implies that our ancestors ate matzah in Egypt as well. The commentators offer several views:

After the Exodus: Maharal maintains that although the verse refers to this dough as having been "taken out of Egypt," the truth is that the Israelites were still traveling in a region that was geographically part of Egypt. Hence it is called "the bread...our ancestors ate *in the land of Egypt*" (see also *Machzor Vitri*).

Just Before the Exodus: Other commentators suggest that the matzah referred to in this passage is the one we were commanded to eat during our first Seder, which was held in Egypt proper along with the Paschal Lamb, before midnight on the night of the Exodus (*Kol Bo*).

Abarbanel, however, asserts that the expression *our ancestors ate in the land of Egypt* implies "not a solitary occurrence but something they regularly did throughout their sojourn."

As Slaves: Abarbanel favors the view that the Egyptians fed their slaves matzah, since it takes longer to digest and keeps one satisfied for longer. As Ibn Ezra reported, he was once held captive in India and was fed only matzah during his captivity (*Avudraham;* see *Sforno* cited below).[34]

❧ INVITING THE POOR ❧

The original custom was to leave the door open and invite the poor. When this became impractical, the custom arose to provide for the Pesach needs of the poor *before* Pesach. Nevertheless, we continue to "invite" the poor as our ancestors did (*Avudraham*).

❧ WHY ARAMAIC? ❧

This passage was composed while the Jews were in Babylonia, where the spoken language was Aramaic. It was therefore written in Aramaic so that even uneducated Jews could understand it. The last phrase, "next year we will be free," was said in Hebrew so that non-Jews would not understand it, lest they think the Jews were planning a rebellion (*Kol Bo*). The rest of the Haggadah was composed in the Land of Israel and was therefore written in Hebrew (*The Rebbe's Haggadah*).

Shaloh writes that this passage was composed during the first exile from the Holy Land. The choice of Aramaic reflects the depressed spiritual state of the Jewish people at that time: they were no longer on the level of "Hebrew," a holy language.

The passage therefore switches partially to Hebrew when speaking of the return to the Holy Land during the Second Temple era, reflecting a semi-return to holiness, and then *completely* to Hebrew when referring to the future redemption—*next year...free*—reflecting the perfectly sacred consciousness of that time.

מסלקין הקערה עם המצות לצד אחר ומוזגין לו כוס ב' וכאן הבן שואל מה נשתנה.

Move the Seder Plate to the side, pour the second cup, and here the child asks,
"Mah Nishtanah..."

❧ LIKE THE LOVE FOR A CHILD ☙

It was handed down in the name of the Baal Shem Tov that there are two versions to the introduction to the Four Questions: 1) "Father, I **want** to ask of you four questions"; 2) "Father, I **will** ask of you four questions." Each version, however, begins in an identical manner—"Father." This refers to our Father in Heaven—to whom all of Israel ask the Four Questions (*Rabbi Yosef Yitzchak of Lubavitch*).[44]

The child's asking stimulates God's love for us, like the love of parents for their *young* child, as in the verse (Hosea 11:1) regarding the time of the Exodus: *For Israel is a youth, [therefore] I love him....*[45]

The Torah in several instances describes us as being God's children. The above verse, however, emphasizes that God's love for us is like a parent's love for a *young* child.

Parents love their children because the parent and child are of one essence. But this love is most felt for young children. As children mature, the parents begin to love them for their accomplishments and qualities as well, for their wisdom, good character, or the honor and care they show to their parents. This latter love obscures to some extent the innate, unconditional *parental* love.

The love for a young child, by contrast, who is not yet wise, or good, or helpful, is pure *parental* love, the unconditional love of two beings that are of one essence. The love for the young child is therefore stronger and more evident, since it is not obscured by a conditional love.

Similarly, when we speak of God's love for us in the way a parent loves a young child, we refer to this essential, unconditional love borne of our inherent bond with God.

Staying Young

When we become "mature" and self-aware because of our wisdom and accomplishments, we obscure our essential oneness with God with our sense of self and separateness. But when we humble ourselves like a small child before God, when we see our wisdom and accomplishments as an extension of our service of God, the oneness is restored—we rediscover our youth and the special Divine attention that comes with it (*The Rebbe*).[46]

Moses said to Joshua: "This nation that I am entrusting you with, they are still young goats, they are still children. Do not be irritated with them for what they do, for their Master too was not irritated with them for what they did." As it is written, "When Israel was a youth, I loved him; from Egypt I summoned My son."

When Israel rebelled against God at the Sea of Reeds, the angels said to God: "They are rebelling and provoking, yet You are silent?!"

God said to the angels: "They are children. And one does not get irritated with children. Just as a child emerges soiled from the womb and is then washed, so too Israel: "I washed your blood from upon you. I anointed you with oil and dressed you in embroidered garments...." (Ezekiel 16:9-10)

—YALKUT SHIMONI §527

ꙮ Provoking The Questions ꙮ

מסלקין הקערה **We move the Seder Plate... to the side.** In Talmudic times, each participant had a small table. At this point in the Seder, the custom was to move this little table away from the Seder leader, in order to intrigue the children and provoke them to ask why the table was being taken away before the meal (*Pesachim* 115b). This in turn would stimulate them to ask the rest of the questions of the *Mah Nishtanah*.

Since we no longer use small tables, and moving a large table is quite burdensome, our custom is to instead intrigue the children by moving away the Seder Plate (*Tosfot*).

Originally, the custom was to move the Seder Plate to the other side of the table. Today, however, this is no longer done since the children do not associate the meal with the Seder Plate. They will therefore not be puzzled by its removal (*Shulchan Aruch HaRav* 473:38 from *Magen Avraham* and *Chok Yaakov*).

מוזגין לו כוס ב' וכאן הבן שואל **Pour the second cup and here the child asks.** The Mishnah (*Pesachim* 116a) connects the *Mah Nishtanah* to the second cup: "After the second cup is poured, *here* the child asks." As the Talmud explains, we pour the cup now—even though we will not need to raise the cup for some time[39]—to provoke the children to ask "*Mah Nishtanah*," i.e., "*What is different* about this night that you are pouring a second cup before eating?" (*Rashi; Rashbam*)

This in turn will stimulate them to ask the other questions of the *Mah Nishtanah*. By eliciting questions and then answering them with the story of the Exodus, we fulfill the verse (Deuteronomy 6:20-21): *When your child will ask you tomorrow, saying: "What are these testimonies, statutes and laws, etc.?" And you shall tell your child: "We were slaves, etc."* (*Shulchan Aruch HaRav* 473:40).

ꙮ Focus on Questions ꙮ

Questions are essential to the Seder. They must therefore be asked even when no child is present.

For example, even at a Seder attended only by two Torah scholars proficient in the laws of Pesach, one scholar must ask the other. One who is alone asks the questions to himself (*Pesachim* 116a).

What is the point of asking oneself the questions? The mitzvah tonight is to tell the story *to another person*. By asking yourself the questions, you become the "other" to whom you will relate the story. Role-playing in this manner helps a person absorb the information with greater clarity and profundity (*The Rebbe*).[40]

ꙮ Questions Repeated ꙮ

Once the children have asked the questions, the leader does not have to repeat them (*Maharil; Shulchan Aruch HaRav*).

Nevertheless, the Rebbes of Chabad, after hearing the children and grandchildren ask the questions,[41] would then recite the questions themselves in an undertone.

This custom coincides with the opinion of *Rambam*, who maintains that the Seder leader recites the *Mah Nishtanah*. It is now the universal Chabad practice for everyone to recite the *Mah Nishtanah* after the children ask the questions (*The Rebbe*).[42]

ꙮ After a Father's Passing ꙮ

It was the custom of the Chabad Rebbes to preface their recitation of *Mah Nishtanah* with the words, "Father, I will ask you the Four Questions." They did so even long after the passing of their fathers (*Sefer Hasichot 5704*, p. 87), which is now the standard Chabad custom (*Torat Menachem—Hitvaaduyot 5743*, vol. 3, p. 1231).[43]

After the Seder Plate is moved aside and the cup is poured, the child recites the traditional rendition of Mah Nishtanah (see below in the commentary). After the child(ren)'s recitation, it is customary for all to recite it in an undertone.

מַה נִּשְׁתַּנָּה הַלַּיְלָה הַזֶּה מִכָּל הַלֵּילוֹת:
שֶׁבְּכָל הַלֵּילוֹת אֵין אָנוּ מַטְבִּילִין אֲפִילוּ פַּעַם אֶחָת הַלַּיְלָה הַזֶּה שְׁתֵּי פְעָמִים. שֶׁבְּכָל הַלֵּילוֹת אָנוּ אוֹכְלִין חָמֵץ אוֹ

∽ TRADITIONAL RENDITION OF MAH NISHTANAH ∼

Father, I will ask you four questions:

Ma nishtana halai-lö ha-ze mikol halay-los? What makes Pesach night different from all nights of the year?

The first question is: *Sheb'chöl halay-los ayn önu matbilin afilu pa-am echös, halai-lö ha-ze sh'tay f'ömim.* On all nights of the year we do not [need to] dip even once, but on Pesach night we dip twice! The first time, we dip *karpas* in salt water, and the second time, *maror* in *charoset*.

The second question is: *Sheb'chöl halay-los önu och'lin chömaytz o matzö, halai-lö ha-ze kulo matzö.* On all nights of the year we eat *chametz* or matzah, but on Pesach night we eat only matzah!

The third question is: *Sheb'chöl halay-los önu och'lin sh'ör y'rökos, halai-lö ha-ze möror.* On all nights of the year we eat various vegetables, but on Pesach night we eat bitter vegetables!

The fourth question is: *Sheb'chöl halay-los önu och'lin bayn yosh'vin uvayn m'subin, halai-lö ha-ze kulönu m'subin.* On all nights of the year we eat either sitting upright or reclining, but on Pesach night we all eat while reclining!

(Father, I have asked you four questions, now please give me an answer.)

טאַטע, איך וועל בּאַ דיר פרעגן פיר קשיות:

מַה נִּשְׁתַּנָּה הַלַּיְלָה הַזֶּה מִכָּל הַלֵּילוֹת וואָס איז אַנדערש די נאַכט פון פּסח פון אַלע נעכט פון אַ גאַנץ יאָר.

די ערשטע קשיא איז: שֶׁבְּכָל הַלֵּילוֹת אֵין אָנוּ מַטְבִּילִין אֲפִילוּ פַּעַם אֶחָת הַלַּיְלָה הַזֶּה שְׁתֵּי פְעָמִים: אַלע נעכט פון אַ גאַנץ יאָר טונקען מיר ניט אַיין אֲפילו איין מאָל, אָבּער די נאַכט פון פּסח טונקען מיר אַיין צוויי מאָל: איין מאָל כַּרפַּס אין זאַלץ וואַסער, דעם צווייטן מאָל מָרוֹר אין חֲרֹסת.

די צווייטע קשיא איז: שֶׁבְּכָל הַלֵּילוֹת אָנוּ אוֹכְלִין חָמֵץ אוֹ מַצָּה, הַלַּיְלָה הַזֶּה כֻּלּוֹ מַצָּה: אַלע נעכט פון אַ גאַנץ יאָר עסן מיר חָמֵץ אָדער מַצָּה, אָבּער די נאַכט פון פּסח עסן מיר נאָר מַצָּה.

די דריטע קשיא איז: שֶׁבְּכָל הַלֵּילוֹת אָנוּ אוֹכְלִין שְׁאָר יְרָקוֹת, הַלַּיְלָה הַזֶּה מָרוֹר: אַלע נעכט פון אַ גאַנץ יאָר עסן מיר אַנדערע גרינסן, אָבּער די נאַכט פון פּסח עסן מיר בּיטערע גרינסן.

די פערטע קשיא איז: שֶׁבְּכָל הַלֵּילוֹת אָנוּ אוֹכְלִין בֵּין יוֹשְׁבִין וּבֵין מְסֻבִּין, הַלַּיְלָה הַזֶּה כֻּלָּנוּ מְסֻבִּין: אַלע נעכט פון אַ גאַנץ יאָר עסן מיר סַיי זיצענדיקערהייט און סַיי אָנגעלענטערהייט, אָבּער די נאַכט פון פּסח עסן מיר אַלע אָנגעלענטערהייט.

(טאַטע, איך האָבּ בּאַ דיר געפרעגט פיר קשיות, יעצט גיב מיר אַן ענטפער.)

~◌ THE FOUR QUESTIONS ◌~

After the Seder Plate is moved aside and the cup is poured, the child recites the traditional rendition of Mah Nishtanah (see below in the commentary). After the child(ren)'s recitation, it is customary for all to recite it in an undertone.

What makes this night different from all other nights?

1. **On all nights** we need not dip even once, and on this night we dip twice!

2. **On all nights** we eat leavened bread or matzah, and on this night, only matzah!

Notes & Insights

❧ THE ORDER ❧

This order of the questions—(1) dipping, (2) matzah, (3) *maror*, (4) reclining—is the order found in the version of the Mishnah as it appears in the Jerusalem Talmud, *Alfassi*, and *Rosh* (though the last two questions do not appear there). This is also the order found in the *Siddurim* of Rav Amram Gaon and Rav Saadiah Gaon, *Rambam*, *Tur*, *Avudraham* (by implication, since his commentary addresses the question about dipping before the others), *Abarbanel*, *Pri Etz Chaim*, *Siddur of the Arizal*, *Mishnat Chasidim*, and others. It is also the order found in the first printed Haggadah (Soncino, 1485).

It also follows the order of the night, where dipping (of the *karpas*, at least) precedes the eating of matzah, which is followed by *maror*. The question about reclining comes last, since it was added long after the first three questions were composed (*The Rebbe's Haggadah*).

הַלַּיְלָה הַזֶּה שְׁתֵּי פְעָמִים On this night we dip twice. Although we also dip the *maror* in *charoset* when eating the *Korech* "sandwich," we do not consider this a separate dipping from the *Maror* dipping, since *Korech* is only performed out of doubt as to how *maror* should be eaten (*Taz, Orach Chaim* 475:6).

❧ FOUR CUPS ❧

We do not ask about the Four Cups because drinking them is not a Biblical requirement, nor does it involve any Biblical requirement—it is entirely Rabbinic in origin. Reclining and dipping, by contrast, although not Biblical requirements *per se*, are connected to Biblical requirements: Reclining is done while fulfilling the Biblical mitzvah of matzah, and dipping, at least the second one, involves the *maror*, likewise a Biblical mitzvah in Temple times (*Maharal*).

From a mystical perspective, the order of the questions follows the order of the spiritual worlds, from the lowest to the loftiest, as follows (*Pri Etz Chaim*):

DIPPING	*Asiyah* – World of Actuality
MATZAH	*Yetzirah* – World of Formation
MAROR	*Beriah* – World of Creation
RECLINING	*Atzilut* – World of Emanation

מַצָּה, הַלַּיְלָה הַזֶּה כֻּלּוֹ מַצָּה. שֶׁבְּכָל הַלֵּילוֹת אָנוּ אוֹכְלִין שְׁאָר יְרָקוֹת, הַלַּיְלָה הַזֶּה מָרוֹר. שֶׁבְּכָל הַלֵּילוֹת אָנוּ אוֹכְלִין בֵּין יוֹשְׁבִין וּבֵין מְסֻבִּין, הַלַּיְלָה הַזֶּה כֻּלָּנוּ מְסֻבִּין.

with the saintly, is an existential and innate devotion, one in which there is no "self" that needs to be overcome. Such a person is not susceptible at all to sin. (This is called *bittul b'metziut* and is associated with the highest world, *Atzilut*, which is entirely permeated with Divine awareness.)

Sitting and reclining are manifestations of these two levels of devotion:

Sitting	Imposed Devotion	(Beriah, Yetzirah, Asiyah)
Reclining	Innate Devotion	(Atzilut)

When we sit down, our heads are brought to a lower position. This symbolizes a *partial* bowing to the Divine, since the head is not *completely* lowered. But when we recline, our heads are nearly if not completely lowered. This symbolizes an absolute and innate "bowing" to the Divine.[51]

Tonight we all recline: Tonight, because of the intensity of the Divine revelation that occurred on this night, and which reverberates each year, *kulanu mesubin*, we *all* recline—we are all imbued with an innate devotion to the Divine. This fleeting revelation that overwhelms us on Pesach gives us a jolt, a jump-start for the work of refining the "self" during the forty-nine days between Pesach and Shavuot (*The Rebbe*).[52]

❧ CUSTOMS ☙

Of all the rituals addressed by the child, dipping seems to be least important. Unlike matzah and *maror*, it is not a Biblical or Rabbinic mitzvah; and unlike reclining, it does not express a central theme of the holiday.

How striking, then, that the *first* of the four questions addresses neither the first ritual the child encounters—reclining while drinking the Kiddush wine—nor the more essential rituals of the night, but a custom!

The Haggadah thereby addresses a misconception regarding the place of custom in Judaism. Some consider customs to be non-essential, a "luxury." They recognize the need to make sacrifices for *mitzvot*, but they would not do the same for "mere" customs. In regards to educating children, they argue, we ought to compromise on the customs so as to better focus on the primary obligations.

The Mah Nishtanah tells us otherwise. What is the first thing that the child asks about? What grabs his or her attention and makes the deepest impression? Jewish customs. Not only are they not expendable, they are central. For the customs have the unique capacity to sensitize a child to the *sanctity* of Torah and *mitzvot*.

The customs give our children a strong Jewish identity and the sense that they are part of a nation chosen by God to be beacons of goodness and holiness in this world (*The Rebbe*).[53]

❧ HOLY QUESTIONS ☙

Questioning is essential to acquiring wisdom. Without critical analysis one's wisdom is incomplete. On the other hand, the quality of faith and simplicity precludes questioning, as in the verse (Deut. 18:13), *You shall be wholehearted with God....* (See p. 42b below, regarding the child who knows not to ask.)

Intellectualization and simplicity are two mutually exclusive traits that cannot possibly coexist. Our Sages therefore instituted questions within the realm of holiness. These have the mystical effect of refining the phenomenon of "questions," enabling us to maintain simplicity even while engaged in intellectual endeavor (*Rabbi Yosef Yitzchak of Lubavitch*).[54]

3. **On all nights** we eat various vegetables, and on this night, *maror*!

4. **On all nights** we eat sitting upright or reclining, and on this night we all recline!

Notes & Insights

הַלַּיְלָה הַזֶּה מָרוֹר **On this night, *maror*.** We do not say "on this night, *only maror*" as we say of the matzah, since we eat other vegetables during the first dipping (*Tosfot* s.v. *Halailah, Pesachim* 115b).

הַלַּיְלָה הַזֶּה כֻּלָּנוּ מְסֻבִּין **On this night we all recline.** This question appears neither in the Mishnah's version of the questions nor in the Talmud. Some have suggested that it was added at a later time when people stopped reclining all year-round (*The Vilna Gaon*).[47]

🙠 DEVELOPMENT OF MAH NISHTANAH 🙢

We find many different versions of the Four Questions in the various manuscripts of the Talmud—not only in the order of the questions but in the number as well. Some versions, for example, omit the question about *maror*, others omit the question about the Paschal lamb even in Temple times.

The above would seem to indicate that initially there were various acceptable versions, or perhaps no fixed version at all. This was because *halachically* one need not ask all the questions.

As the Talmud relates, when Abbaye as a child saw the table being removed from

before Rabbah, he exclaimed: "We haven't eaten yet—and they come and remove the table from before us?!" Rabbah turned to the child and said: "You have *exempted us* from having to say the *Mah Nishtanah*" (*Pesachim* 115b).[48]

At some point, however, the Sages consolidated the various customs and instituted a universal practice of reciting all the questions so that all of Israel would follow the same custom.

Another example of this sort of development is the way we blow the *shofar*:

The requirement is to blow a wailing sound, called a *teruah*, preceded and followed by a simple blast, called a *tekiah*. According to Rav Hai Gaon (cited in *Beit Yosef, Orach Chaim* §590[49]), for many centuries the definition of the "wailing" *teruah* remained unfixed, with various communities performing it in their own way. Some Jewish communities performed it as heavy groans. For others, it was very short "cries," and yet other communities performed it as a combination of both.

In Talmudic times, the Sages sought to unify all of Israel with a universal custom. They therefore instituted that *all* Jews blow the *shofar* in a manner that included all three customs (*The Rebbe's Haggadah*).[50]

🙠 SITTING VS. RECLINING 🙢

Chasidus

Chasidic teachings differentiate between two levels of loyalty and devotion to God: an *imposed* devotion and an *innate* devotion. The first kind is experienced by those who are filled with an awareness of "self," a feeling of being independent from and outside of God. Yet, through study and contemplation, they come to the recognition that it is logical and

good to devote themselves to their Creator, Who is infinite.

They therefore overcome the "self" and devote themselves to God. But the independent "self" remains intact; it is merely suppressed. (This is called *bittul hayesh* and is associated with the lower three worlds, *Beriah, Yetzirah* and *Asiyah*.)

A higher level of devotion, usually associated

ומחזירין הקערה ומגלין מקצת הפת ואומרים עבדים וכו':

Bring back the Seder Plate, uncover the *matzot* partially, and say:

עֲבָדִים הָיִינוּ לְפַרְעֹה בְּמִצְרַיִם, וַיּוֹצִיאֵנוּ יְיָ אֱלֹהֵינוּ
מִשָּׁם בְּיָד חֲזָקָה וּבִזְרֹעַ נְטוּיָה, וְאִלּוּ לֹא הוֹצִיא
הַקָּדוֹשׁ בָּרוּךְ הוּא אֶת אֲבוֹתֵינוּ מִמִּצְרַיִם, הֲרֵי אָנוּ וּבָנֵינוּ
וּבְנֵי בָנֵינוּ מְשֻׁעְבָּדִים הָיִינוּ לְפַרְעֹה בְּמִצְרָיִם. וַאֲפִילוּ כֻּלָּנוּ
חֲכָמִים כֻּלָּנוּ נְבוֹנִים כֻּלָּנוּ יוֹדְעִים אֶת הַתּוֹרָה, מִצְוָה עָלֵינוּ
לְסַפֵּר בִּיצִיאַת מִצְרַיִם, וְכָל הַמַּרְבֶּה לְסַפֵּר בִּיצִיאַת מִצְרַיִם
הֲרֵי זֶה מְשֻׁבָּח.

Egyptian kings.[60] *Avudraham*, however, points out, that in the era of the Mishnah and the time the Haggadah was arranged, Egypt no longer called its kings Pharaoh.[61]

It may be suggested, however, that the demise of the Egyptian "Pharaoh" was a symptom of Egypt's broader fall from greatness, which began with the Exodus. After the Exodus, Egypt was never the same, enduring various ups and downs as well as invasion and conquest.

But *if God would not have taken our ancestors out of Egypt*—had the Israelites remained there, Egypt would have retained its power along with its royal protocols—the king of Egypt would still have been a "Pharaoh."

As recorded in *Yalkut Shimoni* (§230): "Pharaoh's power extended across the world because of the dignity of the Israelites [so that they should be enslaved to a powerful nation]. As soon as they went free, Egypt collapsed" (*The Rebbe's Haggadah*).

❧ A PREMATURE EXIT ❧

Kabbalah
With the sin of Adam and Eve, God's presence became concealed from the world. The behavior of subsequent generations only reinforced this concealment. Abraham began the process of bringing God's presence back into the world. Abraham's descendants would continue what Abraham had begun until God's light would illuminate the world with an intensity greater than ever.[62] God therefore told *Abraham* about the future exile of the Israelites, since the humbling experience of the "iron crucible" of Egypt was meant to fully restore God's presence—the fulfillment of what *Abraham* had begun.

But the rectification was not completed in 400 years. True, the exile had rectified the Israelites and the world to the extent that they were now ready to receive the Torah.[63] But it had not succeeded in ridding the world of future exile and death. Yet God desired to redeem the Israelites prematurely, since they had fallen to the nadir of depravity and would have been forever lost, God forbid, had they not been redeemed immediately.

Because it was premature, the attribute of justice could justifiably argue: How can the Israelites leave Egypt if the mission has not been completed? According to this argument, the Israelites would have had to stay in Egypt until the rectification was completed. The metaphor of a "strong hand" in this context refers to God overriding the persuasive argument of the attribute of justice (*The Rebbe*).[64]

～ THE ANSWER ～

Bring back the Seder Plate, uncover the *matzot* partially, and say:

We were slaves to the despotic **Pharaoh in Egypt** from where no slave could escape, **and God, our God, took us out from there with a strong hand and with an outstretched arm.**

If the Holy One, blessed be He, had not taken our ancestors out of Egypt, then ancient Egypt and its Pharaohs would never have fallen and **we, our children and our children's children would be enslaved to** a **Pharaoh in Egypt.**

Even if we were all wise, perceptive, and knew the Torah, we would still be obligated to discuss the Exodus from Egypt; and everyone who discusses the Exodus from Egypt at length is praiseworthy.

 Notes & Insights

ומחזירין הקערה ומגלין מקצת הפת The...*matzot* are brought back and we reveal part of the matzah. This is done because the Haggadah must be recited over the *matzot*, which are called *lechem oni*—"bread over which many things are recited," as the Talmud (*Pesachim* 115b) explains.

⁂ SHAMEFUL BEGINNINGS ⁂

The Mishnah states that the retelling of the Exodus should "begin with the shame" of the Israelites. The two Talmudic sages, Rav and Shmuel, differed on the definition of this "shame."

According to **Rav**, this refers to our shameful beginnings as idolaters, prior to Abraham. As we say later on in the Haggadah: "In the beginning our ancestors were idolaters...." **Shmuel** says this refers to the shame of our slavery, as we say here, "We were slaves...."[55]

The Haggadah incorporates *both* versions to satisfy the opinions of both Rav and Shmuel (*Rif; Rosh*).[56]

ואלו לא הוציא הקדוש ברוך הוא If the Holy One...would not have taken our ancestors

out of Egypt. God promised Abraham that after 400 years Israel would leave Egypt. Nevertheless, if we had left Egypt on our own, without *God* taking us out, we would have eventually returned to slavery because of the slave mentality we had acquired.[57] As it was, even though God did take us out, we cried with nostalgia for Egypt and several times declared our wish to return there.[58] Had we left Egypt on our own, we would have in fact returned to slavery. It is only because *God* took us out and instilled freedom within us that we are not enslaved today (*The Rebbe*).[59]

Tonight we celebrate not a physical liberation but a spiritual one. At the Exodus, God liberated our souls from *spiritual* bondage. The physical liberation was transient—we have been enslaved and exiled again. But the liberation of our *souls* is eternal. No matter what we have been through, no power has been able to deprive us of our inner freedom (*Maharal*).

מְשֻׁעְבָּדִים הָיִינוּ לְפַרְעֹה בְּמִצְרָיִם We...would be enslaved to Pharaoh in Egypt. Obviously, this does not refer to the Pharaoh of Moses' days. Rather, "Pharaoh" is the title for all

מַעֲשֶׂה בְּרַבִּי אֱלִיעֶזֶר, וְרַבִּי יְהוֹשֻׁעַ, וְרַבִּי אֶלְעָזָר בֶּן־
עֲזַרְיָה, וְרַבִּי עֲקִיבָא, וְרַבִּי טַרְפוֹן, שֶׁהָיוּ מְסֻבִּין
בִּבְנֵי־בְרַק, וְהָיוּ מְסַפְּרִים בִּיצִיאַת מִצְרַיִם, כָּל־אוֹתוֹ
הַלַּיְלָה, עַד שֶׁבָּאוּ תַלְמִידֵיהֶם וְאָמְרוּ לָהֶם: רַבּוֹתֵינוּ, הִגִּיעַ
זְמַן קְרִיאַת שְׁמַע, שֶׁל שַׁחֲרִית.

naturally perceive creation as existing independent of God. We may recognize that God *controls* creation, but as an outside force, like a king ruling a country.

The spiritual "work" of reciting the Shema is to overcome our natural misconception of reality, in which we, along with all of creation, are separate from God. Our goal is to reach a level of awareness where we apprehend God's "oneness"—the fact that only God truly exists and nothing exists outside of Him.

The Evening Shema—Lower Unity

There are two ways of knowing anything—one, intellectually, the other innately. Intellectual knowledge is a detached knowledge. It is not our initial assumption; it is something we attain through the inquiry of reason. The logical conclusion that we reach does not completely displace our initial assumption.

This is the Shema of evening, the Shema recited amid darkness. Despite the spiritual darkness in which we are immersed—our sense of separateness from God—we work to perceive God's oneness.

This is referred to Kabbalistically as "the lower unity," *yichuda tata'a.*

The Morning Shema—Higher Unity

Then there are those times when the light of the Divine reality shines with the brightness of day. There is no assumption of separateness to overcome. We have an *innate* knowledge of God's oneness.

This is what is achieved during the morning Shema, recited in the light of day, which is a reflection of Divine light and spiritual clarity. This is called "the higher unity," *yichuda Ila'a.*

Generally, the master's perception reflects the "higher unity" while the student's is that of the "lower unity." But even the student perceives a "taste" of the higher unity in the morning and the teacher perceives a "taste" of the lower unity in the evening. It is the job of the master to help the student gain that "taste" of the higher unity.

***

With the above introduction, let us return to the end of the Seder in Bnei Brak:

Until their students came and told them, "Our masters...." Why is it important to note *how* the teachers found out the time? And why not state simply: "until their students told them it was morning"?

The Haggadah is conveying that this was not a simple wake-up call or message delivery. Anyone could have done that. Rather, it was a profound communication between the students and their teachers. They therefore did not say, "morning has come," but rather:

"The time has come for reciting the morning Shema...." In its plain sense, this means that the sages were so immersed in their discussion that they did not realize that morning had come.[71] But there is a deeper explanation:

The students were telling their teachers after their night of "illumination": "You have succeeded as teachers. You gave us the spiritual awareness with which to experience the higher unity, the innate knowledge of the morning Shema" (*Rabbi Yosef Yitzchak of Lubavitch*).[72]

⁓ THE ALL-NIGHT SEDER ⌒

It happened that Rabbi Eliezer, Rabbi Yehoshua, Rabbi Elazar ben Azaryah, Rabbi Akiva and Rabbi Tarfon were reclining [at a Seder] in Bnei Brak.

They were discussing the Exodus from Egypt all that night, until their students came and told them: "Our Masters! The time has come for reciting the morning Shema!"

Notes & Insights

🕮 AN ILLUSTRIOUS GROUP 🕮

This episode reinforces the statement of the previous passage "even if we are all wise, etc." These five sages certainly had wisdom, understanding, and knowledge of Torah. Yet they discussed the Exodus at length, even until morning (*Shibolei Haleket*).

Instead of referring simply to "a group of illustrious sages," the Haggadah names each of them. The Haggadah thereby emphasizes its statement in the previous passage, that *"everyone who discusses the exodus from Egypt at length is praiseworthy." Everyone* is meant to include even descendants of the tribe of Levi (Kohanim and Levites), whose ancestors were not enslaved, as well as converts, whose ancestors did not experience the exile or the Exodus. To illustrate this point, the Haggadah names the sages, since Rabbi Yehoshua was a Levi, Rabbi Elazar and Rabbi Tarfon were Kohanim, and Rabbi Akiva was a descendant of converts. Yet they all spent the entire night discussing the Exodus (*Chida*).

כָּל־אוֹתוֹ הַלַּיְלָה **All That Night.** The sages wished to relive the original Exodus, during which the Israelites remained awake all night, circumcising themselves, partaking of the Paschal lamb, and preparing for the Exodus (*Abarbanel*; see p. 50b below).[65]

וְהָיוּ מְסַפְּרִים בִּיצִיאַת מִצְרַיִם **They Were Discussing the Exodus...** The word used here for "discussing"—*mesaprim*—also connotes "illuminating," as in *even sapir* אֶבֶן סַפִּיר, a brilliant gem.

Chasidus

Through their discussion, the sages sought to *illuminate*, to enable their students to transcend their earthly perception—to leave their spiritual "Egypts"—and view reality through a more enlightened, Divine prism.[66]

כָּל־אוֹתוֹ הַלַּיְלָה **All That Night...** The *Zohar*[67] states that the night of the Exodus was filled with light like day, as in the verse: *...the night shines like day, darkness is like light.*[68] Spiritually, this refers to the great Divine revelation that was present on that night.

In reliving the Exodus, these holy sages were able to perceive the "light" of that night.[69]

"Even within the bitterness of exile, Rabbi Akiva was able to perceive the sweetness of the future redemption."

—SEFER HASICHOT 5703, P. 71[70]

🕮 A TALE OF TWO SHEMAS 🕮

The Torah obligates us to recite the Shema twice daily, at night and in the morning. Yet the two recitations express very different perceptions of God's "oneness."

When we say that "God is one," we don't mean only that there are no other gods. We mean that God is the one and only true existence, since everything else exists only because of Him. We

אָמַר רַבִּי אֶלְעָזָר בֶּן עֲזַרְיָה: הֲרֵי אֲנִי כְּבֶן שִׁבְעִים שָׁנָה,
וְלֹא זָכִיתִי שֶׁתֵּאָמֵר יְצִיאַת מִצְרַיִם בַּלֵּילוֹת, עַד
שֶׁדְּרָשָׁהּ בֶּן זוֹמָא, שֶׁנֶּאֱמַר: לְמַעַן תִּזְכֹּר אֶת יוֹם צֵאתְךָ
מֵאֶרֶץ מִצְרַיִם כֹּל יְמֵי חַיֶּיךָ. יְמֵי חַיֶּיךָ; הַיָּמִים, כֹּל יְמֵי חַיֶּיךָ;
לְהָבִיא הַלֵּילוֹת. וַחֲכָמִים אוֹמְרִים: יְמֵי חַיֶּיךָ; הָעוֹלָם הַזֶּה,
כֹּל יְמֵי חַיֶּיךָ; לְהָבִיא לִימוֹת הַמָּשִׁיחַ.

Sages,[78] Rabbi Elazar refutes this misconception: **The Exodus and the future redemption are not two separate redemptions so that one might supersede the other. They form a continuum of *one* redemption that began with the Exodus, continues throughout our history, and culminates with the future redemption. The Exodus, then, is *one* with the future redemption and will therefore be remembered at that time.**

Hence the homiletic reading of the Sages' words: *All the days of your life—to **bring** the days of Moshiach.* Throughout this millennia-long "interruption," we should remain uncomfortable in the exile, remembering that it is not an end in itself.

Remembering the Exodus *all the days of your life*—in this world—brings the spirit of *the days of Moshiach* into our current world of exile, and brings ultimately to the actual *days of Moshiach*.

The Day He Became *Nassi*

A primary function of a Jewish leader is to uplift the people from their exilic mentality, to peel back the façade of exile. Rabbi Elazar ben Azaryah was therefore preoccupied with this teaching—the relevance of the Exodus even during the "night" of exile, and that the Exodus would lead to the future redemption—on the day he became *nassi*.

The leader's role is to imbue our physical lives in this world, even our "nights," with redemption—to unite exile and redemption, to enable a Jew in exile to transcend exile and operate in an atmosphere akin to *the days of Moshiach*.

Upon assuming leadership, Rabbi Elazar removed the guards from the study hall, opening it even to those less pious and formerly ostracized students.[79] Rabbi Elazar succeeded in transforming those students.[80] He thus brought redemption, the "Exodus," to a place of spiritual night (the less pious students), and imbued it with the spirit of *the days of Moshiach* (*The Rebbe*).[81]

✿ SEVENTY AND ע (AYIN) ✿

Kabbalah Seventy represents the perfection of one's *seven* emotions, when each emotion is fully developed and balanced by its *ten* facets.[82] In addition, seventy is associated with earthliness, as in "the seventy nations of the world." Achieving the level of 70 refers to refining one's portion of the world, elevating one's earthly self and sphere of influence.

The Hebrew letter that represents 70 is *ayin*, which means "eye." Attaining the level of "70" is to develop a holy "eye"—the ability to not only understand Godliness as an abstract reality, but to "see" Godliness, to know it as one knows what the eyes can see. (This is the significance of the large *ayin* in the word שְׁמַע *Shema*.)

For Rabbi Elazar to become *nassi*, he had to be "70." This enabled him to "mention the Exodus at night"—to experience Exodus even amid spiritual darkness, and to "include the days of Moshiach," to internalize and project the future world, when the world will be transformed and our *eyes* will see the Divine reality (*The Rebbe*).[83]

∽ DAY & NIGHT; NOW & ALWAYS ⌒

Rabbi Elazar ben Azaryah said: I am like a man of seventy years, yet I did not merit to identify the Biblical source for the obligation to mention the Exodus from Egypt at night—until Ben Zoma derived it from the following verse (Deuteronomy 16:3):

*...that you may remember the day you left Egypt **all the days of your life.***

—*The days of your life* teaches us the daytime obligation; —*all the days of your life* is meant to include the nights.

The Sages said: —*The days of your life* refers to this world; —*all* *the days of your life* is meant to include the days of Moshiach.

Notes & Insights

This passage underscores the gravity of the Exodus, that it is forever central to Jewish life. We are charged with remembering it *all the days of our lives*, by day and at night, as Ben Zoma taught, and both in this world and during the days of Moshiach, as the Sages taught (*The Rebbe*).[73]

הֲרֵי אֲנִי כְּבֶן שִׁבְעִים שָׁנָה **I am like a man of seventy.** Rabbi Elazar made this statement at the age of eighteen, on the day he was appointed *nassi*, leader of the Jewish people. God blessed him that day with an elderly, sagacious appearance. Hence: *"I am **like** a man of seventy years"*—but not actually seventy (*Berachot* 27b-28a and *Rashi* ad loc.).

This external elderliness was a reflection of his inner wisdom: Spiritually, he *was* seventy years old. Generally, there is no shortcut to gaining the wisdom of age. Rabbi Elazar ben Azaryah, however, had the benefit of being a tenth-generation descendant of the prophet Ezra. He therefore inherited from his ancestors the wisdom they had gained through their years. He also inherited an especially keen mind, which enabled him to acquire in eighteen years what normally takes seventy years to acquire (*The Rebbe*).[74]

שֶׁתֵּאָמֵר יְצִיאַת מִצְרַיִם בַּלֵּילוֹת **To mention the Exodus from Egypt at night.** Toward the end of reading the Shema, we add a section from Numbers (15:37) about *tzitzit*, which ends with the verse: *I am God...who took you out of the Land of Egypt...*, thus fulfilling the mitzvah to mention the Exodus at night (see *Rashi* on *Berachot* 12b).[75]

וַהֲכָמִים אוֹמְרִים **The Sages said.** According to some commentators, there is no disagreement in practice between the Sages and Ben Zoma. They differ only on how to interpret the verses.[76] Others maintain that the debate is over practice as well.[77]

✤ THE EXODUS CONTINUUM ✤

Chasidus

The Sages state that we must remember the Exodus even in the messianic age. But why remember the Exodus, which did not transform the world and did not eradicate evil, once we experience the future, eternal and all-encompassing redemption?

This question arises from viewing the future redemption as a *new* and foreign event, a departure from the world we know. But in citing the

בָּרוּךְ הַמָּקוֹם, בָּרוּךְ הוּא, בָּרוּךְ שֶׁנָּתַן תּוֹרָה
לְעַמּוֹ יִשְׂרָאֵל, בָּרוּךְ הוּא, כְּנֶגֶד אַרְבָּעָה
בָנִים דִּבְּרָה תוֹרָה: אֶחָד חָכָם, וְאֶחָד רָשָׁע, וְאֶחָד תָּם,
וְאֶחָד שֶׁאֵינוֹ יוֹדֵעַ לִשְׁאוֹל.

❧ INDIVIDUALITY ❧

Chasidus The Torah generally speaks of one truth and one path for every person. With the Exodus, however, the Torah uncharacteristically provides a *different* explanation for each of the four types of children, thereby conveying a critical lesson in education:

When reaching out to others, to educate them and help them transcend their "Egypts," we should not use a standardized, unvarying approach for all types of students. To reach students and affect them, teachers must tailor their words and method to conform to each individual student.

By providing different answers for each of the four children, the Torah enables and inspires us to find the right words and approach with which to engage every individual and successfully ignite their Godly spark.[85]

❧ FOUR IN ONE ❧

Since all of Torah addresses all of Israel, we must say that all four messages of the Torah are applicable to all of us, since we all possess the "four children" within ourselves. We are therefore all required—even one who does not have children—to recite all four answers, since we are in essence speaking to the wise, wicked, simple, and "unable to ask" elements that exist within every one of us.[86]

❧ THE WISE AND THE WICKED ❧

The Haggadah mentions the wicked immediately after the wise. This teaches the wise that they cannot ignore their "wicked" brethren, for we are all responsible for each other (see *Sanhedrin* 27b; *Tanya*, ch. 32).

Every Jew is like a letter in a Torah scroll: if even one letter is missing, regardless of what that letter is, the holiness of *all* the letters is compromised. Similarly, the condition of the entire nation is dependent on each individual.

Additionally, the wise should not imagine themselves so far removed from the reality of the "wicked." The "wicked"—the potential for self-destructive distractions—is the *immediate* neighbor of the wise.

The wise must therefore remain vigilant against this susceptibility within *themselves* and pray to remain above it.

In fact, the two lessons overlap:

By reaching out to help the "wicked," the wise will gain the spiritual merit that will help them overcome and transform their own, inner "wicked child."[87]

❧ THE FIFTH CHILD ❧

"Unfortunately, there is, in our time of confusion and obscurity, another kind of a Jewish child: the child who is conspicuous by his absence from the Seder Service; the one who has no interest whatsoever in Torah and *mitzvot*...who is not even aware of the Seder, of the Exodus from Egypt and the subsequent Revelation at Sinai.

"This presents a grave challenge, which should command our attention long before Passover and the Seder night, for no Jewish child should be forgotten and given up. We must make every effort to save also that "lost" child, and bring the absentee to the Seder table. Determined to do so, and driven by a deep sense of compassion and responsibility, we need have no fear of failure..." (*The Rebbe*).[88]

◡ FOUR BLESSINGS, FOUR CHILDREN ◡

Blessed is the Omnipresent One, blessed be He!

Blessed is He who gave the Torah to His people Israel, **blessed** be He!

The Torah speaks of four children: One wise, one wicked, one simple, and one who does not know how to ask.

Notes & Insights

בָּרוּךְ הַמָּקוֹם **Blessed is the Omnipresent.** At this point, the Haggadah begins focusing on the explanation of Biblical verses. This passage therefore begins with an exclamation praising God, which is customarily done prior to teaching Torah (*Avudraham*).

In the passage we bless God four times, corresponding to the four Torah passages that instruct us to retell the Exodus. This mitzvah would essentially require a blessing, as do all positive commandments. In practice, we do not recite a blessing over it (see below). Nevertheless, out of affection for the mitzvah, the Sages ordained these four informal blessings (*Shibolei Haleket*).

Why not recite a proper blessing over the mitzvah to relay the Exodus? The following opinions are cited in *The Rebbe's Haggadah*:
• We have already fulfilled the *basic* obligation during the Kiddush with the words "commemorating the Exodus..." (*Rif*).
• We fulfilled the obligation during the reading of the Shema (during which we remember the Exodus), which we prefaced and concluded with blessings (*Shibolei Haleket*).
• According to some, there is no defined measure for the "discussion of the Exodus" and a mere mention is in effect sufficient [and such a mitzvah does not require a blessing] (*Rashba*).
• The entire Haggadah is a blessing and form of praise, especially since it includes the

blessing "Who has redeemed us"—and one does not recite a blessing over a blessing [just as we do not recite a blessing over the blessing after a meal] (*Maaseh Nissim*).
• This mitzvah is fulfilled with interruptions—eating and drinking, etc.—and in such a case one does not recite a blessing (*Shevach Pesach*).

הַמָּקוֹם **The Omnipresent (literally "the Place").** "Why do we provide an appellation for God and call Him 'the Place'? For He is the place of the world, whereas His world is not His place"—the world is contained in Him, not He in it (*Bereishit Rabbah* 68:9).

חָכָם... רָשָׁע... תָּם... שֶׁאֵינוֹ יוֹדֵעַ לִשְׁאוֹל **Wise, wicked, simple, does not know how to ask.** This order conforms neither to the order in which the children are mentioned in the Torah (Wicked, Simple, Does Not Know How to Ask, Wise), nor to the order of their moral standing, in which the wicked child should be last.

Rather, they are listed in order of their intellectual capacities: The wise child; the wicked child, who is also wise but whose insolence leads him to act wickedly; the simple child, who has at least enough intelligence to ask; and finally the one who does not know how to ask (*Avudraham*). Alternatively, the Haggadah first mentions the extremes, then the ones in the middle. See, similarly, *Bava Kama* 4b, *Tosfot* s.v. *Shomer Chinam* (*The Rebbe*).[84]

חָכָם מַה הוּא אוֹמֵר: מָה הָעֵדֹת וְהַחֻקִּים וְהַמִּשְׁפָּטִים אֲשֶׁר צִוָּה יְיָ אֱלֹהֵינוּ אֶתְכֶם. וְאַף אַתָּה אֱמוֹר לוֹ כְּהִלְכוֹת הַפֶּסַח, אֵין מַפְטִירִין אַחַר הַפֶּסַח אֲפִיקוֹמָן.

allude to the four stages of the soul's descent into the world. At each stage, the presence of God becomes less obvious and the illusion of an autonomous self increases.

The highest level, "pure," describes the soul at the highest of the four worlds, the world of *Atzilut*, absolute Divine awareness. At this level, the soul is a "*chacham*," filled with Divine awareness and therefore absolutely free of self-orientation.

The Chacham's Question

The "pure" aspect of our souls, the *chacham* within, therefore asks:

What are the Testimonies, Statutes, and Laws? These three categories of *mitzvot* are distinguished by the extent to which they resonate with human intellect.

This resonance or lack thereof is only relevant to the soul's lower consciousness, not to the *chacham* aspect of the soul. To the *chacham*, a mitzvah is an opportunity to fulfill the Divine will. From this perspective, the particular features of the *mitzvot* are secondary.

This feeling is expressed in the saying: "*If God had commanded us to chop wood, we would do it with the same fervor as when putting on tefillin*" (Rabbi Schneur Zalman of Liadi).[92] For in either case we would be fulfilling God's will.

The *chacham* therefore asks: Why categorize *mitzvot* as if they were somehow different from one another?

This implies, says the *chacham*, that our ability to understand a given mitzvah by reason or intuition matters in some way. Yet to the *chacham*, these features of the mitzvah are irrelevant, since the overriding definition of all *mitzvot* is identical in each one: fulfillment of the Divine will.[93]

Reponse to the Chacham

Instruct him in the laws of Pesach. A true *chacham* already knows the laws. "Instruct him..." alludes to something deeper:

The words "laws" and "Pesach" represent polar opposites. *Pesach*, which means "passing over," represents absolute transcendence; "passing over" the natural order. On Pesach, the very essence of God "descended" to Egypt—"*not an angel....but God Himself.*" And to where did God "descend"? To the lowliest of places, to the coarse and idolatrous land of Egypt. Such a phenomenon completely disregards and "*passes over*" all norms.

Yet the celebration of the transcendent and rule-bending "Pesach" is very much *within* order and structure. There are *laws* of Pesach. The celebration itself is called *Seder*, "order."

For it is God's will that we channel the intensity and loftiness of what transcends the natural order into the world of structure and order.

Internalizing the Transcendent

So we tell the *chacham*:

It is true that the essence of the soul transcends the "natural order" of the person—the intellect and emotions—and therefore is blind to distinctions between *mitzvot*. It is likewise true that one can observe *mitzvot* without understanding them but simply because of the innate, essence-connection between the soul and God. One can "pass over" and bypass the complications and limitations of self.

But it is God's will that we experience *mitzvot* *within* the "natural order" of our psyche, within our intellect and emotions. The transcendent "Pesach" of our souls then finds expression within and permeates the "laws" of our minds and hearts[94] (*The Rebbe*).[95]

ᴖ THE WISE ᴐ

What does the wise one say?

"What are the testimonies, the statutes, and the laws that God, our God, has commanded to you?" (Deut. 6:20)

You should respond to him as the Torah commands, "We were slaves to Pharaoh in Egypt, etc." and also instruct him in all the laws of Pesach, up to and including its final law: "After eating the Pesach offering, one should not then conclude the meal with dessert which would wash away the taste of the Pesach offering."

Notes & Insights

מָה הָעֵדֹת וְהַחֻקִּים וְהַמִּשְׁפָּטִים **What are the testimonies, statutes, laws?** These three terms for *mitzvot* signify three *types* of *mitzvot*:

STATUTES — Chukim	Inexplicable Laws (e.g., not to mix wool and linen)
TESTIMONIES — Edot	Explicable but not Intuitive Laws (e.g., Shabbat and Festivals)
LAWS — Mishpatim	Intuitive Laws (e.g., not to steal)

צִוָּה יְיָ אֱלֹהֵינוּ אֶתְכֶם **God our God has commanded to you.** When the wicked child says "What is this service to *you*?" we assume he is excluding himself. But doesn't the wise child also refer to "the testimonies…that God our God has commanded to *you*"?

The wicked child makes no mention of God; the wise child refers to "God *our* God," clearly *including* himself. He uses "you" in the sense of "you who came out of Egypt and received God's commandments," as opposed to himself who was not yet born when the commandment was given (*Machzor Vitri*).

חָכָם **The wise child.** True wisdom refers to absolute awareness of God—to know that He is the source and sustenance of everything and yet transcends everything. This is the deeper meaning of the Talmudic saying: "Who is wise? The one who sees what is born."[89] Read simply, this means that the wise foresee the consequences of their actions and behave accordingly. On a deeper level it means that the wise perceive that all of existence is "born"—comes into being—and continues to exist by God's will, without which nothing can exist.

We all possess an inner "wise child," a *chacham*. Hence our unbreakable bond with God: We neither desire nor are capable of separating ourselves from God.[90] This is because our inner *chacham* knows that there is no real existence outside of God.

The greater our awareness that God is all, the lesser our awareness of "self," of anything outside of Him. Self-orientation is only possible where God is concealed, where our source and purpose is obscured. Wisdom, then, is the conviction that "God is all, and there is nothing besides Him."[91]

It is Pure

This selfless dimension of the soul is called "pure." In the morning blessings we say: *My God, the soul that you placed within me—it is **pure**. You **created** it, you **formed** it, you **breathed** it into me*…. These four descriptions

רָשָׁע מַה הוּא אוֹמֵר: מָה הָעֲבֹדָה הַזֹּאת לָכֶם. לָכֶם וְלֹא לוֹ, וּלְפִי שֶׁהוֹצִיא אֶת עַצְמוֹ מִן הַכְּלָל, כָּפַר בְּעִקָּר. וְאַף אַתָּה הַקְהֵה אֶת שִׁנָּיו וֶאֱמָר לוֹ: בַּעֲבוּר זֶה עָשָׂה יְיָ לִי בְּצֵאתִי מִמִּצְרָיִם, לִי וְלֹא לוֹ, אִלּוּ הָיָה שָׁם לֹא הָיָה נִגְאָל.

by saying: "In Egypt, your distance from God would have prevented you from being redeemed. But we have since received the Torah. And the Torah speaks of *four* children, including you. God spoke to *you* at Sinai, when He said: 'I am the Lord *Your* God.'[102] At Sinai, God was engraved into the depths of your soul. And so despite your distance, the Torah considers you connected. You would not have been redeemed from Egypt, but you will be redeemed in the future redemption."

As the Talmud states, a Jew cannot lose his Jewishness (*Sanhedrin* 44a). Regardless of the degree of his disengagement from Judaism, the Jewish spark lives on within him.[103]

Kabbalah teaches that the wicked child, *second* of the four children, corresponds to the *second* of the Four Cups.[104] This means that that the bulk of the Haggadah is recited over the cup related to the wicked child! Clearly, befriending and educating the wicked child is a central aspect of the Haggadah. For this effort helps bring about the ultimate realization of the Egyptian Exodus:

The Egyptian Exodus was incomplete. It will only be fully realized in the Messianic age, a time that will be ushered in by uniting all Jews—including those who seem most distant—and revealing their inherent connection to God, their inner "wise child."[105]

✥ WICKED OR IGNORANT? ✥

Today there is the "wicked" child who in reality is not wicked but simply ignorant.

In today's day and age, there is virtually no such thing as a renegade Jew! Those who do not observe Jewish practices and the like, cannot be faulted, since they never received a proper Jewish education. In the past, there were those who had a choice and chose to rebel.... But children born in the last 70 years were never told about Judaism or in such a manner that would translate into observance. They cannot be blamed for their disinterest....[106]

"*The attitude of the Chabad Rebbes, especially my father-in-law, was to befriend all of Israel, even those in the category referred to at the end of chapter 32 of Tanya ('heretics who have no portion...'), to try to bring them back to good...*" (*The Rebbe*).[107]

✥ GETTING TO THE ROOT ✥

הַקְהֵה אֶת־שִׁנָּיו **Blunt his teeth.** The word for tooth, *shen*, is spelled like the Hebrew letter *shin*, the middle letter of the word for wicked, *rasha*. Blunting the "tooth" of the *rasha* alludes to subduing the letter "*shin*" in the word *rasha*.

Everything must have a holy foundation, a spark of holiness, to exist. For example, falsehood must possess some truth in order to be believable—this is the *shin* in *sheker*, falsehood.[108]

The *shin* of *rasha* is the spark of holiness that resides in evil but which is "swallowed" and concealed by the letters *reish* and *ayin* that surround it, letters that embody negativity—*ra*. To blunt the "*shin*" of wickedness means to identify and redeem its spark of holiness (*Arizal*).[109]

In the case of irredeemable evil,[110] this means that the evil entity loses its existence, since its source of existence has been removed. In the case of redeemable evil, such as the *rasha* of the Seder, we apply the teaching:[111] "May sins be removed from the earth, not the sinners" (*The Rebbe*).[112]

∽ THE WICKED ∾

What does the wicked one say?

"What is this service of yours?!"[96] He says *of yours*—implying that it is not for him. By excluding himself from the community, he denies the essential principle of Judaism, the obligation to fulfill the commandments of the Torah.[97]

You should also "blunt his teeth" (speak harshly to him[98]) and say to him:

"It is because of this that I would fulfill His commandments, such as this Pesach offering, matzah and *maror*[99] *that God acted for me when I left Egypt* (Exodus 13:8)—*for me,* but not for **him.** If he [the wicked child] had been there, he would not have been redeemed."[100]

Notes & Insights

וְאַף אַתָּה You should also (blunt his teeth). In addition to giving him the response the Torah gives to his question (Exodus 12:27), *It is a Pesach offering [to God, Who passed over the homes of the Children of Israel in Egypt, when He smote Egypt and saved our homes],* you should *also* blunt his teeth (*Abarbanel*).[101]

בַּעֲבוּר זֶה, עָשָׂה יְיָ לִי It is because of this that God acted for me. This verse appears in the Torah as the response to the child who does not know to ask. But the words *"(God did) for*

me" clearly do not mean to exclude him. We therefore apply the exclusion as a teaching about the wicked child (see *Avudraham* and *Abarbanel*).

לִי וְלֹא לוֹ For me, but not for him. In the *Mechilta* the phrase reads "for me, but not for *you.*" The editor of the Haggadah evidently changed the text out of consideration for the participants at the Seder [so it should not appear as if the leader of the Seder is addressing and insulting them] (*The Rebbe's Haggadah*).

◈ EMBRACING THE WICKED ◈

The Talmud (*Kiddushin* 36a) records a debate between Rabbi Yehudah and Rabbi Meir regarding our designation as God's children. According to Rabbi Yehudah, we are only considered God's children when we behave as God's children. Rabbi Meir, however, holds that either way we are called God's children. He cites several verses in the Prophets where we are chided as foolish, or impious, and yet we are called foolish *children,* impious *children.*

Rashba rules (Responsa §194 and §260) that although Jewish law generally follows Rabbi Yehudah's view, in this case we follow the view

of Rabbi Meir, since the verses from the Prophets clearly confirm Rabbi Meir's view.

Here in the Haggadah, Rabbi Meir's view is likewise displayed: The Torah speaks of four types of Jews, including the wicked child, yet refers to all of them as children, alluding to their status as God's children (see *Chida*).

Yet how do we reconcile this benevolent view with the Haggadah's instruction that we tell the wicked child that he would not have been redeemed from Egypt? The answer is that we are not, God forbid, trying to reject him. To the contrary, we are encouraging him

תָּם מַה הוּא אוֹמֵר: מַה זֹּאת, וְאָמַרְתָּ אֵלָיו: בְּחֹֽזֶק יָד
הוֹצִיאָֽנוּ יְיָ מִמִּצְרַֽיִם מִבֵּית עֲבָדִים:

וְשֶׁאֵינוֹ יוֹדֵֽעַ לִשְׁאוֹל, אַתְּ פְּתַח לוֹ, שֶׁנֶּאֱמַר: וְהִגַּדְתָּ
לְבִנְךָ בַּיּוֹם הַהוּא לֵאמֹר: בַּעֲבוּר זֶה עָשָׂה יְיָ לִי
בְּצֵאתִי מִמִּצְרָֽיִם.

personal "Exodus": Just as God used *a strong hand* to "overcome" the attribute of justice, we too must use *a strong hand* to overcome those aspects of our personalities that impede our spiritual growth. We then experience a spiritual liberation from our personal enslavements (*The Rebbe*).[115]

❧ NOT SO SIMPLE ❧

The four children are introduced with the phrase: "*One* is wise, *one* is wicked, etc."—emphasizing that each of the four children knows and speaks of the *One* God.

(Even the wicked child speaks of God but asserts that God is uninterested in the affairs of man.)

The simpleton perceives God with pure and innocent faith (*Rabbi Yosef Yitzchak of Lubavitch*).[116]

❧ KNOWS NOT HOW TO ASK ❧

The fourth child's inability to ask may be the result of having been deprived of a Jewish education: "By placing this child at the end, the Haggadah emphasizes that the worst thing, even worse than wickedness, is ignorance. This is because the wicked child has studied Torah and performed *mitzvot*. Once he repents, which he can do in the blink of an eye, he knows what to do…. The wicked child has a choice. He can choose good or evil.

"But then there is a place that is *a parched and thirsty land without water*.[117] This is the reality of the ignorant Jew, who was not given a choice…" (*The Rebbe*).[118]

❧ TOO SMART FOR QUESTIONS ❧

This fourth child may be a ritually observant Jew who fulfills all the customs of the Seder. But his Judaism is cold and dry. He does not feel a need for spiritual liberation. He has no questions about or real interest in the Exodus because he does not think of himself as being in exile.

He claims that he is not the excitable type and thus excuses his lifeless Jewish practice. Yet while he cannot muster any excitement for Judaism, he is easily exercised and engaged by material ambitions. He does not realize that his heart and mind are in exile, oblivious to the spiritual content of life.

We cannot begin by telling this Jew what God did (as we tell the simple child); we must first inspire him to seek spiritual liberation. We therefore tell him:

"God did this for me when *I left Egypt*"—you too are in need of leaving Egypt (*The Rebbe*).[119]

❧ THE ANGELIC CHILD ❧

On a deeper level, the fourth child refers to a lofty sort of soul, one that is perfectly in tune with the Divine truth. Though inhabiting this world like the rest of us, such souls maintain a heavenly consciousness in which there are no questions, even when they are faced with personal challenges. They experience none of the dissonance and tension between matter and spirit that is the usual lot of mortals.

On this level, the fourth child's lack of questions is something to admire (*Rabbi Yosef Yitzchak of Lubavitch*).[120]

❧ THE SIMPLE ONE ☙

The Simple One—what does he say?

"What is this celebration about?" You shall say to him: "We are commemorating the fact that with a strong hand God took us out of Egypt, from the house of slaves" (Exodus 13:14).

❧ DOES NOT KNOW HOW TO ASK ☙

As for The One Who Knows Not How To Ask—you must open up [the conversation] for him.

As it is written: *You shall tell your child on that day: "It is because of this that God acted for me when I left Egypt"* (Exodus 13:8).

Notes & Insights

אַתְּ פְּתַח לוֹ **You must open up for him.** The commentators differ on how to define this phrase. Some maintain that our obligation is to provoke this child to ask, so that the story can be told as an answer to a question. "You must *open* for him" then means to create an opening for him through intriguing rituals and by telling him about the Exodus, until he is inspired to ask questions (*Pirush Kadmon*; *Shibolei Haleket*).

Others understand the phrase to mean "*begin* for him," i.e., since he is not asking any questions, we have no choice but to begin relating the story to him, even though he has not asked about it (*Rashbatz*; *Chida*). As we read in Proverbs (31:8), **Open** *your mouth on behalf of the mute* (*Avudraham*).[113] Hence the verse cited, which does not speak of any question, yet states *tell your child...* (*Ritva*). *Rashbatz* thus concludes that tonight's mitzvah of retelling the story of the Exodus can be fulfilled with or without the question and answer form. See, however, *Minchat Chinuch* (*mitzvah 21*), *et al.*, and *The Rebbe's Haggadah*, p. 15.

❧ THE BASHFUL CHILD ☙

The fourth child may actually *want* to ask but lacks confidence and fears being seen as a fool. The Haggadah instructs us to be sensitive to such people and to put them at ease by initiating conversation with them until they are comfortable sharing their thoughts confidently and clearly (*R. Shlomo Alkabetz*; *Chida*).

בְּחֹזֶק יָד **With a strong hand.** The simpleton is the sort who has the sensitivity to get excited over a wondrous occurrence that involves God and Torah. When he sees that so many Jews left Egypt, despite Pharaoh's global power (see *Mechilta, Bo* 14:5), he gets excited, and asks: "What is this?" He wants to know more about the Exodus and how he can connect with it. So we tell him:

Even though we were unworthy of redemption—sunk as we were in "the forty-nine gates of impurity" and serving idols like the Egyptians—God used a "strong hand" to overrule strict justice and redeem us.[114] And although we were supposed to stay in Egypt for 400 years, God used a "strong hand" to recalculate the 400-year decree and take us out after only 210 years (*Chida*; see p. 46a).

We tell the simpleton how the Exodus occurred and how he too can experience a

Chasidus

יָכוֹל מֵרֹאשׁ חֹדֶשׁ, תַּלְמוּד לוֹמַר: בַּיּוֹם הַהוּא. אִי בַּיּוֹם הַהוּא, יָכוֹל מִבְּעוֹד יוֹם, תַּלְמוּד לוֹמַר: בַּעֲבוּר זֶה, בַּעֲבוּר זֶה לֹא אָמַרְתִּי אֶלָּא בְּשָׁעָה שֶׁיֵּשׁ מַצָּה וּמָרוֹר מֻנָּחִים לְפָנֶיךָ:

that is rejected. So even though the Haggadah rejects its first two suggestions, it is hinting to us that these days contain the spirit of Pesach. On the first of the month, the spirit of Pesach, of redemption, enters the world. On this day Moses told the people that their long exile was about to end. On this day, the Jewish people were given their first commandment from God. The day preceding the Seder likewise brings us closer to the spirit of redemption.

But while the potential for redemption exists from the first day of the month, it is *revealed* in the world on the night of the Seder. The mitzvah is therefore reserved for this night (*The Rebbe*).[122]

בַּעֲבוּר זֶה **Because of this God acted for me.** Although this verse is part of the answer to the one who does not know to ask, it also contains an answer to the wise child. The wise child wonders why God commands us to fulfill *physical mitzvot*.[123] We tell the wise child that in order for us to leave Egypt, God's essence had to be revealed.

What evoked this lofty revelation? It was "because of this, when matzah and *maror* are before you"—because of the *physical mitzvot* that would be performed—that "God acted for me when I left Egypt." It is through *mitzvot* performed in the lowest of the low—the physical world—that we evoke God's essence, the highest of the high (*The Rebbe*).[124]

בַּיּוֹם הַהוּא...בַּעֲבוּר זֶה **On that day... because of this.** The expressions "on that day" and "this" represent two opposite realities. The expression *zeh*, "this," can only be said about something that is present and revealed. The Israelites thus said during the

crossing of the sea, "*This* is my God...!"—they were able to point with their fingers and say, "This!" The Messianic age is therefore also associated with the word "this."[125]

By contrast, the expression "on *that* day" speaks of something that is not here. It is *that*, not *this*. It is an expression that conveys the Divine concealment we experience in Exile, where we do not feel God's immediate presence, as in the verse, *And I will surely conceal My face* on that day (Deuteronomy 31:18).

Matzah and *Maror*

How do we progress from the concealment of "on that day" to the future revelation represented by the word "this"? It is through our fulfillment of *mitzvot* now during the time of Divine concealment, a time "when matzah and *maror* are placed before you":

The bitter *maror* represents the opposite of life, a condition of Divine concealment.[126] In the future, this aspect of *maror* will be "swallowed forever," both spiritually and physically, *and God shall wipe away the tears from upon every face* (Isaiah 25:8).

The spiritual notion of matzah will likewise cease to exist: The flatness and blandness of matzah represents the shunning of the inflated and arrogant "*chametz.*" In the future, however, there will be no need to shun "*chametz,*" since only constructive pride will exist, holy pride in doing what is good and Godly.

The *mitzvot* we do today despite our challenges—"when matzah and *maror* are still before you"—create the Divine revelation that we will experience in the future, when the concealment of Exile, "*on that day,*" will be transformed. We will then point and say: "*This* is our God" (*Rabbi Schneur Zalman of Liadi*).[127]

43b

∼ WHEN THE OBLIGATION ∼ CAN BE FULFILLED

Essential to the recounting of the Exodus is its connection to the *mitzvot* of Pesach, as in the verse that mandates the recounting, *You shall tell your child on that day saying: "Because of this [the fulfillment of the Pesach* mitzvot, *like matzah and* maror*] God acted for me when I left Egypt."* How "present" must the *mitzvot* of matzah and *maror* be for the obligation to be fulfilled properly?

One may have suggested that the obligation to recount the Exodus begins **from the first of the month** of Nissan, the day Moses *instructed* Israel regarding the *mitzvot* of Pesach.

The Torah therefore says, *You shall tell your child* **on that day** (i.e., the day the verse spoke of earlier, the day of the Exodus, the 15th of Nissan).

On that day, however, **could mean while it is yet daytime** on the 14th of Nissan, the day we *prepare* the Pesach *mitzvot.*

The Torah therefore says, *You shall tell your child on that day saying:* **"Because of this** (the fulfillment of the Pesach *mitzvot—God acted for me when I left Egypt)".* *Because of* **this** can only be said **when the matzah and** *maror* **are placed before you** at the Seder, when the *mitzvot* can actually be performed.

Notes & Insights

יָכוֹל **One may have suggested.** Having just mentioned the verse *And you shall tell your child...*, the Haggadah cites commentary of our Sages upon it (*Avudraham*). Others suggest that this teaching is part of our response to the child who knows not how to ask (*Abarbanel; Maaseh Nissim*).

בְּשָׁעָה שֶׁיֵּשׁ מַצָּה וּמָרוֹר מֻנָּחִים לְפָנֶיךָ **When the matzah and** *maror* **are placed before you.** In Temple times, the text read: "When the Paschal lamb, the matzah, and the *maror*

are placed before you" (*Shibolei Haleket*; see Rashi on Exodus 13:8).

Clearly, though, even when only *one* of the *mitzvot* is in effect, we can still fulfill the mitzvah of retelling the Exodus. For nowadays, of the three *mitzvot* mentioned above, only the matzah is Biblically mandated: We do not offer a Paschal lamb, and the *maror* obligation today is only Rabbinic. Yet the mitzvah of retelling the Exodus remains a Biblical obligation even today (*The Rebbe's Haggadah;* see *Pesachim* 120a and 116b).

מֵרֹאשׁ חֹדֶשׁ **The first of the month.** One lesson here is that one cannot arbitrarily decide when and how to celebrate Jewish festivals and rituals: one cannot celebrate Pesach on the first of the month. If we reshape Torah to conform to our whims and conve-

nience, we no longer have Torah.[121]

Yet although the practical *mitzvot* of Pesach can only be fulfilled on the night of Pesach, we can experience redemption in the spiritual sense even earlier:

"A theory in Torah is also Torah," even one

מִתְּחִלָּה עוֹבְדֵי עֲבוֹדָה זָרָה הָיוּ אֲבוֹתֵינוּ, וְעַכְשָׁו קֵרְבָנוּ
הַמָּקוֹם לַעֲבֹדָתוֹ, שֶׁנֶּאֱמַר: וַיֹּאמֶר יְהוֹשֻׁעַ אֶל
כָּל הָעָם, כֹּה אָמַר יְיָ אֱלֹהֵי יִשְׂרָאֵל. בְּעֵבֶר הַנָּהָר יָשְׁבוּ
אֲבוֹתֵיכֶם מֵעוֹלָם, תֶּרַח אֲבִי אַבְרָהָם וַאֲבִי נָחוֹר, וַיַּעַבְדוּ
אֱלֹהִים אֲחֵרִים.

קֵרְבָנוּ הַמָּקוֹם **The Omnipresent one has brought us close.** Being drawn close to God changed our connection to God, not only in *degree* but in *kind*. No longer was it defined by our finite efforts to seek and apprehend the Infinite, but by the Infinite's seeking of us. No longer were we part of a creation distinct from God; Godliness became a part of our very being. We became a manifestation of Godliness within creation (*The Rebbe*).[132]

בְּעֵבֶר הַנָּהָר יָשְׁבוּ אֲבוֹתֵיכֶם **Your ancestors used to live on the other side of the river.** In its plain sense, Joshua's prophecy describes Abraham's ascent from lowly beginnings—"from your land, your birthplace and house of your father"—to a higher and holier place, "to the land that I will show you." This describes the journey we must all make in our lifetimes, to transcend our natural tendencies and go to the land that God shows us.

But this journey of ascent is preceded by another journey, one of descent: the descent of the soul from the sublime heights of heaven to this physical world. In this sense, God commands the soul to descend "from your land, your birthplace and house of your father"—the heavenly origins of the soul—"to the land that I will show you," the physical world.[133]

Joshua's prophecy likewise describes not only the ascent of Abraham but the descent of his soul from its sublime origin, "the other side of the river":

The River of Eden

Genesis (2:10) speaks of "the river emanating from Eden." *Eden* represents absolute Divine consciousness (the level of *chochmah*, innate knowledge). The "river" that flows from *Eden* constitutes a diminished spiritual consciousness, one derived through intellectual contemplation and thought. In Eden one *knows* Divinity as one knows what one's eyes have seen. In the "river," knowledge of Divinity is like the knowledge of something one has not *seen* but has only *heard* about.[134]

That our ancestors came from "the other side of the river" means that their souls were rooted in a source *beyond* the "River"—their souls possessed an intuitive and innate knowledge of God that transcends the cognitive process.

Abraham the Hebrew

The Hebrew word for "other side" is *eiver*. Abraham, who came from the "other side (of the river)" was therefore called the *Ivree*, or the "Hebrew" (Genesis 14:13; see on next passage). Like Abraham, we too are called "Hebrews," as Moses said to Pharaoh: *The God of the Hebrews has appeared to us* (Exodus 5:3). This name alludes to the root of our souls in the "other side of the river," in the innate knowledge of God associated with Eden.[135]

We are generally not conscious of this "Hebrew" dimension of our souls.[136] The prophet (Isaiah 11:15), however, tells us that just as we experienced a crossing of water during the redemption of the Exodus, so will we experience a crossing during the future redemption: We will cross back to "the other side of the river" and return to the consciousness of knowing God as one knows what one's eyes can see (*Rabbi Schneur Zalman of Liadi; Rabbi Shmuel of Lubavitch*).[137]

∽ SHAMEFUL BEGINNINGS ∾

In the beginning, our ancestors Terach, father of Abraham, and earlier were idolaters. But now the Omnipresent one has drawn us close to His service, as in the verse (Joshua 24:2-4):

And Joshua said to the entire nation, "So said God, the God of Israel: 'Your ancestors used to live on the other side of the [Euphrates] river—Terach, father of Abraham and father of Nachor—and they worshipped other gods.'"

Notes & Insights

✣ SHAMEFUL BEGINNINGS ✣

As mentioned above, the retelling of the Exodus should begin with the shame of Israel, which, according to Rav, refers to our shameful beginnings as idolaters (*Pesachim* 116a; see p. 36a above).

וְעַכְשָׁו קֵרְבָנוּ הַמָּקוֹם **But now the Omnipresent one has drawn us close.** Although this occurred in the days of Abraham, God continues to draw us close to Him to this day. We too are therefore obliged to thank God for this gift. Hence, "But *now* the Omnipresent one..." and not "But *afterwards* the Omnipresent one...."

See *Zohar* (III:298b): "*And I took your father Abraham...*—and since then God takes Israel *in every generation* and does not separate from them, taking them with compassion..." (*The Rebbe's Haggadah*).

✣ PURE FROM IMPURE ✣

Midrash *Who can produce pure from impure? Is it not the One God?* (Job 14:4)

"Pure from impure—such as Abraham from Terach...Mordechai from Shimi [who cursed David]...the World to Come from this world. Who did this? Who commanded this? Who decreed this? Is it not the One God?"[128] (*Midrash Rabbah, Chukat* 19:1)

Chasidus Though it would seem to detract from our festive mood, remembering our challenging past can increase our celebration. For it is by remembering the depths of depravity from which we emerged that we can appreciate and celebrate the heights to which God has brought us.[129]

The Haggadah also reveals here an essential principle of spiritual work:

When we take an honest look at our deeds, we may encounter a "Terach," an "idolatrous" past of worship of self and material pursuits, of distance from God. We may have assumed that such "shameful beginnings" preclude us from a spiritual future, from a "praiseworthy ending." But our history teaches us otherwise:

Abraham emerged from a depraved beginning. His father was not only an idolater, he created idols for others. Yet he produced the illustrious Abraham. Clearly, an impure beginning does not dictate an impure end. Indeed from the impure, from the challenges and birth pangs, does the pure emerge (*Rabbi Yosef Yitzchak of Lubavitch*).[130]

This was demonstrated again during the Exodus when the idolatrous Israelites were suddenly and abruptly uplifted to the loftiest revelations of Divinity.

So, too, tonight, as we relive the Exodus, if a person feels that "in the beginning he was an idolater," he is assured that "now God has drawn him close"—the Divine revelation of this night enables him to achieve a sudden and radical transformation from darkness to light (*The Rebbe*).[131]

וָאֶקַּח אֶת אֲבִיכֶם אֶת אַבְרָהָם מֵעֵבֶר הַנָּהָר, וָאוֹלֵךְ אוֹתוֹ בְּכָל אֶרֶץ כְּנָעַן, וָאַרְבֶּ(ה) אֶת זַרְעוֹ וָאֶתֶּן לוֹ אֶת יִצְחָק: וָאֶתֵּן לְיִצְחָק אֶת יַעֲקֹב וְאֶת עֵשָׂו, וָאֶתֵּן לְעֵשָׂו אֶת הַר שֵׂעִיר לָרֶשֶׁת אוֹתוֹ, וְיַעֲקֹב וּבָנָיו יָרְדוּ מִצְרָיִם:

existence. (Fear of this transition, of entering a land that "consumes its inhabitants" by burying them in material pursuit, led the spies to reject the land.)

The prophecy through Joshua provided the strength and inspiration for the Jewish people to fulfill their new mandate: to become involved with material existence and transform it into a vehicle for Godliness. Where would they gather the strength to fulfill this charge? God therefore tells them of the sublime source of their souls and what He did with Abraham:

The Unnamable Essence

I took your patriarch, Abraham...and I led him across all of the land of Canaan. "I" is God Himself, without any description—the unnamable essence of God that transcends all categories and "rules." *I took* Abraham, from the sublime and lofty atmosphere of the "the other side of the river" (see on previous passage) and led him across Canaan, giving him the capacity to achieve the impossible: to remain a "chariot" and conduit for Divinity, for the lofty consciousness of the "other side of the river," even while engaged in the very materialistic world of the land of Canaan.

In the prophecy to Joshua, God tells the Jewish people that they are heirs to this capacity that He bestowed upon the Patriarchs. They too can access the power of the infinite—where opposites can abide—to be a conduit for Divinity even as they enter the "real" and challenging world of Canaan (*The Rebbe*).[141]

וָאַרְבֶּה אֶת־זַרְעוֹ, וָאֶתֶּן לוֹ אֶת־יִצְחָק **I made his offspring abundant and gave him Isaac.** At first glance it seems odd that one child, Isaac,

is called abundant offspring.[142] On the simple level, however, the verse means that Abraham's offspring would become abundant *through* Isaac.[143] On a deeper level, Abraham may not have been immediately blessed with many children, but his one child, Isaac, was an *abundant* child, abounding in blessing. Within Isaac was contained blessing and greatness equal to many children, as the Midrash says of Moses: "He was equal to all of Israel"[144] (*The Rebbe*).[145]

> ### ❧ JACOB VS. ESAU ❧
> *Esau receives without effort. But in the realm of holiness there must be toil. One must earn. Hence: "...to Esau I gave Mount Seir as an inheritance; and Jacob and his children went down to Egypt...."* [146]
> —RABBI YOSEF YITZCHAK OF LUBAVITCH

וָאֶתֶּן לוֹ אֶת־יִצְחָק **I...gave him Isaac.** The *gematria* of Isaac (208) is equal to four times the word for "child" (*ben*—52). Isaac thus embodies all four children—the wise, wicked, etc. Joseph, on the other hand, is numerically equivalent to three times "child" (156).

Joseph was so named as Rachel prayed that God "add for me another child."[147] Homiletically, this means that Joseph is associated with the work of transforming one who is distant from God into a child of God—turning an "other" into a "child."[148] His name is therefore equal to *three* times "child," since Joseph transforms the wicked one to righteousness (*The Tzemach Tzedek*).[149]

∾ GOD TAKES ABRAHAM ⌒

Joshua's prophecy continues: **And I took your patriarch, Abraham,** *from the other side of the river, and I led him across all of the land of Canaan; and made his offspring abundant and gave him Isaac. And to Isaac I gave Jacob and Esau; and to Esau I gave Mount Seir as an inheritance; and Jacob and his children went down to Egypt.*

 ∾ Notes & Insights ⌒

וָאַרְבֶּ(ה) אֶת־זַרְעוֹ, וָאֶתֶּן לוֹ אֶת־יִצְחָק **I...made his offspring abundant and gave him Isaac.** The word for "and made abundant" (*va'arbeh*) is spelled in an unusual way (without the letter *hey* at the end).

This spelling also renders: "and I contended" (*va'ariv*). The verse thus alludes to God saying: "I 'contended' with Abraham in many ways, i.e., gave him many tests, before I gave him Isaac" (Jerusalem Talmud, *Pesachim* 10:5).

৪ A LONE FIGURE ৪৪

 Chasidus *Abraham was [only] one and [yet] he inherited the land...* (Ezekiel 33:24).

"Why was Abraham called the Hebrew? Because the entire world was on one side (*eiver*) and Abraham on the other" (*Bereishit Rabbah* 42:12).[138]

Although Abraham was a lone individual, with the entire world opposing his beliefs, he persevered and ultimately triumphed—"he inherited the land." He influenced the entire world by bringing awareness of the Divine to its inhabitants.

Abraham thereby made it possible for all of us to do the same: Even a lone individual in a place that is indifferent or even hostile to God and Torah should not despair of effecting change.

From Abraham we inherit the ability to defy numbers. Though we are the smallest of all nations[139] and, by natural law, should be assimilated into or wiped out by a world that vastly outnumbers us, we remain miraculously distinct.

By our strength alone we would indeed become subservient to those who outnumber us. But we go with the strength of God, who is not limited by the rules of nature, and who has given us the mandate to influence all of

society, bringing the light of God and Torah to the entire world (*The Rebbe*).[140]

৪ WHY JOSHUA? ৪৪

The *Zohar* (III:98b) asks a simple question on this passage and the previous one: "Was not all of Israel aware of this history? Certainly Joshua must have known it." Why then the need for, *So said God*, implying that without this revelation they would not have known the basic history of Abraham and his descendants?

The *Zohar* explains the mystical meaning of the terms in this passage, according to which God informed Joshua of the sublime source from which the souls of the Patriarchs were created, as explained above. (See *Mikdash Melech* on the *Zohar* and *Siddur of Arizal* on the Haggadah.)

But why was it important for Joshua to teach this message about the Patriarchs at that particular time in history?

A Timely Prophecy

Joshua conveyed this prophecy when the Jews entered Canaan. They were leaving the relatively spiritual life of the desert—where all their material needs were miraculously tended to—and entering the "real" world of "plowing and planting," of engagement with material

בָּרוּךְ שׁוֹמֵר הַבְטָחָתוֹ לְיִשְׂרָאֵל, בָּרוּךְ הוּא, שֶׁהַקָּדוֹשׁ בָּרוּךְ הוּא חִשַּׁב אֶת הַקֵּץ לַעֲשׂוֹת כְּמָה שֶׁאָמַר לְאַבְרָהָם אָבִינוּ בִּבְרִית בֵּין הַבְּתָרִים, שֶׁנֶּאֱמַר: וַיֹּאמֶר לְאַבְרָם: יָדֹעַ תֵּדַע כִּי גֵר יִהְיֶה זַרְעֲךָ בְּאֶרֶץ לֹא לָהֶם, וַעֲבָדוּם וְעִנּוּ אֹתָם, אַרְבַּע מֵאוֹת שָׁנָה: וְגַם אֶת הַגּוֹי אֲשֶׁר יַעֲבֹדוּ דָּן אָנֹכִי, וְאַחֲרֵי כֵן יֵצְאוּ בִּרְכֻשׁ גָּדוֹל:

Abraham then walked through the parts and God caused a smoking furnace and flaming torch to pass through as His "representatives" to the covenant. On that day, says the Torah, God made a covenant with Abraham and said: "To your descendants I have given this land, from the Egyptian River to the Euphrates..." (see *The Torah* (Kehot) on Genesis 15:7-21).

✣ TEMPORARY ESTRANGEMENT ✣

Chasidus While developing a new idea, the teacher retreats from the students, who may misconstrue this detachment as abandonment. Yet it is the teacher's love that motivates the retreat. For only by concentrating deeply on the new idea can the teacher develop it to a point where it can be shared with the student.

Similarly, the seeming estrangement and distance from God that occurs in exile is in fact an expression of God's love. For it is the conditions of exile that enable us to attain a deeper, more profound relationship with God. It was therefore precisely during the Covenant—an expression of loyalty between two parties—that God told Abraham about the future exiles.[151]

✣ CREDIT FOR THE EXODUS? ✣

Kabbalah R. Yesse asked: "God reminds Israel repeatedly that He redeemed them from Egypt. Yet, was He not simply fulfilling His promise?" Rabbi Shimon ben Yochai replied: "God promised Abraham that He would take Israel out of the Egyptian exile but not out of the subjection to idolatry. Israel in Egypt fell under 'the 49 forces of impurity,' from which God subsequently redeemed them. Furthermore, He took them into the corresponding '49 gates of understanding.' This is why you will find that the Exodus is mentioned in the Torah 50 times (excluding tangential references—*R. Moshe Cordovero*). And this is why we count the days and weeks following Pesach, since every day of those 49 days God took us out from a force of impurity and brought us into a force of purity" (condensed from *Zohar Chadash*, beg. of Yitro; see also *Tikkunei Zohar* 32 ["Can a master praise himself for freeing one he has enslaved?"]).

R. Moshe Cordovero lists the fifty instances where the Exodus is mentioned in the Torah.[152]

✣ ABRAM TO ABRAHAM ✣

When God told Abram about the future exile of the Israelites to Egypt, He did not not ask for Abram's approval. For perhaps Abram would have declined the 'great wealth' that would come afterward and the whole 'business' of exile. God simply informed him: "Know for certain." As long as his name was Abram, the cosmic significance of the exile could not be revealed to him. But later, when his name became Abraham (and he was thereby granted a new, profound spiritual perception) he understood the significance of the exile on his own.[153]

—RABBI YOSEF YITZCHAK OF LUBAVITCH

∽ THE PROMISE ↶

Blessed is He who keeps His promise to Israel— blessed be He! For the Holy One, blessed be He, calculated the end [of the bondage], to bring about what He told our father Abraham at the Covenant Between the Parts, as it is written: *And He said to Abram: "Know for certain that your descendants will be strangers in a land not their own. [The people of that land] will enslave them and oppress them for 400 years. I will also execute judgment upon the nation whom they shall serve, after which [Israel] will leave with great wealth"* (Genesis 15:13-14).

 Notes & Insights

שׁוֹמֵר הַבְטָחָתוֹ **Keeps His promise**—the promise given to our father Abraham about the Egyptian exile, and the promise given to the prophets about those who rise up against us in every generation. "It was this promise that stood by our ancestors, etc.," as we say in the subsequent passage (*The Rebbe's Haggadah*).

חִשֵׁב אֶת־הַקֵּץ **Calculated the end.** Although God spoke of a 400 year exile, the Israelites were only in Egypt for 210 years. God considered the 190 years from Isaac's birth until Jacob's descent to Egypt as part of the 400 years. After Abraham's first "descendant," Isaac, was born, they, and later Jacob, lived as "foreigners" in the land of Canaan. Isaac was born on the 15ᵗʰ of Nissan, 2048, and the Exodus took place exactly 400 years later, on the 15ᵗʰ of Nissan, 2448 (see *Rashi* on Genesis 15:13).

"Foreigners" in the land of Canaan: Birth of Isaac until Jacob's descent to Egypt	190 years
Descent to Egypt and gradual enslavement there	124 years
Severe enslavement and oppression in Egypt	86 years
Total:	**400 years**

The word for "end," *ketz*, is numerically

equivalent to 190. Thus: God counted the *ketz*, the 190 years from Isaac's birth, as part of the fulfillment of what he told Abraham: "your descendants will be foreigners...." (*Shibolei Haleket*).

בִּבְרִית בֵּין הַבְּתָרִים **Covenant Between the Parts.** On the 15ᵗʰ of Nissan, in the year 2018, when Abraham was seventy years old (and still called "Abram"), God promised him the land of Israel. Abraham asked God for a sign that he would indeed inherit it.¹⁵⁰

In ancient times, a covenant was formalized by cutting something in two and having the two parties walk "between the parts." By doing so, they expressed the interdependence of the two parties, just as the split object is complete only when its parts are united.

To establish His covenant with Abraham and his descendants, to give them the Land of Israel, God told Abraham to arrange parts to walk through. After arranging the parts, a deep sleep overcame Abraham, as well as a dark and ominous dread. This foretold the travails of the various exiles his descendants were destined to experience.

It was then that God told Abraham that his descendants would be strangers in a foreign land and that they would be enslaved and oppressed for four hundred years, etc., as we read in the Haggadah.

צריך להגביה הכוס ולכסות הפת כן כתב האר"י ז"ל.

Cover the *matzot* and then raise your cup (as we do during Kiddush) while reciting the following paragraph.

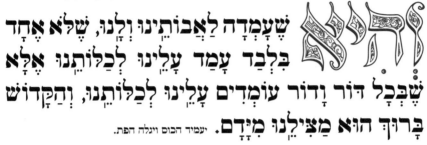

וְהִיא שֶׁעָמְדָה לַאֲבוֹתֵינוּ וְלָנוּ, שֶׁלֹּא אֶחָד בִּלְבָד עָמַד עָלֵינוּ לְכַלּוֹתֵנוּ אֶלָּא שֶׁבְּכָל דּוֹר וָדוֹר עוֹמְדִים עָלֵינוּ לְכַלּוֹתֵנוּ, וְהַקָּדוֹשׁ בָּרוּךְ הוּא מַצִּילֵנוּ מִיָּדָם. יעמיד הכוס ויגלה הפת.

Place the cup on the table and uncover the *matzot*.

---

has failed.[157] Adrianus Caesar compared Israel to a lone sheep surrounded by seventy wolves.[158] Yet unlike many of those "wolves" who are now unknown outside of history books, the lone and continually hounded "sheep" lives on and endures.

For the lone sheep is not truly alone. As Rabbi Yehoshua responded to the Caesar: "Great is the Shepherd Who saves [the lone sheep] and protects it."

Regarding our first exile, God told Jacob: *I will descend with you to Egypt.*[159] As the Talmud puts it: "Exiled to Egypt, the Divine presence was with them…Exiled to Babylon, the Divine presence was with them…."[160]

It is this—God's presence, the manifestation of His promise—that stands by us in every generation. As we say in our prayers (Isaiah 8:10):

Conspire a scheme, but it will be foiled; contrive a plot, but it will not materialize—for God is with us.[161]

וְהַקָּדוֹשׁ בָּרוּךְ הוּא מַצִּילֵנוּ מִיָּדָם **The Holy One blessed be He saves us from their hands.** The first Jewish birth, the miraculous birth of Isaac, set the tone for the future of the Jewish people. Miracles do not merely occur to this people—it is part of its makeup, the foundation of its existence.[162]

Hence, while we engage in conventional measures to protect ourselves—such as Esther lobbying Achashverosh to protect us from Haman—we know that the ultimate source of our survival is not Achashverosh, but a Divine promise and miracle.

Our efforts create the conduit to receive God's salvation—but we must not confuse the conduit with the Source.[163]

We pray that very soon we will no longer need God to "save us from their hands," since we will see the fulfillment of the prophecies: *And the wolf will lie with the lamb* and *swords will be turned into plowshares*[164] (*The Rebbe*).[165]

❧ PERSONAL SURVIVAL ❧

Just as physical enemies continually rise up to destroy us, so do our inner "foes," our negative impulses, rise up to destroy us every day. And just as God protects us from our collective enemies, so does He help us overcome our personal "enemy." As the Talmud teaches:

The negative impulse rises up against us each day to cause us to sin. And were it not for the fact that God comes to our aid, we would be unable to overcome our negative impulse.[166]

God's promise to Israel is an unconditional one, extending to every generation, in any place and any time and any condition. His promise to protect us from our inner "enemy" is likewise unconditional:

Even if we have lapsed and failed morally, His promise to protect us is not rescinded, and He continues to help us overcome our inner challenges (*The Rebbe*).[167]

47b

ᴖ THE MIRACLE OF JEWISH SURVIVAL ᴗ

Cover the *matzot* and then raise your cup (as we do during Kiddush) while reciting the following paragraph.

It was this [promise] that stood by our ancestors and by us. For it was not only one enemy, (i.e., Pharaoh) that rose up against us to destroy us—in every single generation they rise up against us to destroy us, and the Holy One Blessed be He saves us from their hands.

Place the cup on the table and uncover the *matzot*.

 Notes & Insights

ולכסות הפת **Cover the *matzot*—**so that it is not "shamed" by seeing us raise the cup of wine (*Agur; Shulchan Aruch HaRav* 473:44).

צריך להגביה הכוס **Raise your cup.** The Talmud states that praise of God should be recited over wine (*Berachot* 35a). Some suggest that this is why we raise our cups here, as we do later during the paragraph of "We are therefore obligated to give praise..." (*Shaar Hakollel*).

It seems, however, that this passage is less a song of praise and more a statement of fact and would not require raising the cup. Rather, raising the cup during *this* paragraph is of Kabbalistic significance and associated with the verse (Psalms 116:13): *I will raise a cup of salvations...* (see *Shaloh* and *Yaavetz*).

Rabbi Schneur Zalman therefore writes in his instructions prior to this paragraph:

"One must raise the cup and cover the bread—so writes the [kabbalist] Arizal"—hinting that this custom is a Kabbalistic one (*The Rebbe's Haggadah*).

(Rabbi Yosef Yitzchak of Lubavitch offers a homiletic interpretation of the above instruction: The word for "cup" (*kos*) is numerically equivalent to "nature" (*hateva*). In life, one must raise up one's "cup," i.e., one's *natural* existence,

and dedicate it to a higher purpose. One must also "cover the bread," i.e., overcome the materialistic allure of the natural world. One can then harness nature for its spiritual purpose.

Where do we derive the strength to accomplish this? From the Arizal and his mystical teachings.[154])

שֶׁלֹא אֶחָד בִּלְבַד עָמַד עָלֵינוּ לְכַלּוֹתֵנוּ **Not only one [Pharaoh] rose up against us to destroy us.** Some versions (*Rav Saadiah Gaon, Rambam, Shibolei Haleket*) omit the words "to destroy us," since Pharaoh did not seek to eliminate all of us, as we say in the following paragraph, Pharaoh's decree of death applied only to the males (*Abarbanel*).

To explain our version (which is the version of *Arizal, Shaloh* and *Yaavetz*) one may suggest that although Pharaoh did not initially intend to eliminate all Jews, he later egged on the Egyptians to chase after the Jews by saying: *...I will unsheathe my sword, my hand will despoil them.*[155]

This implies that Pharaoh's intention was to destroy all of them, as *Maharal* writes. This seems to be the understanding of both *Targum Onkelus* and *Targum Yonatan* on the above verse as well (*The Rebbe's Haggadah*).

৪ THE LONE SHEEP ৪

Chasidus
In this passage we declare that no threat to our people can lead us to despair.[156] For the attempt to destroy the Jewish nation is

not new. It occurred a generation ago, and two generations ago, going back all the way to Pharaoh and Laban, and even before that, to the time of Abraham, the first Jew. Yet each attempt

צֵא וּלְמַד מַה בִּקֵּשׁ לָבָן הָאֲרַמִּי לַעֲשׂוֹת לְיַעֲקֹב אָבִינוּ,
שֶׁפַּרְעֹה לֹא גָזַר אֶלָּא עַל הַזְּכָרִים, וְלָבָן בִּקֵּשׁ לַעֲקוֹר
אֶת הַכֹּל, שֶׁנֶּאֱמַר: אֲרַמִּי אֹבֵד אָבִי, וַיֵּרֶד מִצְרַיְמָה וַיָּגָר
שָׁם בִּמְתֵי מְעָט, וַיְהִי שָׁם לְגוֹי גָּדוֹל עָצוּם וָרָב:

צֵא וּלְמַד Go out and learn. With this seemingly superfluous phrase, the author of the Haggadah alludes to a profound teaching: If one wishes to truly learn, one must "go out"—one must transcend the limitations of the self. Only then can one truly acquire knowledge.[172]

> When Rabbi Schneur Zalman returned from Mezritch, after studying with his master Rabbi DovBer, people asked him what he had gained there. He replied:
>
> "We were taught that one must 'go out and learn.' One must transcend the self and learn from one's fellow. [This can be achieved by] perceiving your own flaws and the virtues of your fellow." [173]
>
> —Rabbi Yosef Yitzchak of Lubavitch

וְלָבָן בִּקֵּשׁ לַעֲקֹר אֶת־הַכֹּל Laban sought to uproot everything. Jacob and Laban could not have been further apart in outlook and philosophy. Laban was a sly materialist who viewed the material domain as completely independent of the spiritual.

Jacob dreamt of a ladder standing on the ground, in the material world, but whose head reached the heavens. He dreamt of uniting the two worlds, of elevating the physical and imbuing it with the heavenly.

Laban sought to educate his grandchildren with his materialist worldview; Jacob sought to give his children a Torah education. A Torah education is the "foundation of everything"; an

education from a Laban "uproots everything."

True, our Sages teach (*Avot* 2:2), "It is good [to combine] the study of Torah with an occupation." Significantly, however, they mention Torah first. For Torah is primary; "occupation," secondary. Laban seeks to switch the order around.

The study of the inner dimension of Torah helps one see the danger of Laban's outlook. Hence: *Go out and learn what Laban sought to do*—by bringing out and revealing the inner aspect of Torah, you will perceive and understand the dangers of Laban's intentions (*Rabbi Yosef Yitzchak of Lubavitch*).[174]

אֲרַמִּי אֹבֵד אָבִי An Aramean sought to destroy my father. As mentioned, this passage is the beginning of the declaration made when bringing *Bikkurim*, the first fruits, to the Temple.

Mystically, *Bikkurim*, the *first* fruits, represent the sublime consciousness of the soul as it exists in its first manifestation, before it descends into this world. As Hosea (9:10) prophesied: *I [God] perceived your ancestors like the first of the dates....*

Bringing the *Bikkurim* represents our attempt to 1) *raise up* our earthly selves toward our heavenly consciousness, and 2) *draw down* our heavenly consciousness to infuse our earthly reality. The first is accomplished through bringing the fruits, the second through the declaration (The *Tzemach Tzedek*).[175]

The allusion to *Bikkurim* during the Seder underscores once again the sublime source of the soul, as mentioned above (p. 44b) regarding "the other side of the river" (*The Rebbe*).[176]

⌒ SAVED FROM LABAN ⌒

Go out and learn what Laban the Aramean sought to do to our father Jacob: Pharaoh issued a decree only against the males (i.e., male newborns); but Laban sought to uproot everything. As it is written: *An Aramean [Laban, sought to] destroy my father [Jacob], and he went down to Egypt and sojourned there, few in number; [yet] he grew there into a great nation, mighty and numerous* (Deut. 26:5).

 Notes & Insights

The Mishnah instructs (*Pesachim* 116a): "Expound the verses beginning with *An Aramean sought to destroy my father* to the end of that section."

Thus we proceed to do so now, following the interpretations given in the *Sifrei* (*Avudraham*).

The passage beginning "An Aramean sought..." is the declaration made by the Jew when bringing the *Bikkurim*, the first fruits of the harvest, to the Holy Temple in Jerusalem. Over the next ten passages (until page 59), the Haggadah will analyze the first four verses of that declaration, which relate to the Exodus. The four verses in succession are as follows:

...An Aramean [sought to] destroy my father and he went down to Egypt and sojourned there, few in number; and he grew there into a great nation, mighty and numerous. The Egyptians persecuted us and oppressed us, and imposed harsh labor upon us. And we cried out to God, the God of our fathers, and God heard our voice and saw our suffering, our toil, and our oppression. God took us out of Egypt with a strong hand and an outstretched arm, and with a great revelation, and with signs and wonders (Deut. 26:5-8).

וּלְמַד **And learn**—that God saves us from the hands of those who rise up against us. For "Laban sought to uproot everything" and failed only because of God's intervention. God likewise protected Jacob when he moved to Egypt (*Machzor Vitri; Shibolei Haleket; Avudraham*).

צֵא וּלְמַד **Go out and learn.** This figurative expression can also be found in the Talmud (e.g., *Kiddushin* 37a, *Sanhedrin* 86a, *Chullin* 63a) and occurs many times in the Midrashic works.

Abarbanel explains its meaning in the present context as follows:

"*Go out* from the subject of Egypt in which you are engaged *and learn* from the stories of Laban and Jacob" (*The Rebbe's Haggadah*).

אֲרַמִּי אֹבֵד אָבִי, וַיֵּרֶד מִצְרָיְמָה **An Aramean... and he went down to Egypt.** Through the gift of *Bikkurim* we show our thanks to God for His kindness of enabling us to settle the Land of Israel and enjoy its produce.[168] We therefore begin the declaration by thanking God for His kindness during our *prior* settlements, which were in Aram and Egypt.[169]

הַזְּכָרִים **The males.** Pharaoh's astrologers told him that a boy would be born who would redeem Israel. He therefore commanded that all Jewish newborn males be drowned in the Nile.[170]

וְלָבָן בִּקֵּשׁ לַעֲקֹר אֶת־הַכֹּל **Laban sought to uproot everything.** After Jacob took his family and fled from Laban's home, Laban pursued Jacob intending to kill them all. It was only because God appeared to Laban in a dream, warning Laban not to harm them, that they were saved (*Machzor Vitri*).[171]

וַיֵּרֶד מִצְרַיְמָה, אָנוּס עַל פִּי הַדִּבּוּר.

וַיָּגָר שָׁם, מְלַמֵּד שֶׁלֹּא יָרַד יַעֲקֹב אָבִינוּ לְהִשְׁתַּקֵּעַ בְּמִצְרַיִם אֶלָּא לָגוּר שָׁם, שֶׁנֶּאֱמַר: וַיֹּאמְרוּ אֶל פַּרְעֹה לָגוּר בָּאָרֶץ בָּאנוּ, כִּי אֵין מִרְעֶה לַצֹּאן אֲשֶׁר לַעֲבָדֶיךָ, כִּי כָבֵד הָרָעָב בְּאֶרֶץ כְּנָעַן, וְעַתָּה יֵשְׁבוּ נָא עֲבָדֶיךָ בְּאֶרֶץ גֹּשֶׁן.

❧ A RELUCTANT DESCENT ☙

Jacob, like the other Patriarchs, is described as a chariot of God, a conduit to the fulfillment of God's will, with no agenda of his own.[180] How, then, can his descent to Egypt, by which he was fulfilling God's will, be described as "forced," as if he went reluctantly?

Of course Jacob willingly and joyfully fulfilled God's desire and with joy. But when God gives us a mission that requires us to leave a place of holiness—the Land of Israel, in Jacob's case—and descend to an "Egypt," a place of Divine concealment, there must be an element of reluctance in that descent. We should be happy to fulfill God's will, but we cannot be happy about the descent per se.

This reluctance is integral to the success of our mission. If spiritual descent is not unappealing to us, our chances of subsequent spiritual ascent become less likely. How can we fulfill our mission of bringing light to a spiritual desert if we have grown comfortable there, if we no longer think of it as a parched land and no longer yearn to return home?

Jacob was happy to fulfill God's will. But he knew that God's will could only be done if he would descend reluctantly—forced by Divine decree. Only then would Israel succeed in its Egyptian sojourn and emerge with the "great wealth," the spiritual benefits for which the descent was decreed (The Rebbe).[181]

בְּאֶרֶץ גֹּשֶׁן **The land of Goshen.** According to the *Midrash*, Goshen was the property of the Jewish people, since the Pharaoh in the days of Abraham had given it to Sarah as a gift.[182] Nonetheless, their stay in their own property, the "choicest part" of Egypt,[183] was still counted as part of their preordained exile and servitude.

The purpose of the exile was to refine the Jewish people by putting them through "the iron crucible"[184] of Egyptian slavery.

Before Joseph and his brothers died, the Jewish people went through this "crucible" through the intense intellectual "labor" of Torah study[185] and the pain of yearning for the Holy Land. Once Joseph and his brothers died, however, the peoples' spiritual awareness deteriorated.

They no longer applied themselves laboriously to the study of the Torah and became complacent in their new land.[186] They failed to utilize the choice land of Goshen for holy living and instead became coarsened by its material abundance.[187]

The servitude to Egypt therefore began in earnest at that point, replacing spiritual toil with physical labor.

As the *Mishnah* states (*Avot* 3:5): when we engage in the toil of spiritual growth and Torah study, God removes from us the yoke and toil of the material world (The Rebbe; The Torah (Kehot), Genesis 47:27).[188]

Kabbalah וַיֵּרֶד מִצְרַיְמָה, אָנוּס עַל פִּי הַדִּבּוּר **He went down to Egypt—forced by the decree [lit., the "speech"].** The mystics teach that defilement in speech causes spiritual defilement of the body.

Thus: One descends to "Egypt," to the unholy *kelipot*, experiencing a "forced" spiritual descent of the body that one cannot control.

How does this occur? "By the speech"—because of defilement in speech (*Rabbi DovBer of Mezritch*).[189]

~ DESCENT TO SOJOURN IN EGYPT ~

And he went down to Egypt—forced by the decree of God to Abraham that his descendants would be exiled.

And he sojourned there—this teaches that our father Jacob did not descend to settle permanently in Egypt (lit., "to be submerged in Egypt,") but only to stay there temporarily. As it is written: *Joseph's brothers* said to Pharaoh: "We have come to sojourn in the land, because there is no pasture for your servants' flocks in Canaan, since the famine is severe in the land of Canaan. So now, please, let your servants settle in the land of Goshen" (Genesis 47:4).

 Notes & Insights

אָנוּם עַל פִּי הַדִּבּוּר **Forced by the decree [of God].** As the Talmud states (*Shabbat* 89b): "Our father Jacob was destined to descend to Egypt in iron chains"—to fulfill *the decree of God* made to Abraham that his descendants would be exiled to an alien land.

[Generally, as was the case in our other exiles, those exiled are taken away in chains. Because of Jacob's merit, God arranged it so that he would descend honorably, invited by the king of Egypt (*Shabbat* ibid., and *Rashi* there). In any case, we see from the Talmudic statement that Jacob's descent to Egypt was a fulfillment of the decree made to Abraham and the beginning of the Egyptian exile.[177]]

In this teaching, the Haggadah informs us of the manner in which Jacob "went down to Egypt." But, unlike the second teaching in this paragraph, this one is not derived from the verse's choice of words ("he went down to Egypt").

The Haggadah thus does not say "*this teaches us* (that he went down by Divine decree)," as it does in the second teaching (*The Rebbe's Haggadah*).[178]

כִּי כָבֵד הָרָעָב **The famine is severe.** Their explanation of their desire to reside in Egypt suggests that they did not intend to settle in Egypt permanently. Rather, they planned to return to Canaan once the famine ended (*Shibolei Haleket; Machzor Vitri*).

אָנוּם עַל פִּי הַדִּבּוּר **Forced by the decree.** The fulfillment of the utopian promises of our prophets, a time of world peace and Divine knowledge, can at times feel unachievable, an unrealistic fantasy. The world we perceive does not seem capable of such transformation.

Truthfully, however, what *should* be unfathomable to us is not our promised future, but the current world we have come to accept as the norm. It is the endurance of the condition of exile, which includes the "exile," i.e., the concealment of the Divine presence, that should be incomprehensible to us.

The Haggadah thus reminds us: Jacob's descent to Egypt, which began the Egyptian exile—as well as the exile of the Divine presence that abides to this day—is an anomaly, an impossibility. It occurred only because the Creator, who is not restrained by the laws of the possible, has so decreed for the sake of the spiritual benefits of this descent.

The future prophesied by our prophets describes a far more logical reality for a world created by God. It is the descent to Egypt, as well as the world's current state of spiritual darkness, that is unnatural and illogical—forced by Divine decree (*The Rebbe*).[179]

בִּמְתֵי מְעָט, כְּמָה שֶׁנֶּאֱמַר: בְּשִׁבְעִים נֶפֶשׁ יָרְדוּ אֲבֹתֶיךָ
מִצְרָיְמָה, וְעַתָּה שָׂמְךָ יְיָ אֱלֹהֶיךָ כְּכוֹכְבֵי הַשָּׁמַיִם לָרֹב.

וַיְהִי שָׁם לְגוֹי, מְלַמֵּד שֶׁהָיוּ יִשְׂרָאֵל מְצֻיָּנִים שָׁם.

גָּדוֹל עָצוּם, כְּמָה שֶׁנֶּאֱמַר: וּבְנֵי יִשְׂרָאֵל פָּרוּ וַיִּשְׁרְצוּ וַיִּרְבּוּ
וַיַּעַצְמוּ בִּמְאֹד מְאֹד וַתִּמָּלֵא הָאָרֶץ אֹתָם.

וָרָב, כְּמָה שֶׁנֶּאֱמַר: וָאֶעֱבֹר עָלַיִךְ וָאֶרְאֵךְ מִתְבּוֹסֶסֶת
בְּדָמָיִךְ, וָאֹמַר לָךְ בְּדָמַיִךְ חֲיִי, וָאֹמַר לָךְ בְּדָמַיִךְ חֲיִי.
רְבָבָה כְּצֶמַח הַשָּׂדֶה נְתַתִּיךְ, וַתִּרְבִּי וַתִּגְדְּלִי וַתָּבֹאִי בַּעֲדִי
עֲדָיִים, שָׁדַיִם נָכֹנוּ וּשְׂעָרֵךְ צִמֵּחַ, וְאַתְּ עֵרֹם וְעֶרְיָה.

"turn from evil." Circumcision is a fundamental "do good" mitzvah, through which we establish a covenant with God. Taking the Paschal lamb was a fundamental act of "turn from evil," since by slaughtering the lamb, Israel was rejecting the god of Egypt and the idolatry in which they had become so immersed. Had they failed to sever themselves from the idolatry of Egypt, they may have left Egypt during the Exodus but "Egypt" would not have left them.[199]

Having performed these two *mitzvot*, Israel could now experience not just a physical liberation, but an internal transformation and redemption.

Clothing the Naked Today

The above speaks to us in our current exile, which we have endured for nearly two thousand years, and which leads us to wonder: How much longer can the Jewish people endure the travails of Exile?!

But just as God sought "clothing" for us prior to the first redemption, He wishes for each and every one of us to have the "clothing" to experience the future redemption. Thus, when we see a fellow Jew who lacks the "clothing" of *mitzvot*, let us clothe him—to give him at least one mitzvah (which will multiply into many others) with which to merit redemption (*The Rebbe*).[200]

❧ THE TANTALIZING AROMA ❧

On the night of the Exodus, God caused the aroma of Moses' Paschal offering to reach those Israelites who did not want to undergo circumcision. They were drawn irresistibly to Moses and begged to partake of his offering. Moses told them they would have to circumcise themselves, which they agreed to do immediately (*Shemot Rabbah* 19:5).[201] Although Torah law stipulates that circumcision must be done by day,[202] the law that circumcision performed after the eighth day must be done by day was not yet in effect (see *Tosfot, s.v. Mar, Yevamot* 72b).

Furthermore, it was preferable that the circumcision occur on that night, when the revelation of Godliness dissolved the distinctions between day and night—*the night was bright like day*.[203] God's shattering the conditions of the natural order was mirrored by the Israelites—in their unconditional and supra-rational commitment expressed by the covenant of circumcision.

Those who relive the Exodus properly likewise overcome the distinctions between "night" and "day." Even in a state of spiritual "night"—despite crippling inertia or unholy obsessions and cravings—they find the strength to overcome all inner impediments and cleave to God with an eternal covenant (*The Rebbe*).[204]

∽ Miraculous Growth in Egypt ∾

Few in number—as it is written: *Your ancestors went down to Egypt with seventy people, and now, God, your God, has made you as numerous as the stars of heaven* (Deut. 10:22).

And he became there a nation—this teaches that the Israelites were distinctive there retaining their Hebrew names, language, religion, and garb. *Great, mighty*—as it is written: *And the children of Israel were fertile* (miscarriages and infant mortality were nonexistent[190]) and prolific (bearing sextuplets[191]); *they multiplied and became exceedingly mighty, and the land became filled with them* (Ex. 1:7).

And numerous—as it is written, in a passage comparing Israel in Egypt to a newborn: *I passed over you and saw you wallowing in your bloods* in the Egyptian persecution, *and I said to you, "By your blood you shall live," and I said to you, "By your blood you shall live*—the more Egypt persecutes you the more you will become numerous!" *As numerous as the plants of the field did I make you, and you thrived, and matured, and reached the age of adornment* of becoming a bride,[192] *your bosom fashioned* alluding to Moses and Aaron, who were ready to redeem you[193] *and your hair grown*—the ending of your exile had arrived,[194] *but you were* as if *naked and bare* in the tattered clothing of captives and metaphorically "naked" of mitzvot to merit redemption[195] (Ezekiel 16:6-7).

בְּשִׁבְעִים נֶפֶשׁ **With seventy people**— corresponding to the seventy primary nations of the world (*Zohar*).[196] For our descent to Egypt, as seventy souls, began the process through which we would receive the Torah and bring its light and teachings to the seventy nations of the world (*The Rebbe*).[197]

כְּצֶמַח הַשָּׂדֶה **As the plants of the field.** Before a seed can germinate and grow into a plant it must first dissolve. Similarly, through their suffering in Egypt Israel was "dissolved" and thus enabled to blossom. Hence: *As numerous as the plants of the field did I make you*—whose seeds germinate only after decomposing—which prepared you to *thrive, mature, and reach the age of adornment*, i.e., to receive two crowns at the Giving of the Torah (*Rabbi Shalom DovBer of Lubavitch*).[198]

מִתְבּוֹסֶסֶת בְּדָמָיִךְ **Wallowing in your bloods.** *Rabbi Matya ben Charash would teach: "I passed over you and saw you and behold your time for love had come* (Ezekiel 16:8)—*the time had come to fulfill the promise to Abraham that I redeem his children, but they lacked* mitzvot *to engage in with which to be redeemed." As it is written: "You were naked and bare."*

God then gave them two mitzvot, *the blood of the Paschal lamb and that of circumcision—they circumcised on that night—as it is written, "wallowing in your bloods (pl.)," in the two bloods [of the Paschal lamb and circumcision]* (*Rashi* on Exodus 12:6 from *Mechilta*).

The question arises: Would not one mitzvah have sufficed to remove them from a state of "nakedness"?

These two *mitzvot* are fundamental: one in the realm of "do good," the other in the realm of

וַיָּרֵעוּ אֹתָנוּ הַמִּצְרִים וַיְעַנּוּנוּ, וַיִּתְּנוּ עָלֵינוּ עֲבֹדָה קָשָׁה.

וַיָּרֵעוּ אֹתָנוּ הַמִּצְרִים, כְּמָה שֶׁנֶּאֱמַר: הָבָה נִתְחַכְּמָה לוֹ, פֶּן יִרְבֶּה, וְהָיָה כִּי תִקְרֶאנָה מִלְחָמָה, וְנוֹסַף גַּם הוּא עַל שֹׂנְאֵינוּ, וְנִלְחַם בָּנוּ וְעָלָה מִן הָאָרֶץ.

וַיְעַנּוּנוּ, כְּמָה שֶׁנֶּאֱמַר: וַיָּשִׂימוּ עָלָיו שָׂרֵי מִסִּים לְמַעַן עַנֹּתוֹ בְּסִבְלֹתָם, וַיִּבֶן עָרֵי מִסְכְּנוֹת לְפַרְעֹה, אֶת פִּתֹם וְאֶת רַעַמְסֵס.

וַיִּתְּנוּ עָלֵינוּ עֲבֹדָה קָשָׁה, כְּמָה שֶׁנֶּאֱמַר: וַיַּעֲבִדוּ מִצְרַיִם אֶת בְּנֵי יִשְׂרָאֵל בְּפָרֶךְ. וַיְמָרְרוּ אֶת חַיֵּיהֶם בַּעֲבֹדָה קָשָׁה בְּחֹמֶר וּבִלְבֵנִים וּבְכָל עֲבֹדָה בַּשָּׂדֶה, אֵת כָּל עֲבֹדָתָם אֲשֶׁר עָבְדוּ בָהֶם בְּפָרֶךְ.

✣ FINANCIAL FIXATIONS ✣

The shop is closed; customers and employees have gone home for the night. But the owner remains. His mind continues to trawl for yet another way to increase profits.

Even as he finally makes his way home, he never really leaves the business. Instead of setting aside time for prayer or study, he continues to strategize. And even as he lies down to sleep, his thoughts turn again to his business, which become the subject of his dreams.[209]

The Torah prohibits us from subjecting a servant to "crushing labor" (*avodat perech*). Maimonides defines this as "endless and purposeless labor"—the sort of grinding drudgery the Egyptians imposed upon us to embitter our lives.[210] Yet, in today's exile, we can become our own taskmasters, enslaving ourselves to our work like the apocryphal business owner above.

And financial ambitions are not our only fixations. At times we obsess over perceived offenses to our honor, or spend many hours nursing old wounds or jealousies.

We all have fears, insecurities, and inclinations that can saturate our lives *endlessly* and *purposelessly*.

How are we—*finite* creatures in a *finite* world—able to obsess *infinitely* and *unconditionally*? Ironically, we do so by usurping the infinite energy of the Divine soul that we each possess. Being one with the infinite God, the soul has the capacity for endless and unconditional goodness and holiness. Its altruistic drive is without limit and without concern for personal gain.

Yet the soul can only watch in pain as we exploit its unique capacity and direct it toward empty or transient concerns.

To break out of this cycle, we need to exercise the soul's limitless energy in an appropriate way. In Egypt, the Israelites did so by offering a lamb, the idol of the Egyptians. To defy Egypt so boldly in following the command of their true Master, the Israelites had to access that infinite and unconditional energy of the soul. Likewise today, the path to personal freedom lies in restoring the soul's energy to its proper place—accessing it to fulfill our mission in this world (*The Rebbe*).[211]

∽ THE EGYPTIAN PERSECUTION ৲

The Egyptians harmed us and afflicted us, and they imposed hard labor upon us.

The Egyptians harmed us—as it is written: *Come, let us deal wisely with them, lest they multiply and, if a war breaks out, they will join our enemies, fight against us and leave the land* (Exodus 1:10).

They afflicted us—as it is written: *They appointed taskmasters over [the Israelites] to afflict them with their burdens, and they built storage cities for Pharaoh: Pitom and Ramses* (Exodus 1:11).

And they imposed hard labor upon us—as it is written: *The Egyptians enslaved the children of Israel with crushing harshness. They embittered their lives with hard labor, involving mortar and bricks, as well as all kinds of labor in the field—with all their enslavements, which they imposed upon them with crushing harshness* (Exodus 1:13-14).

Notes & Insights

וַיְמָרֲרוּ אֶת חַיֵּיהֶם **They embittered their lives.** The style of the Haggadah is to elaborate upon the verses from Deuteronomy by drawing upon more descriptive verses elsewhere in the Torah. Accordingly, we can understand why Rabbi Schneur Zalman's version of the Haggadah includes the verse *They embittered, etc.* at the conclusion of this passage, even though it does not appear in any other version of the Haggadah (with the apparent exception of Rabbi Moshe Cordovero's *Siddur Tefillah L'Moshe*).[205]

For without this second verse, the Haggadah does not elaborate on *hard labor*. The first verse—*the Egyptians enslaved the children of Israel with crushing harshness*—is clearly not a sufficient elaboration, since it provides only a general description, namely, that the labor was crushing. It is certainly insufficient according to Rabbi Elazar, who maintains that the first occurrence of "crushing harshness"—*b'farech*—means "with soft-spoken words"—*b'feh rach*, i.e., the Egyptians used soft-spoken words to lure us into volunteer labor and then made it mandatory (*Sotah* 11b). Rabbi Schneur Zalman therefore includes the second verse, which details the nature of the "hard labor" (*The Rebbe's Haggadah*).[206]

וַיָּרֵעוּ אֹתָנוּ הַמִּצְרִים **The Egyptians harmed us.** Or, "they corrupted us" (*Shaloh*).[207]

This interpretation helps us understand a puzzling feature of the narrative: How is it that the Israelites were capable of falling to the nadir of impurity, such that God had to remove them prematurely before they were forever lost?

The answer is that "the Egyptians corrupted us." Our own weaknesses and proclivities would not have led us to such depravity. But the Egyptians dragged us to new levels of impurity that were alien and unnatural to us.

On Yom Kippur we express a similar idea, when we ask God to forgive us for "sins committed with the evil inclination." But are not all sins committed because of our evil inclination? The answer is that at times we become so immersed in selfish pursuits that we intensify our "evil inclination," causing it to lead us to misdeeds that are completely alien and foreign to our true selves (*The Rebbe*).[208]

וַנִּצְעַק אֶל יְיָ אֱלֹהֵי אֲבֹתֵינוּ, וַיִּשְׁמַע יְיָ אֶת קֹלֵנוּ, וַיַּרְא אֶת עָנְיֵנוּ וְאֶת עֲמָלֵנוּ וְאֶת לַחֲצֵנוּ.

וַנִּצְעַק אֶל יְיָ אֱלֹהֵי אֲבֹתֵינוּ, כְּמָה שֶּׁנֶּאֱמַר: וַיְהִי בַיָּמִים הָרַבִּים הָהֵם וַיָּמָת מֶלֶךְ מִצְרַיִם, וַיֵּאָנְחוּ בְנֵי יִשְׂרָאֵל מִן הָעֲבֹדָה וַיִּזְעָקוּ, וַתַּעַל שַׁוְעָתָם אֶל הָאֱלֹהִים מִן הָעֲבֹדָה.

God in prayer, to emerge from the darkness of our enslavement (*Rabbi Schneur Zalman of Liadi*).[215]

וַתַּעַל שַׁוְעָתָם אֶל הָאֱלֹהִים מִן הָעֲבֹדָה **And their prayerful cry…ascended to God**. According to the Midrash, this alludes to the cry of the small children who were taken by the Egyptians and who endured great suffering (*Yalkut Shimoni, Shemot* §169).

In addition to its plain meaning, the Midrash also alludes to the children of today who are taken by "Egypt," i.e., deprived of a Jewish upbringing.

If the subjugation of the body is bitter, how much more so the subjugation of the soul. It is therefore incumbent upon each of us, when we come to celebrate the Season of our Liberation, to first of all liberate ourselves from our entrapment in "Egypt"; but we must especially do all we can, each in his or her way, to liberate the sons and daughters of Israel from spiritual subjugation by providing them with a proper Jewish education (From a letter of the Rebbe, 11 Nissan 5711 [1951]).[216]

Kabbalah וַתַּעַל שַׁוְעָתָם אֶל הָאֱלֹהִים מִן הָעֲבֹדָה **And their prayerful cry, evoked by their labor, ascended to God.** The Arizal taught that the people who were enslaved in Egypt possessed the souls of the Generation of the Dispersion, those who constructed the tower of Babel. Their experience in Egypt was meant to rectify their earlier behavior. They therefore were made to work with mortar and bricks, just as they had done to build their tower, as the

Torah relates (Gen. 11:3), *…they said to one another, "Come, let us mold bricks and fire them." The bricks were as [hard as] stone, and the clay served them for mortar.*

Furthermore, their essential sin was arrogance. They wished to receive sustenance from God without curbing their egos and desires. Their rectification was therefore to be broken by the hardships of Egypt. Once the hardships had humbled them and broken their egos, they called out to God and were redeemed (*Rabbi Shmuel of Lubavitch*).[217]

❧ WE CRIED OUT TO GOD ☙

"My Beloved is to me, and I to Him…"

He is to me a God, and I am to Him a nation.… He is to me a Father, and I am to Him a child.… He is to me a Shepherd, and I am to Him a flock.…

Whenever I was in need, I called only upon Him, as it is written: It was during those many years that the king of Egypt died.… And God heard their anguished cry.… And God saw the children of Israel.…

Whenever He was "in need," He called only upon me, as it is written: "Speak to the entire community of Israel, saying: 'On the tenth of this month, each man among them shall take for himself a lamb or a kid….'" [218]

—SHIR HASHIRIM RABBAH 2:16:1

~ ISRAEL CRIES OUT TO GOD ~

And we cried out to God, the God of our fathers, and God heard our voice and saw our suffering, our labor and our oppression.

And we cried out to God, the God of our fathers—as it is written: *It was during those many years that the king of Egypt died; and the children of Israel groaned because of their labor, and they cried out; and their prayerful cry, evoked by their labor, ascended to God* (Exodus 2:23).

 Notes & Insights

בַּיָּמִים הָרַבִּים הָהֵם **Those many years.** This refers to the sixty or so years during which Moses was a fugitive from Egypt (see *Rashi, et al.*). He escaped from Egypt (after killing an Egyptian taskmaster) while still a teen, and returned to Egypt when he was close to eighty years old (see *Ramban* on Exodus, ibid.).

They are called "*many* years" because they were years of pain (*Shemot Rabbah* 1:35).

וַיָּמָת מֶלֶךְ מִצְרַיִם **The king of Egypt died.** What is the connection between the king's death and the subsequent events?

Several explanations are given:
• As long as the king was alive, the Israelites hoped that upon his death his decree of enslavement would be softened. After his death, they saw that the new king not only did not alleviate their suffering, he increased it.

They therefore began groaning intensely and realized that their only hope was to pray to the God of their ancestors to save them (*Rashbatz*).[212]
• The Israelites were generally forbidden from bemoaning their fate. But when the king died,

all of Egypt, including the Israelites, went out into the streets to cry out and mourn as is the custom in monarchies. The Israelites too cried out in mourning, but in their hearts they were crying out to God to save them (*Me'am Loez* from *Abarbanel*).
• The king did not die but rather became ill. This led to a new decree, which caused the Israelites to cry out (see *Rashi* from the *Midrash*).
• The earlier king, because of his affection for Joseph, engaged in only a relatively mild religious persecution of the Israelites.

After his death, a new king arose who intensified the religious coercion and forced them to worship idols. They therefore "groaned because of their labor"—"labor" in the sense of worship, i.e., their forced *worship* of idols (*Pirush Kadmon*).[213]

וַתַּעַל שַׁוְעָתָם **Their prayerful cry...ascended.** The translation of *shavatam* as "prayerful cry" follows *Or Hachaim* in his second interpretation, according to which their cry was not simply a cry of pain but a prayer to God. (See, however, his first interpretation and *Kli Yakar*.)[214]

৪ THE FALL OF REASON ৪

Chasidus Enslavement to "Egypt"—to the transient and ultimately empty concerns of this world—begins with a quasi-rational foundation. But it can degenerate into an irrational obsession that defies even the logic of "Egypt."

Metaphorically, "the king of Egypt" is the wisdom or logic of "Egypt." In our own lives, we can become so attached to "Egypt" that the "king of Egypt"—the logic of Egypt—"dies": we descend into an *irrational* attachment to "Egypt." At that point we must cry out to

וַיִּשְׁמַע יְיָ אֶת קֹלֵנוּ, כְּמָה שֶׁנֶּאֱמַר: וַיִּשְׁמַע אֱלֹהִים אֶת נַאֲקָתָם, וַיִּזְכֹּר אֱלֹהִים אֶת בְּרִיתוֹ אֶת אַבְרָהָם אֶת יִצְחָק וְאֶת יַעֲקֹב.

וַיַּרְא אֶת עָנְיֵנוּ, זוֹ פְּרִישׁוּת דֶּרֶךְ אֶרֶץ, כְּמָה שֶׁנֶּאֱמַר: וַיַּרְא אֱלֹהִים אֶת בְּנֵי יִשְׂרָאֵל, וַיֵּדַע אֱלֹהִים.

✣ PRAISES OF ISRAEL ✣

Another Midrash enumerates four virtues for which Israel was redeemed:

1) they maintained their Hebrew names, 2) continued to use their Hebrew language, 3) did not gossip, and 4) were (with only one exception) completely free of adultery (*Vayikra Rabbah* 32:5).

"Although they were lowly in *mitzvot* like a hyssop, nevertheless, they were united in a bond of friendship—and therefore they were saved. They also possessed the 'scent' of Torah and were humble..." (*Ritva*).[224]

✣ PHARAOH'S FAILED PLOT ✣

Pharaoh commanded the taskmasters to pressure the Israelites to complete their daily quota and to ensure that they did not go home to sleep at night. He intended to thereby minimize their procreation, assuming they would not procreate if they did not sleep at home.

So the taskmasters said to the Israelites:

"If you go home to sleep—by the time we call for you in the morning you will have lost one or two hours of the day and will not be able to finish your quota." Subsequently, the Israelites began sleeping on the floor near their worksites.

Said God to the Egyptian taskmasters: "I told Abraham their father that I would cause his offspring to proliferate like the stars...and you are plotting to prevent their proliferation?! Let us see whose word will endure—Mine or yours." Immediately—*the more they afflicted them the more they proliferated*... (*Shemot Rabbah* 1:12).

✣ FISH AND WINE ✣

Pharaoh did not take into account the dedication of the Israelite women. What did the daughters of Israel do? They would go down to the river to draw water. God would ensure that small fish [which aid in procreation—*Etz Yosef*] would providentially enter their pitchers. They would cook some of the fish, sell a portion of it for wine, then go out to the work fields to feed their husbands.

After their husbands had partaken of the food and drink, the women would take out their copper mirrors and have their husbands look at their reflections together with them. The wives thus brought their husbands to admire their beauty and aroused their marital passion, from which, with God's blessing, they would conceive. In this way, the people continued to miraculously proliferate.

When the time came to build the Tabernacle, the women donated these mirrors and brought them to Moses who initially rejected them. God told Moses: "Are you mocking these mirrors? These mirrors produced all these multitudes of Israel in Egypt! Use them to make the copper lever from which the priests will consecrate themselves..." (*Tanchuma, Pekudei* 9).

> *Rabbi Akiva taught: It was in the merit of the righteous women of that generation that Israel was redeemed from Egypt.*
> —SHEMOT RABBAH 1:12

⊷ God Hears...and Sees ↄ

And God heard our voice—as it is written: *And God heard their anguished cry, and God remembered His covenant with Abraham, Isaac and Jacob* (Exodus 2:24).

And He saw our suffering—this refers to abstinence from "the way of the land"—as it is written: *God saw the children of Israel, and God knew* (Exodus 2:25).

 Notes & Insights ↄ

וַיִּזְכֹּר אֱלֹהִים אֶת בְּרִיתוֹ **God remembered His covenant.** God's hearing our voice was not the sole reason for our redemption, and on its own would have been insufficient. Rather, the redemption came because of 1) our crying out and returning to God, and 2) God's covenant with the Patriarchs (*Abarbanel*; see *Midrash* below).

וַיַּרְא אֶת־עָנְיֵנוּ: זוֹ פְּרִישׁוּת דֶּרֶךְ אֶרֶץ **He saw our suffering—this refers to abstinence from the way of the land**—i.e., abstinence from marital intimacy, as in Genesis 13:31 (*Pirush Kadmon*). This too was part of Pharaoh's plan to suppress Jewish growth, as our Sages relate in the Midrash (*Shemot Rabbah* 1:12, see below; see also *Sefer Halikkutim* (Arizal) on Exodus 1:12).

The Haggadah interprets *anyeinu*—translated as "our suffering"—as deriving from *eenoi*, which is a biblical term that refers to abstinence (see Genesis 31:50[219] and *Yoma* 74b in connection with the Torah's command regarding Yom Kippur, "*v'initem et nafshotechem*"—"and you

shall afflict yourselves."). The commentators attempt to show how the proof text cited by the Haggadah—*God saw...and God knew*—alludes to abstinence [see below]. However, one can argue that the proof text is meant to show that God saw and paid attention to our suffering, *not* to prove that *anyeinu* means abstinence, which comes as a parenthetical insertion (*The Rebbe's Haggadah*).

וַיֵּדַע אֱלֹהִים **And God knew.** He paid attention to them and did not conceal His eyes from them (*Rashi* on Exodus 2:25).

"And He knew" alludes to marital intimacy, since it is concealed from others and is known only to God (*R. Yehudah ben Yakar*). Marital intimacy is also referred to biblically as "knowing" (as in Genesis 4:25, I Samuel 1:19—*Ritva, et al.*).[220]

Some commentators suggest that the Israelites deliberately refrained from procreating because of Pharaoh's decree to kill all the newborns (see *Rashi* on Exodus 2:1—*Shibolei Haleket; Abarbanel, et al.*).

וַיִּשְׁמַע אֱלֹהִים אֶת־נַאֲקָתָם, וַיִּזְכֹּר אֱלֹהִים אֶת־בְּרִיתוֹ **God heard their anguished cry...and God remembered His covenant.** "They were not fit to be redeemed since they were wicked, but they were redeemed in the merit of the Patriarchs, as in the verse, *God remembered His covenant...*" (*Shemot Rabbah* 2:34).

According to *Devarim Rabbah* (2:23), five conditions facilitated the Exodus:

1. **Oppression of the Israelites** (*the children of Israel groaned*)
2. **Their repentance** (*their prayerful cry ascended to God*)[221]
3. **Merit of the Patriarchs** (*God remembered His covenant*)[222]
4. **Divine mercy** (*God saw the children of Israel*)
5. **Arrival of the time of the redemption** (*God knew*).[223]

וְאֶת עֲמָלֵנוּ, אֵלּוּ הַבָּנִים, כְּמָה שֶׁנֶּאֱמַר: כָּל הַבֵּן הַיִּלּוֹד הַיְאֹרָה תַּשְׁלִיכֻהוּ, וְכָל הַבַּת תְּחַיּוּן.

וְאֶת לַחֲצֵנוּ, זֶה הַדְּחַק, כְּמָה שֶׁנֶּאֱמַר: וְגַם רָאִיתִי אֶת הַלַּחַץ אֲשֶׁר מִצְרַיִם לֹחֲצִים אֹתָם.

❧ MIRIAM SPEAKS UP ☙

After Pharaoh's decree against the new-born males, the Jewish leader of the time, Amram, father of Moses, decided to cease procreating, saying, "We toil in vain!" The other Israelites followed his example.

But his young daughter, Miriam, said to him: "You are worse than Pharaoh! For he only decreed against the males, but you have decreed against males and [the potential birth of] females. Pharaoh deprives them of this world, but you deprive them of both this world and the next [since those who are never born cannot enter the World to Come]. Pharaoh is wicked and his decree may or may not endure, but you are righteous and your decree will endure."

Amram listened to his daughter and reunited with his wife, leading the rest of Israel to follow suit (*Sotah* 12a).

❧ TAKING THE BEATING ☙

Despite the pressure from their taskmasters, the Israelite foremen had pity on the people and did not pressure them to meet their daily quota of bricks. The Egyptians then beat the Israelite foremen for failing to pressure their brethren. As a reward for their self-sacrifice, God later told Moses in the desert to choose these foremen to receive prophetic vision (Exodus 5:14; *Shemot Rabbah* 5:20).

❧ TODAY'S NILE ☙

The Egyptians worshiped the Nile as a god. They saw it as the source of Egypt's sustenance, since it was the waters of the Nile that irrigated Egypt's soil.

In addition to literally drowning the Jewish children in the Nile, Egypt also sought to tear the Jewish people away from the true God, the Creator of heaven and earth, and "drown" them in the worship of the Nile.

Pharaoh therefore added a seemingly super-fluous instruction: "And every girl you shall keep alive." To be kept alive in Pharaoh's view was to be immersed in the lifestyle of Egyptian culture. If the males were to be physically destroyed, the girls were to be spiritually destroyed.

In this sense, Pharaoh's decree is sadly alive and well to this day. It is the impulse to immerse our children in the "Nile" of material pursuit and the worship of the idols and obsessions of our day. It is the sense that without a certain type of education a child cannot succeed in life and that giving a child a Jewish education may impede his future success.

Responding to Pharaoh

The Jewish women—the midwives whom Pharaoh initially charged with the task of killing the Jewish newborns—defied Pharaoh's decree, putting their faith in God. Likewise, Miriam told her father not to be influenced by Pharaoh's decree but to trust in God. The Jewish "midwives" succeeded in raising a generation of Jewish children under the most adverse conditions. It was in their merit that we were redeemed from Egypt.

The faith of the women should inspire us today:

Let us resolve to educate our children in the traditional Jewish way and God will take care of them and their parents. Let us remember that our sustenance comes not from the Nile but from God (*The Rebbe*).[229]

54b

⁓ GOD SEES OUR TOIL ⁓
AND OPPRESSION

Our toil—this refers to the children, as it is written: *Every boy that is born you shall throw into the river, and every girl you shall keep alive* (Exodus 1:22).

And our oppression—this refers to the pressure—as it is written: *I have seen the oppression with which the Egyptians oppress them* (Exodus 3:9).

 Notes & Insights

וְאֶת־עֲמָלֵנוּ, אֵלוּ הַבָּנִים **Our toil—this refers to the children.** Children are called "our toil" because they are produced from our strength and virility. As Jacob said of his firstborn Reuben (Genesis 49:3), *Reuben, you are...my strength, the first of my virility* (*Machzor Vitri*). Our Sages teach (*Shabbat* 32b): What is the "handiwork" of people? Their children (*Shibolei Haleket—The Rebbe's Haggadah*).

Parents toil to raise their children, educate them, and teach them Torah. They also toil to earn money to bequeath after their passing (*Ritva*).

God saw our "toil"—our children—and how they had been thrown into the Nile (*Raavan*).[225]

Some commentators explain this passage of the Haggadah to mean that God saw our children being drowned and intervened to save them. As the Midrash relates:

The Nile would not swallow the children—it would spit them out into the desert, where God would sustain them with milk and honey. When these children grew up and later were present during the splitting of the Sea—a time when God's presence was revealed—it was they who recognized God's presence first and said: "This is my God!" (*Rabbi Yehudah ben Yakar; Ritva*).[226]

כְּמָה שֶׁנֶּאֱמַר **As it is written.** The cited verse is not meant to prove that children are called "toil," but to show that there was a decree against the children (*The Rebbe's Haggadah*).[227]

וְאֶת לַחֲצֵנוּ **Our oppression.** The term *lachatz*, "oppression," can mean 1) a physical pressing, or 2) a non-physical coercion and pressure, which our Sages call *dochak*.

The Haggadah is telling us that in our context it has the second meaning: not only did the Egyptians enslave the Israelites, they allowed them no respite from their work, as the Torah relates (Exodus 5:13):

And the taskmasters pressured them [and said, "You must complete your daily quota of work, just as before, when straw was provided"] (*Abarbanel—The Rebbe's Haggadah*).[228]

The Egyptian taskmasters held the Israelite "policemen"—the foremen appointed by the Egyptians to oversee the Israelites—accountable for this quota and would beat them if it were not completed (Exodus 5:14; *Pirush Kadmon*).

☙ OPPRESSION OF IDOLATRY ❧

The Egyptians pressured the Israelites in other ways as well. When they saw that the Israelites continued to proliferate, they began pressuring them to worship the Egyptian gods and assimilate.

Hence: God saw the *lachatz*, that Egypt was pushing them to become idolaters, which was another reason to expedite their redemption for fear that they would not withstand the pressure. In fact they had already begun to adopt Egyptian customs, ceased circumcising themselves, and were dabbling in witchcraft (*Ritva*).

וַיּוֹצִאֵנוּ יְיָ מִמִּצְרַיִם בְּיָד חֲזָקָה וּבִזְרֹעַ נְטוּיָה וּבְמֹרָא גָּדֹל וּבְאֹתוֹת וּבְמֹפְתִים.

וַיּוֹצִאֵנוּ יְיָ מִמִּצְרַיִם, לֹא עַל יְדֵי מַלְאָךְ וְלֹא עַל יְדֵי שָׂרָף וְלֹא עַל יְדֵי שָׁלִיחַ, אֶלָּא הַקָּדוֹשׁ בָּרוּךְ הוּא בִּכְבוֹדוֹ וּבְעַצְמוֹ, שֶׁנֶּאֱמַר: וְעָבַרְתִּי בְאֶרֶץ מִצְרַיִם בַּלַּיְלָה הַזֶּה, וְהִכֵּיתִי כָל בְּכוֹר בְּאֶרֶץ מִצְרַיִם מֵאָדָם וְעַד בְּהֵמָה, וּבְכָל אֱלֹהֵי מִצְרַיִם אֶעֱשֶׂה שְׁפָטִים, אֲנִי יְיָ. וְעָבַרְתִּי בְאֶרֶץ מִצְרַיִם, אֲנִי וְלֹא מַלְאָךְ. וְהִכֵּיתִי כָל בְּכוֹר בְּאֶרֶץ מִצְרַיִם, אֲנִי וְלֹא שָׂרָף. וּבְכָל אֱלֹהֵי מִצְרַיִם אֶעֱשֶׂה שְׁפָטִים, אֲנִי וְלֹא הַשָּׁלִיחַ. אֲנִי יְיָ, אֲנִי הוּא וְלֹא אַחֵר.

৪ঀ THE KING & THE PAUPER ৪ঀ

Chasidus Human nature is to reciprocate, to react lovingly when a friend acts lovingly towards us. How much more so if a great and mighty king would show great love for a despised and lowly commoner cast upon a garbage heap. Imagine that the king descends from his glorious palace, followed by his entire retinue, and descends to this commoner, lifts him from his garbage heap and brings him into the royal palace, into the innermost chamber, a place where no servant or lord ever enters, and there shares with him the closest companionship with embraces and kisses and profound spiritual attachment.

The heart of this humble individual would of course be stirred with a deep love for the king. Even if his heart were like stone and not given to tender feelings of love, it would surely melt—his soul would pour itself out with longing for the love of the king.

Raised From The Heap

The above describes what God did for us, though to an infinitely greater degree: Israel was brought out of Egypt by the King Himself—*"Not through an angel…nor through a messenger…but the Holy One, blessed be He, Himself in His glory and essence"* descended there.

And just as the king in the parable, after raising the individual from the garbage heap, takes him into his palace and shares with him the closest companionship, so did God draw the Children of Israel to Him in true closeness and unity, by giving them His Torah and *mitzvot* (*Tanya*, ch. 46).

৪ঀ IMITATIO DEI ৪ঀ

God's behavior serves as a model and inspiration for how we are to engage in saving our fellow from a spiritual Egypt. Without God's example, a Jewish educator, for instance, may say that he is willing to teach Torah to others, but only to those who will come to the synagogue to study. He refuses to leave his place of holiness to seek out those would-be students who are not inclined to enter the synagogue. Likewise, we may be tempted to discharge our obligation to help others with a perfunctory involvement—engaging only our external selves, our "angels" and "messengers," and reserving our essence for other activities.

God's behavior teaches us that we can and should personally descend to the depths of "Egypt" to help our fellow, and to do so with the very essence of our beings (*The Rebbe*).[237]

∽ GOD HIMSELF TAKES US OUT ∾

God took us out of Egypt with a strong hand and an outstretched arm, and with a great revelation, and with signs and wonders.

God took us out of Egypt—not through an angel, not through a seraph [a fiery angel of judgment], and not through a messenger—rather it was the Holy One, blessed be He, in His glory and essence! As it is written: *I will pass through the land of Egypt on that night, and I will smite every firstborn in the land of Egypt, from man to beast* [since the Egyptians deified the animals[230]]*, and I will carry out judgments against all the gods of Egypt* [the wooden idols would rot, the metal ones would melt[231]]*—I, God* (Exodus 12:12).

I will pass through the land of Egypt—I and not an angel. *And I will smite every firstborn in the land of Egypt*—I and not a seraph. *And I will carry out judgments against all the gods of Egypt*—I and not a messenger. *I, God*—it is I, and none other.

∽ Notes & Insights ∾

לֹא עַל־יְדֵי מַלְאָךְ Not through an angel... God wanted to show his great love for Israel by redeeming them Himself (*Alshich*). Angels were unfit for the job since angels of judgment would have punished unworthy Israel along with Egypt. Only God, who transcends both judgment and mercy, could employ both at the same time (*Rabbenu Bachaye*).

וְהִכֵּיתִי כָל־בְּכוֹר בְּאֶרֶץ־מִצְרַיִם. אֲנִי וְלֹא שָׂרָף I will smite every firstborn...I and not a seraph. Who, then, was the *mashchit* ("destroyer") that God promised to protect Israel from on that night?[232] Among the answers: The *mashchit* is the plague itself (*Shibolei Haleket*); it refers to the Egyptians, who would seek to kill the Israelites in retaliation for the death of the Egyptian firstborn (*Abarbanel*).

לֹא עַל־יְדֵי מַלְאָךְ, וְלֹא עַל־יְדֵי שָׂרָף, וְלֹא עַל־יְדֵי שָׁלִיחַ Not through an angel...messenger. The role of Moses (and Aaron) was to speak to Pharaoh and administer the first nine plagues. But the redemption itself, and the last plague, which directly led to the redemption, could only be done by God Himself (*Shibolei Haleket*).[233] Below are some of the opinions regarding the three terms *angel, seraph*, and *messenger*:

	ANGEL	SERAPH	MESSENGER
Abarbanel citing Kabbalists	The angel Michael	The angel Gavriel	The angel Matatron
Maharal Redemption could have occurred in three ways:	Supernatural redemption carried out by an angel	Redemption through destruction—the "burning up (*seraph*)" of Egypt	Redemption through the "agency" (*shelichut*) of natural events
Alshich: Three aspects to the redemption, which could have been done by angels:[234]	An angel to keep Israel distinct and unharmed during the destruction	An angel of judgment to smite the Egyptians	An angel of impurity to smite the Egyptian gods
Rabbi Schneur Zalman of Liadi [235]	Of the World of Asiyah[236]	Of the World of Yetzirah	Of the World of Beriah

See also *Ramban* and *Rabbeinu Bachaye* (on Exodus 12:12); *Siddur Kol Yaakov*; *Yaavetz*; and the *Vilna Gaon* (*The Rebbe's Haggadah*).

בְּיָד חֲזָקָה, זֶה הַדֶּבֶר, כְּמָה שֶׁנֶּאֱמַר: הִנֵּה יַד יְיָ הוֹיָה בְּמִקְנְךָ אֲשֶׁר בַּשָּׂדֶה, בַּסּוּסִים בַּחֲמֹרִים בַּגְּמַלִּים בַּבָּקָר וּבַצֹּאן, דֶּבֶר כָּבֵד מְאֹד.

וּבִזְרֹעַ נְטוּיָה, זוֹ הַחֶרֶב, כְּמָה שֶׁנֶּאֱמַר: וְחַרְבּוֹ שְׁלוּפָה בְּיָדוֹ נְטוּיָה עַל יְרוּשָׁלָיִם.

וּבְמֹרָא גָדֹל, זֶה גִּלּוּי שְׁכִינָה, כְּמָה שֶׁנֶּאֱמַר: אוֹ הֲנִסָּה אֱלֹהִים לָבוֹא לָקַחַת לוֹ גוֹי מִקֶּרֶב גּוֹי בְּמַסֹּת בְּאֹתֹת וּבְמוֹפְתִים וּבְמִלְחָמָה וּבְיָד חֲזָקָה וּבִזְרוֹעַ נְטוּיָה וּבְמוֹרָאִים גְּדֹלִים, כְּכֹל אֲשֶׁר עָשָׂה לָכֶם יְיָ אֱלֹהֵיכֶם בְּמִצְרַיִם לְעֵינֶיךָ.

וּבְאֹתוֹת, זֶה הַמַּטֶּה, כְּמָה שֶׁנֶּאֱמַר: וְאֶת הַמַּטֶּה הַזֶּה תִּקַּח בְּיָדֶךָ, אֲשֶׁר תַּעֲשֶׂה בּוֹ אֶת הָאֹתֹת.

and everything Moses has said about this nation has come to pass, let us go and remove these Hebrews from amongst us, otherwise, we will die! Don't you want us to live?"

The elders replied: "The Hebrews will not leave here, even it means that all of Egypt will die." So the firstborn went to Pharaoh, who himself was a firstborn, and cried out to him: "We beg of you, send out this nation, since it is because of them that calamity will fall upon us and upon you."

But Pharaoh remained stubborn and commanded his servants: "Go out and beat the shins of these people!" Hearing this, the firstborn unsheathed their swords and killed 600,000 of their elders.

This is the meaning of the verse (Psalms 136:10), *Who struck Egypt through their first-born, for His kindness is everlasting.* The verse does not say "Who struck Egypt's firstborn"—rather, it says God struck Egypt *through* their firstborn, as explained above (*Yalkut Shimoni* on Psalm 136; *Pesikta d'Rav Kahana* cited in *Shibolei Haleket*).

וּבְאֹתוֹת זֶה הַמַּטֶּה **Signs—this refers to the staff.** Moses used this staff as a *sign* before Pharaoh, by turning it into a snake, then returning it to a staff that swallowed the snakes/staffs of Pharaoh's wizards.

This staff was also used for other "signs," namely to administer many of the ten plagues.

The word for "signs" (*otot*) also means "letters." The Haggadah thus alludes to the Midrashic teaching that the staff was engraved with the letters *d'tzach adash b'achav,* the acronym of the ten plagues (*Shibolei Haleket;* see below on page 59).

The staff was also engraved with the names of the Patriarchs, the Matriarchs, the Twelve Tribes, and the Divine Name (*Targum Yeho-natan*). When God told Moses to take the staff to administer the plagues, He alluded to him that the plagues would be done in the merit of Israel's ancestors, whose names were engraved on the staff (*Chida*).

This staff was one of the ten things God created at twilight on the sixth day of creation (*Avot* 5:6; *Ritva*).

⟶ ELEMENTS OF THE EXODUS ⟵

With a strong hand—this refers to the pestilence, as it is written: *Behold, the **hand** of God will be upon your livestock in the field, upon the horses, the donkeys, the camels, the herds and the flocks, a very severe **pestilence*** (Exodus 9:3).

And with an outstretched arm—this refers to the sword with which God struck the firstborn, as it is written: *His **sword** was drawn in his hand, **outstretched** over Jerusalem* (I Chronicles 21:16).

And with a great revelation—this refers to the revelation of the Divine Presence during the destruction of the firstborn and the redemption—as it is written: *Has any god ever tried to take for himself a nation from the midst of another nation, with trials, signs and wonders, with war and with a strong hand and an outstretched arm, and with **great revelations**, like all that God, your God, did for you in Egypt before your eyes!* (Deuteronomy 4:34)

And with signs—this refers to the staff of Moses, as it is written: *Take into your hand this **staff**, with which you shall perform the **signs*** (Exodus 4:17).

(Note: This passage concludes on the following page.)

 Notes & Insights

דֶּבֶר Pestilence—the fifth of the ten plagues. This passage highlights three of the ten plagues: pestilence (5ᵗʰ plague), death of the firstborn (10ᵗʰ plague), and the Nile turning to blood (1ˢᵗ plague). The commentators wonder why these plagues are highlighted and why in this non-chronological order.

Perhaps the verse highlights the progressive sequence in the scope of God's deeds: He destroyed Egypt's assets (their cattle). Greater yet, He struck their firstborn. Still greater, He executed justice upon their gods by striking the Nile, which the Egyptians worshipped (*The Rebbe's Haggadah*).

וְחַרְבּוֹ שְׁלוּפָה בְּיָדוֹ, נְטוּיָה עַל־יְרוּשָׁלָיִם **His sword…outstretched over Jerusalem.** We thus find the expression "outstretched arm" used in the context of wielding a sword (*Shibolei Haleket; Abarbanel*).

(In its original context, the verse speaks of King David seeing an angel wielding a sword over Jerusalem. This came as a punishment for David's counting the Jewish people, which the Torah forbids. The angel tells David to build an altar on what is now the "Temple Mount." David purchases the land, builds the altar, offers sacrifices and prays to God, after which the angel returns his sword to its sheath.)

הַחֶרֶב **The sword.** *Shibolei Haleket* cites an opinion that this refers to the sword that the Egyptian firstborn raised against their elders. This occurred when Moses warned of the tenth plague, in which all the firstborn would die. Upon hearing this warning, the firstborn turned to their fathers and said: "Since Moses has warned that all the firstborn will die,

באמירת דם ואש ותמרות עשן ישפוך ג' שפיכות ואין ליטול באצבע לשפוך כ"א בכוס עצמו וישפוך לתוך כלי שבור
(ויכוין שהכום הוא סוד המלכות ושופך מהיין שבתוכו סוד האף והזעם שבה ע"י כח הבינה לתוך כלי שבור סוד הקליפה
שנקראת ארור):

• When saying the words "דָם וָאֵשׁ וְתִימְרוֹת עָשָׁן", spill three times from the wine in your cup—once during each phrase, preferably into a damaged dish. (It is not the Chabad custom to remove wine by dipping in a finger.)

• Have in mind that the cup symbolizes the attribute of *malchut* (kingship), which contains an element of "anger and indignation." Using our faculty of *binah* (understanding), we pour out that element of "anger and indignation" by spilling from the wine in the cup into a broken dish, which represents *kelipah*, i.e., that which is called "accursed." The remaining wine is called "wine that brings joy."

וּבְמוֹפְתִים, זֶה הַדָּם, כְּמָה שֶׁנֶּאֱמַר: וְנָתַתִּי מוֹפְתִים בַּשָּׁמַיִם
וּבָאָרֶץ —

Spill while saying:

דָם וָאֵשׁ וְתִימְרוֹת עָשָׁן:

Israelite would turn to blood. Even if they were drinking water from the same cup, the Egyptian would come up with blood and the Israelite with water (*Ritva*).

וְנָתַתִּי מוֹפְתִים... דָם וָאֵשׁ וְתִימְרוֹת עָשָׁן **I shall show wonders...blood...fire...smoke.** The prophet Joel tells of a great war that will occur prior to the Messianic age, the war of Gog and Magog. During this war: 1) much **blood** will be spilled, 2) God will rain **fire** upon the attackers of Israel, from which will rise 3) **pillars of smoke** (*Metzudot David*).

The Haggadah cites this verse to demonstrate that "wonders" includes an allusion to blood (*Rashbatz*).

According to *Ritva*, "blood, fire, and pillars of smoke" also alludes to the plague of blood in Egypt, since it was a fiery blood that filled Egypt with smoke.

❧ THE ROTTEN FISH ❦

A man once instructed his servant to bring him a fish from the market. The servant went out to the market and returned with a rotten fish. As a punishment, the servant was offered three choices: 1) eat the rotten fish, 2) take 100 lashes, or 3) pay a 100 maneh (10,000 zuz) fine.

The servant decided to eat the fish. He forced himself to take bite after bite, but in the end was so repulsed that he couldn't finish it. At that point, the lashes looked more appealing than finishing the fish, so he changed his mind and decided to take the lashes. After sixty lashes, the pain was so unbearable that he couldn't take it anymore and decided to pay the fine (Mechilta 14:5).[239]

The above is an analogy for the the folly of Egypt: They first "ate the fish"—they suffered the first three plagues. Then they were "whipped" with the next three plagues. In the last four plagues, they were forced to "pay"— their crops were destroyed by the hail and locust; their possessions were discovered (and later taken out of Egypt) by the Israelites during the plague of darkness; and they were forced to let the Israelites free after the plague of the firstborn (*Me'am Loez*).

Rebuke penetrates the wise, more than a hundred blows to the fool.[240]

—PROVERBS 17:10

- When saying the words *"blood, fire, and pillars of smoke,"* spill three times from the wine in your cup—once during each phrase, preferably into a damaged dish. (It is not the Chabad custom to remove wine by dipping in a finger.)

- Have in mind that the cup symbolizes the attribute of *malchut* (kingship), which contains an element of "anger and indignation." Using our faculty of *binah* (understanding), we pour out that element of "anger and indignation" by spilling from the wine in the cup into a broken dish, which represents *kelipah*, i.e., that which is called "accursed." The remaining wine is called "wine that brings joy."

And wonders—this refers to the blood i.e., when the Nile turned to blood during the first plague, **as it is written** (Joel 3:3): *And I shall show **wonders** in heaven and on earth—*

Spill while saying:

blood, fire, and pillars of smoke.

Notes & Insights

☙ SPILLING WINE ❧

Normally, Rabbi Schneur Zalman of Liadi, whose version of the Haggadah is used in this edition, did not include Kabbalistic meditations. In this case, however, he felt compelled to do so for the following reason: The Talmud teaches that one should not recite a blessing over a cup associated with calamity (*Berachot* 51b). Indeed some authorities suggest that after reciting the plagues, one should spill out the remaining wine from the cup, clean out the cup, and refill it with fresh wine (*Pesach Me'ubin* cited by *Chok Yaakov* 473:37).

To address the above concern, it is important to keep in mind [while reciting the plagues and spilling the wine] that the element of retribution, of "anger and indignation," is associated *only* with the wine that is being spilled and that the wine that remains in the cup is "wine that brings joy" (*The Rebbe's Haggadah*, based on *Shaar Hakollel*).

The above explains the Kabbalistic custom, which we follow. In his book of law, Rabbi Schneur Zalman provides a different approach: It is customary to remove a small amount of wine when one reaches the phrase "blood, fire, etc." One should also do so when mentioning the plagues individually...and when mentioning them collectively in the phrase *"D'tzach,*

Adash, B'achav." This totals sixteen pourings, corrresonding to God's "sword," i.e., the angel called יוה"ך (*Yoha"ch*), who administers revenge. [The first two letters of the angel's name "יו" equal 16; the second two letters form the word "הך", which means "strike"—*Machatzit Hashekel*.]

It is customary to remove the wine with one's index finger, alluding to the verse, *it is the finger of God.* Some have the custom to use the ring finger, since it was with this "finger" that God struck Egypt. And some have the custom, for the [Kabbalistic] reason known to them, to pour from the cup itself and not to use a finger.[238]

וּבְמוֹפְתִים, זֶה הַדָּם **Wonders—this refers to the blood.** According to most commentators, this refers to the first plague in which the Nile turned to blood. Others maintain that this refers to the miraculous feat that Moses demonstrated to Israel when he first appeared to them in Egypt: he poured water onto the ground and it turned to blood (Exodus 4:9). It was because of this "wonder" that the Israelites believed in him (*Kol Bo*).

The plague of blood is called "wonders," plural, since it included several wonders: Not only did the waters of the Nile turn to blood, any water purchased by an Egyptian from an

דָּבָר אַחֵר: בְּיָד חֲזָקָה שְׁתַּיִם, וּבִזְרֹעַ נְטוּיָה שְׁתַּיִם, וּבְמֹרָא גָּדֹל שְׁתַּיִם, וּבְאֹתוֹת שְׁתַּיִם, וּבְמֹפְתִים שְׁתַּיִם:

אֵלּוּ עֶשֶׂר מַכּוֹת שֶׁהֵבִיא הַקָּדוֹשׁ בָּרוּךְ הוּא עַל הַמִּצְרִים בְּמִצְרַיִם, וְאֵלּוּ הֵן:

באמירת עשר מכות ישפוך עשר שפיכות מהכוס מהכום עצמו כנ"ל (ויכוין בשפיכה גם כן כנ"ל) ומה שנשאר בכוס (נעשה סוד יין המשמח לכך) לא ישפוך אלא יוסיף יין:

When saying the ten plagues, spill ten times, once during each plague, into the broken dish, with the same meditation as above.

דָּם, צְפַרְדֵּעַ, כִּנִּים, עָרוֹב, דֶּבֶר, שְׁחִין, בָּרָד, אַרְבֶּה, חֹשֶׁךְ, מַכַּת בְּכוֹרוֹת:

is unholy before introducing holiness into our lives. We should "do good" even before achieving a complete "turn from evil." We can attain passion for holiness—the "plague of blood"— even if our passion for the unholy has not yet been cooled—the "plague of frogs." And in the end, the darkness of the unholy that we may possess will be displaced by this increase in holy light, leading us to our personal and collective redemption (*The Rebbe*).[241]

ᛘ HAIL ᛘ

There was…flaming fire within the hail (Exodus 9:24). This can be compared to two legions of the king that hated each other. When the king needed to go to war, what did he do? He made peace between them, and they went and fought the king's war. Fire and hail are similarly at odds. But when it came time to battle Egypt, God made peace between them and they struck Egypt (*Tanchuma, Va'era* 14).

The integration of fire and water during this plague demonstrates a spiritual integration of kindness, which is the spiritual antecedent of water, and judgment, which is the spiritual antecedent of fire (*Maskil L'David*).[242]

This integration can also be seen in the uniqueness of this plague: On the one hand, it was the beginning of an *intensification* of the plagues, as in the verse, *This time* I am sending *all* of My plagues to your heart… (Exodus 9:14). On the other hand, this was the only plague in which God provided the Egyptians a means to escape by fleeing into their houses.

This plague demonstrated another sort of integration: When warning Pharaoh of the plague of hail, Moses made a scratch on the wall of the palace where the sun had cast its shadow. He then said in the name of God: "Tomorrow, when the sun's shadow reaches this mark, I will rain down a very heavy hail…."

This was the only plague in which God conveyed to Pharaoh through Moses the precise moment when the plague would begin. (This would prove decisively that the plague was indeed the hand of God, since no wizard or magician could predict the precise timing of an occurrence.)

Now, the hail, like the other miraculous plagues, was a manifestation of God's *transcendence from* time and space. Yet this transcendent phenomenon occurred at a *precise time*, demonstrating the synthesis of God's powers of transcendence and immanence (*The Rebbe*).[243]

THE TEN PLAGUES

Another interpretation in which the verse alludes to the Ten Plagues: (1) **Strong** (2) **hand** indicates two [plagues]; (3) **Outstretched** (4) **arm**—two; (5) **Great** (6) **revelation**—two; (7-8) **Signs**—two (since "signs" is plural); and (9-10) **Wonders**—two.

These are the Ten Plagues that the Holy One, blessed be He, brought upon the Egyptians. They are:

 When saying the ten plagues, spill ten times, once during each plague, into the broken dish, with the same meditation as above.

1) Blood. 2) Frogs. 3) Lice. 4) Wild Beasts. 5) Pestilence. 6) Boils. 7) Hail. 8) Locust. 9) Darkness. 10) Slaying of the Firstborn.

❧ HOLY APATHY ☙

Each of the plagues also has its parallel in our own spiritual Exodus. Take the first two plagues, for example: The transformation of cold water to hot blood symbolizes the transformation of cold apathy to warm passion. The invasion of cold frogs into Egypt, even into their hot ovens, symbolizes the cooling of passion.

Holiness is characterized by life and therefore warmth. The first step toward spiritual emancipation must therefore be an assault on coldness and apathy. Even one who does everything right but does so without excitement and passion is enslaved to Egypt. If he is not animated by holiness, he will in the end be animated by the unholy.

Our unholy impulse therefore expends much energy to prevent us from getting excited about Godliness. When we see a miracle, for example, the unholy impulse argues that even if it was a miracle, why get excited? Since God created nature, why should we be surprised when He chooses to suspend it?

In our first blow to our inner Egypt, we must attack this coldness—we must transform the cold waters of the idolatrous Nile to passion and warmth.

Unholy Passion

In order to provide us with freedom of choice, God created an unholy parallel to everything that exists in the realm of holiness. We therefore have the option of being passionate about unholy things. The second step in the Exodus is to recover our misplaced, unholy passions. What are those things that we get excited about but are not necessarily in the best interest of our spiritual growth?

In the first plague we seek to replace our unholy apathy with holy passion; in the second plague we seek to cool our unholy passions with holy apathy.

First Things Second

The conventional order of things is to first "turn from evil" and then "do good." The metaphor used for this describes the method for preparing a home for a king: one would first thoroughly clean the house, get rid of the garbage, and only then bring in attractive furnishings. Likewise, conventionally, we ought to clear out our "garbage" before bringing holiness into our "palace."

But the order of the first two plagues teaches us otherwise. There are times to reverse the order—not to wait until we are cleansed of what

רַבִּי יְהוּדָה הָיָה נוֹתֵן בָּהֶם סִמָּנִים:

When saying the following three acronyms, spill three times into the broken dish, once during each acronym, with the same meditation as above.

דְּצַ"ךְ, עֲדַ"שׁ, בְּאַחַ"ב.

Replenish your cup with wine.

Israelites, despite their close proximity. Regarding the third plague, the Torah emphasizes how the wizards were particularly overwhelmed by the plague. The Torah therefore uses the expression "so that you will know that I am God *within the land*" regarding this set of plagues.

God is Supreme: The third set demonstrated God's dominance over the gods of Egypt, the "sun god" and the constellation Aries, the ram: 1) the sun failed to melt the hail, 2) the rays of the sun were concealed by the cloud of locust and by 3) the plague of darkness. The death of the firstborn demonstrated the weakness of Aries, which was considered the "firstborn" of the zodiac and thought to protect the firstborn. Furthermore, the plague occurred during the month of Nissan, when Aries is dominant. The Torah therefore states prior to the third set, *so that you will know that there is none like Me…* (*Me'am Loez* from *Abarbanel*, et al.).[245]

❧ THREE WARNINGS ❧

By grouping the plagues into three sets, Rabbi Yehudah also alludes to a pattern: The third plague of each set came to Egypt without any warning from Moses. In contrast, the first two plagues in each of the three sets were preceded by warnings.[246]

This teaches us that one who commits a crime twice forfeits his right to a third warning (*Raavan*).

Why then did they receive a warning for the fourth plague and beyond? Since each set of plagues was a different type of punishment (see *Rashbam*, above), Pharaoh therefore deserved a separate warning for each set (*Chida*, as per *Ketuvot* 33b).

❧ THREE ADMINISTRATORS ❧

Three of the plagues were administered by Aaron, three by Moses, three by God, and one by all three.

The plagues of the first set were administered by **Aaron**.[247]

The first two of the second set were administered by **God**, the third by all three.

The first three of the third set were administered by **Moses**, the final one by God (*Shibolei Haleket*; cf. *Avudraham* and *Abarbanel*).

	Rashbam	Shibolei Haleket	Abarbanel
D.TZa.Ch.	From the land	By Aaron	Showed God's existence
A.Da.Sh.	Natural occurrences	By God (primarily)	God's particular providence
B.A.Cha.V	From the skies	By Moses (primarily)	Supreme over all gods

❧ GEMATRIA ❧

In the coming passages we read of three opinions regarding how many plagues the Egyptians suffered at the sea: 50, 200, or 250. With his mnemonic, which are numerically equivalent to 501, Rabbi Yehudah suggests that all opinions are correct, since the Egyptians in fact suffered a total of 500 plagues at the sea, a number that incorporates all three opinions: 50+200+250=500 (*Pirush Kadmon*). (One extra or missing number is considered negligible in Gematria (*Shibolei Haleket*).)

THE MNEMONICS

Rabbi Yehudah would coin mnemonics for the plagues (i.e., a learning and memory aid. He coined three "words" made up of the Hebrew initials of the ten plagues):

When saying the following three acronyms, spill three times into the broken dish, once during each acronym, with the same meditation as above.

D'tzach. Adash. B'ahchav.

Replenish your cup with wine.

Notes & Insights

The mnemonics stand for the following:

D'TZaCh: *Dam*—blood, *Tzfardea*—frogs, *Kinim*—lice [the letters *Chaf* and *Kaf* are interchangeable]; **ADaSh:** *Arov*—wild beasts, *Dever*—pestilence, *Shechin*—boils; **B'AhChaV:** *Barad*—hail, *Arbeh*—locust, *Choshech*—darkness, *Bechorot*—firstborn [the letters *Bet* and *Vet* are two forms of one letter].

"The vowelization of these acronyms is universal in all the *Haggadot* I have seen. I have not yet found an explanation for this particular vowelization" (*The Rebbe's Haggadah*).

What was the purpose of these mnemonics? In Psalms, chapters 78 and 105, the chronology of the plagues is different from the chronology in Exodus. [In Psalm 78, the order is: blood, wild beasts, frogs, locust, hail, pestilence, plague of the firstborn (the other three plagues are not mentioned). In Psalm 105, the order is: darkness, blood, frogs, wild beasts, lice, hail, locust, plague of the firstborn.] Rabbi Yehudah therefore provided these mnemonics to demonstrate that the plagues occurred according to the chronology recorded in Exodus (*Shibolei Haleket*; *Avudraham*; see other reasons there—*The Rebbe's Haggadah*).

THREE TYPES

The mnemonics divide the plagues into three sets: The first set came from the land (blood and frogs from the water and lice from the soil); the second set included occurrences that also occur naturally; the third set came from the skies (*Rashbam*).[244]

EGYPT'S 3 LESSONS

Midrash

Egyptian paganism included three general groups: The first group completely denied the existence of a Creator. The second accepted the existence of a Creator but placed Him "in the heavens," detached from and disinterested in this lowly world. The third group accepted the existence of the God of Israel, but considered Him to be of limited power, like the other "gods."

By grouping the plagues into three sets, Rabbi Yehudah alludes to the three "lessons" of the plagues, which came to demonstrate the fallacy of the above beliefs.

God Exists: The first set taught Egypt of the existence of God, as the Egyptian wizards stated after the third plague "it is the finger of God!" The Torah therefore uses the expression "so that Egypt will know *that I am God*" regarding these plagues.

Particular Divine Providence: The second set emphasized the extent of God's detailed and precise providence over this world. Regarding the first two of these plagues, the Torah emphasizes that the plagues miraculously affected only the Egyptians and not the

רַבִּי יוֹסֵי הַגְּלִילִי אוֹמֵר: מִנַּיִן אַתָּה אוֹמֵר שֶׁלָּקוּ הַמִּצְרִים
בְּמִצְרַיִם עֶשֶׂר מַכּוֹת וְעַל הַיָּם לָקוּ חֲמִשִּׁים מַכּוֹת,
בְּמִצְרַיִם מַה הוּא אוֹמֵר: וַיֹּאמְרוּ הַחַרְטֻמִּם אֶל פַּרְעֹה
אֶצְבַּע אֱלֹהִים הִיא: וְעַל הַיָּם מַה הוּא אוֹמֵר: וַיַּרְא יִשְׂרָאֵל
אֶת הַיָּד הַגְּדֹלָה אֲשֶׁר עָשָׂה יְיָ בְּמִצְרַיִם, וַיִּירְאוּ הָעָם אֶת
יְיָ, וַיַּאֲמִינוּ בַּיְיָ וּבְמֹשֶׁה עַבְדּוֹ: כַּמָּה לָקוּ בְאֶצְבַּע, עֶשֶׂר
מַכּוֹת, אֱמוֹר מֵעַתָּה: בְּמִצְרַיִם לָקוּ עֶשֶׂר מַכּוֹת, וְעַל הַיָּם
לָקוּ חֲמִשִּׁים מַכּוֹת:

☙ ONE, FOUR, OR FIVE ☙

Kabbalah Every object can be viewed at its most external form, or one can delve deeper into its elemental properties. The Sages taught that everything includes four basic *yesodot*: fire, water, air, and earth.

Rabbi Yosai maintains that the plague only affected its recipient in the most external form. According to Rabbi Eliezer and Rabbi Akiva, the plagues penetrated even the elemental aspects of the recipients.

According to Rabbi Eliezer, the plagues overwhelmed their "recipient" to such a degree that each of its four *yesodot* was permeated. Hence each plague was in fact "four."

Rabbi Akiva says that the plague extended even further; it reached a fifth dimension called *hiyuli*. *Hiyuli* refers to the formless matter that existed at the beginning of creation and from which all beings were formed. In Rabbi Akiva's opinion the plague went beyond even the four *yesodot* and permeated the *essence* of the thing—its most primal core (*Kol Bo; Ritva, et al.*).

Delving Deeper

The function of the plagues was to destroy the impurity of Egypt. So the question of how deeply the plagues penetrated Egypt depends on how deeply the impurity had penetrated Egypt. Rabbi Yosai says the impurity only affected the external aspect of Egypt; according to Rabbi Eliezer, Egypt had become corrupt down to its elemental level; and according to Rabbi Akiva, even the essence of Egypt had become corrupt.

The Chametz Parallel

We find a similar debate regarding how *chametz* must be destroyed.[249] According to most sages, it is enough to crumble the *chametz* and scatter its crumbs to the wind. Rabbi Akiva follows the minority opinion of Rabbi Yehudah that *chametz* must be burned. [250]

What is the underlying debate here between these sages? The argument is about the degree of *chametz's* "impurity": does it affect only the form of the *chametz* or does it affect its substance as well? If the impurity only penetrates the form, it would be sufficient to destroy the form, even if the substance remains.

The Sages (and Rabbi Eliezer among them) maintain that the impurity of *chametz* only permeates its form. So as long as one destroys the form—rendering the *chametz* no longer edible or usable—one has "destroyed" the *chametz*, even if its substance still exists.

Rabbi Yehudah and Rabbi Akiva maintain that the impurity of *chametz* extends to its substance. So crumbling it and destroying its form is insufficient; one must burn it so that even its substance is destroyed.

Continued on next spread.

60b

∽ FIFTY PLAGUES AT SEA ∾

Rabbi Yosai of the Galilee said: Where does the Torah indicate that in Egypt the Egyptians were struck by ten plagues and at the sea by fifty plagues?

Regarding Egypt, what does it say? *The magicians said to Pharaoh, "This is the **finger** of God"* (Exodus 8:15).

And regarding the sea, what does it say? *Israel saw the great **hand** that God laid against Egypt; and the people feared God, and they believed in God and in His servant Moses* (Exodus 14:31).

Now, with how many plagues were they struck by "the finger"? Ten plagues. Deduce, then, that in Egypt they were struck by ten plagues, and by fifty plagues at the sea since a hand has five fingers.

∽ Notes & Insights ∾

With the previous passage, the Haggadah concluded its citation from the *Sifrei*, which began on page 48 with the passage "Go out and learn."

The current section describing the opinions of Rabbi Yosai, Rabbi Eliezer, and Rabbi Akiva, appears in the *Mechilta* on Exodus 14:31.

This section does not appear in Rambam's Haggadah. However, his son, Rabbi Avraham, writes (cited in *Maaseh Rokeach*) that the reason his father did not include it is because its recitation was not widely practiced and it was not obligatory. But it was Rambam's personal custom to recite it. In his son's words: "...this is our custom and the custom of our predecessor, my father and master of blessed memory, as well as his predecessors and the Sages of the West [in the Land of Israel]" (*The Rebbe's Haggadah*).

וְעַל־הַיָּם לָקוּ חֲמִשִּׁים מַכּוֹת... **Fifty at the sea... 200...250.** The following two passages cite Rabbi Eliezer and Rabbi Akiva, who agree with Rabbi Yosai that the plagues at the sea were fivefold those in Egypt. However, Rabbi Eliezer

and Rabbi Akiva add that in fact each plague in Egypt was more than one plague. Thus the plagues at the sea are multiplied accordingly (*Shibolei Haleket*).[248]

Regardless of how many plagues there were, they were all derivatives of the ten that descended upon Egypt. At the sea, these ten prototypes were divided into many different afflictions (*Rambam's* commentary on *Avot* 5:4).

Our text, therefore, does not conflict with *Avot* 5:4 and *Avot d'Rabbi Nattan* ch. 33, where it is stated that God brought *ten* plagues upon the Egyptians at the sea, since this can be understood to mean that God brought ten *types* of plagues at the sea (*Abarbanel*).

Rabbi Moshe Cordovero in his *Tefillah L'Moshe* specifies the 50, 200, and 250 plagues (*The Rebbe's Haggadah*).

וַיֹּאמְרוּ הַחַרְטֻמִּם... אֶצְבַּע אֱלֹהִים הִוא **The magicians said...This is the finger of God.** Although they said this after seeing the plague of lice (and failing to replicate it), the implication is that they realized that *all* of the plagues came from the finger of God (*Abarbanel*)

רַבִּי אֱלִיעֶזֶר אוֹמֵר: מִנַּיִן שֶׁכָּל מַכָּה וּמַכָּה שֶׁהֵבִיא הַקָּדוֹשׁ בָּרוּךְ הוּא עַל הַמִּצְרִים בְּמִצְרַיִם הָיְתָה שֶׁל אַרְבַּע מַכּוֹת, שֶׁנֶּאֱמַר: יְשַׁלַּח בָּם חֲרוֹן אַפּוֹ, עֶבְרָה, וָזַעַם, וְצָרָה, מִשְׁלַחַת מַלְאֲכֵי רָעִים. עֶבְרָה אַחַת, וָזַעַם שְׁתַּיִם, וְצָרָה שָׁלשׁ, מִשְׁלַחַת מַלְאֲכֵי רָעִים אַרְבַּע. אֱמוֹר מֵעַתָּה: בְּמִצְרַיִם לָקוּ אַרְבָּעִים מַכּוֹת, וְעַל הַיָּם לָקוּ מָאתַיִם מַכּוֹת.

❧ RABBI YOSAI ❧

Rabbi Yosai was among the illustrious Rabbinic leaders of his generation. Though younger than his colleagues, such as Rabbi Akiva and Rabbi Tarfon, he was considered their equal and in fact bested Rabbi Akiva in debate.

He was a saintly man whose prayers were answered, as the Talmud reports: "When the Jews sin…and rain is withheld, they bring an elder such as Rabbi Yosai of the Galilee, who prays for them and the rain falls."[254]

❧ RABBI ELIEZER ❧

As a youth, young Eliezer showed no interest in Torah study. He was an exceptionally strong lad and worked for his father plowing on the mountainous terrain while his brothers plowed the flatlands.

In his twenties, he was suddenly overcome with a desire to learn Torah. He left his father's home and made his way, on foot, to the academy of Rabban Yochanan ben Zakkai, where he became one of his five outstanding students.[255]

Rabban Yochanan compared him to "a cemented cistern that does not lose a drop." He also said: "If all the sages of Israel were on one side of the scale and Rabbi Eliezer on the other, he would outweigh them all!"[256]

Rabbi Yehoshua once kissed the stone that Rabbi Eliezer would sit upon and said: "This stone is like Mount Sinai and the one who sat upon it like the Ark of the Covenant!"[257]

Rabbi Eliezer considered generosity of spirit to be the essential attribute of spiritual work. He used to say: "Let the honor of your fellow be as dear to you as your own and do not be easily angered…."[258]

❧ RABBI AKIVA ❧

Until the age of forty, Rabbi Akiva, a descendant of converts to Judaism, was an ignorant shepherd who despised the Sages. Rachel, the daughter of his wealthy employer, saw greatness in him, married him, and encouraged him to study.

After being disinherited by her father, Rachel and Rabbi Akiva lived in abject poverty. Yet with Rachel's encouragement, Rabbi Akiva became one of the greatest sages and leaders of Israel. He credited the vision and self-sacrifice of his wife Rachel for his achievements.[259]

Aside from his scholarship, Rabbi Akiva was a communal leader who raised funds for the needy.[260]

Despite the efforts of the Romans to ban Torah study, Rabbi Akiva continued teaching, saying that a Jew without Torah is like a fish without water. The Romans arrested Rabbi Akiva and eventually killed him as one of the Ten Martyrs.

Yet even while being brutally tortured to death by his captors, Rabbi Akiva remained unfazed. He recited the verse *Shema Yisrael*, and his soul left him as he said the word *echad*, [God is] "one."[261]

He passed away at the age of 120.

∾ FOUR PLAGUES ∾

Rabbi Eliezer said: Where does the Torah indicate that each individual plague that the Holy One, blessed be He, brought upon the Egyptians in Egypt consisted of four plagues?

For it is written, *He sent against them His fierce anger* which expressed itself in:[251] *fury, and rage, and affliction, a contingent of messengers of evil* (Psalms 78:49):

Fury is one; *rage*—two; *affliction*—three; *contingent of messengers of evil*—four. Deduce, then, that in Egypt they were struck by forty plagues, and at the sea by 200 plagues.

Continued from previous spread:

(Another example of Rabbi Yehudah's view: The Torah states that in the Messianic age God will *remove predatory beasts from the land* (Leviticus 26:6). Rabbi Shimon maintains that this means predatory beasts will become peaceful, as in the verse *The wolf shall lie with the lamb...* (Isaiah 11:6). Yet they are considered to be "removed from the land," since their "form," their predatory nature, will have been removed.

Rabbi Yehudah, however, maintains that "removal" means a literal one, not just of form but of substance as well.) (*The Gaon of Rogachov* cited in *Likkutei Sichot*, vol. 7, p. 189).

Rabbi Yosai's Lenient View

Rabbi Yosai is most lenient about *chametz*. In contrast to the majority opinion, he maintains that one is allowed to derive benefit from *chametz* even on Pesach [as long as one does not eat it or own it].[252]

In other words, in his view the impurity of *chametz* reaches only its most external aspect— its use as a food. In Rabbi Yosai's view, one can therefore have benefit from *chametz* in other ways as long as one does not eat it.

The chart below demonstrates how the three views of the sages in regard to the number of plagues are reflected in their three views in regard to *chametz*.[253]

	Each Plague	Extent of Egypt's Impurity	Degree of Chametz Prohibition
Rabbi Yosai	1	External	One may derive benefit from it
Rabbi Eliezer	4	Penetrated its four *yesodot*	Sufficient to destroy its form by crumbling it and scattering it to the wind
Rabbi Akiva	5	Penetrated four *yesodot* and essence	Must be burnt, since even its substance is forbidden

רַבִּי עֲקִיבָא אוֹמֵר: מִנַּיִן שֶׁכָּל מַכָּה וּמַכָּה שֶׁהֵבִיא הַקָּדוֹשׁ בָּרוּךְ הוּא עַל הַמִּצְרִים בְּמִצְרַיִם הָיְתָה שֶׁל חָמֵשׁ מַכּוֹת, שֶׁנֶּאֱמַר: יְשַׁלַּח בָּם חֲרוֹן אַפּוֹ, עֶבְרָה, וָזַעַם, וְצָרָה, מִשְׁלַחַת מַלְאֲכֵי רָעִים. חֲרוֹן אַפּוֹ אַחַת, עֶבְרָה שְׁתַּיִם, וָזַעַם שָׁלשׁ, וְצָרָה אַרְבַּע, מִשְׁלַחַת מַלְאֲכֵי רָעִים חָמֵשׁ. אֱמוֹר מֵעַתָּה: בְּמִצְרַיִם לָקוּ חֲמִשִּׁים מַכּוֹת, וְעַל הַיָּם לָקוּ חֲמִשִּׁים וּמָאתַיִם מַכּוֹת.

world—our own intellect. Our connection to God is stifled by a cerebral detachment and to the constraints of what our limited minds can grasp.

Innate Knowledge (water)—On an even higher level, we may have overcome the impediments of intellect but remain self-aware, as in the following vignette:

When reciting the verse "Hear O Israel, etc.," it is customary to meditate upon the all-pervasiveness of God and our readiness for self-sacrifice. A self-deceiving worshiper once boasted that he had recited the Shema and meditated for nearly a minute! While supposedly meditating on the all-pervasiveness of God and his readiness for self-sacrifice, this worshipper still had the presence of mind to keep his eye on the clock....

The above vignette is a caricature of a more refined syndrome: one who is truly prepared for selfless self-sacrifice but is aware of this selflessness and self-sacrifice. In this quasi-selflessness, the individual has not completely transcended the limitations of self to a state where he is oblivious to his own selflessness (see page 35a above regarding the difference between sitting and reclining, and page 37a above regarding the two types of Shema).

The Troubled Essence

Rabbi Akiva goes even further: even one who has overcome any possible enslavements of the four dimensions of the soul—as described above—must still be concerned with the soul's essence. Rabbi Akiva perceived that the infinite capacity of the soul's essence can be hijacked and misused. Since God always provides balance between good and evil, the soul's supra-rational attachment to God is mirrored by a capacity for a supra-rational attachment to the transient and trivial (see page 51a above and page 52b regarding the deeper meaning of the "death of the king of Egypt").

Rabbi Eliezer descended from holy ancestors. He therefore could not fathom how the soul's essence could be corrupted. Rabbi Akiva, on the other hand, descended from pagans. He saw the darker side of the world and knew that even the soul's essence can be exploited.

Hence a fifth "plague" upon our personal Egypt: the spiritual work of fixing the soul's essence (*The Rebbe*).[262]

Crown of the Yud	Soul's Essence	Hiyuli	Keter
י (Y)	Innate knowledge of God, which leads to self-sacrifice	Water	Chochmah
ה (H)	Intellect	Fire	Binah
ו (V)	Emotion	Air	Z'eyr Anpin
ה (H)	Behavior (thought, speech, deed)	Earth	Malchut

∽ A Fifth Dimension ∾

Rabbi Akiva said: Where does the Torah indicate that each individual plague that the Holy One, blessed be He, brought upon the Egyptians in Egypt consisted of five plagues?

For it is written: *He sent against them His fierce anger, fury, and rage, and affliction, a contingent of messengers of evil* (Psalms, ibid.):

His fierce anger is one; *fury*—two; *rage*—three; *affliction*—four; *contingent of messengers of evil*—five. Deduce, then, that in Egypt they were struck by fifty plagues, and at the sea they were stricken by 250 plagues.

∽ Notes & Insights ∾

שֶׁכָּל־מַכָּה וּמַכָּה... הָיְתָה שֶׁל חָמֵשׁ מַכּוֹת **Each indvidual plague... consisted of five plagues.** As mentioned, Rabbi Moshe Cordovero describes the five dimensions of each plague. For example, in regard to the plague of darkness, he explains the five plagues and how they correspond to the five expressions of the verse, as follows:

His fierce anger: During the plague of darkness, the Egyptians could not see.

Fury: During the last three days of the plague, they could not move. One who was seated remained seated, and one who was standing remained standing.

Rage: They were hungry and thirsty but could not eat or drink.

Affliction: They remained conscious throughout.

A contingent of messengers of evil: They could hear the Israelites moving about and worried that the Israelites would loot all their possessions.

❧ Four vs. Five ☙

Kabbalah As we have seen, Rabbi Eliezer and Rabbi Akiva differ about the extent of Egypt's corruption. Rabbi Eliezer maintains that only the form of Egypt—which is defined by the four *yesodot* of fire, water, air, and earth—had become corrupt, but not its essence, which transcends its four *yesodot*. Therefore only a four-dimensional plague was necessary. Rabbi Akiva, however, perceived that even the essence of Egypt had become corrupt and that a five-dimensional plague was therefore necessary.

In our personal Exodus, what does it mean to "plague" and overcome the four dimensions of our "Egypt"? And what is the fifth dimension?

Bashful, Cerebral, and Self-Aware

The soul is also composed of four *yesodot*: 1) behavior (thought, speech, and deed); 2) emotion, 3) intellect, 4) innate knowledge of God, which gives the soul its capacity for self-sacrifice (see page 40 regarding the "wise child"). These correspond to the four *yesodot* and the four letters in the Divine Name (see chart).

In our personal Exodus we must confront potential enslavements that can occur in each of the four *yesodot* of our souls:

Behavior (earth)—On this level, we can be enslaved to any improper behavior, whether in thought, speech, or deed.

Emotion (air)—On a higher level, we may be entirely free of unholy behaviors but our feelings and emotions enslave us. We lack the freedom of conviction. We remain shy about our Judaism, worrying about popular opinion.

Intellect (fire)—On yet a higher level, we are free of emotional enslavement to the world around us but remain enslaved by our inner

כַּמָּה מַעֲלוֹת טוֹבוֹת לַמָּקוֹם עָלֵינוּ:

It is customary not to interrupt the recital of the fourteen stanzas of *"Dayenu."*

אִלּוּ הוֹצִיאָנוּ מִמִּצְרַיִם וְלֹא עָשָׂה בָהֶם שְׁפָטִים, דַּיֵּנוּ.

אִלּוּ עָשָׂה בָהֶם שְׁפָטִים וְלֹא עָשָׂה בֵאלֹהֵיהֶם, דַּיֵּנוּ.

אִלּוּ עָשָׂה בֵאלֹהֵיהֶם וְלֹא הָרַג אֶת בְּכוֹרֵיהֶם, דַּיֵּנוּ.

אִלּוּ הָרַג אֶת בְּכוֹרֵיהֶם וְלֹא נָתַן לָנוּ אֶת מָמוֹנָם, דַּיֵּנוּ.

אִלּוּ נָתַן לָנוּ אֶת מָמוֹנָם וְלֹא קָרַע לָנוּ אֶת הַיָּם, דַּיֵּנוּ.

אִלּוּ קָרַע לָנוּ אֶת הַיָּם וְלֹא הֶעֱבִירָנוּ בְּתוֹכוֹ בֶּחָרָבָה, דַּיֵּנוּ.

אִלּוּ הֶעֱבִירָנוּ בְּתוֹכוֹ בֶּחָרָבָה וְלֹא שִׁקַּע צָרֵינוּ בְּתוֹכוֹ, דַּיֵּנוּ.

אִלּוּ שִׁקַּע צָרֵינוּ בְּתוֹכוֹ וְלֹא סִפֵּק צָרְכֵּנוּ בַּמִּדְבָּר אַרְבָּעִים שָׁנָה, דַּיֵּנוּ.

אִלּוּ סִפֵּק צָרְכֵּנוּ בַּמִּדְבָּר אַרְבָּעִים שָׁנָה וְלֹא הֶאֱכִילָנוּ אֶת הַמָּן, דַּיֵּנוּ.

אִלּוּ הֶאֱכִילָנוּ אֶת הַמָּן וְלֹא נָתַן לָנוּ אֶת הַשַּׁבָּת, דַּיֵּנוּ.

אִלּוּ נָתַן לָנוּ אֶת הַשַּׁבָּת וְלֹא קֵרְבָנוּ לִפְנֵי הַר סִינַי, דַּיֵּנוּ.

אִלּוּ קֵרְבָנוּ לִפְנֵי הַר סִינַי וְלֹא נָתַן לָנוּ אֶת הַתּוֹרָה, דַּיֵּנוּ.

אִלּוּ נָתַן לָנוּ אֶת הַתּוֹרָה וְלֹא הִכְנִיסָנוּ לְאֶרֶץ יִשְׂרָאֵל, דַּיֵּנוּ.

אִלּוּ הִכְנִיסָנוּ לְאֶרֶץ יִשְׂרָאֵל וְלֹא בָנָה לָנוּ אֶת בֵּית הַבְּחִירָה, דַּיֵּנוּ.

Notes & Insights

כַּמָּה מַעֲלוֹת **How many levels...** "This passage does not appear in the Haggadah of the Rambam.... I have not found a source for this passage in any *Midrash*, as of this time. But Abarbanel seems to imply that it is the conclusion of the statement of Rabbi Akiva!" (*The Rebbe's Haggadah*).

לִפְנֵי הַר סִינַי **Before Mount Sinai.** At Sinai, God revealed to us His glory and greatness (Deuteronomy 5:21). As we say in the Rosh Hashanah liturgy, "You revealed Yourself in Your cloud of glory upon Mount Sinai." If God had done only this and not given us the Torah— *Dayenu* (*The Rebbe's Haggadah*).

∽ LAYERS OF DIVINE KINDNESS: ↶
EGYPT TO JERUSALEM

It is customary not to interrupt the recital of the fourteen stanzas of *"Dayenu."*

How many levels of favors has the Omnipresent One bestowed upon us!

If He had brought us out from Egypt, and had not carried out
judgments against them—   (it would have sufficed for us) *Dayenu!*

If He had carried out judgments against them,
and not against their idols—   *Dayenu!*

If He had destroyed their idols,
and had not struck their firstborn—   *Dayenu!*

If He had struck their firstborn,
and had not given us their wealth—   *Dayenu!*

If He had given us their wealth, and had not split the
sea for us [and not hardened Pharaoh's heart to chase us]—   *Dayenu!*

If He had split the sea for us, and had not taken us through
it on dry land [instead leaving the seabed muddy]—   *Dayenu!*

If He had taken us through the sea on dry land,
and had not drowned our oppressors in it—   *Dayenu!*

If He had drowned our oppressors in it, and had not supplied
our needs in the desert for forty years [and we would have
bought provisions from traveling merchants]—   *Dayenu!*

If He had supplied our needs in the desert for forty years,
and had not fed us the manna—   *Dayenu!*

If He had fed us the manna,
and had not given us the Shabbat—   *Dayenu!*

If He had given us the Shabbat, and had not brought us
before Mount Sinai [and revealed His presence]—   *Dayenu!*

If He had brought us before Mount Sinai,
and had not given us the Torah—   *Dayenu!*

If He had given us the Torah,
and had not brought us into the Land of Israel—   *Dayenu!*

If He had brought us into the Land of Israel,
and had not built for us the Holy Temple —   *Dayenu!*

עַל אַחַת כַּמָּה וְכַמָּה טוֹבָה כְפוּלָה וּמְכֻפֶּלֶת לַמָּקוֹם עָלֵינוּ, שֶׁהוֹצִיאָנוּ מִמִּצְרַיִם, וְעָשָׂה בָהֶם שְׁפָטִים, וְעָשָׂה בֵאלֹהֵיהֶם, וְהָרַג אֶת בְּכוֹרֵיהֶם, וְנָתַן לָנוּ אֶת מָמוֹנָם, וְקָרַע לָנוּ אֶת הַיָּם, וְהֶעֱבִירָנוּ בְתוֹכוֹ בֶּחָרָבָה, וְשִׁקַּע צָרֵינוּ בְּתוֹכוֹ, וְסִפֵּק צָרְכֵּנוּ בַּמִּדְבָּר אַרְבָּעִים שָׁנָה, וְהֶאֱכִילָנוּ אֶת הַמָּן, וְנָתַן לָנוּ אֶת הַשַּׁבָּת, וְקֵרְבָנוּ לִפְנֵי הַר סִינַי, וְנָתַן לָנוּ אֶת הַתּוֹרָה, וְהִכְנִיסָנוּ לְאֶרֶץ יִשְׂרָאֵל, וּבָנָה לָנוּ אֶת בֵּית הַבְּחִירָה לְכַפֵּר עַל כָּל עֲוֹנוֹתֵינוּ:

through the sea on dry land—i.e., He revealed His essence, which transcends the conflicting properties of "sea" and "dry land," thereby enabling us to remain conscious during this revelation (*Rabbi DovBer of Lubavitch*).[264]

בֶּחָרָבָה **On dry land.** In contrast to the above interpretation, another perspective is that we are thanking God for 1) splitting the sea and providing us an escape from Egypt and 2) for drying the seabed for us so we would not have to walk in mud (*Abarbanel*; *Avudraham*; *Maharal*).

But sparing us a muddy walk seems a relatively insignificant miracle in comparison to the other miracles enumerated here. Why then is it included?

As mentioned, the splitting of the sea represented a revelation of the Godly reality that is usually hidden. In a personal sense, we also have times when God's presence is revealed and times when God seems concealed from us. There are times when we are spiritually inspired and feel close to God, and times when we are uninspired and feel distant from God. Generally, we experience Divine "revelation"—awareness and inspiration—during the times of prayer, especially through meditative prayer. But this inspiration slowly escapes once we close the prayer book and enter the "real" world, where God is concealed.

A Personal Revelation

A "splitting of the sea" in our lives would mean that the inspiration of prayer stays with us throughout the day—that we experience Divine awareness and revelation even in a time and place where Godliness is typically concealed.

But this can occur in two ways:

In the first, the perspective gained during prayer is enough to affect our *behavior* during the day but does not transform our feelings and inclinations. This can be compared to a splitting of the sea in which the waters of concealment have not been completely removed from the seabed—it remains wet and muddy. This means that the hidden has been revealed, but not entirely—a residue of the waters of concealment remains.

Yet, as we say in the Haggadah, even if God only granted us this "small" spiritual achievement—*Dayenu*!

But God accorded us an even greater kindness: He gave us the ability to experience an absolute "splitting of the sea," a revelation of the concealed, where no "water" remains at all and we can walk on "dry land." Our meditative prayers can "part the sea," enabling us to see through the "concealing waters" of the world even outside the times of prayer. We are then able to see the world as the handiwork of its Creator and to perceive the purpose He intended for it in its creation (*The Rebbe*).[265]

64b

⌐ DOUBLED & REDOUBLED GOODNESS ⌐

How much more so should we be grateful to the Omnipresent One for the doubled and redoubled goodness that He has bestowed upon us! For He brought us out of Egypt,

and carried out judgments against the Egyptians,

and acted against their idols,

and smote their firstborn,

and gave us their wealth,

and split the sea for us,

and took us through it on dry land,

and drowned our oppressors in it,

and supplied our needs in the desert for forty years,

and fed us the manna,

and gave us the Shabbat,

and brought us before Mount Sinai,

and gave us the Torah,

and brought us into the Land of Israel,

and built for us the Holy Temple to atone for all our sins.

Split the sea...and took us through it. וְקָרַע לָנוּ אֶת־הַיָּם, וְהֶעֱבִירָנוּ בְּתוֹכוֹ The Psalmist (136:13-14) likewise portrays the splitting of the sea as two separate acts of Divine kindness:

1) *Who split the Sea...for His kindness is everlasting; and 2) led Israel through it, for His kindness is everlasting.*

But is there any significance to the splitting of the sea independent of God taking us through it? Is it not essentially one act of kindness? Chasidus explains that the splitting of the sea was more than a utilitarian measure to save the Israelites. Indeed God could have saved us in another way. Why did God choose this method?

The answer is that the splitting of the sea was the manifestation of a profound revelation of God at that time. As our Sages taught, even the most spiritually illiterate amongst us experienced prophetic visions at the sea of the sort that our later prophets never experienced.[263] This revelation of the concealed was mirrored by the splitting of the waters, where what is normally concealed (the seabed) was revealed.

Generally, Divine revelation of this kind would cause a person to be so overwhelmed that he would cease to exist with an independent consciousness. Yet the Israelites did not lose their consciousness at all. How was this possible?

More Than Prophecy

At the sea, God revealed more than what is revealed in prophecy—He revealed His essence, which transcends all rules. The Israelites were therefore able to remain conscious—to walk through the sea during this immense revelation.

Hence the two acts of kindness: 1) He split the sea for us—i.e., revealed to us the Divine reality that is normally concealed; 2) He led us

רַ בָּן גַּמְלִיאֵל הָיָה אוֹמֵר: כָּל שֶׁלֹּא אָמַר שְׁלֹשָׁה דְבָרִים אֵלוּ בַּפֶּסַח לֹא יָצָא יְדֵי חוֹבָתוֹ. וְאֵלוּ הֵן: פֶּסַח, מַצָּה, וּמָרוֹר.

offering, and today we are not required nor allowed to offer the Pesach offering.) Rabbinic obligations are established to "make a fence around the Torah," to create conditions that encourage the fulfillment of Torah laws.

On a personal level, we all know that certain behaviors, though technically permitted, create a condition where we are less likely to fulfill our Jewish obligations. Those who are truly committed to Torah will therefore enact their own customized "Rabbinic obligations" to ensure their adherence to the *mitzvot*.

Maror therefore represents our commitment to living a lifestyle that will be most conducive to fulfillment of Torah and *mitzvot*.

Pesach: Today, the Pesach offering is neither a Biblical nor Rabbinic duty. The Pesach therefore represents actions that are neither *mitzvot* nor sins—they are neutral acts, such as engaging in business or eating and drinking. In such things the Torah's approach is: *Know Him in all your ways* (Proverbs 3:6). Instead of engaging in business purely as a material pursuit, we should do so with a Divine awareness, recognizing even seemingly secular and mundane activities as opportunities for "knowing God."

These three essential points are reiterated at the end of *Maggid* so that we remain aware of them throughout the rest of the year: 1) *Matzah*—our Jewish obligations; 2) *Maror*—creating the conditions for Jewish observance; 3) *Pesach*—sanctifying even our mundane affairs (*The Rebbe*).[268]

❧ THREE TYPES OF FOOD ❧

As we have seen, the hierarchy of obligation in regard to Pesach, matzah, and *maror* is: 1) *matzah*, which is Biblically mandated in all times; 2) *maror*, which is not Biblically required when the Temple is not standing, but is required

Rabbinically; 3) *Pesach*, which is not required at all when the Temple is not standing.

Matzah, *Maror*, and *Pesach* represent three types of food:
- *Matzah* (bread): Essential nourishment.
- *Maror*: Toxic substances to stay away from.
- *Pesach*: Supplemental nutrition and enjoyment (since the Pesach is to be eaten when one is already satisfied).

If we think of educating a child as spiritual feeding, the above three types represent the following:
- **Matzah** (bread): Our foremost obligation and focus is providing spiritual nourishment for our children. We do so by teaching them Torah, which is compared to bread, as in the verse (Proverbs 9:5): *Come eat bread from My bread.*

The twice-mentioned bread alludes to: 1) the Written Torah and 2) the Oral Torah, as well as: 1) the legal aspects of Torah and 2) its mystical dimension.

This bread should be "matzah," humble bread—Torah study should be infused with humility.[269]
- **Maror:** The bitter *maror* represents the nourishment we provide through chastisement, by steering our children clear of negative deeds and behaviors. The primacy of *matzah* (positive teaching) over *maror* (chastisement) reflects the Talmudic principle that one should always discipline with the left (weaker) hand and show affection with the right (stronger) hand (*Sotah* 47a).
- **Pesach:** When we raise our children (and ourselves) in this manner, they are fully infused ("sated") with Torah and *mitzvot*, which leads them to intensify and beautify their study and practice, and to do so with enjoyment and pleasure (*The Rebbe*).[270]

∾ Pesach's Three Essentials ᐸ

Rabban Gamliel used to say: Whoever does not discuss the significance of **the following three things on Pesach has not** properly **fulfilled his duty** to recount the Exodus.[266] They are:

The **Pesach** offering, **Matzah**, and **Maror**.

Notes & Insights

The source for this section—beginning with "Rabban Gamliel" and concluding with "Praise God!" on p. 70 below—is a *Mishnah* in tractate *Pesachim* (116a-b). However, the phrases "that our ancestors used to eat" and "that we eat" were added by the editor of the Haggadah and are not part of the Mishnaic text (see *Chida* and *Rashbatz* cited below—*The Rebbe's Haggadah*).

רַבָּן גַּמְלִיאֵל **Rabban Gamliel.** According to Rashbatz, this refers to Rabban Gamliel II, since his grandfather, Rabban Gamliel I, passed away eighteen years before the destruction of the Temple and would not have said, as we read in the next passage, "This is the Pesach *that our ancestors used to eat* while the Holy Temple stood." *Chida*, however, questions this assertion, since the phrase "that our ancestors used to eat" is not part of the original statement of Rabban Gamliel, as mentioned above.

פֶּסַח מַצָּה וּמָרוֹר **Pesach, Matzah, and Maror.** As we near the end of *Maggid*, retelling the Exodus, we make sure to reiterate the main points of Pesach, which can be obscured by our lengthy discussions.[267]

כָּל שֶׁלֹּא אָמַר שְׁלֹשָׁה דְּבָרִים אֵלּוּ **Whoever does not discuss the following three things—** i.e., one who does not explain what they represent (*Rashbam* on *Pesachim*, ibid.).

לֹא יָצָא יְדֵי חוֹבָתוֹ **Has not fulfilled his duty**—to recount the Exodus (*Raavan, Machzor Vitri, et al.*).

Others explain that if one does not verbalize the significance of *Pesach, matzah,* and *maror,* one does not fulfill the *mitzvah* to eat them (see *Pirush Meyuchas l'Rashbam; Ramban (Milchamot)* on *Berachot* 20b).

לֹא יָצָא יְדֵי חוֹבָתוֹ **Has not fulfilled his duty**—as he should, but he has fulfilled his basic Biblical obligation (*Ran* on *Pesachim*, ibid.). This seems to be the opinion of *Rif, Rashba, Avudraham, et al.*, who maintain that a mere mention of the Exodus is sufficient to fulfill the mitzvah of retelling the Exodus (*The Rebbe's Haggadah*).

(*Aruch l'Ner* (commenting on *Sukkah* 28a) suggests that *Tosfot* (s.v. *V'amartem, Pesachim* 116a) maintain that one who does not discuss *Pesach, matzah* and *maror* does not fulfill his obligation *at all*.)

פֶּסַח מַצָּה וּמָרוֹר **Pesach, Matzah, and Maror.** In our spiritual Exodus, we must also make sure not to forget these three principles:

Matzah: Today, matzah is the only one of these *mitzvot* that is Biblically required. Matzah therefore represents our Jewish *obligations,* which include laws stated explicitly in the Torah or those mandated by our Sages and adopted by our people over the centuries, as recorded in the Code of Jewish Law.

Maror: Today, we fulfill this mitzvah as a Rabbinic obligation. (Biblically, one is only required to eat *maror* together with the Pesach-

פֶּסַח שֶׁהָיוּ אֲבוֹתֵינוּ אוֹכְלִים בִּזְמַן שֶׁבֵּית הַמִּקְדָּשׁ קַיָּם עַל שׁוּם מָה, עַל שׁוּם שֶׁפָּסַח הַמָּקוֹם עַל בָּתֵּי אֲבוֹתֵינוּ בְּמִצְרַיִם, שֶׁנֶּאֱמַר: וַאֲמַרְתֶּם זֶבַח פֶּסַח הוּא לַייָ אֲשֶׁר פָּסַח עַל בָּתֵּי בְנֵי יִשְׂרָאֵל בְּמִצְרַיִם בְּנָגְפּוֹ אֶת מִצְרַיִם וְאֶת בָּתֵּינוּ הִצִּיל, וַיִּקֹּד הָעָם וַיִּשְׁתַּחֲווּ.

Leaping Over the Set Time: Although they were meant to be in Egypt for 400 years, God "leaped over" the calculations for the appointed time and redeemed them early (*Shir Hashirim Rabbah* 2:19).

Leaping Over Spiritual Norms: Normally, Divine revelation is experienced in proportion to one's spiritual level and capacity. On this night, however, God was revealed in all His glory to the Israelites, who were not at all fit for such a revelation. In doing so, God "skipped over" all rules (*Rabbi Schneur Zalman of Liadi*).[276]

Israel's Leap from Egypt: The Israelites, who had fallen to the nadir of the Egyptian depravity, were suddenly redeemed by God and embarked on the path toward the highest revelation of God: the Giving of the Torah at Mount Sinai. This, too, was a quantum leap.

Leaping Today: God asks us to offer the Pesach offering to parallel His "leaping." This means that on this night we have the ability to make our own leap—to "skip over" the environment of exile in which we are immersed and leap toward true redemption of the spirit.

We are empowered to take more than a step or two towards living a more Jewish and Godly life; we can leap toward the highest rungs.

Leaping to Unity: The notion of "leaping over" relates also to Jewish unity, to overcoming the false barriers that stand between one person and another, and between the individual and the community.

By "leaping over" our egos and liberating our Godly core, we are able to unite with those around us, the greater community, and all of Israel (*The Rebbe*).[277]

🙖 AN ABSURD SCENARIO 🙖

Rashi (on Exodus 12:13) cites an astounding Midrash:

"If an Israelite was in an Egyptian home on that night, I might assume that he would be struck like the Egyptian. The Torah therefore states: *There will be no plague among you.*

Consider the absurdity of this scenario: The Israelites had suffered miserably under the Egyptians, who had repaid Joseph's kindness with cruelty and sought ways to destroy his descendants. They then witnessed the nine plagues that God had brought upon Egypt, each time sparing the Israelites. Furthermore, Moses had informed them that a tenth plague was coming and that these were the very last moments of their exile, for soon the King of kings would reveal Himself. Moses had also warned them not to leave their homes.

Yet, the above Midrash implies, there may have been an Israelite, who on the night of the Exodus did not want to be among fellow Israelites—he preferred to be in an Egyptian home, placing himself at risk.

Some Israelites suffered from such an inferiority complex and were so enslaved to Egyptian culture that even after nine plagues they still did not learn a lesson, and on this holiest of nights chose to be in an Egyptian home!

One might have assumed, says the Midrash, that such an Israelite does not merit special protection and deserves to be struck along with the Egyptian. The Torah therefore states: *There will be no plague among you*—God's love for his people is such that He will "personally" descend to this Egyptian home and save even this Israelite from any ill fate (*The Rebbe*).[278]

✑ Pesach: Skipping & Leaping ✐

The Pesach-lamb that our ancestors would eat while the Holy Temple stood—what does it commemorate?

It commemorates the fact that the Omnipresent One *skipped over* (*pasach*) our ancestors' homes in Egypt, as it is written (Exodus 12:27):

*You shall say, "It is a **Pesach offering** to God, because He **skipped over** the homes of the Children of Israel in Egypt when He struck the Egyptians with a plague and saved our homes." And the people bowed and prostrated themselves.*

✑ Notes & Insights ✐

וַאֲמַרְתֶּם זֶבַח פֶּסַח הוּא **You shall say, It is a Pesach offering, etc.** This verse is from the passage in which Moses tells the people about the plague of the firstborn and how they can spare themselves from it through the Pesach offering. He then commanded them to continue offering the Pesach offering annually once they would reach the Land of Israel.[271] Moses then told them that they would have children who would ask about the Pesach offering, to which they were to respond: *You shall say, "It is a Pesach offering, etc."*

The people bowed and prostrated: They bowed in gratitude for the three promises Moses had reiterated at that time: The promise of redemption from Egypt, entry to the Land of Israel, and that they would later have offspring (who would ask them about their Pesach-offering).[272]

שֶׁפָּסַח **Skipped over.** *Pesach* connotes "skipping (*dilug*)" or "leaping (*kefitzah*)"—meaning that God skipped over the Israelite homes, leaping from Egyptian home to Egyptian home and sparing the Israelite homes that stood between them. (Some of the Israelite homes were in Egyptian neighborhoods.)

Likewise, God asked the Israelites to perform the rites of the Pesach offering in an energetic, hasty manner, reflecting God's "leaping" from house to house to rescue them (*Rashi*, Exodus 12:11,13).

❧ A Night of Leaping ❧

Midrash The word *Pesach*, which means to "skip" or "leap," represents taking a quantum "leap" and "skipping over" the usual step-by-step process. The fact that this is the name of the holiday—as per Jewish custom—indicates that this is its central theme.

This theme is expressed in many ways. Among them:

Leaping Over Justice: God redeemed Israel from Egypt, not in their own merit, but in the merit of their Patriarchs and Matriarchs.

Hence the verse in Song of Songs (2:8): *The voice of my Beloved is coming, skipping (m'daleg)* upon the mountains, leaping (m'kapetz) upon the hills. "My Beloved is coming" means that God is coming to redeem Israel from Egypt—"skipping upon the mountains"—i.e., in the merit of the "mountains" and the "hills," the Patriarchs and the Matriarchs.[273]

As the *Midrash* puts it: God said, "Were I to look at the deeds of Israel, they would never be redeemed. Rather to whom do I look? To their holy ancestors…."[274]

God skipped over the normal calculations of justice—by which Israel would not merit redemption—and redeemed them in the merit of their ancestors.[275]

נוטל הפרוסה בידו ויאמר:

Hold on to the second and third matzah (leaving them in the matzah cover) until after the second "שׁוּם".

מַצָּה זוֹ שֶׁאָנוּ אוֹכְלִים עַל שׁוּם מָה, עַל שׁוּם שֶׁלֹּא הִסְפִּיק בְּצֵקָת שֶׁל אֲבוֹתֵינוּ לְהַחֲמִיץ עַד שֶׁנִּגְלָה עֲלֵיהֶם מֶלֶךְ מַלְכֵי הַמְּלָכִים הַקָּדוֹשׁ בָּרוּךְ הוּא וּגְאָלָם, שֶׁנֶּאֱמַר: וַיֹּאפוּ אֶת הַבָּצֵק אֲשֶׁר הוֹצִיאוּ מִמִּצְרַיִם עֻגֹת מַצּוֹת, כִּי לֹא חָמֵץ, כִּי גֹרְשׁוּ מִמִּצְרַיִם וְלֹא יָכְלוּ לְהִתְמַהְמֵהַּ, וְגַם צֵדָה לֹא עָשׂוּ לָהֶם.

all future Pesachs. Firstly, its *chametz* laws were only applicable for one day, the fifteenth of Nissan. Secondly, although they could not eat *chametz* during that time, they were allowed to bake and own *chametz*.

Consequently, if the Israelites had not been rushed out of Egypt, they would have allowed their dough to rise and baked leavened bread on the fifteenth of Nissan to eat *after* the fifteenth (*Ran*).[281]

❧ INTO THE WILDERNESS ❧

וְגַם צֵדָה לֹא עָשׂוּ לָהֶם **They had also not prepared any other provisions.** The Torah tells us that the Israelites did not prepare any other provisions (aside from the matzah) in order to praise them: They did not say to Moses, "How can we go out into the desert when we have no provisions for the road?" Rather, they trusted in God and followed Moses (*Yalkut Shimoni* §209).

> *Thus said God: "I remember for you the devotion of your youth, the love of your bridal days, as you went after Me in the wilderness, in an uncultivated land."*
>
> —JEREMIAH 2:2

Miraculously, the matzah they made from the dough that they took of Egypt was as tasty as the *manna* (*Kiddushin* 38a) and lasted for one month (61 meals), until the fifteenth of Iyar. The next day, on the sixteenth of Iyar, they began receiving the *manna* (see *Rashi* on Exodus 16:1).

❧ DOUGH THAT COULDN'T RISE ❧

As mentioned above, the dough that the Israelites prepared after midnight did not rise because of the hasty exit. But why did the dough not rise while the Israelites traveled?[282]

At midnight, God was revealed in the souls of the Israelites. When God is revealed in the soul, there is no room for spiritual *chametz*—arrogance and separateness from God. This spiritual condition caused the physical dough to become insusceptible to leavening.

(The pre-midnight matzah, which was made before the Divine revelation, was susceptible to leavening. God therefore commanded the Israelites to actively prevent it from leavening.)[283]

The Haggadah is telling us that the matzah that we eat tonight (although we eat it before midnight) commemorates the *post*-midnight matzah. Tonight, we not only *suppress* our inner "leavening"—we have the ability to experience a Divine awareness in which *chametz* becomes an impossibility (*Rabbi Schneur Zalman of Liadi*).[284]

∽ MATZAH: A HASTY REDEMPTION ⌒

Hold on to the second and third matzah (leaving them in the matzah cover) until after the word *"commemorates."*

This matzah that we eat—what does it commemorate?

It commemorates the fact that the dough of our ancestors did not have a chance to become leavened before the King of the supernal **kings** who are the kings of the mortal **kings**, the Holy One, blessed be He, revealed Himself to them and redeemed them. As it is written: *They baked matzah-cakes from the dough that they had brought out of Egypt, because it was not leavened; for they had been driven out of Egypt and could not delay, and they had also not prepared any [other] provisions* (Exodus 12:39).

Notes & Insights

נוטל הפרוסה **Hold on to the...matzah.** The Talmud indicates that one must *lift up* the matzah and *maror* (Pesachim 116b).[279] However, the *Siddur* of *Rashi* and *Machzor Vitri* indicate that one should *place one's hand* upon them. (Perhaps their version of the Talmud differed from ours in this matter.) The custom of the Chabad Rebbes was to hold the second and third *matzot* (by means of the cloth). While reciting the section about *maror*, they would place their hands upon both portions of *maror* on the Seder Plate (*The Rebbe's Haggadah*).

שֶׁלֹא הִסְפִּיק בְּצֵקֶת שֶׁל אֲבוֹתֵינוּ לְהַחֲמִיץ **The dough...did not have a chance to become leavened.** The Haggadah seems to imply that the origin of the matzah obligation is our hasty Exodus. But didn't God command us to eat matzah two weeks *before* the Exodus?

The commentators explain that God foresaw that the Egyptians would chase out the Israelites, who would then not have time for their dough to rise. He therefore commanded them to eat matzah to commemorate the miraculous, hasty Exodus that would yet occur (*Shibolei Haleket*).

The Israelites prepared matzah twice. The first was for their evening Pesach meal, which

was to be completed before midnight. The Israelites prevented this dough from rising in fulfillment of God's command. The Israelites prepared dough a second time, after midnight, as provisions for the way. This time, the verse tells us, the dough did not rise because there was no time. The Israelites took this dough with them out of Egypt and baked it on the way as matzah (see *Likkutei Torah, Tzav* 13a).[280]

כִּי גֹרְשׁוּ מִמִּצְרַיִם **They had been driven out of Egypt**—by the Egyptians, who, overwhelmed by the Plague of the Firstborn, pressured the Israelites and rushed them out of Egypt (Exodus 12:33).

The Divine revelation that initiated the redemption was so overwhelming that it caused the Egyptians, who had previously enslaved the Israelites, and Pharaoh, who had stubbornly refused to release them, to come full circle and *urge* them to leave (see *Me'am Loez*).

כִּי גֹרְשׁוּ מִמִּצְרַיִם, וְלֹא יָכְלוּ לְהִתְמַהְמֵהַּ **They had been driven out of Egypt and could not delay.** But would they not have baked matzah in any case, since it was Pesach? The laws governing the first celebration of Pesach, which occurred in Egypt, were different from those of

נוטל המרור בידו ויאמר:

Place one hand on each of the *maror* portions on the Seder Plate until after the second "שׁוּם".

מָרוֹר זֶה שֶׁאָנוּ אוֹכְלִים עַל שׁוּם מָה, עַל שׁוּם שֶׁמֵּרְרוּ הַמִּצְרִים אֶת חַיֵּי אֲבוֹתֵינוּ בְּמִצְרָיִם, שֶׁנֶּאֱמַר: וַיְמָרֲרוּ אֶת חַיֵּיהֶם בַּעֲבֹדָה קָשָׁה בְּחֹמֶר וּבִלְבֵנִים וּבְכָל עֲבֹדָה בַּשָּׂדֶה, אֵת כָּל עֲבֹדָתָם אֲשֶׁר עָבְדוּ בָהֶם בְּפָרֶךְ.

toward God. But in a time of Divine concealment, our soul's intellect is imprisoned by the thoughts, speech and deed of the mundane.

This is the deeper meaning of "the Egyptians embittered our *ancestors'* lives"—the Divine concealment of Egypt destroyed our intellectual connection to God.[291]

Nevertheless, our connection to God was not completely severed. For we also possess a knowledge of God that transcends intellect—we are a people of faith. This is the deeper meaning of God's promise to descend with us to Egypt[292]: even in "Egypt," when our intellectual connection to God is embittered, God's presence remains with us.

Where? In our supra-rational faith and devotion (*The Tzemach Tzedek*).[293]

בַּעֲבֹדָה קָשָׁה **Hard labor.** This alludes to the spiritual work of prayer. In an exile environment, in "Egypt," this work is extremely difficult, requiring us to fight an intense inner battle to overcome the many impediments to Divine awareness.

Yet, as mentioned above, God promises to descend with us to "Egypt." Even when Godliness is concealed, God gives us the tools to connect with Him. God says, "*I will descend with you*"—the Divine "I," God's essence, which transcends all categories, descends with us. This gives us the ability to employ a holy stubbornness (קָשֵׁה עוֹרֶף), to battle and defeat the cold stubbornness of Pharaoh (פַּרְעֹה) (*The Tzemach Tzedek*).[294]

HOLY HARSHNESS

Kabbalah As we have seen, Miriam was so called because she was born at the beginning of the bitterest time of the exile.

Miriam embodies holy bitterness, i.e., a healthy feeling of discontent with a spiritually deficient state of affairs. This feeling is harsh and unpleasant—especially when thinking about one's own spiritual deficiencies and distance from God—but it is a bitterness that leads to beseeching God for mercy and ultimately to joy (see above, p. 25a and below on pp. 78a-b).

Miriam was therefore the one to battle and "sweeten" the unholy bitterness of Egypt. This accords with the Kabbalistic teaching that unholy harshness (*gevurot kashot*) can only be sweetened with its antecedent, namely, holy harshness (*gevurot d'kedusha*).

Similarly, when the Israelites came across bitter waters in the desert [just after Miriam's song at the sea], God instructed Moses to throw a *bitter* branch into the waters in order to sweeten them.[295]

Sweeter Than Sweet

When bitterness is sweetened it becomes even sweeter than natural sweetness. This is alluded to in the phrase regarding Torah: *sweeter than honey*.[296] The sweetness of honey is associated with a time when God is revealed, such as when the Temple stood in Jerusalem. Only in the time of exile, when God is concealed, in a time of bitterness, can we achieve a sweetness that is "*sweeter* than honey" (*The Tzemach Tzedek*).[297]

‿ MAROR: THE BITTERNESS ↼

Place one hand on each of the maror *portions on the Seder Plate until after the word* "commemorates."

This *maror* that we eat—what does it commemorate?

It commemorates the fact that the Egyptians embittered our ancestors' lives in Egypt. As it is written: *They embittered their lives with hard labor, involving mortar and bricks, as well as all kinds of labor in the field—with all their enslavements, which they imposed upon them with crushing harshness* (Exodus 1:14).[285]

✥ CRUSHING HARSHNESS ✥

Midrash When Moses matured, he went out to his brethren, saw their suffering and cried, "I wish I could give my life for you!" He saw a large load on a small person, the load of a man on a woman, the load of young man on the elderly.... Moses would leave his royal retinue and help the Israelites rearrange their loads (*Vayikra Rabbah* 37:2).[286]

Moses saw their shoulders, bloody from their burdens, and made them bandages for their wounds. When cement dust flew into their eyes, Moses went and helped to clean their eyes.

He saw them suffering under the heaviness of their burdens, and put forth his shoulder to help carry their loads (*Midrash* cited in *Torah Shleimah*, Exodus 2:11).

✥ MIRIAM: ANTIDOTE TO BITTERNESS ✥

Chasidus The Israelites were in Egypt for 210 years. But it was in the last 86 years that the slavery became particularly bitter.[287] It was then that God sent a redeemer to Israel—Miriam, older sister of Moses, who was born at that time. She was therefore called *Miriam*, which connotes bitterness (*Shemot Rabbah* 26:1).

But aren't bitterness and redemption two opposites? Why then is Miriam the redeemer called "bitterness"?

Miriam, more than anyone else, was deeply pained by the bitterness of the exile and therefore yearned constantly for the redemption.

So it was she who prophesied that her mother would give birth to a son who would lead the people out of Egypt. And it was she who looked on as Moses was placed in the Nile, to see what would become of him—to see the fulfillment of her prophecy.

(Miriam's celebratory song after the redemption was therefore especially joyful—including musical instruments—since her joy in the redemption was proportionate to her pain during the exile.[288])

It was in the merit of her "bitterness"—her sensitivity to the pain of exile and yearning for redemption—that the redemption eventually came.[289]

The Future

The Midrash teaches that in the merit of Miriam's self-sacrifice in defying Pharaoh's command to kill the Jewish newborns, God blessed her that King David would descend from her (*Shemot Rabbah* 1:17).

Thus, just as the redemption from Egypt occurred through Miriam, so will the future redemption occur through her descendant, Moshiach ben David (*The Rebbe*).[290]

שֶׁמֵּרְרוּ הַמִּצְרִים אֶת־חַיֵּי אֲבוֹתֵינוּ **Embittered our ancestors' lives.** In Kabbalah, the intellect is referred to as parents, since intellect is the progenitor, the "ancestors," of emotion. Ideally, our intellectual appreciation of God's greatness gives birth to the emotions of love and awe

בְּכָל דּוֹר וָדוֹר חַיָּב אָדָם לִרְאוֹת אֶת עַצְמוֹ כְּאִלּוּ הוּא יָצָא מִמִּצְרַיִם, שֶׁנֶּאֱמַר: וְהִגַּדְתָּ לְבִנְךָ בַּיּוֹם הַהוּא לֵאמֹר בַּעֲבוּר זֶה עָשָׂה יְיָ לִי בְּצֵאתִי מִמִּצְרָיִם. לֹא אֶת אֲבוֹתֵינוּ בִּלְבָד גָּאַל הַקָּדוֹשׁ בָּרוּךְ הוּא מִמִּצְרַיִם, אֶלָּא אַף אוֹתָנוּ גָּאַל עִמָּהֶם, שֶׁנֶּאֱמַר: וְאוֹתָנוּ הוֹצִיא מִשָּׁם לְמַעַן הָבִיא אוֹתָנוּ לָתֶת לָנוּ אֶת הָאָרֶץ אֲשֶׁר נִשְׁבַּע לַאֲבוֹתֵינוּ.

exiles could not undo. Yes, we may feel as if subjugated to the superficial consciousness of exile, but at our *core* we are free—the essence of the soul can never again be enslaved.[299]

❧ PARTING WORDS ❧

In 5687 (1927), Rabbi Yosef Yitzchak of Lubavitch was imprisoned in the infamous Spalerno prison in Leningrad for his extensive work to keep Judaism alive in Soviet Russia. He was sentenced to death, a sentence that was later commuted to life in exile (which was later commuted to deportation).

On the way to Kostroma, the city of his exile, he was permitted to stop at his home for a few hours. Afterward, he proceeded to the train station where a large group awaited him. Before boarding the train, the Rebbe turned and spoke to the crowd, citing the words of his father:

"...All the nations on the face of the earth must know: Only our bodies have been subjected to exile, to be ruled by the nations of the world—but not our souls....

"We must openly declare for all to hear, that with regard to everything involving our religion—the Torah of the people of Israel, with its commandments and customs—no one can impose his views upon us, and no power has the right to subjugate us....

"We must always bear in mind that prisons and hard-labor camps are transient; Torah, its mitzvot, and the Jewish people, are eternal...."[300]

❧ EGYPT TO JERICHO ❧

Rabbi Schneur Zalman of Liadi writes that we are meant to see ourselves as leaving Egypt every single day (*Tanya*, chapter 45). But what does it mean to leave "Egypt" each day? How can I leave Egypt today, if I already left it yesterday?

Each "Exodus" provides a new, more mature perspective, in which the old freedom will no longer do. The clothes that were perfectly suited for the child look foolish on the adult. So, for example, if we achieve behavioral freedom—our actions no longer contradict the yearnings of our soul—we have left an "Egypt."

But while we may have achieved behavioral freedom, are our emotions perhaps still in "Egypt"? Leaving Egypt each day means to recognize and seize the opportunity for growth that each new day provides.

The Last Journey

The Torah records forty-two journeys of the Israelites from Egypt to the Promised Land. The last of these took them to the river of Jericho.

Throughout our history—personally, and collectively—we continually "leave Egypt" for the Promised Land. The final journey will also lead us to "Jericho," an allusion to the Messianic age. "Jericho" is etymologically related to the word for scent (*rei'ach*), the quality ascribed to Moshiach who will judge by a spiritual intuition referred to as the power of "smell."[301] At that time we will have fully left Egypt and attained true and eternal freedom (*The Rebbe*).[302]

∽ A PERSONAL EXODUS ∾

In every generation, we are required to view ourselves as having personally left Egypt, as it is written: *You shall tell your child on that day* (even many generations after the Exodus), *"It is because of this that God acted for **me** when **I** left Egypt"* (Exodus 13:8). It was not only our ancestors that the Holy One, blessed be He, redeemed from Egypt. He redeemed us as well along with them, as it is written: *It was **us** that He brought out of there, to bring us to and give us the land that He promised to our ancestors* (Deuteronomy 7:23).

∽ Notes & Insights ∾

This paragraph is a continuation of the Mishnah (*Pesachim* 116a-b) that begins with "Rabban Gamliel...." The second paragraph of this passage, beginning "Not only, etc.," was added by the editor of the Haggadah, based on the teaching of Rava in the Talmud (*Pesachim*, ibid.) that one is required to say during the Seder: "It was us that He brought out of there...."

לְרְאוֹת אֶת־עַצְמוֹ, כְּאִלּוּ הוּא יָצָא מִמִּצְרַיִם **View ourselves as having personally left Egypt.** Each and every Jew must view himself or herself as having been a slave in Egypt and being released to freedom (*Ritva*). As it is written, *Remember that **you** were a slave in Egypt, etc.* (Deuteronomy 16:12; *Avudraham*).

וְהִגַּדְתָּ לְבִנְךָ בַּיּוֹם הַהוּא לֵאמֹר: בַּעֲבוּר זֶה עָשָׂה יְיָ לִי **And you should tell your child on that day...God acted for me.** This verse proves that even many generations later—"on that day"—the parent must refer to the Exodus as having happened to "me" (*Maharsha* on *Pesachim* 116a).[298]

לֹא אֶת־אֲבוֹתֵינוּ בִּלְבָד, גָּאַל הַקָּדוֹשׁ בָּרוּךְ הוּא **It was not only our ancestors that God redeemed from Egypt.** For if God had not redeemed our ancestors, *we* would still be slaves in Egypt. We therefore view the miracles of the Exodus as if they had occurred to us (*Rashi, Shibolei Haleket, et al.*), since we, too, are its beneficiaries.

৪ MAHARAL'S METAPHOR ৪

A seer tells his friend to flee the country because of an impending war. The man follows this advice, emigrates, and raises many generations of offspring. One would not refer to the seer as having saved all of his friend's future offspring. Rather, the seer saved the patriarch, and this salvation *resulted* in the possibility for future offspring.

Why then do we say that God redeemed *all* generations? When God redeemed us, He implanted a sense of freedom in the souls of our people for *all* generations. Thus, even when we are persecuted, we remain internally free.

This is why it was God Himself who carried out the salvation—not an angel—since only God could have effected this eternal transformation of the Jewish soul. So our freedom today is not only the result of our *ancestors'* freedom but because of the freedom *we* were granted during the Exodus (*Maharal*; see above, p. 36a).

৪ INNER FREEDOM ৪

In Egypt, we were immersed in the materialism and paganism of Egypt. Even the *essence* of the Jewish soul had become enslaved. With the Exodus, God implanted an inner freedom within us, one that the later

יכסה את הפת ויגביה את הכוס ואוחזו בידו עד סיום ברכת אשר גאלנו.

Cover the *matzot* and hold the cup as during Kiddush while reciting the following:

לְפִיכָךְ אֲנַחְנוּ חַיָּבִים: לְהוֹדוֹת לְהַלֵּל לְשַׁבֵּחַ לְפָאֵר לְרוֹמֵם לְהַדֵּר לְבָרֵךְ לְעַלֵּה וּלְקַלֵּס, לְמִי שֶׁעָשָׂה לַאֲבוֹתֵינוּ וְלָנוּ אֶת כָּל הַנִּסִּים הָאֵלוּ. הוֹצִיאָנוּ מֵעַבְדוּת לְחֵרוּת, מִיָּגוֹן לְשִׂמְחָה, וּמֵאֵבֶל לְיוֹם טוֹב, וּמֵאֲפֵלָה לְאוֹר גָּדוֹל, וּמִשִּׁעְבּוּד לִגְאֻלָּה, וְנֹאמַר לְפָנָיו הַלְלוּיָהּ.

Place the cup on the table.

Some versions of the Haggadah have only seven expressions of praise[304] corresponding to the "seven heavens" (*Tosfot* on *Pesachim* 116a; *Avudraham*), and to the seven "shepherds" of our people: Abraham, Isaac, Jacob, Moses, Aaron, David, and Solomon (*Abarbanel*).

מִיָּגוֹן לְשִׂמְחָה **From sorrow to joy.** The sorrow of the enslavement came from the fact that the Israelites were not conditioned to being slaves (*Abarbanel*) and from the crushing harshness of the enslavement—doing work that was beyond their strength and which therefore broke their spirit (*Maharal*). Additionally, they were always worried that the Egyptians might come up with some new form of persecution (*Midrash B'chidush*).[305]

וּמֵאֵבֶל לְיוֹם טוֹב **From mourning to festivity—** since in Egypt they were unable to celebrate Shabbat and the festivals (*Abarbanel*). Additionally, their lives were "mournful" and bitter because the Egyptians had deprived them of the normal patterns of life (*Maharal*).

וּמֵאֲפֵלָה לְאוֹר גָּדוֹל **From deep darkness to light.** In Egypt, the Israelites were immersed in the darkness of ignorance and lack of faith. With the redemption, they were immersed in the light of faith and the Torah (*Abarbanel*). While in Egypt, they were like a fetus in the womb. With the Exodus, they were "born" as a nation and entered the light of existence (*Maharal*).

❧ THE FIVE REDEMPTIONS ❧

The Haggadah employs five expressions of transformation. These correspond to the five redemptions of Jewish history: from domination by 1) Egypt, 2) Babylon, 3) Media/Persia, 4) Greece, and 5) "Rome" (which includes our current Exile which began under Roman domination).[306]

These expressions also correspond to various redemptions and salvations that we experience now, during the Exile. At times, we are spared cruelty and torture, but we are "slaves," subjugated to the rule of others. Even in the best of times, we do not have complete independence. At times, we experience much worse—periods of "sorrow." In some cases we are prohibited from celebrating our holidays and can only experience "mourning."

Just as God redeemed us in five ways from Egypt, so does He redeem us during the Exile from these various persecutions.[307] Thus, we must all view ourselves as having been redeemed by God, since we all, in one form or another, experience God's salvation through His constant protection. "It is therefore our duty to thank…the One who did all these miracles for our ancestors *and for us*" (*Abarbanel*).

～ OUR DUTY TO THANK ～

Cover the *matzot* and hold the cup as during Kiddush while reciting the following:

It is therefore our duty to **thank, laud, praise, glorify, exalt, adore, bless, elevate,** and **honor** the One who did all these miracles for our ancestors and for us:

He took us from slavery to freedom, from sorrow to joy, from mourning to festivity, from deep darkness to great light, and from bondage to redemption. Let us therefore recite before Him: *Halleluyah*—Praise God!

Place the cup on the table.

～ Notes & Insights ～

יכסה את הפת **Cover the matzah**—so that it is not "shamed" by seeing us raise the cup of wine (*Agur; Shulchan Aruch HaRav* 473:44).

ויגביה את הכוס **Raise your cup**—in fulfillment of the Talmudic dictum to the effect that praise of God should be recited over wine (*Berachot* 35a; *Shaar Hakollel*).

Some have the custom to continue holding the cup through the blessing *Borei Pri Hagafen* on p. 73 (*Tur* and *Shulchan Aruch*). The custom of the Chabad Rebbes was to put down the cup after reciting this paragraph (a custom cited by *Hagahot Maimoniot*) and pick it up again for the blessing of redemption on p. 73 (which is the opinion of *Aruch Hashulchan* as well—*The Rebbe's Haggadah*).

לְפִיכָךְ אֲנַחְנוּ חַיָּבִים לְהוֹדוֹת **It is therefore our duty, etc.** This paragraph is a continuation of the Mishnah (*Pesachim* 116a-b) that begins with "Rabban Gamliel used to say...."

On Purim and Chanukah, we recite the blessing *She'asah Nissim*, thanking God for performing "miracles for our ancestors in those

days in this season." It would seem appropriate to recite this blessing on Pesach as well. According to some, this paragraph—in which we mention that God "did all these miracles for our ancestors, etc."—takes the place of the blessing *She'asah Nissim* (*Shibolei Haleket*).

Others maintain that this paragraph takes the place of the usual blessing that precedes the *Hallel* (*Orchot Chaim*).

לְפִיכָךְ אֲנַחְנוּ חַיָּבִים **It is therefore our duty, etc.** Since it is as if we ourselves had left Egypt, it is our duty to sing God's praise just as our ancestors did (*Rashbam; Avudraham;* cf. *Rabbi Yehudah ben Yakar* and *Ritva*). It would be improper for us to be ungrateful to God for all the miracles He did for us (*Rashbatz*).

לְשַׁבֵּחַ **To praise....** The Mishnah states that the Haggadah must begin with the negative ("We were slaves in Egypt" or "In the beginning our ancestors were idolaters") and conclude with praise. This paragraph is one of the passages in which we fulfill the obligation to "conclude with praise" (*Rashbatz*).[303]

Midrash לְהוֹדוֹת...וּלְקַלֵּס **To thank...honor the One...** King David uses ten expressions of praise in the Psalms. We therefore use ten expressions of praise in this paragraph. The tenth expression used—*Halleluyah*—surpasses the others, since it contains God's Name, *Y-ah,*

and His praise, *Hallelu,* in one word (*Pesachim* 117a; *Machzor Vitri*).

(The ten expressions of praise used in Psalms are: *ashrei, nitzuach, nigun, shir, maskil, mizmor, tefillah, tehillah, hoda'ah,* and *halleluyah* (*Raavan* from *Pesachim,* ibid.).)

הַֽלְלוּיָהּ, הַֽלְלוּ עַבְדֵי יְיָ, הַֽלְלוּ אֶת שֵׁם יְיָ. יְהִי שֵׁם יְיָ
מְבֹרָךְ, מֵעַתָּה וְעַד עוֹלָם. מִמִּזְרַח שֶׁמֶשׁ עַד
מְבוֹאוֹ, מְהֻלָּל שֵׁם יְיָ. רָם עַל כָּל גּוֹיִם יְיָ, עַל הַשָּׁמַיִם כְּבוֹדוֹ.
מִי כַּיְיָ אֱלֹהֵינוּ, הַמַּגְבִּיהִי לָשָׁבֶת. הַמַּשְׁפִּילִי
לִרְאוֹת, בַּשָּׁמַיִם וּבָאָרֶץ. מְקִימִי מֵעָפָר דָּל, מֵאַשְׁפֹּת יָרִים
אֶבְיוֹן. לְהוֹשִׁיבִי עִם נְדִיבִים, עִם נְדִיבֵי עַמּוֹ. מוֹשִׁיבִי עֲקֶרֶת
הַבַּיִת, אֵם הַבָּנִים שְׂמֵחָה, הַֽלְלוּיָהּ.

a lamp before him to illuminate his path. But God behaved differently with His servants Israel after the Exodus: He tended to their needs—washed them, anointed them with oil, clothed them, carried them, and lit a path before them (*Shemot Rabbah* 20:11).

הַֽלְלוּ עַבְדֵי יְיָ **Offer praise servants of God.** When the children of Israel went down to Egypt, they were seventy souls. Since God descended with them, the total number was 71. The word for *offer praise* (הַֽלְלוּ) equals 71. The verse can thus be read: "Seventy-one were the servants of God" (*Yalkut Shimoni, Tehillim* §873).

מִמִּזְרַח שֶׁמֶשׁ עַד מְבוֹאוֹ מְהֻלָּל שֵׁם יְיָ **From the rising of the sun to its setting, God's Name is praised.** Through the miracles of the Exodus, God's Name became known in the world (*Rashbam*).

✤ BEYOND TRANSCENDENCE ✤

Just as God's loftiness is awesome, so is His "humility": He Himself descended to punish the Egyptians on behalf of a humiliated nation of slaves (*Rashbam*).

The nations of the world relegated God to the heavens. They defined God by His transcendence and assumed that He could not be concerned with earthly matters—*His glory is upon the heavens.*

But in truth, God is not limited by His "transcendence." Despite His inherent exaltedness,

He lowers Himself to examine the affairs of the earthly—*He dwells on high yet looks down so low (Abarbanel).*[310]

God's true greatness is reflected not in His transcendence but in His humility. Likewise, in our lives, we achieve greatness not by escaping and transcending the world but by "descending" and dwelling within it in a holy manner (*Rabbi Schneur Zalman of Liadi*).[311]

מְקִימִי מֵעָפָר דָּל **He raises the poor from the dust**—i.e., Israel from enslavement. *To seat them with nobles*—with Moses and Aaron. *With the nobles of His people*—with the Israelite elders (*Rashbam*).

מוֹשִׁיבִי עֲקֶרֶת הַבַּיִת **He restores the barren woman to her home.** The Egyptians assumed that the Israelites were unable to procreate because of the hardships of the enslavement. But during the Exodus, the Egyptians saw the Israelites leaving with many children—they saw that the Israelite woman "was a joyful mother of children" (*Rashbam*; see above on p. 53b).

When Pharaoh decreed that all newborn boys should be thrown in the Nile, Amram, the future father of Moses, ceased procreating. Only when his daughter convinced him otherwise did he reunite with his wife and Moses was born.

He restores the barren woman to her home—this refers to Yocheved, the mother of Moses (*Pesikta Rabbati*,[312] see above on p. 54b).

◝ RAISED FROM THE DUST ◜

Halleluyah*—Praise God!** Offer praise, you servants of God; praise the name of God. May God's Name be blessed from now and to all eternity. From the rising of the sun to its setting, God's Name is praised. God is exalted above all nations; His glory is upon the heavens. Who is like God, our God, Who dwells on high, yet looks down so low upon heaven and earth! He raises the poor from the dust, He lifts the needy from the garbage heap, to seat them with nobles, with the nobles of His people. He restores the barren woman to her home, [and makes her] a joyful mother of children—Halleluyah*—praise God!**

Notes & Insights

The following two passages are the first two Psalms of the *Hallel*, Psalms 113-114. The rest of the *Hallel*, Psalms 114-118, are recited after the meal. At the Seder we are required to recite *Hallel* just as our ancestors did when they left Egypt, as the Talmud relates—*Pesachim* 117a (*Machzor Vitri*).[308]

❧ AN UNUSUAL READING ❧

Unlike all other recitations of *Hallel*, this recitation is not preceded by the usual blessing ("Blessed are You...Who...commanded us to recite the *Hallel*.") According to Rav Tzemach Gaon, this is because its recitation is divided by the meal. According to Rav Hai Gaon, the blessing is omitted because we are not reciting it in fulfillment of the mitzvah to recite *Hallel*, but rather as one reading Scripture (*Or Zarua*, vol. 1, §43).[309]

❧ THE DIVISION ❧

Hallel's first two psalms relate to the past—to the Exodus, the splitting of the sea, and the Giving of the Torah. The rest of *Hallel* relates to the future redemption (*Pesachim* 118a). The first two psalms are therefore read on their own, followed by the blessing over the redemption and eating matzah, both of which commemorate the Exodus. The rest, which has a different focus, is recited after the meal (*Abarbanel*).

❧ THE EGYPTIAN HALLEL ❧

This *Hallel*—who recited it? Moses and the Israelites recited it when they stood at the sea (*Pesachim* 117a). The Talmud (*Berachot* 56a) refers to this *Hallel* as "The Egyptian Hallel," since it relates to the Exodus. It is forbidden to read it in its entirety on a typical day; one can only recite it on the festivals in commemoration of the miracles God has done for us (*Shabbat* 118b; *Rashbatz*).

❧ PHARAOH'S RETREAT ❧

When Pharaoh came to Moses during the plague of the firstborn, Moses told him he would be spared if he declared that the Israelites were free and servants of God. Pharaoh began to shout: "Until now you were my servants; now you are free—you are rather the servants of God!" (*Yalkut Shimoni, Tehillim* §872). At that moment, the Israelites called out: "*Praise God! Offer praise, you servants of God*—servants of God and not of Pharaoh" (Jerusalem Talmud, *Pesachim* 5:5).

❧ AN UNUSUAL MASTER ❧

God treated His servants in an unusual manner: A conventional master buys servants who will tend to his needs, transport him, and hold

בְּצֵאת יִשְׂרָאֵל מִמִּצְרָיִם, בֵּית יַעֲקֹב מֵעַם לֹעֵז. הָיְתָה יְהוּדָה לְקָדְשׁוֹ, יִשְׂרָאֵל מַמְשְׁלוֹתָיו. הַיָּם רָאָה וַיָּנֹס, הַיַּרְדֵּן יִסֹּב לְאָחוֹר. הֶהָרִים רָקְדוּ כְאֵילִים, גְּבָעוֹת כִּבְנֵי צֹאן. מַה לְּךָ הַיָּם כִּי תָנוּס, הַיַּרְדֵּן תִּסֹּב לְאָחוֹר. הֶהָרִים תִּרְקְדוּ כְאֵילִים, גְּבָעוֹת כִּבְנֵי צֹאן. מִלִּפְנֵי אָדוֹן חוּלִי אָרֶץ, מִלִּפְנֵי אֱלוֹהַּ יַעֲקֹב. הַהֹפְכִי הַצּוּר אֲגַם מָיִם, חַלָּמִישׁ לְמַעְיְנוֹ מָיִם.

Midrash הָיְתָה יְהוּדָה לְקָדְשׁוֹ **Judah became His holy one.** All the Israelites were afraid to enter the sea until Nachshon ben Aminadav, the leader of the tribe of Judah, jumped in, trusting in God. He was followed by all of Israel. (It was only after the Israelites had entered the waters that the sea split.)[315]

The verse therefore singles out Judah as God's sanctified one, since Judah sanctified God's name amid all of Israel (*Radak*; see *Sotah* 37a and *Yalkut Shimoni, Tehillim* §799).

❧ JOSEPH'S COFFIN ❧

The verse states that the sea saw and fled. But what exactly did it see? According to one Midrash, it saw the coffin of Joseph descending into the waters. Said God to the sea: "Flee before the one who fled." As it is written (Genesis 39:12), *[Joseph] left his garment in her hand and **fled**...* (*Yalkut Shimoni*, ibid.; see *Bereishit Rabbah* 87:8).

❧ ROCK TO WATER ❧

Chasidus There are two methods of sweetening bitter waters, of overcoming negativity. In the first, the bitter waters are overwhelmed by an abundance of sweet waters. In this case, although the bitter waters are no longer perceptible, they remain in existence. The second method is to transform the bitterness itself to sweetness.

This sort of transformation is alluded to in the transformation of the rock into a pool of water. The rock represents brute strength; the water represents kindness. When the rock turns into water, this means that severity has not only been overwhelmed and subdued by kindness, it has been *transformed* into kindness. The curse has become a blessing, the prosecutor has become the defender, the flaw has become a merit (*Rabbi Shalom DovBer of Lubavitch*).[316]

Kabbalah הַיָּם רָאָה וַיָּנֹס **The sea saw and fled.** The waters of the sea symbolize Divine concealment. Just as the waters of the sea conceal the contents of the sub-aquatic world, so does the *tzimtzum*, the hiding of God's presence, conceal the world's true "content"—the Divine energy that brings it all into existence.

In Kabbalistic terms, the waters of the sea are associated with *malchut*, whose function is to conceal Divinity. This is alluded to in the name of the sea, *Yam Suf*. *Suf* connotes "end," since *malchut* is the last, the *sof*, of the ten *sefirot*. This concealment facilitates the existence of self-aware beings—souls and angels. For if God's presence were not obscured, the soul would not have any sense of self. It would be like the light of the sun as it exists within the sun, nullified and subsumed within the sun.

As we have seen (above on p. 64a), the splitting of the sea was the result of an overwhelming Godly revelation. The "waters of the sea"—the attribute of concealment—was overwhelmed by this revelation and ceased to function (*Rabbi Schneur Zalman of Liadi*).[317]

⸙ WHY THE SEA FLED ⸙

When Israel went out of Egypt, the House of Jacob from a nation that speaks a foreign tongue, Judah became His holy one, Israel, His dominion. The sea saw and fled, the Jordan turned backward. The mountains leapt like rams, the hills like young sheep.

"What is with you, O sea, that you flee, O Jordan, that you turn backward? What is with you O Mountains, that you leap like rams, O hills, like young sheep?"

"We do so in trepidation before the Master, Creator of earth, before the God of Jacob—who turns the rock into a pool of water, the flintstone into a spring of water (when Israel was in the desert)."[313]

Notes & Insights

מֵעַם לֹעֵז **A nation that speaks a foreign tongue**—i.e., the Egyptians. Conversing in any language besides Hebrew, the Holy Tongue, is called *lo'ez*, speaking a foreign tongue (*Abarbanel; Metzudot, et al.*).

The phrase *"am lo'ez"*—translated as *a nation of a foreign tongue*—also suggests: a shameless (as in *"azut"*—*Abarbanel*) and scandalous (as in *"l'hotzi la'az"*—*Ibn Ezra*) nation.

הָיְתָה יְהוּדָה לְקָדְשׁוֹ **Judah became His holy one.** God extricated them from the midst of an impure nation and made them a holy nation. *Israel became His dominion*—they were no longer under the dominion of Egypt, only God's (*Radak*).

⸙ DIVIDING JUDAH & ISRAEL ⸙

Why are Judah and Israel mentioned separately? The Jewish people were always divided into two general groups: the tribe of Judah, and the rest of the nation. This division began long before the division that occurred in the days of Rechavam (son of King Solomon) and Yeravam. (At that time, two kingdoms arose in Israel: the kingdom of Judah and the kingdom of Israel.)

Even at the time of the Exodus, the tribe of Judah took a leadership position and traveled in front of all the tribes in fulfillment of Jacob's blessing that Judah would lead the other tribes.

Even when the Israelites had one king, they remained two distinct groups. Thus, in the days of King Saul and King David, Judah and Israel were counted separately in the census (*Abarbanel*).

הַיָּם רָאָה **The sea saw**—the Israelites coming into the sea—*and fled* from its place revealing dry land (*Metzudot*).

הַיַּרְדֵּן יִסֹּב לְאָחוֹר **The Jordan turned backward.** This occurred when Joshua led the Israelites to the Land of Israel (Joshua 3:16). The River Jordan stopped flowing in its usual current, allowing Israel to pass. Hence: *the Jordan turned backward* (*Metzudot*).

Alternatively, the Psalmist is still referring to the moment the sea split. As our Sages tell us, at that time *all* waters of the world split (*Rashi*).

הֶהָרִים רָקְדוּ **The mountains leapt.** During the Giving of the Torah, the mountains and hills—Mount Sinai and neighboring mountains (*Radak*)—leapt in great fear and trepidation (*Metzudot*). They raised a tumult for the glory of God (*Ibn Ezra*).[314]

Hold the cup as during Kiddush and say the following two blessings:

בָּרוּךְ אַתָּה יְיָ, אֱלֹהֵינוּ מֶלֶךְ הָעוֹלָם, אֲשֶׁר גְּאָלָנוּ וְגָאַל אֶת אֲבוֹתֵינוּ מִמִּצְרַיִם, וְהִגִּיעָנוּ הַלַּיְלָה הַזֶּה לֶאֱכָל בּוֹ מַצָּה וּמָרוֹר, כֵּן יְיָ אֱלֹהֵינוּ וֵאלֹהֵי אֲבוֹתֵינוּ יַגִּיעֵנוּ לְמוֹעֲדִים וְלִרְגָלִים אֲחֵרִים הַבָּאִים לִקְרָאתֵנוּ לְשָׁלוֹם, שְׂמֵחִים בְּבִנְיַן עִירֶךָ, וְשָׂשִׂים בַּעֲבוֹדָתֶךָ, וְנֹאכַל שָׁם

On Saturday night:	On all nights except Saturday night:
מִן הַפְּסָחִים וּמִן הַזְּבָחִים	מִן הַזְּבָחִים וּמִן הַפְּסָחִים

אֲשֶׁר יַגִּיעַ דָּמָם עַל קִיר מִזְבַּחֲךָ לְרָצוֹן, וְנוֹדֶה לְךָ שִׁיר חָדָשׁ עַל גְּאֻלָּתֵנוּ וְעַל פְּדוּת נַפְשֵׁנוּ. בָּרוּךְ אַתָּה יְיָ, גָּאַל יִשְׂרָאֵל.

ומברך ושותה בהסיבה.

Drink the entire cup (or at least most of it) without interruption while seated and reclining on the left side.

בָּרוּךְ אַתָּה יְיָ, אֱלֹהֵינוּ מֶלֶךְ הָעוֹלָם, בּוֹרֵא פְּרִי הַגָּפֶן.

---

himself went voluntarily), and who saw firsthand the suffering of Israel, writes as follows:

"From the many troubles that have befallen us we have nearly been wiped off the earth; it is by God's kindness that we have not disappeared. And He, in His kindness, enables us to reach this day....

"...Remembering the Exodus provides us a great hope and an indicator for the future redemption. For the two redemptions are interconnected, as we can see from the words of our prophets:

"As in the days of your Exodus from Egypt, I will show you wonders.... Behold I have redeemed you at the end of days as I have at the beginning.... God shall set His hand again, the second time to acquire the remnant of His people....[318]

"Likewise our Sages taught that God told Moses at the burning bush: I shall be Whom I shall be—meaning, 'I will be with them [Israel] in this exile and I will be with them in their future exile.'[319]

"In this vein do our Sages interpret the words of Moses to God (when Moses was demurring from being the redeemer) as saying: Please send the one whom you will ultimately send—referring to Moshiach, who would redeem Israel at the end of days.[320]

"The Sages therefore ordained that we diligently perform all the Pesach statues and laws. For they provide an unmistakable testimony regarding the future redemption...."

⌁ THE BLESSING OF REDEMPTION ⌁

Hold the cup as during Kiddush and say the following two blessings:

Blessed are You, God, our God, King of the universe, who has redeemed us and redeemed our ancestors from Egypt, and brought us to this night to eat matzah and *maror*.

So too, God our God, and God of our fathers, bring us to other holidays (Rosh Hashanah and Yom Kippur) and pilgrimages (Pesach, Shavuot, and Sukkot) that are approaching us in peace—celebrating the rebuilding of Your city, and rejoicing in Your service [in the Holy Temple].

On all nights except Saturday night:	On Saturday night:
Then we shall eat of the sacrifices and of the Pesach offerings—	Then we shall eat of the Pesach offerings and of the sacrifices—

whose blood shall be brought upon the wall of Your altar for acceptance. And we shall thank You with a new song for our redemption and for the deliverance of our souls. Blessed are You, God, who redeemed Israel.

BLESSING OVER THE WINE

Drink the entire cup (or at least most of it) without interruption while seated and reclining on the left side.

Blessed are You, God, our God, King of the universe, who creates the fruit of the vine.

⌁ Notes & Insights ⌁

This blessing is from the Mishnah in *Pesachim* 116b, in accordance with the opinion of Rabbi Akiva cited there.

According to some, this blessing takes the place of the blessing *She'asah Nissim*, thanking God for performing "miracles for our ancestors in those days in this season" (*Rashi* in *Sefer Ha'orah*; *Avudraham*—The Rebbe's Haggadah).

במוצאי שבת אומרים On Saturday night say. On a regular year, we will eat the "sacrifices"

first, referring to the *Chagigah* offering, followed by the Pesach offering. When Pesach coincides with Shabbat, the *Chagigah* is not offered until the next day. Hence: We will eat from the Pesach offering and *then* from the "sacrifices" (*Shulchan Aruch HaRav* 473:49).

אֲשֶׁר גְּאָלָנוּ... וְהִגִּיעָנוּ הַלַּיְלָה הַזֶּה Redeemed us...and enabled us to reach this night. Abarbanel, one of the Jews who left Spain during the expulsion of 1492 (though Abarbanel

⌇ WASHING HANDS FOR MATZAH ⌇

רחצה   ואחר כך נוטל ידיו ומברך על נטילת ידים.

The hands are now washed in the following manner:

- Pick up the cup containing the water in the right hand. Pass it to the left hand, and pour three times on the right hand. Then pass the cup to the right hand and pour three times on the left hand. It is customary to hold the cup with a towel when pouring on the left hand.

- A little water from the final pouring should remain in the left hand. Rub this water over both hands together, while reciting the following blessing:

בָּרוּךְ אַתָּה יְיָ, אֱלֹהֵינוּ מֶלֶךְ הָעוֹלָם, אֲשֶׁר קִדְּשָׁנוּ בְּמִצְוֹתָיו, וְצִוָּנוּ עַל נְטִילַת יָדָיִם.

Blessed are You, God, our God, King of the universe, who has sanctified us with His commandments, and commanded us concerning the washing of the hands.

- Dry your hands completely. Do not talk from this point until after eating the matzah (preferably until after eating the *Korech* "sandwich").

⅋ HEALING THE PRINCE ⅋

Kabbalah

"*There was once a king who had an only son, who became ill. One day the child wished to eat. It was said: 'Let the son of the king eat this medicine. And until he does, let no other food be found in the home.'*

"*Once he had eaten the medicine, it was said: 'From here on he can eat whatever he desires and he will not be harmed.'*

"Similarly, when the Israelites left Egypt they were ignorant of the principle and secret of faith. Said God: 'Let them eat [a food of] healing; and until then, let no other food be visible to them.' Once they ate the matzah, a food of healing that enables one to come to know the secret of faith, God said: 'From here on, they can see and eat *chametz*, since it can no longer harm them'" (*Zohar* II:41a and 183b).

⅋ INGESTING GODLINESS ⅋

When we eat matzah for the sake of the mitzvah, we are deriving physical sustenance from something that is a Godly entity.

The matzah not only affects the faith of our souls, it affects our animalistic consciousness, our "animal soul," and changes the way it thinks. The animal soul becomes less resistant to holiness and allows the Godly soul to believe with complete faith—even in that which transcends intellect.[326]

—RABBI SHMUEL OF LUBAVITCH

◌ THE MITZVAH OF MATZAH ◌

❧ THE MITZVAH ❧

There is a Biblical commandment to eat matzah on the night of the Seder, as the Torah states: *...in the evening, you shall eat* matzot... (Exodus 12:18).[321]

• **During the Rest of Pesach.** During the rest of Pesach, other than the night of the Seder, eating matzah is considered *"reshut,"* optional (*Pesachim* 120a).

Many authorities understand this to mean that even though it is not a full-fledged mitzvah, it is a quasi-mitzvah and is therefore encouraged (see *Otzar Minhagei Chabad, Nissan* §19).[322]

The spiritual effect of eating matzah (i.e., that one is "ingesting Godliness"—see previous page), while more pronounced on the night of the Seder, occurs throughout Pesach.[323]

• **A Biblical Command.** "Rava said: 'The mitzvah of matzah nowadays (i.e., even when the *Beit Hamikdash* lies in ruins) remains a Biblical command" (*Pesachim* 120a).

In contrast, the mitzvah of *maror* is only Biblically required when it can accompany the Pesach offering, which cannot be done until the *Beit Hamikdash* is rebuilt (see below on *Maror*).

• **How Much Matzah Do I Have To Eat?** Jewish law defines "eating" as consuming one *kezayit*, approximately one ounce (*Berachot* 49b). So if one eats less than a *kezayit* of matzah, one has not fulfilled the commandment to eat matzah (*Pesachim* 40a).

There is some debate, however, as to whether this *kezayit* should be taken from the first or the second matzah. It is therefore best to eat two *kezeitim* of matzah at this point, one from each of the two top *matzot*, to satisfy both opinions (*Pri Chadash; Taz*).

However, after the fact, one who only ate one *kezayit* has fulfilled the obligation (*Shulchan Aruch HaRav, Orach Chaim* 475:8).

❧ THE BLESSING ❧

• **Remaining Silent.** The recitation of any blessing should be immediately followed by the action for which the blessing was said. Speaking before the action invalidates the blessing. One should therefore not speak at all between the recitation of the blessing and partaking of the matzah.

Since the blessing over the mitzvah of matzah applies to the *Korech* sandwich as well, it is best not to speak until after eating the sandwich (*R. Yechiel*, brother of the *Baal Haturim; Even Hayarchi*).[324] Although we also bear the *afikoman* in mind when reciting the blessing (*Shaloh*), doing so is considered an exceptional stringency (*Chok Yaakov*). It is therefore not our custom to refrain from speaking before the *afikoman* is eaten (*The Rebbe's Haggadah*).

• **Holding the Matzot.** When saying a blessing over any food, we are required to hold the food during the blessing. There is some debate as to which of the two blessings applies to which of the two top *matzot*. We therefore hold both *matzot* during the recitation of both blessings (*Shulchan Aruch HaRav* 475:5).

• **The Third Matzah.** As on every Shabbat and festival, we are required to say the *Hamotzi* tonight over two *whole* "loaves" (*Rosh, Mordechai*, et al; cf. *Rif*). We therefore hold the third matzah during the blessing [even though the blessing refers *primarily* to the first two *matzot*] so that we are holding two whole *matzot* during the blessing (see *Shulchan Aruch HaRav* 475:3).

• **Releasing the Bottom Matzah.** Although we bear this matzah in mind during the blessing, we release it during the second blessing so as not to mistakenly partake of it at this time. (This concern is also cited as the reason we hide the *afikoman*.[325]) Additionally, we thereby emphasize that the blessing relates primarily to the top two *matzot* (*The Rebbe's Haggadah*).

מוֹצִיא מַצָּה
Motzi-Matzah

∾ MOTZI ∿

מוֹצִיא   וִיקַח הַמַּצּוֹת כְּסֵדֶר שֶׁהִנִּיחָם הַפְּרוּסָה בֵּין שְׁתֵּי הַשְּׁלֵמוֹת וְיֹאחֲזֵם בְּיָדוֹ וִיבָרֵךְ:

Hold the three *matzot* (while still covered by the cloth) and recite the following:

בָּרוּךְ אַתָּה יְיָ, אֱלֹהֵינוּ מֶלֶךְ הָעוֹלָם, הַמּוֹצִיא לֶחֶם מִן הָאָרֶץ.

Blessed are You, God, our God, King of the universe, who brings forth bread from the earth.

Do not break the *matzot* until after saying the second blessing:

∾ MATZAH ∿

מַצָּה   וְלֹא יִבְצַע מֵהֶן אֶלָּא יַנִּיחַ הַמַּצָּה הַשְּׁלִישִׁית לְהִשָּׁמֵט מִיָּדוֹ וִיבָרֵךְ עַל הַפְּרוּסָה עִם הָעֶלְיוֹנָה טֶרֶם יִשְׁבְּרֵם בִּרְכָה זוֹ. וִיכַוֵּן לִפְטוֹר ג"כ אֲכִילַת הַכְּרִיכָה שֶׁמֵּהַמַּצָּה הַשְּׁלִישִׁית וְגַם אֲכִילַת הָאֲפִיקוֹמָן יִפְטוֹר בְּבִרְכָה זוֹ:

• Let go of the bottom matzah and recite the following blessing, bearing in mind that it also applies to the eating of the "sandwich" of *Korech*—which will be made with the third (bottom) matzah—and also to the eating of the *afikoman* at the end of the meal:

בָּרוּךְ אַתָּה יְיָ, אֱלֹהֵינוּ מֶלֶךְ הָעוֹלָם, אֲשֶׁר קִדְּשָׁנוּ בְּמִצְוֺתָיו, וְצִוָּנוּ עַל אֲכִילַת מַצָּה.

Blessed are You, God, our God, King of the universe, who has sanctified us with His commandments, and commanded us concerning the eating of matzah.

וְאח"כ יִבְצַע כַּזַּיִת מִכָּל אֶחָד מִשְּׁתֵּיהֶן, וְיֹאכְלֵם בְּיַחַד וּבַהֲסִבָּה.

• Break off a *kezayit* (approx. one ounce, which is approx. half of a *shmurah* matzah or a whole machine matzah—see above, pp. 11-12) from each of the top two *matzot*, and eat the two pieces together while reclining on your left side.

• The entire amount (i.e., two ounces) should be eaten within approximately four to seven minutes. • One should not speak of anything unrelated to the Seder until after eating the sandwich.

• Each participant is required to eat at least a *kezayit* of matzah. Since it is impossible for all to receive the sufficient amount from the two *matzot* of the Seder Plate, other *matzot* should be available. However, it is preferable that all receive at least a small piece of the two *matzot* of the Seder Plate.

• The matzah is not dipped in salt.

～ THE MYSTICAL MATZAH ～

❧ HOW MATZAH WORKS ❧

 Human beings are conditioned by their deeds. What we *do* affects how we *feel*. Hence the power of the rituals of the Seder: Eating matzah and doing the other rituals to remember the Exodus reinforces our belief in God as the Creator, His sovereignty over nature, and His ability to suspend nature at any time, as He did in Egypt (*Sefer Hachinuch, mitzvah 21 and 16*).

The above explanation of the *Sefer Hachinuch* describes the perspective of the "body" of Torah, its external dimension. But from the perspective of the inner dimension of Torah, the "soul" of Torah, matzah is more than a *symbolic* reminder of the Exodus—its very ingestion contains a mystical power to strengthen our faith (*The Tzemach Tzedek*).[327]

❧ TASTE OF GRAIN ❧

The Talmud teaches that babies don't know to call out "Father" or "Mother" until they "taste the taste of grain" (*Berachot* 40a; *Sanhedrin* 70b).

This alludes to the idea that the food we ingest affects our psyche. In a similar vein, when we eat matzah (which is made of grain), we gain the ability to "recognize" our "parent," our Father in heaven and call out to Him.

Now, babies at that age don't understand how their parents are their parents and why they should love them. They react with an intuitive knowledge, not a rational one.

Our recognition of God gained through the matzah is likewise a non-rational one. For it enables us to "know" God even as He transcends the limits of our intellect.

Such knowledge is possible only through the humility of faith, which we acquire by ingesting the humble matzah (*Rabbi Schneur Zalman of Liadi*).[328]

❧ BODY & SOUL ❧

"*Matzah shemurah* is called by two intrinsic and inherent names: Food of Faith and Food of Healing. It strengthens the faculty of *daat* (internalization)." –THE BAAL SHEM TOV

"Matzah strengthens the health of the body by helping it perceive the purpose of the soul's descent into the body. Matzah is therefore also the Food of Faith, meaning that it causes the unshakable faith [of the soul] to permeate every aspect of our lives."[329] –RABBI YOSEF YITZCHAK OF LUBAVITCH

❧ FAITH & HEALING ❧

Food of Faith relates [primarily] to the first night of Pesach; Food of Healing relates [primarily] to the second night.
　—RABBI SCHNEUR ZALMAN OF LIADI

Healing that leads to faith implies a situation where the person was at first ill and after being healed thanks God. But healing that comes about through faith implies that the person was not ill to begin with.[330]
　—RABBI DOVBER OF LUBAVITCH

Faith and healing are interdependent: Simple faith is the elixir for every type of ill.[331]
　—RABBI YOSEF YITZCHAK OF LUBAVITCH

❧ A LOFTY NIGHT ❧

Pesach is distinguished from all other holidays, since on Pesach we receive our physical sustenance through a Godly food. Our lives are uplifted to the loftiest heights during Pesach, and especially on the night of the Seder (*Rabbi Shmuel of Lubavitch*).[332]

Harvest: As long as the wheat stalk is attached to the ground (and continues to be nourished from the ground—*Rashba*), it is not susceptible to fermentation, even if water falls upon it. The moment the wheat is harvested, it becomes susceptible to fermentation through contact with water.

Some authorities therefore maintain that according to Rabbinic law the obligation to eat matzah can only be fulfilled with matzah made of wheat that was guarded from the moment of harvest (*Rif; Rambam*). Such matzah is colloquially known as "*matzah shemurah*," "guarded matzah." In consideration of this view, it is best to use "*matzah shemurah*" for the obligatory *matzot* (*Ran; Shulchan Aruch HaRav*).[336]

❧ HAND VS. MACHINE ❧

For thousands of years, Jews baked their *matzot* by hand. The introduction of *matzot* made by a machine elicited mixed reactions in the rabbinic community. Many rabbis strongly opposed eating such *matzot* on Pesach. Others were more permissive, but insisted that only handmade *matzot* be used for the fulfillment of the obligation to eat matzah on the night of the Seder. The proponents of handmade *matzot* cited several concerns. Among them:

Depriving the Poor

The "machine *matzot*" deprived the many poor Jews, who were employed in the preparation of matzah, from the income they would have normally earned prior to Pesach. This is especially troubling since Pesach is a time when we emphasize providing the poor with funds for the holiday. We also invite the poor during the first passage of *Maggid*. In a similar vein, the Sages ensured that we do not read the Scroll of Esther if Purim occurs on Shabbat so that the poor would not be deprived of their traditional Purim alms (since it is forbidden to handle money on Shabbat) (*Rabbi Shlomo Kluger*).

The Human Touch

Human involvement and effort is essential to the preparation of matzah. Ideally, every Jew should be *personally* involved in preparing the matzah. Delegating the preparation of the matzah to a machine strips the process of human involvement and effort (*Rabbi Mordechai Ettinger*). It may even create the impression that we consider the *mitzvot* a yoke and look for ways to get away with less work (*Responsa Bar Levai*).

The rabbis also pointed to many aspects of the machine matzah process that they felt compromised the halachic requirements for ensuring that dough does not become *chametz*. Even some of the rabbis who permitted the use of machine *matzot* did so reluctantly, while for their own Seder they used handmade *matzot* (see at length *Moadim Lesimcha* and *Pardes Eliezer*).

❧ ROUND VS. SQUARE ❧

Rabbi Yehudah Assad (leading rabbi in 19th century Hungary) writes that the tradition of baking *round matzot* stems from the Torah itself, which describes the *matzot* the Israelites made as *oogot* (usually translated as "cakes"). Rabbi Yehudah goes to great length, citing many Biblical and Talmudic references, to demonstrate that *oogot* implies *round* cakes. The fact that the Torah tells us the shape of the *matzot*, a seemingly irrelevant point, indicates that the shape is essential.

Rabbi Assad suggests several reasons for this, including the following:

The Egyptians believed in many gods or forces. They may have therefore used square or triangular breads, whose multiple points would symbolize their many gods. The Torah therefore emphasizes that the *matzot* were round, with no beginning or end, symbolizing the oneness of God (*Yehudah Yaaleh, Orach Chaim* 157).

SOME LAWS OF MATZAH

The Torah requires us to eat a portion of matzah on the night of the Seder. For the rest of Pesach, or even during the meal of the Seder, there is no requirement to eat matzah. The laws below, drawn from *Shulchan Aruch HaRav* (Laws of Pesach §453 and §462), relate primarily to the *matzot mitzvah*, the "obligatory matzah" used for the mitzvah.

THE IDEAL GRAIN

It is best to use wheat for the matzah that one is required to eat on the night of the Seder. However, when wheat is not available, matzah may be made from any of the following grains: barley, spelt, oats, and rye (*Pesachim* 35a; *Maharil; Rema*).[333]

MUST BE SUSCEPTIBILE TO LEAVENING

The Torah juxtaposes the prohibition of *chametz* and the obligation of matzah (Deuteronomy 16:3): *Do not eat...chametz; for seven days you shall eat matzot....* This indicates that the obligatory matzah must be made from grains that are susceptible to becoming *chametz*.

Now, the Talmud differentiates between two types of fermentation: *chimutz* ("leavening") and *sirchon* ("spoiling"). Dough that is made from rice, millet, or other legumes can achieve *sirchon* but not *chimutz*. The latter grains are therefore unfit to be used to fulfill the mitzvah of matzah (*Pesachim* 35a).[334]

[For Ashkenazic Jews, the latter grains are prohibited on Pesach, in any case.]

WHAT IS RICH MATZAH?

Matzah made with fruit juices, oil, honey, milk, or eggs is called *matzah ashirah*, "rich matzah." Such matzah is unsuitable for the fulfillment of the mitzvah, since the Torah requires us to eat "poor bread," the bland matzah of flour and water (*Pesachim* 35a and *Rashi* ad loc.).

Furthermore, if such matzah contains no water at all, it is also disqualified because it is not susceptible to leavening, one of the matzah requirements, as stated above (see Jerusalem Talmud, *Pesachim* 2:4).[335]

SHEMURAH MATZAH

The Torah obligates us to "guard the *matzot*" from becoming *chametz* (Exodus 12:17), and to do so with the intention that one is doing so for the sake of the mitzvah of matzah (*Pesachim* 40a, and *Rashi* ad loc.).

But at what point in the process of making matzah does this obligation begin? Jewish law speaks of three stages:

Kneading: By the letter of the law, the obligation to "guard the matzah" for the sake of the mitzvah begins when the *need* to guard it occurs. This is defined as when the flour is mixed with water, which is when leavening would normally begin to occur (*Pesachim*, ibid. and *Rashi* ad loc.).

It must then be guarded from leavening by quickly kneading, rolling, and baking it for the sake of the mitzvah. These three activities must therefore be done by those who can be relied upon to have this intention, i.e., Jewish adults (*Magen Avraham*).

Grinding: Jewish custom, however, has been, at the very least, to guard the obligatory *matzot*—as well as the non-obligatory *matzot* (*Chok Yaakov*)—beginning with the grinding of the wheat into flour, since it is not uncommon for the flour to come into contact with water at that time (*Tur*). (The grinding itself, however, need not be done by a Jew (*Taz*).)

In extreme circumstances, one would be allowed to follow the letter of the law and buy flour from the market and use it even for the obligatory *matzot* (*Tur*), unless it is known or assumed that the wheat or flour had previously been in contact with water (*Magen Avraham*).

מרור
Maror

~ BITTER HERBS ~

מרור   ואחר כך יקח כזית מרור ויטבל בחרוסת וינער החרוסת מעליו כדי שלא יתבטל טעם המרירות ויברך ברכה זו:

• Soften the *charoset* with wine. Take at least a *kezayit* of *maror* (approximately 2/3 of an ounce—see above, p. 12) from the Seder Plate and dip it into the *charoset*. Shake off the *charoset* so that the bitter taste of the *maror* will not be neutralized. When reciting the following blessing, bear in mind that it is also for the *chazeret* of the "sandwich" of *Korech*.

בָּרוּךְ אַתָּה יְיָ, אֱלֹהֵינוּ מֶלֶךְ הָעוֹלָם, אֲשֶׁר קִדְּשָׁנוּ בְּמִצְוֹתָיו, וְצִוָּנוּ עַל אֲכִילַת מָרוֹר. ויאכלנו בלי הסיבה.

Blessed are You, God, our God, King of the universe, who has sanctified us with His commandments, and commanded us concerning the eating of *maror*.

• Eat the *maror* without reclining. The entire *kezayit* should be eaten within approximately four to seven minutes.

• Each participant is required to eat a *kezayit* of *maror*. Since it is impossible for all to receive the sufficient amount from the *maror* on the Seder Plate, other *maror* should be available.

during the Egyptian exile, where we had been thoroughly corrupted by Egyptian culture.

This was because of the unique evil of Egypt, the most depraved nation of its time.[341] Egypt embodied the very *core of evil*, from which all manifestations of evil emerge, including the evil we suffered during our subsequent exiles.

Core of Good: The fruits of the *charoset*, which remind us of God's love for us, evoke the core of holiness—the pure, Godly essence of our souls. For it is this aspect of ourselves—not what we think, feel or do, but who we are in essence—that inspires God's unconditional, "parental" love for us.

Egypt, the core of evil, was able to overcome this core of good. Hence the eternal significance of our redemption from Egypt: the soul's essential goodness would never again be overcome—it remains eternally free.

Essence & Expression. *Charoset* is used 1) as a prop during the retelling of the Exodus, and 2)

as a dip. This parallels the *essence* vs. the *expression* of the cores of evil and good:

Core of Evil: Having the *charoset* on the table recalls Egypt as the core of evil. Using it later as a dip recalls that this core is "put to use" and expressed in all subsequent exiles.

Core of Good: Likewise, having the *charoset* on the table evokes the *innate* value of the soul's essence, independent of any manifestation. But its true purpose is to be "put to use"—to permeate and influence all of one's consciousness, which is symbolized by its use as a dip.

Today, after all the persecutions we have endured and all the *mitzvot* we have performed over the centuries, we have been sufficiently refined so as to be able to consciously experience—in our minds and hearts, as well as our thoughts, speech and deeds—the innate goodness and freedom of our soul's essence. The "*charoset* of the soul" ought no longer be a mere "prop"—we can and should put it to use....[342]

 Notes & Insights

❧ MAROR ☙

The Torah links the eating of *maror* to the eating of the Pesach offering: *...they shall eat [the Pesach] with matzot and bitter herbs* (Numbers 9:11). Most authorities do not consider *maror* to be an independent mitzvah. It is seen rather as an *accessory* to be eaten together with the Pesach offering (*Pesachim* 90a), to accentuate the freedom by contrasting it with the bitter slavery from which it emerged.[337]

Since we do not have the Pesach offering today, there is no Biblical requirement to eat *maror*. (Regarding matzah, on the other hand, the Torah refers to it in another verse: *...in the evening, you shall eat matzot...*, indicating that matzah is an independent mitzvah and remains obligatory even in the absence of the Pesach-offering.) There is, however, a Rabbinic mitzvah to eat *maror* by itself today (*Pesachim* 120a) as a remembrance of what was done in the days when the *Beit Hamikdash* stood (*Shulchan Aruch HaRav, Orach Chaim* 475:15).[338]

The Blessing. Although eating *maror* today is a Rabbinic mitzvah, the blessing we recite over it, as in all blessings over Rabbinic *mitzvot* (such as lighting the Shabbat or Chanukah lights), refers to it as something commanded to us by God.

For it is God's command that we fulfill the *mitzvot* instituted by the Sages, as in the verse (Deuteronomy 17:11): *...you should fulfill that which they tell you [do not stray, right or left, from that which they will instruct you]* (see *Rambam, Hilchot Berachot* 11:3, from *Shabbat* 23a).

❧ CHAROSET ☙

Whereas the *maror* evokes the *general* bitterness of enslavement, the cement-like texture of the *charoset* commemorates the *particular* bitterness of the Egyptian slavery, which involved cement. As the *Midrash* states (*Shemot Rabbah* 1:27), no labor is more crushing than working with cement (*Maharal*). We therefore do not recite a separate blessing for the mitzvah of eating *charoset*, since this mitzvah is subsidiary to the mitzvah of *maror* (see *Pesachim* 116a; *The Rebbe's Haggadah* explaining *Avudraham*).

Charoset also recalls a positive event: When Egypt sought to kill all Jewish newborns, the Israelite women went out under the apple trees to give birth, so as to evade the Egyptian guards. Miraculously, they bore their children there without birth pangs. The above is alluded to in the verse (Song of Songs 8:5): *Under the apple tree, I [God] awakened you*—God awakened the fetuses to emerge. The *charoset*, which contains apples, commemorates this miracle (*Pesachim*, ibid.; *Sotah* 11b and *Rashi* ad loc.).

Two Functions. *Charoset* functions as a "prop" and then as a dip: As Rabbi Schneur Zalman writes: "The Sages instituted that we have *charoset* before us while reciting the Haggadah, since the *charoset* commemorates the cement...and must therefore *be on the table* while we relate the Egyptian bondage" (*Orach Chaim* 473:20). Only in a later chapter does he write of its function as a dip: "We dip the *maror* in *charoset*...to commemorate the clay" (ibid., 475:11; see also *Rambam*[339]—*The Rebbe*).[340]

❧ CHAROSET OF THE SOUL ☙

The *charoset* evokes two opposites. Its cement-like texture commemorates the unique suffering we endured in Egypt (see *Maharal*, cited above). Yet *charoset* is made of fruits to which God lovingly compares us in Song of Songs. Its apples likewise recall an event that reflects God's loving care of the mothers and babies born in Egypt (see above on "*Charoset*").

Another *charoset* oddity: There is no pre-scribed volume for the *charoset*; even a minuscule amount is technically sufficient.

Charoset does not require volume because it represents essence—the indivisible core of a thing. It thus recalls both the core of evil and the core of good, which parallel each other:

Core of Evil: Charoset evokes our unique suffering in Egypt, which [in certain elements] surpassed anything we endured as a people in our subsequent exiles. It likewise evokes our spiritual distress, which was also most severe

~ THE SANDWICH ~

כורך   ואח"כ יקח מצה הג' וחזרת עמה כשיעור כזית ויטבול בחרוסת ויכרכם ביחד ויאמר זה:

Take a *kezayit* of the third matzah and a *kezayit* of the *chazeret*. Place some dry *charoset* on the *chazeret* and then shake it off. Combine the two—like a sandwich— and recite the following:

כֵּן עָשָׂה הִלֵּל בִּזְמַן שֶׁבֵּית הַמִּקְדָּשׁ הָיָה קַיָם, הָיָה כּוֹרֵךְ פֶּסַח מַצָּה וּמָרוֹר וְאוֹכֵל בְּיַחַד, כְּמוֹ שֶׁנֶּאֱמַר: עַל מַצּוֹת וּמְרוֹרִים יֹאכְלֻהוּ.

Thus did Hillel do at the time of the *Beit Hamikdash*: he would combine the Pesach offering, matzah and *maror* and eat them together, as it is written: *They shall eat it with matzot and bitter herbs.*

ויאכלם ביחד [ובהסיבה. טוש"ע סימן תע"ה. הגהה מסדור אדמו"ר בעל צ"צ ז"ל].

- Eat the *korech* "sandwich" while reclining on the left side. The *korech* should be eaten within approximately four to seven minutes.

- Each participant is required to eat a *kezayit* of matzah and a *kezayit* of *chazeret*. Since it is impossible for all to receive the sufficient amount from the matzah and *chazeret* of the Seder Plate, other *matzot* and *chazeret* should be available.

emotions, thoughts, speech, and deeds, that distance us even further from God. Done properly, this sort of brutally honest introspection causes one to cry bitter tears, to call out to God from the depths of one's broken heart and ask for Divine mercy.

The law is that one who swallows *maror* without chewing it does not fulfill the obligation, since one must *taste* the bitterness of the *maror*. Similarly, one must ensure that the bitterness of the *maror* is not overwhelmed by the sweetness of the *charoset* (*Pesachim* 115b). In a spiritual sense, "swallowing *maror*" refers to one who emits a superficial sigh of regret, avoiding the true bitterness of his situation.[343] Or he "swallows it whole," by limiting his reflection to a vague recognition of his imperfection without considering the particular behaviors that need correction. Likewise, instead of thinking about the bitterness of his situation, he submerges himself instead in the sweetness of Torah study.[344] On a higher level, there is one who, after some introspection, is inspired to change and indeed does so. But he "swallows the *maror* whole," he does not allow the bitterness of his situation to linger long enough to move him to call out for Divine mercy, so that he might attain innate humility.

Yet only by chewing and absorbing the bitter taste of the "*maror*" and allowing it to transform us do we fulfill our obligation and become a cleansed vessel for the Divine revelation.[345]

Notes & Insights

❧ HILLEL'S SANDWICH ❧

Hillel's opinion is as follows:

Temple Times: In times when the *Pesach*-offering is offered, one fulfills the *mitzvot* of the Seder only if one wraps the *Pesach*, matzah and *maror* together and eats them as one.

Non-Temple Times: When the Pesach is not offered, Hillel distinguishes between matzah and *maror*:

Matzah must be eaten alone—without *maror*—since the matzah obligation is Biblical, while the *maror* obligation is Rabbinic (in non-Temple times). Matzah can only be mixed with *maror* when both are equally obligatory, such as in Temple times, when both are Biblically required.

Maror, which is eaten nowadays to commemorate what was done in Temple times, must be eaten together with matzah since that is how the *maror* was eaten in Temple times.

Evidently, Hillel holds that there is a Rabbinic obligation nowadays to eat matzah a second time (to accompany the *maror*).

Other sages disagreed with Hillel. They held that in Temple times one did not need to wrap the items together. Hence the sages' opinion regarding non-Temple times:

Matzah must be eaten alone, since the matzah obligation is Biblical while the *maror* obligation is Rabbinic. In this they agree with Hillel.

Maror cannot be eaten with matzah, since the matzah of such a sandwich would not be obligatory—even Rabbinically—and would therefore invalidate the *maror*.

Jewish law never came down on either side of the argument. We therefore eat the matzah and *maror* in a way that satisfies both opinions, as follows:

Matzah: We eat the matzah alone. According to Hillel and the sages, this is the only way to fulfill the mitzvah in non-Temple times.

Maror: We eat the *maror* twice. First alone, to satisfy the opinion of the sages who maintain that *maror* eaten with matzah is invalid. We then eat *maror* with matzah to satisfy the opinion of Hillel, who maintains that the mitzvah of *maror* is fulfilled only when wrapped with matzah (*Pesachim* 115a; *Shulchan Aruch HaRav, Orach Chaim* 475:16-18; *The Rebbe's Haggadah*).

❧ CLEANSING THE VESSEL ❧

Chasidus The spiritual significance and connection between the *Pesach*, matzah, and *maror* is as follows:

Pesach: The *Pesach* recalls the Divine revelation that occurs on Pesach.

Matzah: Matzah symbolizes humility before God, a trait that enables a person to be a receptive "vessel" to receive and internalize the Divine revelation of Pesach.

Maror: Maror symbolizes sincere introspection, which "cleanses the vessel."

The humility symbolized by matzah is an imposed humility, not an innate one. (The matzah must therefore be guarded from becoming leavened.) It therefore requires the introspection symbolized by *maror*, which "cleanses the vessel." Introspection moves one to ask for Divine mercy to be strong enough to attain innate humility and thereby merit the Divine revelation of Pesach.

The two portions of bitter herbs signify two types of introspective meditations that lead to "bitterness," i.e., a feeling of sadness over one's distance from God:

First Maror: This *maror* signifies the meditation on the distance of *all* of creation from God, since creation can only come into being through the concealment of God. As the Kabbalah teaches, God created and sustains the world through a filtered "ray" of His light. In higher spiritual worlds, the worlds of souls and angels, this light is somewhat perceptible. But in our physical world, this light is nearly entirely obscured.

Second Maror: This *maror*, eaten with the matzah, signifies a more personal meditation, in which we think about our un-Godly

שולחן עורך
Shulchan Orech
~ THE MEAL ~

שלחן עורך   ואחר כך אוכל ושותה כדי צרכו ויכול לשתות יין בין כוס ב' לג'.

- **The Egg.** Begin the meal by eating the egg from the Seder Plate, dipped in salt water.

- **Reclining.** Chabad custom is not to recline while eating the meal.

- **How Much to Eat.** Eat enough so that you will be satiated before eating the *afikoman*. (The *afikoman* commemorates the Pesach offering, which was to be eaten when satiated.) However, do not overeat to the degree that you would not have any appetite *at all* for the *afikoman*. On the first night, bear in mind that the *afikoman* should be eaten before midnight.

- **Wet Matzah.** It is Chabad custom to prevent the matzah from coming in contact with water during the first seven days of Pesach. The *matzot* on the table should therefore be kept covered to protect them from possible spills.

צפון
Tzafun
~ EATING THE AFIKOMAN ~

צפון   ואח"כ יקח האפיקומן ויחלקו לכל בני ביתו לכל אחד כזית ויזהר שלא ישתה אחר אפיקומן ויאכל בהסיבה וצריך לאכלו קודם חצות.

- **Midnight Deadline.** On the first night of Pesach, the *afikoman* should be eaten before midnight. • **Final Drink.** One should not eat or drink anything (even water) after eating the *afikoman* for the rest of the night. One should therefore make sure to have had enough liquids so as not to be thirsty after eating the *afikoman*.

- **Level of Appetite.** Ideally one should at least have some desire to eat while eating the *afikoman*, since eating it without *any* appetite is not the ideal way to fulfill the mitzvah. Nevertheless, one fulfills the obligation even without any appetite.

- **Two *Kezeitim*.** There is a debate among the rabbis as to whether the *afikoman* commemorates the Pesach offering or the matzah that was eaten along with it. Ideally, one should therefore eat two *kezeitim* of the *afikoman*—one *kezayit* to commemorate the Pesach offering, and the other *kezayit* to commemorate the matzah that was eaten along with it. One who finds this too difficult, however, may eat the amount of one *kezayit*, bearing in mind that this *kezayit* should serve as a remembrance in accordance with whichever of the two opinions is the correct one (i.e., whether the *afikoman* commemorates the Pesach offering, or the matzah eaten with it). Each participant receives a piece of the *afikoman*. Since it is impossible for all to receive a full *kezyait* from the matzah put away for the *afikoman*, other *matzot* should be used as well.

- Eat the *afikoman* while reclining on the left side. The *afikoman* should be eaten within approximately four to seven minutes.

Notes & Insights

❦ THE MEAL ❧

From the morning of *Erev Pesach* until after the *Korech* of the second Seder, we do not eat any of the ingredients of the *charoset* and *maror* (*The Rebbe's Haggadah*).

The Egg. On both nights we begin the meal by eating the egg (from the Seder Plate) after dipping it in salt water.

This is done to remember the mourning for the destruction of the *Beit Hamikdash*. When it stood, we would eat the Pesach offering on this night, whereas now we cannot do so (*Shulchan Aruch HaRav, Orach Chaim* 476:6; *The Rebbe's Haggadah*).

❦ AFIKOMAN ❧

The *afikoman* is eaten to commemorate the eating of the Pesach offering, which was done at the end of the meal, when satiated (*Rosh, et al*). However, *Rashi* and *Rashbam* maintain that the *afikoman* does not commemorate the Pesach, but the matzah that accompanied the Pesach. Furthermore, in their opinion, it is with our *afikoman* matzah that we fulfill the mitzvah of matzah. (They agree that the blessing "*al achilat matzah*" is recited earlier, but maintain that that blessing applies to the *afikoman* matzah we eat now.)

We therefore eat two *kezeitim*: one to commemorate the Pesach, and one to commemorate the matzah that accompanied the Pesach, to account for both opinions (*Bach*; *Magen Avraham*).

One who finds it difficult to eat two *kezeitim* should eat at least one (*Maharil*), with the intention that it serve as a remembrance in accordance with whichever of the two opinions is the correct one (*The Rebbe's Haggadah*).

❦ LAST DRINK ❧

From a strictly legal point of view there is no prohibition on eating or drinking on the second night of Pesach after the third or fourth cups.

However, the *mehadrin*, i.e., those who are fervent in the performance of *mitzvot*, treat the second night as the first. Thus one who eats or drinks cannot be held culpable in any way, from a strictly legal point of view.

Nonetheless, by eating or drinking one excludes oneself from the body of the *mehadrin* and thus violates the edict of the Sages (*Berachot* 49b) that one should never exclude oneself from the general body (*Shibolei Haleket* cited in *Shulchan Aruch HaRav*).

The Rebbe notes in his commentary on the Haggadah: "Here we have an explicit legal ruling about the extent to which we are all obligated to be fervent in the observance of *mitzvot* (in the most beautified manner possible), even where there is absolutely no legal obligation!"

❦ NOT OPEN FOR DISCUSSION ❧

The chasid Rabbi Shalom Kadaner, a brilliant Torah scholar, once asked Rabbi Shmuel of Lubavitch: "Why must we hide the *afikoman*?"

The Rebbe replied: "Because it says in the Haggadah (in reference to the *afikoman*): *tzafun* (which means 'hidden')."

Rabbi Shalom was not satisfied with this reply, so the Rebbe explained:

"The *afikoman* gives us the strength to eradicate that which is hidden in the heart of man, namely the evil inclination. As the prophet says (Joel 2:20), *I will distance the* tzafoni *from upon you…*—alluding to the evil inclination."

The Rebbe explained further that the evil inclination is not subdued by reason but with firmness, by the firm resolution that "what should not be done must not be done, and what must be done, must be done."

The Hebrew word for taste and reason is identical (*taam*). The *afikoman*, which is not tasty, represents that which transcends reason, i.e., the steely firmness that banishes the hidden one (*Rabbi Yosef Yitzchak of Lubavitch*).[346]

ברך
Beirach

בְּרֵךְ וְאח"כ מוֹזְגִין כּוֹס שְׁלִישִׁי וְאוֹמֵר עָלָיו בהמ"ז.

The third cup is poured, and the Blessing After Meals is recited. An additional cup, the "Cup of Elijah," is also filled.

שִׁיר הַמַּעֲלוֹת, בְּשׁוּב יְיָ אֶת שִׁיבַת צִיּוֹן, הָיִינוּ כְּחֹלְמִים. אָז יִמָּלֵא שְׂחוֹק פִּינוּ וּלְשׁוֹנֵנוּ רִנָּה, אָז יֹאמְרוּ בַגּוֹיִם, הִגְדִּיל יְיָ לַעֲשׂוֹת עִם אֵלֶּה. הִגְדִּיל יְיָ לַעֲשׂוֹת עִמָּנוּ, הָיִינוּ שְׂמֵחִים. שׁוּבָה יְיָ אֶת שְׁבִיתֵנוּ, כַּאֲפִיקִים בַּנֶּגֶב. הַזֹּרְעִים בְּדִמְעָה, בְּרִנָּה יִקְצֹרוּ. הָלוֹךְ יֵלֵךְ וּבָכֹה נֹשֵׂא מֶשֶׁךְ הַזָּרַע, בֹּא יָבֹא בְרִנָּה נֹשֵׂא אֲלֻמֹּתָיו.

לִבְנֵי קֹרַח מִזְמוֹר שִׁיר, יְסוּדָתוֹ בְּהַרְרֵי קֹדֶשׁ. אֹהֵב יְיָ שַׁעֲרֵי צִיּוֹן, מִכֹּל מִשְׁכְּנוֹת יַעֲקֹב. נִכְבָּדוֹת מְדֻבָּר בָּךְ, עִיר הָאֱלֹהִים סֶלָה. אַזְכִּיר רַהַב וּבָבֶל לְיֹדְעָי, הִנֵּה פְלֶשֶׁת וְצוֹר עִם כּוּשׁ, זֶה יֻלַּד שָׁם. וּלְצִיּוֹן יֵאָמַר אִישׁ וְאִישׁ יֻלַּד בָּהּ, וְהוּא יְכוֹנְנֶהָ עֶלְיוֹן. יְיָ יִסְפֹּר בִּכְתוֹב עַמִּים, זֶה יֻלַּד שָׁם סֶלָה. וְשָׁרִים כְּחֹלְלִים, כָּל מַעְיָנַי בָּךְ.

אֲבָרְכָה אֶת יְיָ בְּכָל עֵת, תָּמִיד תְּהִלָּתוֹ בְּפִי. סוֹף דָּבָר הַכֹּל נִשְׁמָע, אֶת הָאֱלֹהִים יְרָא וְאֶת מִצְוֹתָיו שְׁמוֹר כִּי זֶה כָּל הָאָדָם. תְּהִלַּת יְיָ יְדַבֶּר פִּי וִיבָרֵךְ כָּל בָּשָׂר שֵׁם קָדְשׁוֹ לְעוֹלָם וָעֶד. וַאֲנַחְנוּ נְבָרֵךְ יָהּ מֵעַתָּה וְעַד עוֹלָם הַלְלוּיָהּ.

זֶה חֵלֶק אָדָם רָשָׁע מֵאֱלֹהִים וְנַחֲלַת אִמְרוֹ מֵאֵל.

Rinse the fingertips (but do not pass them over the lips as during the rest of the year), then recite the following:

וַיְדַבֵּר אֵלַי זֶה הַשֻּׁלְחָן אֲשֶׁר לִפְנֵי יְיָ.

Avoteinu Beyadeinu, vol. 2, p. 392). There are several customs as to when this cup should be poured. Some do so prior to the Seder, others before saying *Pour out Your wrath*, etc. It is now Chabad custom to do so before the Blessing After Meals (see *Otzar Minhagei Chabad*).

Chasidus We pour Elijah's Cup at *this* point in the Seder because Elijah is the harbinger of the future redemption, the theme of the latter part of the Seder.

(Elijah so thoroughly refined his body that upon his passing he was able to retain his physical form—it rose to heaven and did not need to be buried. Elijah is therefore identified with the Messianic age, a time when our physical being will be completely refined and capable of apprehending Godliness.)

This explains why the custom to pour Elijah's Cup gained widespread observance in the relatively recent past. For the belief in and yearning for the future redemption *intensifies* as we move closer to that time (*The Rebbe*).[347]

ᴖ Beirach: Blessing After Meals ᴗ

The third cup is poured, and the Blessing After Meals is recited. An additional cup, the "Cup of Elijah," is also filled.

A Song of Ascents. When God will return the exiles of Zion, we will have been like dreamers. Then our mouth will be filled with laughter, and our tongue with joyous song. Then will they say among the nations, "God has done great things for these." God has done great things for us; we were joyful. God, return our exiles as streams in the Negev. Those who sow in tears will reap with joyous song. He goes along weeping, carrying the bag of seed; he will surely come [back] with joyous song, carrying his sheaves.

A Psalm by the sons of Korach, a song whose foundation is in the holy mountains. God loves the gates of Zion more than all the dwelling places of Jacob. Glorious things are spoken of you, O city of God. I will make mention of Rahab and Babylon unto those that know me; behold Philistia and Tyre, as well as Cush, "This one was born there." But of Zion it will be said, "This man and that man was born there," and He, the Most High, will establish it. God will count the register of the nations, "This one was born there." Selah. Singers and dancers alike [will chant], "All my inner thoughts are of you."

I will bless God at all times; His praise is always in my mouth. The ultimate conclusion, all having been heard: fear God and observe His commandments, for this is the whole of man. My mouth will utter the praise of God, and all flesh shall bless His holy Name forever and ever. And we will bless God from now and forever. *Halleluyah*—praise God!

This is the portion of a wicked man from God, and the heritage assigned to him by God.

Rinse the fingertips (but do not pass them over the lips as during the rest of the year), then recite the following:

And he said to me: This is the table that is before God.

 Notes & Insights

⸸ THE CUP OF ELIJAH ⸸

The custom to pour the "Cup of Elijah" is a relatively recent one. One of the first to mention it is the 15th century scholar Rabbi Zelikman of Binga: "I have observed that some people pour a special cup and place it on the table and say that it is for Elijah the Prophet." After stating that he does not know the reason for the custom, Rabbi Zelikman suggests that since we hope that Elijah will appear on this night to herald the redemption, we prepare a cup for him to fulfill the mitzvah of drinking the Four Cups. (The custom is later cited in the Sefardic work *Pesach Me'ubin* as an Ashkenazic custom, which the author had adopted.) *Rabbi Moshe Chagiz* suggests that just as Elijah is charged with witnessing every circumcision, he likewise "comes to every Jewish home to witness the mitzvah of Pesach, which depends upon circumcision [since an uncircumcised person cannot partake of the Paschal offering], and he ascends to heaven to pray on our behalf, to usher in the final redemption" (see *Minhag*

Hold the cup as during Kiddush until after the blessing וּבְנֵה, page 83.

ZIMMUN—INVITATION

If there are less than three men at the Seder, continue with בָּרוּךְ אַתָּה, below. When three or more men eat together, one of them leads the rest in the blessing. When ten or more eat together, add אֱלֹהֵינוּ as indicated.

Leader:
רַבּוֹתַי מִיר וֶועלִין בֶּענְטְשִׁין.

The others respond:
יְהִי שֵׁם יְיָ מְבֹרָךְ מֵעַתָּה וְעַד עוֹלָם.

The leader repeats the response and continues:
יְהִי שֵׁם יְיָ מְבֹרָךְ מֵעַתָּה וְעַד עוֹלָם.
בִּרְשׁוּת מָרָנָן וְרַבָּנָן וְרַבּוֹתַי נְבָרֵךְ (אֱלֹהֵינוּ) שֶׁאָכַלְנוּ מִשֶּׁלּוֹ.

The others (who have eaten) respond:
בָּרוּךְ (אֱלֹהֵינוּ) שֶׁאָכַלְנוּ מִשֶּׁלּוֹ וּבְטוּבוֹ חָיִינוּ.

The leader repeats:
בָּרוּךְ (אֱלֹהֵינוּ) שֶׁאָכַלְנוּ מִשֶּׁלּוֹ וּבְטוּבוֹ חָיִינוּ.

The leader concludes each blessing aloud, and the others respond אָמֵן.

בָּרוּךְ אַתָּה יְיָ אֱלֹהֵינוּ מֶלֶךְ הָעוֹלָם, הַזָּן אֶת הָעוֹלָם כֻּלּוֹ בְּטוּבוֹ בְּחֵן בְּחֶסֶד וּבְרַחֲמִים הוּא נוֹתֵן לֶחֶם לְכָל בָּשָׂר כִּי לְעוֹלָם חַסְדּוֹ. וּבְטוּבוֹ הַגָּדוֹל עִמָּנוּ תָּמִיד לֹא חָסַר לָנוּ וְאַל יֶחְסַר לָנוּ מָזוֹן לְעוֹלָם וָעֶד. בַּעֲבוּר שְׁמוֹ הַגָּדוֹל כִּי הוּא אֵל זָן וּמְפַרְנֵס לַכֹּל וּמֵטִיב לַכֹּל וּמֵכִין מָזוֹן לְכָל בְּרִיּוֹתָיו אֲשֶׁר בָּרָא, כָּאָמוּר: פּוֹתֵחַ אֶת יָדֶךָ וּמַשְׂבִּיעַ לְכָל חַי רָצוֹן. בָּרוּךְ אַתָּה יְיָ, הַזָּן אֶת הַכֹּל.

נוֹדֶה לְךָ יְיָ אֱלֹהֵינוּ עַל שֶׁהִנְחַלְתָּ לַאֲבוֹתֵינוּ אֶרֶץ חֶמְדָּה טוֹבָה וּרְחָבָה וְעַל שֶׁהוֹצֵאתָנוּ יְיָ אֱלֹהֵינוּ מֵאֶרֶץ מִצְרַיִם וּפְדִיתָנוּ מִבֵּית עֲבָדִים וְעַל בְּרִיתְךָ שֶׁחָתַמְתָּ בִּבְשָׂרֵנוּ וְעַל תּוֹרָתְךָ שֶׁלִּמַּדְתָּנוּ וְעַל חֻקֶּיךָ שֶׁהוֹדַעְתָּנוּ וְעַל חַיִּים חֵן וָחֶסֶד שֶׁחוֹנַנְתָּנוּ וְעַל אֲכִילַת מָזוֹן שָׁאַתָּה זָן וּמְפַרְנֵס אוֹתָנוּ תָּמִיד בְּכָל יוֹם וּבְכָל עֵת וּבְכָל שָׁעָה.

Hold the cup as during Kiddush until after the blessing *Rebuild*, page 83.

ZIMMUN—INVITATION

If there are less than three men at the Seder, continue with *Blessed are You*, below. When three or more men eat together, one of them leads the rest in the blessing. When ten or more eat together, add (*our God*) as indicated.

Leader:
Gentlemen, let us say the Blessings.

The others respond:
May the Name of God be blessed from now and to all eternity.

The leader repeats the response and continues:
With your permission, esteemed gentlemen,
let us bless Him (*our God*) of whose bounty we have eaten.

The others respond:
Blessed be He (*our God*) of whose bounty we have
eaten and by whose goodness we live.

[The leader repeats this response.]

The leader concludes each blessing aloud, and the others respond "Amen."

Blessed are You, God, our God, King of the universe, who, in His goodness, feeds the whole world with grace, with kindness and with mercy. He gives food to all flesh, for His kindness is everlasting. Through His great goodness to us, continuously, we are not lacking, and may we never lack food, for the sake of His great Name. For He is a [benevolent] God who feeds and sustains all, does good to all, and prepares food for all His creatures whom He has created, as it is written: "You open Your hand and satisfy the desire of every living thing." Blessed are You, God, who provides food for all.

We thank You, God, our God, for having given as a heritage to our fathers a precious, good and spacious land; for having brought us out, God our God, from the land of Egypt, and redeemed us from the house of slaves; for Your covenant which You have sealed in our flesh; for Your Torah which You have taught us; for Your statutes which You have made known to us; for the life, favor and kindness which You have graciously bestowed upon us; and for the food we eat with which You constantly feed and sustain us every day, at all times and at every hour.

וְעַל הַכּל יְיָ אֱלֹהֵינוּ אֲנַחְנוּ מוֹדִים לָךְ וּמְבָרְכִים אוֹתָךְ יִתְבָּרַךְ שִׁמְךָ בְּפִי כָּל חַי תָּמִיד לְעוֹלָם וָעֶד, כַּכָּתוּב: וְאָכַלְתָּ וְשָׂבָעְתָּ וּבֵרַכְתָּ אֶת יְיָ אֱלֹהֶיךָ עַל הָאָרֶץ הַטּבָה אֲשֶׁר נָתַן לָךְ. בָּרוּךְ אַתָּה יְיָ, עַל הָאָרֶץ וְעַל הַמָּזוֹן.

רַחֵם יְיָ אֱלֹהֵינוּ עַל יִשְׂרָאֵל עַמֶּךָ וְעַל יְרוּשָׁלַיִם עִירֶךָ וְעַל צִיּוֹן מִשְׁכַּן כְּבוֹדֶךָ וְעַל מַלְכוּת בֵּית דָּוִד מְשִׁיחֶךָ וְעַל הַבַּיִת הַגָּדוֹל וְהַקָּדוֹשׁ שֶׁנִּקְרָא שִׁמְךָ עָלָיו. אֱלֹהֵינוּ אָבִינוּ רוֹעֵנוּ זוֹנֵנוּ פַּרְנְסֵנוּ וְכַלְכְּלֵנוּ וְהַרְוִיחֵנוּ וְהַרְוַח לָנוּ יְיָ אֱלֹהֵינוּ מְהֵרָה מִכָּל צָרוֹתֵינוּ. וְנָא אַל תַּצְרִיכֵנוּ יְיָ אֱלֹהֵינוּ, לֹא לִידֵי מַתְּנַת בָּשָׂר וָדָם וְלֹא לִידֵי הַלְוָאָתָם כִּי אִם לְיָדְךָ הַמְּלֵאָה הַפְּתוּחָה הַקְּדוֹשָׁה וְהָרְחָבָה שֶׁלֹּא נֵבוֹשׁ וְלֹא נִכָּלֵם לְעוֹלָם וָעֶד:

On Friday night, add this paragraph:

רְצֵה וְהַחֲלִיצֵנוּ יְיָ אֱלֹהֵינוּ בְּמִצְוֹתֶיךָ וּבְמִצְוַת יוֹם הַשְּׁבִיעִי הַשַּׁבָּת הַגָּדוֹל וְהַקָּדוֹשׁ הַזֶּה כִּי יוֹם זֶה גָּדוֹל וְקָדוֹשׁ הוּא לְפָנֶיךָ, לִשְׁבָּת בּוֹ וְלָנוּחַ בּוֹ בְּאַהֲבָה כְּמִצְוַת רְצוֹנֶךָ, וּבִרְצוֹנְךָ הָנִיחַ לָנוּ יְיָ אֱלֹהֵינוּ שֶׁלֹּא תְהֵא צָרָה וְיָגוֹן וַאֲנָחָה בְּיוֹם מְנוּחָתֵנוּ, וְהַרְאֵנוּ יְיָ אֱלֹהֵינוּ בְּנֶחָמַת צִיּוֹן עִירֶךָ, וּבְבִנְיַן יְרוּשָׁלַיִם עִיר קָדְשֶׁךָ, כִּי אַתָּה הוּא בַּעַל הַיְשׁוּעוֹת וּבַעַל הַנֶּחָמוֹת.

The leader says the phrases from זָכְרֵנוּ to טוֹבִים aloud, and the others respond אָמֵן as indicated.

אֱלֹהֵינוּ וֵאלֹהֵי אֲבוֹתֵינוּ, יַעֲלֶה וְיָבוֹא וְיַגִּיעַ, וְיֵרָאֶה וְיֵרָצֶה וְיִשָּׁמַע, וְיִפָּקֵד וְיִזָּכֵר זִכְרוֹנֵנוּ וּפִקְדוֹנֵנוּ, וְזִכְרוֹן אֲבוֹתֵינוּ, וְזִכְרוֹן מָשִׁיחַ בֶּן דָּוִד עַבְדֶּךָ, וְזִכְרוֹן יְרוּשָׁלַיִם עִיר קָדְשֶׁךָ, וְזִכְרוֹן כָּל עַמְּךָ בֵּית יִשְׂרָאֵל לְפָנֶיךָ, לִפְלֵיטָה לְטוֹבָה, לְחֵן וּלְחֶסֶד וּלְרַחֲמִים וּלְחַיִּים טוֹבִים

For all this, God, our God, we thank You and bless You. May Your Name be blessed by the mouth of every living being, constantly and forever. As it is written: "When you have eaten and are satiated, you shall bless God, your God, for the good land which He has given you." Blessed are You, God, for the land and for the food.

Have mercy, God, our God, upon Israel Your people, upon Jerusalem Your city, upon Zion the abode of Your glory, upon the kingship of the house of David Your anointed, and upon the great and holy House which is called by Your Name. Our God, our Father, our Shepherd, feed us, sustain us, nourish us and give us comfort; and speedily, God, our God, grant us relief from all our afflictions. God, our God, please do not make us dependent upon the gifts of mortal men nor upon their loans, but only upon Your full, open, holy and generous hand, that we may not be shamed or disgraced forever and ever.

On Friday night, add this paragraph:

May it please You, God, our God, to strengthen us through Your commandments, and through the precept of the Seventh Day, this great and holy Shabbat. For this day is great and holy before You, to refrain from work and to rest thereon with love, in accordance with the commandment of Your will. In Your will, God, our God, bestow upon us tranquility, that there shall be no trouble, sadness or grief on the day of our rest. God, our God, let us see the consolation of Zion Your city, and the rebuilding of Jerusalem Your holy city, for You are the Master of [all] salvations and the Master of [all] consolations.

The leader says the phrases from *Remember us to good life* aloud, and the others respond Amen as indicated.

Our God and God of our fathers, may there ascend, come and reach, be seen, accepted and heard, recalled and remembered before You, the remembrance and recollection of us, the remembrance of our fathers, the remembrance of Moshiach, the son of David Your servant, the remembrance of Jerusalem Your holy city, and the remembrance of Your entire people, the House of Israel, for deliverance, well-being, grace, kindness,

וּלְשָׁלוֹם, בְּיוֹם חַג הַמַּצּוֹת הַזֶּה, בְּיוֹם טוֹב מִקְרָא קֹדֶשׁ הַזֶּה, זָכְרֵנוּ יְיָ אֱלֹהֵינוּ בּוֹ לְטוֹבָה (אָמֵן), וּפָקְדֵנוּ בּוֹ לִבְרָכָה (אָמֵן), וְהוֹשִׁיעֵנוּ בּוֹ לְחַיִּים טוֹבִים (אָמֵן), וּבִדְבַר יְשׁוּעָה וְרַחֲמִים, חוּס וְחָנֵּנוּ, וְרַחֵם עָלֵינוּ וְהוֹשִׁיעֵנוּ, כִּי אֵלֶיךָ עֵינֵינוּ, כִּי אֵל מֶלֶךְ חַנּוּן וְרַחוּם אָתָּה.

וּבְנֵה יְרוּשָׁלַיִם עִיר הַקֹּדֶשׁ בִּמְהֵרָה בְיָמֵינוּ. בָּרוּךְ אַתָּה יְיָ, בּוֹנֵה בְרַחֲמָיו יְרוּשָׁלָיִם. אָמֵן.

Place the cup on the table.

בָּרוּךְ אַתָּה יְיָ, אֱלֹהֵינוּ מֶלֶךְ הָעוֹלָם, הָאֵל, אָבִינוּ מַלְכֵּנוּ, אַדִּירֵנוּ בּוֹרְאֵנוּ גּוֹאֲלֵנוּ יוֹצְרֵנוּ, קְדוֹשֵׁנוּ קְדוֹשׁ יַעֲקֹב, רוֹעֵנוּ רוֹעֵה יִשְׂרָאֵל הַמֶּלֶךְ הַטּוֹב וְהַמֵּטִיב לַכֹּל בְּכָל יוֹם וָיוֹם, הוּא הֵטִיב לָנוּ, הוּא מֵטִיב לָנוּ, הוּא יֵיטִיב לָנוּ, הוּא גְמָלָנוּ הוּא גוֹמְלֵנוּ הוּא יִגְמְלֵנוּ לָעַד, לְחֵן וּלְחֶסֶד וּלְרַחֲמִים, וּלְרֶוַח הַצָּלָה וְהַצְלָחָה, בְּרָכָה וִישׁוּעָה, נֶחָמָה פַּרְנָסָה וְכַלְכָּלָה וְרַחֲמִים וְחַיִּים וְשָׁלוֹם וְכָל טוֹב וּמִכָּל טוּב לְעוֹלָם אַל יְחַסְּרֵנוּ. הָרַחֲמָן הוּא יִמְלוֹךְ עָלֵינוּ לְעוֹלָם וָעֶד. הָרַחֲמָן הוּא יִתְבָּרַךְ בַּשָּׁמַיִם וּבָאָרֶץ. הָרַחֲמָן הוּא יִשְׁתַּבַּח לְדוֹר דּוֹרִים וְיִתְפָּאַר בָּנוּ לָעַד וּלְנֵצַח נְצָחִים וְיִתְהַדַּר בָּנוּ לָעַד וּלְעוֹלְמֵי עוֹלָמִים. הָרַחֲמָן הוּא יְפַרְנְסֵנוּ בְּכָבוֹד. הָרַחֲמָן הוּא יִשְׁבּוֹר עֹל גָּלוּת מֵעַל צַוָּארֵנוּ וְהוּא יוֹלִיכֵנוּ קוֹמְמִיּוּת לְאַרְצֵנוּ. הָרַחֲמָן הוּא יִשְׁלַח בְּרָכָה מְרֻבָּה בַּבַּיִת הַזֶּה וְעַל שֻׁלְחָן זֶה שֶׁאָכַלְנוּ עָלָיו. הָרַחֲמָן הוּא יִשְׁלַח לָנוּ אֶת אֵלִיָּהוּ הַנָּבִיא זָכוּר לַטּוֹב וִיבַשֶּׂר לָנוּ בְּשׂוֹרוֹת טוֹבוֹת יְשׁוּעוֹת וְנֶחָמוֹת. הָרַחֲמָן הוּא יְבָרֵךְ אֶת אָבִי מוֹרִי בַּעַל הַבַּיִת הַזֶּה וְאֶת אִמִּי מוֹרָתִי בַּעֲלַת הַבַּיִת הַזֶּה אוֹתָם וְאֶת

mercy, good life, and peace, on this day of the Festival of Matzot, on this Festival of holy convocation. Remember us on it, God, our God, for good (Amen); recollect us on it for blessing (Amen); help us on it for good life (Amen). With the matter of salvation and compassion, spare us and be gracious to us; have mercy upon us and deliver us; for our eyes are directed to You, for You, God, are a gracious and merciful King.

Rebuild Jerusalem the holy city speedily in our days. Blessed are You, God, who in His mercy rebuilds Jerusalem. Amen.

Place the cup on the table.

Blessed are You, God, our God, King of the universe, benevolent God, our Father, our King, our Might, our Creator, our Redeemer, our Maker, our Holy One, the Holy One of Jacob, our Shepherd, the Shepherd of Israel, the King who is good and does good to all, each and every day. He has done good for us, He does good for us, and He will do good for us; He has bestowed, He bestows, and He will forever bestow upon us grace, kindness and mercy, relief, salvation and success, blessing and help, consolation, sustenance and nourishment, compassion, life, peace and all goodness; and may He never cause us to lack any good. May the Merciful One reign over us forever and ever. May the Merciful One be blessed in heaven and on earth. May the Merciful One be praised for all generations, and be glorified in us forever and all eternity, and honored in us forever and ever. May the Merciful One sustain us with honor. May the Merciful One break the yoke of exile from our neck, and may He lead us upright to our land. May the Merciful One send abundant blessing into this house and upon this table at which we have eaten. May the Merciful One send us Elijah the prophet—may he be remembered for good—and may he bring us good tidings, salvations, and consolations. May the Merciful One bless my father, my teacher, the master of this house, and my mother, my teacher, the mistress of this house; them, their household,

בֵּיתָם וְאֶת זַרְעָם וְאֶת כָּל אֲשֶׁר לָהֶם אוֹתָנוּ וְאֶת כָּל אֲשֶׁר
לָנוּ. כְּמוֹ שֶׁבֵּרַךְ אֶת אֲבוֹתֵינוּ אַבְרָהָם יִצְחָק וְיַעֲקֹב בַּכֹּל
מִכֹּל כֹּל, כֵּן יְבָרֵךְ אוֹתָנוּ (בְּנֵי בְרִית) כֻּלָּנוּ יַחַד בִּבְרָכָה
שְׁלֵמָה וְנֹאמַר אָמֵן.

מִמָּרוֹם יְלַמְּדוּ עָלָיו וְעָלֵינוּ זְכוּת שֶׁתְּהֵא לְמִשְׁמֶרֶת
שָׁלוֹם וְנִשָּׂא בְרָכָה מֵאֵת יְיָ וּצְדָקָה מֵאֱלֹהֵי
יִשְׁעֵנוּ וְנִמְצָא חֵן וְשֵׂכֶל טוֹב בְּעֵינֵי אֱלֹהִים וְאָדָם.

On Shabbat add this paragraph:
הָרַחֲמָן הוּא יַנְחִילֵנוּ לְיוֹם שֶׁכֻּלּוֹ שַׁבָּת וּמְנוּחָה לְחַיֵּי הָעוֹלָמִים.

הָרַחֲמָן הוּא יַנְחִילֵנוּ לְיוֹם שֶׁכֻּלּוֹ טוֹב.

הָרַחֲמָן הוּא יְזַכֵּנוּ לִימוֹת הַמָּשִׁיחַ וּלְחַיֵּי הָעוֹלָם הַבָּא.
מִגְדּוֹל יְשׁוּעוֹת מַלְכּוֹ וְעֹשֶׂה חֶסֶד לִמְשִׁיחוֹ לְדָוִד
וּלְזַרְעוֹ עַד עוֹלָם. עֹשֶׂה שָׁלוֹם בִּמְרוֹמָיו הוּא יַעֲשֶׂה שָׁלוֹם
עָלֵינוּ וְעַל כָּל יִשְׂרָאֵל וְאִמְרוּ אָמֵן.

יְראוּ אֶת יְיָ קְדֹשָׁיו, כִּי אֵין מַחְסוֹר לִירֵאָיו. כְּפִירִים רָשׁוּ
וְרָעֵבוּ, וְדֹרְשֵׁי יְיָ לֹא יַחְסְרוּ כָל טוֹב. הוֹדוּ לַיְיָ כִּי
טוֹב, כִּי לְעוֹלָם חַסְדּוֹ. פּוֹתֵחַ אֶת יָדֶךָ, וּמַשְׂבִּיעַ לְכָל חַי
רָצוֹן. בָּרוּךְ הַגֶּבֶר אֲשֶׁר יִבְטַח בַּיְיָ, וְהָיָה יְיָ מִבְטַחוֹ.

ומברך על הכוס ושותה בהסיבה

Hold the cup as during Kiddush and recite the following blessing for the wine. Then
drink the entire cup (or at least most of it) without interruption while seated and
reclining on the left side.

בָּרוּךְ אַתָּה יְיָ, אֱלֹהֵינוּ מֶלֶךְ הָעוֹלָם, בּוֹרֵא פְּרִי
הַגָּפֶן.

their children, and all that is theirs; us, and all that is ours. Just as He blessed our forefathers, Abraham, Isaac and Jacob, "in everything," "from everything," with "everything," so may He bless all of us (the children of the Covenant) together with a perfect blessing, and let us say, Amen.

From On High, may there be invoked upon him and upon us such merit which will bring a safeguarding of peace. May we receive blessing from God and just kindness from the God of our salvation, and may we find grace and good understanding in the eyes of God and man.

> On Shabbat add this paragraph:
>
> **May** the Merciful One cause us to inherit that day which will be all Shabbat and rest for life everlasting.

May the Merciful One cause us to inherit that day which is all good.

May the Merciful One grant us the privilege of reaching the days of Moshiach and the life of the World to Come. He is a tower of salvation to His king, and bestows kindness upon His anointed, to David and his descendants forever. He who makes peace in His heights, may He make peace for us and for all Israel; and say, Amen.

Fear God, you His holy ones, for those who fear Him suffer no want. Young lions are in need and go hungry, but those who seek God shall not lack any good. Give thanks to God, for He is good, for His kindness is everlasting. You open Your hand and satisfy the desire of every living thing. Blessed is the man who trusts in God, and God will be his trust.

BLESSING OVER THE WINE

Hold the cup as during Kiddush and recite the following blessing for the wine. Then drink the entire cup (or at least most of it) without interruption while seated and reclining on the left side.

Blessed are You, God, our God, King of the universe, who creates the fruit of the vine.

מוזגין כוס ד' ופותחין הדלת ואומר.

- The fourth cup is poured.

- All doors between where the Seder is being conducted and the outside are opened, and the following paragraph is recited. Those sent to open the doors recite the paragraph at the front door. All others recite it while seated.

- On weeknights, it is customary to take lit candles to the front door.

שְׁפֹךְ חֲמָתְךָ אֶל הַגּוֹיִם אֲשֶׁר לֹא יְדָעוּךָ, וְעַל מַמְלָכוֹת אֲשֶׁר בְּשִׁמְךָ לֹא קָרָאוּ. כִּי אָכַל אֶת יַעֲקֹב, וְאֶת נָוֵהוּ הֵשַׁמּוּ. שְׁפָךְ עֲלֵיהֶם זַעְמֶךָ וַחֲרוֹן אַפְּךָ יַשִּׂיגֵם. תִּרְדֹּף בְּאַף וְתַשְׁמִידֵם מִתַּחַת שְׁמֵי יְיָ.

The doors are closed.
When those sent to open the doors return, continue with Hallel.

❧ OPENING THE DOOR ❧

"Although Elijah the Prophet can find his way into a Jewish home on his own, we must nevertheless go and open the doors ourselves to let him in...."

"Once, as a child, I went to open the door, which consisted of two sections. I first opened the bottom section, and then I stood on a stool to open the top section. But I still couldn't reach the top, so my father lifted me up. As I climbed down from the stool, I breathed heavily, as if tired from the exertion. My father then remarked, 'To welcome a fellow Jew into one's home—[and in this case] Elijah the Prophet—requires exertion..." *(Rabbi Yosef Yitzchak of Lubavitch).*[354]

❧ GOD'S DOORS ❧

Our Sages teach that God does whatever He commands Israel to do (*Shemot Rabbah* 30:9). That God commands us to open our doors on this night implies that He opens His "doors" as well. Generally, we must climb the ladder of spiritual advancement one step at a time. If we are not worthy, we are held back by the "doors" of the heavenly protocol. Tonight, those doors are swung wide open, allowing everyone, regardless of their spiritual caliber, to "skip over" all impediments and attain the highest levels of spiritual growth and closeness with God (*The Rebbe*).[355]

❧ HOLY THIEVES ❧

In the Russian town of Lubavitch, there were two wagon drivers, Shaul and Shlomo, who were also professional thieves. They used to say:

"On the Seder night we don't steal—even though the doors are left open. We just canvass the homes, eyeing the merchandise we'll be stealing later...."

The above story was related to us not just as a humorous anecdote but as a profound teaching: Even a thief feels the holiness of the night and cannot bring himself to commit a crime.

The hallmark of a thief is deception. To varying degrees, we are all guilty of deception—*self*-deception.

This human frailty clouds our moral vision and impedes our spiritual growth. But the Divine revelation of this night causes us to become honest and stop fooling ourselves—we cease to be "thieves" (*The Rebbe*).[356]

∿ Opening the Door ࿐

- The fourth cup is poured.

- All doors between where the Seder is being conducted and the outside are opened, and the following paragraph is recited. Those sent to open the doors recite the paragraph at the front door. All others recite it while seated.

- On weeknights, it is customary to take lit candles to the front door.

Pour out Your wrath upon the nations that do not acknowledge You, and upon the kingdoms that do not call upon Your Name. For they have devoured Jacob and laid waste his Temple. Pour out Your indignation upon them, and let the wrath of Your anger overtake them. Pursue them with anger, and destroy them from beneath the heavens of God.

The doors are closed.
When those sent to open the doors return, continue with Hallel.

Notes & Insights

❧ Celebrating the Future ☙

Until this point, the Seder focuses primarily on the first redemption, the Exodus from Egypt. This includes telling the story of the Exodus, eating the matzah and *maror*, etc. From this point on (and in a sense even from *Korech*, when we remember how things were done in the *Beit Hamikdash*) the Seder focuses also on the future redemption. This has several ramifications:

Hallel: As we have seen, the first two psalms of Hallel, which relate to the first redemption, are read before the meal. The rest of Hallel, which relates to the subsequent exiles and the future redemption, is read after the meal (see *Pesachim* 118a; *Abarbanel*).

Justice: We read the paragraph *Pour out Your wrath*, asking God to bring the redemption, which will be initiated by the execution of justice on the evildoers of the world.

Opening the Door: Tonight is *Leil Shimurim* ("Night of Watching"), a night of Divine protection, as it was in Egypt during the Exodus. Opening the door demonstrates our faith in God and our lack of fear of anything but Him. The merit of this faith helps bring the world closer to the future redemption.[348]

God also "watches over" this night as an auspicious time to initiate the future redemption.[349] By opening the doors, we welcome Elijah the Prophet, herald of the future redemption, into our homes, in the hope and belief that he will deliver his long-awaited announcement.[350] Indeed the spirit of Elijah does enter our home as a "participant" at our Seder (see *Shulchan Aruch HaRav* 480:4-5[351]).

Elijah's Cup: At this point, many have the custom to pour the Cup of Elijah the Prophet. While the first four cups relate to the four verbs used in the Torah to describe the Exodus from Egypt and the experience at Sinai, Elijah's Cup relates to a fifth verb that alludes to the future redemption: "*V'heveti*"—and I shall bring you into the Land (Exodus 6:8; *Taamei Haminhagim* citing *Toldot Esther*; see *Minhag Avoteinu Beyadeinu* ibid.).[352]

שְׁפֹךְ חֲמָתְךָ **Pour out Your wrath.** This prayer obviously is not directed towards benevolent nations, such as the United States, which has not only been a haven for Jews and Judaism but which assists us in the observance of our faith (*The Rebbe*).[353]

הלל נרצה
Hallel Nirtzah

לֹא לָנוּ, יְיָ, לֹא לָנוּ, כִּי לְשִׁמְךָ תֵּן כָּבוֹד, עַל חַסְדְּךָ עַל אֲמִתֶּךָ: לָמָּה יֹאמְרוּ הַגּוֹיִם, אַיֵּה נָא אֱלֹהֵיהֶם: וֵאלֹהֵינוּ בַשָּׁמָיִם, כֹּל אֲשֶׁר חָפֵץ עָשָׂה: עֲצַבֵּיהֶם כֶּסֶף וְזָהָב, מַעֲשֵׂה יְדֵי אָדָם: פֶּה לָהֶם וְלֹא יְדַבֵּרוּ, עֵינַיִם לָהֶם וְלֹא יִרְאוּ: אָזְנַיִם לָהֶם וְלֹא יִשְׁמָעוּ, אַף לָהֶם וְלֹא יְרִיחוּן: יְדֵיהֶם וְלֹא יְמִישׁוּן, רַגְלֵיהֶם וְלֹא יְהַלֵּכוּ, לֹא יֶהְגּוּ בִּגְרוֹנָם: כְּמוֹהֶם יִהְיוּ עֹשֵׂיהֶם, כֹּל אֲשֶׁר בֹּטֵחַ בָּהֶם: יִשְׂרָאֵל בְּטַח בַּיְיָ, עֶזְרָם וּמָגִנָּם הוּא: בֵּית אַהֲרֹן בִּטְחוּ בַיְיָ, עֶזְרָם וּמָגִנָּם הוּא: יִרְאֵי יְיָ בִּטְחוּ בַיְיָ, עֶזְרָם וּמָגִנָּם הוּא:

יְיָ זְכָרָנוּ יְבָרֵךְ, יְבָרֵךְ אֶת בֵּית יִשְׂרָאֵל, יְבָרֵךְ אֶת בֵּית אַהֲרֹן: יְבָרֵךְ יִרְאֵי יְיָ, הַקְּטַנִּים עִם הַגְּדֹלִים: יֹסֵף יְיָ עֲלֵיכֶם, עֲלֵיכֶם וְעַל בְּנֵיכֶם: בְּרוּכִים אַתֶּם לַיְיָ, עֹשֵׂה שָׁמַיִם וָאָרֶץ: הַשָּׁמַיִם שָׁמַיִם לַיְיָ, וְהָאָרֶץ נָתַן לִבְנֵי אָדָם: לֹא הַמֵּתִים יְהַלְלוּ יָהּ, וְלֹא כָּל יֹרְדֵי דוּמָה: וַאֲנַחְנוּ נְבָרֵךְ יָהּ, מֵעַתָּה וְעַד עוֹלָם, הַלְלוּיָהּ:

❧ HEAVEN AND EARTH ❧

The heavens are the heavens of God. *This can be compared to a king who decreed that citizens of Rome must not descend to Syria and citizens of Syria must not ascend to Rome. Similarly, when God created the world He decreed:* The heavens are the heavens of God, but the earth He gave to people. *But when He gave the Torah to Israel, the original decree was abolished: those below ascended on High and those on High descended below, as it is written (Exodus 19:3, 20):* God descended upon Mount Sinai...Moses ascended to God.... —Midrash Tanchuma, Va'eira 15

∼ HALLEL NIRTZAH ∽
PRAISE / ACCEPTED FAVORABLY

Not to us, God, not to us, but to Your Name give glory, for the sake of Your kindness and Your truth. Why should the nations say, "Where, now, is their God?" Our God is in heaven, He does whatever He pleases. Their idols are of silver and gold, the product of human hands: they have a mouth, but cannot speak; they have eyes, but cannot see; they have ears, but cannot hear; they have a nose, but cannot smell; their hands cannot feel; their feet cannot walk; they can make no sound with their throat. Like them should be their makers, everyone that trusts in them. Israel, trust in God! He is their help and their shield. House of Aaron, trust in God! He is their help and their shield. You who fear God, trust in God! He is their help and their shield.

God, mindful of us, will bless. He will bless the House of Israel; He will bless the House of Aaron; He will bless those who fear God, the small with the great. May God increase [blessing] upon you, upon you and upon your children. You are blessed unto God, the Maker of heaven and earth. The heavens are the heavens of God, but the earth He gave to the children of man. The dead do not praise God, nor do those that go down into the silence [of the grave]. But we will bless God, from now to eternity. *Halleluyah*—Praise God!

Notes & Insights

৪ HALLEL ৪৪

The paragraphs beginning "Not to us" through "His kindness is everlasting" on p. 89 below comprise the rest of the psalms of Hallel—Psalms 115-118. As the Mishnah states: "The Hallel is concluded over the fourth cup" (*Pesachim* 117b).

৪ ACCEPTED FAVORABLY ৪৪

The fifteenth "step" of the Seder, "Accepted Favorably," is not something we do. Rather, one who has completed all the required observances is favorably accepted by God (*Shaloh*).

It would seem more appropriate, however, for the word *Nirtzah* (Accepted Favorably) to appear at the conclusion of the whole Seder and not here.

A number of versions (*Siddur of Rabbi Shabbetai* and *Shaloh*) do indeed have it at the end (*The Rebbe's Haggadah*).

אָהַבְתִּי, כִּי יִשְׁמַע יְיָ אֶת קוֹלִי תַּחֲנוּנָי: כִּי הִטָּה אָזְנוֹ לִי, וּבְיָמַי אֶקְרָא: אֲפָפוּנִי חֶבְלֵי מָוֶת, וּמְצָרֵי שְׁאוֹל מְצָאוּנִי, צָרָה וְיָגוֹן אֶמְצָא: וּבְשֵׁם יְיָ אֶקְרָא, אָנָּה יְיָ מַלְּטָה נַפְשִׁי: חַנּוּן יְיָ וְצַדִּיק, וֵאלֹהֵינוּ מְרַחֵם: שֹׁמֵר פְּתָאִים יְיָ, דַּלּוֹתִי וְלִי יְהוֹשִׁיעַ: שׁוּבִי נַפְשִׁי לִמְנוּחָיְכִי, כִּי יְיָ גָּמַל עָלָיְכִי: כִּי חִלַּצְתָּ נַפְשִׁי מִמָּוֶת, אֶת עֵינִי מִן דִּמְעָה, אֶת רַגְלִי מִדֶּחִי: אֶתְהַלֵּךְ לִפְנֵי יְיָ, בְּאַרְצוֹת הַחַיִּים: הֶאֱמַנְתִּי כִּי אֲדַבֵּר, אֲנִי עָנִיתִי מְאֹד: אֲנִי אָמַרְתִּי בְחָפְזִי, כָּל הָאָדָם כֹּזֵב:

מָה אָשִׁיב לַיְיָ, כָּל תַּגְמוּלוֹהִי עָלָי: כּוֹס יְשׁוּעוֹת אֶשָּׂא, וּבְשֵׁם יְיָ אֶקְרָא: נְדָרַי לַיְיָ אֲשַׁלֵּם, נֶגְדָה נָּא לְכָל עַמּוֹ: יָקָר בְּעֵינֵי יְיָ, הַמָּוְתָה לַחֲסִידָיו: אָנָּה יְיָ כִּי אֲנִי עַבְדֶּךָ, אֲנִי עַבְדְּךָ בֶּן אֲמָתֶךָ, פִּתַּחְתָּ לְמוֹסֵרָי: לְךָ אֶזְבַּח זֶבַח תּוֹדָה, וּבְשֵׁם יְיָ אֶקְרָא: נְדָרַי לַיְיָ אֲשַׁלֵּם, נֶגְדָה נָּא לְכָל עַמּוֹ: בְּחַצְרוֹת בֵּית יְיָ, בְּתוֹכֵכִי יְרוּשָׁלַיִם, הַלְלוּיָהּ:

הַלְלוּ אֶת יְיָ כָּל גּוֹיִם, שַׁבְּחוּהוּ כָּל הָאֻמִּים: כִּי גָבַר עָלֵינוּ חַסְדּוֹ, וֶאֱמֶת יְיָ לְעוֹלָם, הַלְלוּיָהּ:

The four verses in larger type are recited aloud by the leader. After each verse, all others respond הוֹדוּ לַיְיָ כִּי טוֹב כִּי לְעוֹלָם חַסְדּוֹ, and then recite the subsequent verse in an undertone as indicated. (The leader recites הוֹדוּ after each of the last three verses.) When reading *Hallel* alone, omit the verses in larger type.

—Leader	הוֹדוּ לַיְיָ כִּי טוֹב, כִּי לְעוֹלָם חַסְדּוֹ:
—All Others	הוֹדוּ לַיְיָ כִּי טוֹב, כִּי לְעוֹלָם חַסְדּוֹ:
	יֹאמַר נָא יִשְׂרָאֵל, כִּי לְעוֹלָם חַסְדּוֹ:
—Leader	יֹאמַר נָא יִשְׂרָאֵל, כִּי לְעוֹלָם חַסְדּוֹ:
—All Others	הוֹדוּ לַיְיָ כִּי טוֹב, כִּי לְעוֹלָם חַסְדּוֹ:
	יֹאמְרוּ נָא בֵית אַהֲרֹן, כִּי לְעוֹלָם חַסְדּוֹ:

I love God, because He hears my voice, my prayers. For He turned His ear to me; all my days I will call [upon Him]. The pangs of death encompassed me, and the agonies of the grave came upon me, trouble and sorrow I encounter and I call upon the Name of God: "Please, God, deliver my soul!" God is gracious and just; our God is compassionate. God watches over the simpletons; I was brought low and He saved me. Return, my soul, to your rest, for God has dealt kindly with you. For You have delivered my soul from death, my eyes from tears, my foot from stumbling. I will walk before God in the lands of the living. I had faith even when I said, "I am greatly afflicted"; [even when] I said in my haste, "All men are deceitful."

What can I repay God for all His kindness to me? I will raise the cup of salvation and call upon the Name of God. I will pay my vows to God, now, in the presence of all His people. Precious in the eyes of God is the death of His pious ones. I thank you, God, for I am Your servant. I am Your servant the son of Your handmaid; You have loosened my bonds. To You I will bring an offering of thanksgiving, and I will call upon the Name of God. I will pay my vows to God, now, in the presence of all His people, in the courtyards of the House of God, in the midst of Jerusalem. *Halleluyah*—Praise God!

Praise God, all nations! Extol Him, all peoples! For His kindness was mighty over us, and the truth of God is everlasting. *Halleluyah*—Praise God!

The four verses in larger type are recited aloud by the leader. After each verse, all others respond *Give thanks to GOD, for He is good, for His kindness is everlasting,* and then recite the subsequent verse in an undertone as indicated. (The leader recites *Give thanks* after each of the last three verses.) When reading *Hallel* alone, omit the verses in larger type.

Leader— **Give thanks to GOD, for He is good, for His kindness is everlasting.**

All Others— Give thanks to GOD, for He is good, for His kindness is everlasting. Let Israel say [it], for His kindness is everlasting.

Leader— **Let Israel say [it], for His kindness is everlasting.**

All Others— Give thanks to GOD, for He is good, for His kindness is everlasting. Let the House of Aaron say [it], for His kindness is everlasting.

יֹאמְרוּ נָא בֵית אַהֲרֹן, כִּי לְעוֹלָם חַסְדּוֹ: —Leader
הוֹדוּ לַיְיָ כִּי טוֹב, כִּי לְעוֹלָם חַסְדּוֹ: —All Others
יֹאמְרוּ נָא יִרְאֵי יְיָ, כִּי לְעוֹלָם חַסְדּוֹ:

יֹאמְרוּ נָא יִרְאֵי יְיָ, כִּי לְעוֹלָם חַסְדּוֹ: —Leader
הוֹדוּ לַיְיָ כִּי טוֹב, כִּי לְעוֹלָם חַסְדּוֹ: —All Others

מִן הַמֵּצַר קָרָאתִי יָּהּ, עָנָנִי בַמֶּרְחָב יָהּ: יְיָ לִי לֹא אִירָא, מַה יַּעֲשֶׂה לִי אָדָם: יְיָ לִי בְּעֹזְרָי, וַאֲנִי אֶרְאֶה בְשֹׂנְאָי: טוֹב לַחֲסוֹת בַּיְיָ, מִבְּטֹחַ בָּאָדָם: טוֹב לַחֲסוֹת בַּיְיָ, מִבְּטֹחַ בִּנְדִיבִים: כָּל גּוֹיִם סְבָבוּנִי, בְּשֵׁם יְיָ כִּי אֲמִילַם: סַבּוּנִי גַם סְבָבוּנִי, בְּשֵׁם יְיָ כִּי אֲמִילַם: סַבּוּנִי כִדְבוֹרִים דֹּעֲכוּ כְּאֵשׁ קוֹצִים, בְּשֵׁם יְיָ כִּי אֲמִילַם: דָּחֹה דְחִיתַנִי לִנְפֹּל, וַיְיָ עֲזָרָנִי: עָזִּי וְזִמְרָת יָהּ, וַיְהִי לִי לִישׁוּעָה: קוֹל רִנָּה וִישׁוּעָה בְּאָהֳלֵי צַדִּיקִים, יְמִין יְיָ עֹשָׂה חָיִל: יְמִין יְיָ רוֹמֵמָה, יְמִין יְיָ עֹשָׂה חָיִל: לֹא אָמוּת כִּי אֶחְיֶה, וַאֲסַפֵּר מַעֲשֵׂי יָהּ: יַסֹּר יִסְּרַנִּי יָּהּ, וְלַמָּוֶת לֹא נְתָנָנִי: פִּתְחוּ לִי שַׁעֲרֵי צֶדֶק, אָבֹא בָם אוֹדֶה יָהּ: זֶה הַשַּׁעַר לַיְיָ, צַדִּיקִים יָבֹאוּ בוֹ: אוֹדְךָ כִּי עֲנִיתָנִי, וַתְּהִי לִי לִישׁוּעָה: אוֹדְךָ כִּי עֲנִיתָנִי, וַתְּהִי לִי לִישׁוּעָה: אֶבֶן מָאֲסוּ הַבּוֹנִים, הָיְתָה לְרֹאשׁ פִּנָּה: אֶבֶן מָאֲסוּ הַבּוֹנִים, הָיְתָה לְרֹאשׁ פִּנָּה: מֵאֵת יְיָ הָיְתָה זֹּאת, הִיא נִפְלָאת בְּעֵינֵינוּ: מֵאֵת יְיָ הָיְתָה זֹּאת, הִיא נִפְלָאת בְּעֵינֵינוּ: זֶה הַיּוֹם עָשָׂה יְיָ, נָגִילָה וְנִשְׂמְחָה בוֹ: זֶה הַיּוֹם עָשָׂה יְיָ, נָגִילָה וְנִשְׂמְחָה בוֹ:

Midrash אֶבֶן מָאֲסוּ הַבּוֹנִים **The stone scorned by the builders.** This refers to David, and the Jewish people in general (*Rashi; Radak*).

The Talmud applies this verse to a person who sins and repents. Such a person may be scorned by some for his past behavior. This verse tells us that those who have overcome challenges stand in a place that even the completely righteous—who have never sinned—cannot stand (*Berachot* 34b).

Leader— **Let the House of Aaron say [it], for His kindness is everlasting.**

All Others— Give thanks to GOD, for He is good, for His kindness is everlasting.

Let those who fear GOD say [it], for His kindness is everlasting.

Leader— **Let those who fear GOD say [it], for His kindness is everlasting.**

All Others— Give thanks to GOD, for He is good, for His kindness is everlasting.

Out of narrow confines I called to God; God answered me with abounding relief. God is with me, I will not fear—what can man do to me? God is with me, through my helpers, and I can face my enemies. It is better to rely on God, than to trust in man. It is better to rely on God, than to trust in nobles. All nations surround me, but I cut them down in the Name of God. They surrounded me, they encompassed me, but I cut them down in the Name of God. They surrounded me like bees, yet they are extinguished like a fire of thorns; I cut them down in the Name of God. You [my foes] pushed me again and again to fall, but God helped me. God is my strength and song, and this has been my salvation. The sound of joyous song and salvation is in the tents of the righteous: "The right hand of God performs deeds of valor. The right hand of God is exalted; the right hand of God performs deeds of valor!" I shall not die, but I shall live and relate the deeds of God. God has chastised me, but He did not give me over to death. Open for me the gates of righteousness; I will enter them and give thanks to God. This is the gate of God, the righteous will enter it. I thank You, for You have answered me, and You have been a help to me. I thank You, for You have answered me, and You have been a help to me. The stone scorned by the builders has become the main cornerstone. The stone scorned by the builders has become the main cornerstone. This was indeed from God; it is wondrous in our eyes. This was indeed from God; it is wondrous in our eyes. This day God has made; let us be glad and rejoice on it. This day God has made; let us be glad and rejoice on it.

Each of the following four lines is recited aloud by the leader,
followed by all others.

אָנָּא יְיָ הוֹשִׁיעָה נָּא:

אָנָּא יְיָ הוֹשִׁיעָה נָּא:

אָנָּא יְיָ הַצְלִיחָה נָא:

אָנָּא יְיָ הַצְלִיחָה נָא:

בָּרוּךְ הַבָּא בְּשֵׁם יְיָ, בֵּרַכְנוּכֶם מִבֵּית יְיָ: בָּרוּךְ הַבָּא בְּשֵׁם
יְיָ, בֵּרַכְנוּכֶם מִבֵּית יְיָ: אֵל יְיָ וַיָּאֶר לָנוּ, אִסְרוּ חַג
בַּעֲבֹתִים, עַד קַרְנוֹת הַמִּזְבֵּחַ: אֵל יְיָ וַיָּאֶר לָנוּ, אִסְרוּ חַג
בַּעֲבֹתִים, עַד קַרְנוֹת הַמִּזְבֵּחַ: אֵלִי אַתָּה וְאוֹדֶךָּ, אֱלֹהַי
אֲרוֹמְמֶךָּ: אֵלִי אַתָּה וְאוֹדֶךָּ, אֱלֹהַי אֲרוֹמְמֶךָּ: הוֹדוּ לַייָ כִּי
טוֹב, כִּי לְעוֹלָם חַסְדּוֹ: הוֹדוּ לַייָ כִּי טוֹב, כִּי לְעוֹלָם חַסְדּוֹ:

יְהַלְלוּךָ יְיָ אֱלֹהֵינוּ (עַל) כָּל מַעֲשֶׂיךָ, וַחֲסִידֶיךָ צַדִּיקִים
עוֹשֵׂי רְצוֹנֶךָ, וְכָל עַמְּךָ בֵּית יִשְׂרָאֵל, בְּרִנָּה
יוֹדוּ וִיבָרְכוּ, וִישַׁבְּחוּ וִיפָאֲרוּ, וִירוֹמְמוּ וְיַעֲרִיצוּ, וְיַקְדִּישׁוּ
וְיַמְלִיכוּ אֶת שִׁמְךָ מַלְכֵּנוּ. כִּי לְךָ טוֹב לְהוֹדוֹת, וּלְשִׁמְךָ
נָאֶה לְזַמֵּר, כִּי מֵעוֹלָם וְעַד עוֹלָם אַתָּה אֵל:

❧ THE STORY OF DAVID ❧

The Talmud reads the ending of Hallel as the story of David's humiliation at the hands of his brothers and his ultimate triumph, when he was anointed by Samuel.

The verses are attributed to the various characters in the story accordingly: *The stone scorned by the builders has become the main cornerstone*—this was said by David's father, Jesse. *This was indeed from God...*—David's brothers. *Blessed is he who comes in the Name of God*—Jesse, when David came in to meet Samuel. *We bless you from the House of God*—Samuel. *You are my God and I will thank You*—David. *Give thanks to God, for He is good...*—this was said by all (*Radak* from *Pesachim* 119a).

Each of the following four lines is recited aloud by the leader,
followed by all others.

We implore You, God, deliver us now.

We implore You, God, deliver us now.

We implore You, God, grant us success now.

We implore You, God, grant us success now.

Blessed is he who comes in the Name of God; we bless you from the House of God. Blessed is he who comes in the Name of God; we bless you from the House of God. God is Almighty, He gave us light; bind the festival-offering with cords until [you bring it to] the horns of the altar. God is Almighty, He gave us light; bind the festival-offering with cords until [you bring it to] the horns of the altar. You are my God and I will thank You; my God, I will exalt You. You are my God and I will thank You; my God, I will exalt You. Give thanks to God, for He is good, for His kindness is everlasting. Give thanks to God, for He is good, for His kindness is everlasting.

∽ ALL YOUR WORKS ⌒

God, our God, all Your works shall praise You; Your pious ones, the righteous who do Your will, and all Your people, the House of Israel, with joyous song will thank and bless, laud and glorify, exalt and adore, sanctify and proclaim the sovereignty of Your Name, our King. For it is good to thank You, and befitting to sing to Your Name, for from the beginning to the end of the world You are Almighty God.

 Notes & Insights

יְהַלְלוּךְ יְיָ אֱלֹהֵינוּ כָּל מַעֲשֶׂיךָ **All Your works shall praise.** The liturgy from this point until the end of the Haggadah follows the instructions of the Mishnah and Talmud (*Pesachim*, ibid.). There are various opinions on how to interpret those instructions and various versions of the liturgy. These opinions have been summarized by *Pri Megadim—Eishel Avraham*

(beginning of *Shulchan Aruch, Orach Chaim* §480).

Our version, i.e., the one chosen by Rabbi Schneur Zalman of Liadi, follows that of *Rosh* and *Tur* (as explained by *Taz*, end of *Orach Chaim* §486). This is also the opinion of *Levush, Chok Yaakov, Ba'er Heitev, Siddur Yaavetz*, and *Chayei Adam* (*The Rebbe's Haggadah*).

There are twenty-six verses in this Psalm, corresponding to the numeric equivalent of the Tetragrammaton. When saying the first ten verses, one should have in mind (but not articulate) the letter י of the Tetragrammaton; for the next five verses, have in mind the letter ה of the Tetragrammaton; for the next six verses, the letter ו of the Tetragrammaton; and for the last five verses, the second ה of the Tetragrammaton.

כִּי לְעוֹלָם חַסְדּוֹ:   **ה**וֹדוּ לַייָ כִּי טוֹב,

כִּי לְעוֹלָם חַסְדּוֹ:   הוֹדוּ לֵאלֹהֵי הָאֱלֹהִים,

כִּי לְעוֹלָם חַסְדּוֹ:   הוֹדוּ לַאֲדֹנֵי הָאֲדֹנִים,

כִּי לְעוֹלָם חַסְדּוֹ:   לְעֹשֵׂה נִפְלָאוֹת גְּדֹלוֹת לְבַדּוֹ,

כִּי לְעוֹלָם חַסְדּוֹ:   לְעֹשֵׂה הַשָּׁמַיִם בִּתְבוּנָה,

כִּי לְעוֹלָם חַסְדּוֹ:   לְרוֹקַע הָאָרֶץ עַל הַמָּיִם,

כִּי לְעוֹלָם חַסְדּוֹ:   לְעֹשֵׂה אוֹרִים גְּדֹלִים,

כִּי לְעוֹלָם חַסְדּוֹ:   אֶת הַשֶּׁמֶשׁ לְמֶמְשֶׁלֶת בַּיּוֹם,

אֶת הַיָּרֵחַ וְכוֹכָבִים לְמֶמְשְׁלוֹת בַּלָּיְלָה, כִּי לְעוֹלָם חַסְדּוֹ:

כִּי לְעוֹלָם חַסְדּוֹ:   (י)   לְמַכֵּה מִצְרַיִם בִּבְכוֹרֵיהֶם,

כִּי לְעוֹלָם חַסְדּוֹ:   וַיּוֹצֵא יִשְׂרָאֵל מִתּוֹכָם,

כִּי לְעוֹלָם חַסְדּוֹ:   בְּיָד חֲזָקָה וּבִזְרוֹעַ נְטוּיָה,

כִּי לְעוֹלָם חַסְדּוֹ:   לְגֹזֵר יַם סוּף לִגְזָרִים,

כִּי לְעוֹלָם חַסְדּוֹ:   וְהֶעֱבִיר יִשְׂרָאֵל בְּתוֹכוֹ,

Notes & Insights

❧ THE GREAT HALLEL ☙

This psalm, 136, is called "The Great Hallel" (as distinguished from the "Egyptian" Hallel—see above, p. 71a). It is so called because it describes a great and awesome feat of God, namely, that He *gives food to all flesh* (*Pesachim* 118a; see *Berachot* 4b). It contains twenty-six verses of thanksgiving, corresponding to the numeric equivalent of God's Name. Hence an additional reason for the name "The Great Hallel," since its verses praise (**hallel**) the **great** Name, as in the verse: *God is **great** and exceedingly **praised*** (Psalms 96:4; *Avudraham*).

In Kabbalistic sources, this psalm is referred to as "the great Hallel of the ministering angels" (*Siddur Shaloh—The Rebbe's Haggadah*).

ᴗ THE GREAT HALLEL ᴄ

There are twenty-six verses in this Psalm, corresponding to the numeric equivalent of the Tetragrammaton (Y-H-V-H). When saying the first ten verses, one should have in mind (but not articulate) the letter ' (YUD) of the Tetragrammaton; for the next five verses, have in mind the letter ה (HEY) of the Tetragrammaton; for the next six verses, the letter ו (VAV) of the Tetragrammaton; and for the last five verses, the second ה (HEY) of the Tetragrammaton.

Give thanks to God, for He is good,
for His kindness is everlasting;

Give thanks to the God of Gods,
for His kindness is everlasting;

Give thanks to the Lord of lords,
for His kindness is everlasting;

Who alone does great wonders,
for His kindness is everlasting;

Who made the heavens with understanding,
for His kindness is everlasting;

Who stretched out the earth above the waters,
for His kindness is everlasting;

Who made the great lights,
for His kindness is everlasting;

The sun to rule by day,
for His kindness is everlasting;

The moon and stars to rule by night,
for His kindness is everlasting;

Who struck Egypt through their firstborn,
(ְ – Yud) for His kindness is everlasting;

And brought Israel out of their midst,
for His kindness is everlasting;

With a strong hand and with an outstretched arm,
for His kindness is everlasting;

Who split the Sea of Reeds into sections,
for His kindness is everlasting;

And led Israel through it,
for His kindness is everlasting;

וַיְנַעֵר פַּרְעֹה וְחֵילוֹ בְיַם סוּף, ‏(ה)‏ כִּי לְעוֹלָם חַסְדּוֹ:

לְמוֹלִיךְ עַמּוֹ בַּמִּדְבָּר, כִּי לְעוֹלָם חַסְדּוֹ:

לְמַכֵּה מְלָכִים גְּדֹלִים, כִּי לְעוֹלָם חַסְדּוֹ:

וַיַּהֲרֹג מְלָכִים אַדִּירִים, כִּי לְעוֹלָם חַסְדּוֹ:

לְסִיחוֹן מֶלֶךְ הָאֱמֹרִי, כִּי לְעוֹלָם חַסְדּוֹ:

וּלְעוֹג מֶלֶךְ הַבָּשָׁן, כִּי לְעוֹלָם חַסְדּוֹ:

וְנָתַן אַרְצָם לְנַחֲלָה, ‏(ו)‏ כִּי לְעוֹלָם חַסְדּוֹ:

נַחֲלָה לְיִשְׂרָאֵל עַבְדּוֹ, כִּי לְעוֹלָם חַסְדּוֹ:

שֶׁבְּשִׁפְלֵנוּ זָכַר לָנוּ, כִּי לְעוֹלָם חַסְדּוֹ:

וַיִּפְרְקֵנוּ מִצָּרֵינוּ, כִּי לְעוֹלָם חַסְדּוֹ:

נֹתֵן לֶחֶם לְכָל בָּשָׂר, כִּי לְעוֹלָם חַסְדּוֹ:

הוֹדוּ לְאֵל הַשָּׁמָיִם, ‏(ה)‏ כִּי לְעוֹלָם חַסְדּוֹ:

✥ TWENTY-SIX GENERATIONS ✥

This psalm contains twenty-six occurrences of the phrase *for His kindness is everlasting*, alluding to the twenty-six generations (from Adam to Moses) during which the world existed without the merit of Torah and was sustained by God's kindnesss (*Avudraham* from *Pesachim* 118a).[357]

✥ KABBALISTIC INTENTIONS ✥

The Arizal taught that one should keep in mind the letters of God's Name while reciting this psalm, as explained in the instructions above (*Pri Etz Chaim, Shaar HaShabbat,* ch. 19).

Generally, Rabbi Schneur Zalman of Liadi did not include Kabbalistic intentions of this sort in his version of the Siddur, since such practices are not meant for the average person.

The fact that he *did* insert the letters of God's Name in his rendition of this psalm (in the prayers of Shabbat) suggests that he considered the Kabbalistic intention for this psalm to be one that everyone should practice (*The Rebbe's Haggadah*).

שֶׁבְּשִׁפְלֵנוּ זָכַר לָנוּ...וַיִּפְרְקֵנוּ מִצָּרֵינוּ...נֹתֵן לֶחֶם לְכָל בָּשָׂר *Who remembered us in our lowliness... delivered us from our oppressors...gives food to all flesh. Remembered us in our lowliness—*this refers to our redemption from the exile in Babylonia (see *Radak* as well, who explains that the prophets spoke of future events in past tense); *delivered us from our oppressors—*this refers to the Messianic redemption; *gives food to all flesh—*this alludes to the universal knowledge of God that will permeate all nations at that time (*Tola'at Yaakov*, cited in *Siddur Shaloh*).

And cast Pharaoh and his army into the Sea of Reeds,
(הַ – Hey) for His kindness is everlasting;

Who led His people through the desert,
for His kindness is everlasting;

Who struck great kings,
for His kindness is everlasting;

And slew mighty kings,
for His kindness is everlasting;

Sichon, king of the Amorites,
for His kindness is everlasting;

And Og, king of Bashan,
for His kindness is everlasting;

And gave their land as a heritage,
(וְ – Vav) for His kindness is everlasting;

A heritage to Israel, His servant,
for His kindness is everlasting;

Who remembered us in our lowliness,
for His kindness is everlasting;

And delivered us from our oppressors,
for His kindness is everlasting;

Who gives food to all flesh,
for His kindness is everlasting;

Thank the God of heaven,
(הַ – Hey) for His kindness is everlasting.

Notes & Insights

לְמוֹלִיךְ עַמּוֹ בַּמִּדְבָּר **Who led His people through the desert**. God in His kindness led them with a cloud by day and a pillar of fire at night, showing them the way and providing their needs in a barren desert (*Radak*).

לְמַכֵּה מְלָכִים גְּדֹלִים...אַדִּירִים **Who struck great...mighty kings**—i.e., the thirty-one kings who ruled Canaan and were subsequently conquered by Israel (*Metzudot*).

לְסִיחוֹן...וּלְעוֹג **Sichon...and Og**. We thank God for smiting the two kings, Sichon and Og, who attacked the Israelites on their way to the Land of Israel. They are singled out because of their awesome might (*Metzudot*).

וְנָתַן אַרְצָם לְנַחֲלָה **And gave their land as a heritage**—i.e., those of Sichon and Og, which were on the Jordan's east side, and not included in God's promise to Abraham (*Radak*).

נִשְׁמַת כָּל חַי תְּבָרֵךְ אֶת שִׁמְךָ יְיָ אֱלֹהֵינוּ, וְרוּחַ כָּל בָּשָׂר תְּפָאֵר וּתְרוֹמֵם זִכְרְךָ מַלְכֵּנוּ תָּמִיד, מִן הָעוֹלָם וְעַד הָעוֹלָם אַתָּה אֵל, וּמִבַּלְעָדֶיךָ אֵין לָנוּ מֶלֶךְ גּוֹאֵל וּמוֹשִׁיעַ, פּוֹדֶה וּמַצִּיל וּמְפַרְנֵס וְעוֹנֶה וּמְרַחֵם בְּכָל עֵת צָרָה וְצוּקָה, אֵין לָנוּ מֶלֶךְ אֶלָּא אָתָּה, אֱלֹהֵי הָרִאשׁוֹנִים וְהָאַחֲרוֹנִים. אֱלוֹהַּ כָּל בְּרִיּוֹת, אֲדוֹן כָּל תּוֹלָדוֹת, הַמְהֻלָּל בְּרֹב הַתִּשְׁבָּחוֹת, הַמְנַהֵג עוֹלָמוֹ בְּחֶסֶד וּבְרִיּוֹתָיו בְּרַחֲמִים. וַיְיָ הִנֵּה לֹא יָנוּם וְלֹא יִישָׁן, הַמְעוֹרֵר יְשֵׁנִים, וְהַמֵּקִיץ נִרְדָּמִים, וְהַמֵּשִׂיחַ אִלְּמִים, וְהַמַּתִּיר אֲסוּרִים, וְהַסּוֹמֵךְ נוֹפְלִים, וְהַזּוֹקֵף כְּפוּפִים, לְךָ לְבַדְּךָ אֲנַחְנוּ מוֹדִים. אִלּוּ פִינוּ מָלֵא שִׁירָה כַּיָּם, וּלְשׁוֹנֵנוּ רִנָּה כַּהֲמוֹן גַּלָּיו, וְשִׂפְתוֹתֵינוּ שֶׁבַח כְּמֶרְחֲבֵי רָקִיעַ, וְעֵינֵינוּ מְאִירוֹת כַּשֶּׁמֶשׁ וְכַיָּרֵחַ, וְיָדֵינוּ פְרוּשׂוֹת כְּנִשְׁרֵי שָׁמָיִם, וְרַגְלֵינוּ קַלּוֹת כָּאַיָּלוֹת, אֵין אָנוּ מַסְפִּיקִים לְהוֹדוֹת לְךָ יְיָ אֱלֹהֵינוּ וֵאלֹהֵי אֲבוֹתֵינוּ, וּלְבָרֵךְ אֶת שְׁמֶךָ עַל אַחַת מֵאֶלֶף אַלְפֵי אֲלָפִים, וְרִבֵּי רְבָבוֹת פְּעָמִים, הַטּוֹבוֹת נִסִּים וְנִפְלָאוֹת שֶׁעָשִׂיתָ עִמָּנוּ וְעִם אֲבוֹתֵינוּ מִלְּפָנִים. מִמִּצְרַיִם גְּאַלְתָּנוּ, יְיָ אֱלֹהֵינוּ, מִבֵּית עֲבָדִים פְּדִיתָנוּ, בְּרָעָב זַנְתָּנוּ, וּבְשָׂבָע כִּלְכַּלְתָּנוּ, מֵחֶרֶב הִצַּלְתָּנוּ, וּמִדֶּבֶר מִלַּטְתָּנוּ, וּמֵחֳלָיִם רָעִים וְנֶאֱמָנִים דִּלִּיתָנוּ. עַד הֵנָּה עֲזָרוּנוּ רַחֲמֶיךָ, וְלֹא עֲזָבוּנוּ חֲסָדֶיךָ, וְאַל תִּטְּשֵׁנוּ יְיָ אֱלֹהֵינוּ, לָנֶצַח. עַל כֵּן, אֵבָרִים שֶׁפִּלַּגְתָּ בָּנוּ, וְרוּחַ וּנְשָׁמָה שֶׁנָּפַחְתָּ בְּאַפֵּינוּ, וְלָשׁוֹן אֲשֶׁר שַׂמְתָּ בְּפִינוּ. הֵן הֵם: יוֹדוּ וִיבָרְכוּ וִישַׁבְּחוּ וִיפָאֲרוּ, וִירוֹמְמוּ וְיַעֲרִיצוּ, וְיַקְדִּישׁוּ וְיַמְלִיכוּ אֶת שִׁמְךָ מַלְכֵּנוּ. כִּי כָל פֶּה לְךָ יוֹדֶה, וְכָל לָשׁוֹן לְךָ תִשָּׁבַע, וְכָל עַיִן לְךָ תְצַפֶּה, וְכָל בֶּרֶךְ לְךָ תִכְרַע, וְכָל קוֹמָה לְפָנֶיךָ תִשְׁתַּחֲוֶה, וְכָל הַלְּבָבוֹת יִירָאוּךָ, וְכָל קֶרֶב

Notes & Insights

נִשְׁמַת כָּל חַי **The soul of every living being.** According to some opinions (commentary on *Siddur Kol Bo*), this prayer was composed by Shimon ben Shatach (a sage who lived during the era of the Second *Beit Hamikdash*). His name is thus alluded to in the first letters of its verses, starting from the end of the prayer:

שׁוֹכֵן עַד, מִי יִדְמֶה, עַד הֵנָּה, וְאִלּוּ פִינוּ, נִשְׁמַת

See also Zohar II:138a and *Avudraham* (*The Rebbe's Haggadah*).[358]

∾ SOUL OF EVERY LIVING BEING ๛

The soul of every living being shall bless Your Name, God, our God; and the spirit of all flesh shall always glorify and exalt Your remembrance, our King. From the beginning to the end of the world You are Almighty God; and other than You we have no King, Redeemer and Savior who delivers, rescues, sustains, answers and is merciful in every time of trouble and distress; we have no King but You. [You are] the God of the first and of the last [generations], God of all creatures, Lord of all events, who is extolled with manifold praises, who directs His world with kindness and His creatures with compassion. Behold, God neither slumbers nor sleeps. He arouses the sleepers and awakens the slumberers, gives speech to the mute, releases the bound, supports the falling, and raises up those who are bowed. To You alone we give thanks. Even if our mouths were filled with song as the sea, and our tongues with joyous singing like the multitudes of its waves, and our lips with praise like the expanse of the sky; and our eyes were shining like the sun and the moon, and our hands spread out like the eagles of heaven, and our feet swift like deer—we would still be unable to thank You, God, our God and God of our fathers, and to bless Your Name, for even one of the thousands of millions, and myriads of myriads, of favors, miracles, and wonders which You have done for us and for our fathers before us. God, our God, You have redeemed us from Egypt, You have freed us from the house of bondage, You have fed us in famine and nourished us in plenty; You have saved us from the sword and delivered us from pestilence, and raised us from evil and lasting maladies. Until now Your mercies have helped us, and Your kindnesses have not forsaken us; and do not abandon us, God our God, forever! Therefore, the limbs which You have arranged within us, and the spirit and soul which You have breathed into our nostrils, and the tongue which You have placed in our mouth—they all shall thank, bless, praise, glorify, exalt, adore, sanctify, and proclaim the sovereignty of Your Name, our King. For every mouth shall offer thanks to You, every tongue shall swear by You, every eye shall look to You, every knee shall bend to You, all who stand erect shall bow down before You, all hearts shall fear You, and

וּכְלָיוֹת יְזַמְּרוּ לִשְׁמֶךָ, כַּדָּבָר שֶׁכָּתוּב: כָּל עַצְמוֹתַי תֹּאמַרְנָה, יְיָ, מִי כָמוֹךָ, מַצִּיל עָנִי מֵחָזָק מִמֶּנּוּ, וְעָנִי וְאֶבְיוֹן מִגֹּזְלוֹ. מִי יִדְמֶה לָּךְ, וּמִי יִשְׁוֶה לָּךְ, וּמִי יַעֲרָךְ לָךְ, הָאֵל הַגָּדוֹל, הַגִּבּוֹר וְהַנּוֹרָא, אֵל עֶלְיוֹן, קֹנֵה שָׁמַיִם וָאָרֶץ. נְהַלֶּלְךָ, וּנְשַׁבֵּחֲךָ, וּנְפָאֶרְךָ, וּנְבָרֵךְ אֶת שֵׁם קָדְשֶׁךָ, כָּאָמוּר: לְדָוִד, בָּרְכִי נַפְשִׁי אֶת יְיָ, וְכָל קְרָבַי אֶת שֵׁם קָדְשׁוֹ.

הָאֵל בְּתַעֲצֻמוֹת עֻזֶּךָ, הַגָּדוֹל בִּכְבוֹד שְׁמֶךָ, הַגִּבּוֹר לָנֶצַח, וְהַנּוֹרָא בְּנוֹרְאוֹתֶיךָ, הַמֶּלֶךְ הַיּוֹשֵׁב עַל כִּסֵּא רָם וְנִשָּׂא.

שׁוֹכֵן עַד, מָרוֹם וְקָדוֹשׁ שְׁמוֹ, וְכָתוּב: רַנְּנוּ צַדִּיקִים בַּיְיָ, לַיְשָׁרִים נָאוָה תְהִלָּה. בְּפִי יְשָׁרִים תִּתְרוֹמָם, וּבְשִׂפְתֵי צַדִּיקִים תִּתְבָּרַךְ, וּבִלְשׁוֹן חֲסִידִים תִּתְקַדָּשׁ, וּבְקֶרֶב קְדוֹשִׁים תִּתְהַלָּל.

וּבְמַקְהֲלוֹת רִבְבוֹת עַמְּךָ בֵּית יִשְׂרָאֵל, בְּרִנָּה יִתְפָּאֵר שִׁמְךָ מַלְכֵּנוּ בְּכָל דּוֹר וָדוֹר. שֶׁכֵּן חוֹבַת כָּל הַיְצוּרִים, לְפָנֶיךָ יְיָ אֱלֹהֵינוּ וֵאלֹהֵי אֲבוֹתֵינוּ. לְהוֹדוֹת, לְהַלֵּל, לְשַׁבֵּחַ, לְפָאֵר, לְרוֹמֵם, לְהַדֵּר, לְבָרֵךְ, לְעַלֵּה וּלְקַלֵּם, עַל כָּל דִּבְרֵי שִׁירוֹת וְתִשְׁבְּחוֹת דָּוִד בֶּן יִשַׁי עַבְדְּךָ מְשִׁיחֶךָ.

וּבְכֵן יִשְׁתַּבַּח שִׁמְךָ לָעַד מַלְכֵּנוּ, הָאֵל, הַמֶּלֶךְ הַגָּדוֹל וְהַקָּדוֹשׁ בַּשָּׁמַיִם וּבָאָרֶץ. כִּי לְךָ נָאֶה יְיָ אֱלֹהֵינוּ וֵאלֹהֵי אֲבוֹתֵינוּ לְעוֹלָם וָעֶד. שִׁיר וּשְׁבָחָה, הַלֵּל וְזִמְרָה, עֹז וּמֶמְשָׁלָה, נֶצַח, גְּדֻלָּה וּגְבוּרָה, תְּהִלָּה וְתִפְאֶרֶת, קְדֻשָּׁה וּמַלְכוּת. בְּרָכוֹת וְהוֹדָאוֹת לְשִׁמְךָ הַגָּדוֹל וְהַקָּדוֹשׁ, וּמֵעוֹלָם עַד עוֹלָם אַתָּה אֵל. בָּרוּךְ אַתָּה יְיָ, אֵל מֶלֶךְ גָּדוֹל וּמְהֻלָּל

every innermost part shall sing praise to Your Name, as it is written: "All my bones will say, God, who is like You; You save the poor from one stronger than he, the poor and the needy from one who would rob him!" Who can be likened to You, who is equal to You, who can be compared to You, the great, mighty, awesome God, God most high, Possessor of heaven and earth! We will laud You, praise You, and glorify You, and we will bless Your holy Name, as it is written: "[A Psalm] by David; bless God, O my soul, and all that is within me, [bless] His holy Name."

You are the Almighty God in the power of Your strength; the Great in the glory of Your Name; the Mighty forever, and the Awesome in Your awesome deeds; the King who sits upon a lofty and exalted throne.

He who dwells for eternity, lofty and holy is His Name. And it is written: "Sing joyously to God, you righteous; it befits the upright to offer praise." By the mouth of the upright You are exalted; by the lips of the righteous You are blessed; by the tongue of the pious You are sanctified; and among the holy ones You are praised.

In the assemblies of the myriads of Your people, the House of Israel, Your Name, our King, shall be glorified with song in every generation. For such is the obligation of all creatures before You, God, our God and God of our fathers, to thank, to laud, to praise, to glorify, to exalt, to adore, to bless, to elevate, and to honor You, even beyond all the words of songs and praises of David son of Yishai, Your anointed servant.

And therefore may Your Name be praised forever, our King, the great and holy God and King in heaven and on earth. For to You, God, our God and God of our fathers, forever befits song and praise, laud and hymn, strength and dominion, victory, greatness and might, glory, splendor, holiness and sovereignty; blessings and thanksgivings to Your great and holy Name; from the beginning to the end of the world You are Almighty God. Blessed are You, God, Almighty God, King, great and extolled

בַּתִּשְׁבָּחוֹת, אֵל הַהוֹדָאוֹת, אֲדוֹן הַנִּפְלָאוֹת, בּוֹרֵא כָּל הַנְּשָׁמוֹת, רִבּוֹן כָּל הַמַּעֲשִׂים, הַבּוֹחֵר בְּשִׁירֵי זִמְרָה, מֶלֶךְ יָחִיד חֵי הָעוֹלָמִים.

הנוהגים לומר פזמונים אין להפסיק בהם בין ברכה זו ובין ברכת הכוס אלא מיד אחר כך יברך על כוס ד'.

Hold the cup as during Kiddush and recite the following blessing for the wine (immediately after saying the previous paragraph, without interruption). Then drink the entire cup (or at least most of it) without interruption while seated and reclining on the left side.

בָּרוּךְ אַתָּה יְיָ, אֱלֹהֵינוּ מֶלֶךְ הָעוֹלָם, בּוֹרֵא פְּרִי הַגָּפֶן. • ושותה בהסיבה.

CONCLUDING BLESSING FOR WINE

On Friday night, add the words in shaded parentheses.

בָּרוּךְ אַתָּה יְיָ, אֱלֹהֵינוּ מֶלֶךְ הָעוֹלָם, עַל הַגֶּפֶן וְעַל פְּרִי הַגֶּפֶן וְעַל תְּנוּבַת הַשָּׂדֶה וְעַל אֶרֶץ חֶמְדָּה טוֹבָה וּרְחָבָה שֶׁרָצִיתָ וְהִנְחַלְתָּ לַאֲבוֹתֵינוּ לֶאֱכֹל מִפִּרְיָהּ וְלִשְׂבּוֹעַ מִטּוּבָהּ. רַחֶם נָא יְיָ אֱלֹהֵינוּ עַל יִשְׂרָאֵל עַמֶּךָ וְעַל יְרוּשָׁלַיִם עִירֶךָ וְעַל צִיּוֹן מִשְׁכַּן כְּבוֹדֶךָ וְעַל מִזְבְּחֶךָ וְעַל הֵיכָלֶךָ, וּבְנֵה יְרוּשָׁלַיִם עִיר הַקֹּדֶשׁ בִּמְהֵרָה בְיָמֵינוּ, וְהַעֲלֵנוּ לְתוֹכָהּ וְשַׂמְּחֵנוּ בָהּ וּנְבָרֶכְךָ בִּקְדֻשָּׁה וּבְטָהֳרָה. (וּרְצֵה וְהַחֲלִיצֵנוּ בְּיוֹם הַשַּׁבָּת הַזֶּה.) וְזָכְרֵנוּ לְטוֹבָה בְּיוֹם חַג הַמַּצּוֹת הַזֶּה. כִּי אַתָּה יְיָ טוֹב וּמֵטִיב לַכֹּל וְנוֹדֶה לְּךָ עַל הָאָרֶץ וְעַל פְּרִי הַגָּפֶן. בָּרוּךְ אַתָּה יְיָ, עַל הָאָרֶץ וְעַל פְּרִי הַגָּפֶן.

If you drank other drinks besides wine or grape juice after reciting the Grace After Meals, recite the following:

בָּרוּךְ אַתָּה יְיָ, אֱלֹהֵינוּ מֶלֶךְ הָעוֹלָם, בּוֹרֵא נְפָשׁוֹת רַבּוֹת וְחֶסְרוֹנָן, עַל כָּל מַה שֶׁבָּרֵאתָ לְהַחֲיוֹת בָּהֶם נֶפֶשׁ כָּל חָי, בָּרוּךְ חֵי הָעוֹלָמִים.

in praises, God of thanksgivings, Lord of wonders, Creator of all souls, Master of all creatures, who takes pleasure in songs of praise; the only King, the Life of all worlds.

BLESSING OVER THE WINE

Hold the cup as during Kiddush and recite the following blessing for the wine (immediately after saying the previous paragraph, without interruption). Then drink the entire cup (or at least most of it) without interruption while seated and reclining on the left side.

Blessed are You, God, our God, King of the universe, who creates the fruit of the vine.

CONCLUDING BLESSING FOR WINE

On Friday night, add the words in shaded parentheses.

Blessed are You, God our God, King of the universe, for the vine and the fruit of the vine, for the produce of the field, and for the precious, good and spacious land which You have favored to give as a heritage to our fathers, to eat of its fruit and be satiated by its goodness. Have mercy, God our God, on Israel Your people, on Jerusalem Your city, on Zion the abode of Your glory, on Your altar and on Your Temple. Rebuild Jerusalem, the holy city, speedily in our days, and bring us up into it, and make us rejoice in it, and we will bless You in holiness and purity. (May it please You to strengthen us on this Shabbat day.) And remember us for good on this day of the Festival of Matzot. For You, God, are good and do good to all, and we thank You for the land and for the fruit of the vine. Blessed are You, God, for the land and for the fruit of the vine.

If you drank other drinks besides wine or grape juice after reciting the Grace After Meals, recite the following:

Blessed are You, God, our God, King of the universe, Who created numerous living beings and their needs, for all the things You have created with which to sustain the soul of every living being. Blessed is He who is the Life of all worlds.

Afterwards say:

לְשָׁנָה הַבָּאָה בִּירוּשָׁלָיִם.

The wine in the "Cup of Elijah" is poured back into the bottle to the singing of *Keili Attah*.

❧ AT THE REBBE'S SEDER ❧

From the notes of a chasid:

"*The Rebbe would pour from Elijah's Cup into his cup, from his cup into the bottle, and from the bottle into his cup. From time to time he would pour from his coaster into his cup and from the coaster under Elijah's Cup into Elijah's Cup. He would repeat these enigmatic 'pourings' many, many times.*

"*All who were present during that astounding event recognized that it was no simple matter but rather an entire* avodah *[spiritual practice] unto itself....*"[361]

❧ ALL NIGHT ❧

"*When we were young, we would stay up the entire night of the first Seder. Ah! There is much [spiritual insight] to receive on this night! The gates [of Heaven] are open....*"[362]

—RABBI YOSEF YITZCHAK OF LUBAVITCH

❧ HORSES WANT STRAW ❧

A skeptic was once traveling with Rabbi Shalom DovBer of Lubavitch and questioned the Rebbe about the existence of a spiritual reality. The skeptic declared that he could not believe in what he had not seen. The Rebbe responded:

"*We are traveling now on a horse-drawn wagon. Along for the ride are three parties: the passengers, the driver, and the horses, each party with its own intentions.*

"*The passengers are hurrying to get to their destination and carry out their business there. The driver is thinking about the rubles he will earn with which he can buy provisions for Shabbat. And the horses are thinking about the straw they will soon get to eat. Should we allow the horses to define the purpose of this journey?*

"*Likewise, does the fact that 'horses' can only think of 'straw' negate the existence of the spiritual reality?*"

Like the skeptic of the above tale, we too fail to see a higher reality. We think of the present world as an end unto itself. We fail to see that it is purely a means toward laying the groundwork for the fulfillment of God's plan for Creation, which will come to its fruition in the Days of Moshiach. But does our fixation on "straw" negate the true purpose of our journey?

When Rabbi Schneur Zalman of Liadi was libeled by the opponents of Chasidism, the Czarina sent a minister named Derzhavin, a virulent Jew-hater, to investigate Rabbi Schneur Zalman. Derzhavin reported as follows: "The Chasidim believe in the concept of Moshiach and believe he will arrive soon. Since they will then need huge sums of money to rebuild their Temple, Rabbi Schneur Zalman is collecting money now for this purpose." (The truth was that Rabbi Schneur Zalman did collect money to send to the Holy Land to support the Jewish communities there.)

This story demonstrates that even a Jew-hating Gentile perceives that a chasid is one who believes in the concept of Moshiach and that he will come soon, and the chasid is already preparing himself for that time (*The Rebbe*).[363]

❧ THE SEDER NEVER ENDS ❧

The Rebbe—the Alter Rebbe—did not insert in the Siddur, at the end of the Haggadah, the phrase "The Order of Pesach is now completed." For with Chabad, Pesach does not end, but extends continuously![364]

—RABBI YOSEF YITZCHAK OF LUBAVITCH

Afterwards say:

NEXT YEAR IN JERUSALEM!

The wine in the "Cup of Elijah" is poured back into the bottle to the singing of *Keili Attah*.

❧ YOM KIPPUR & PESACH ❧

There are two times during the year that we utter this prayer: at the conclusion of the Seder and the conclusion of Yom Kippur. The commonality between the two is that both are days when the forces of judgment are not given a voice (see *Pesachim* 109b; *Yoma* 20a).

The Seder night in fact transcends Yom Kippur in this aspect, since only the Seder night is referred to as a "Night of Watching." Even while one is asleep, one need not fear any danger from the forces of judgment, since it is a night of Divine protection.

At such a time, we certainly have the capacity to declare and bring about that "Next year in Jerusalem!"

❧ ONCE IS ENOUGH ❧

According to *Siddur Shaloh*, one should recite this declaration three times, since in Jewish tradition a threefold repetition creates permanence, a "*chazakah*."

Rabbi Schneur Zalman of Liadi, however, did not include this instruction in his Haggadah and so our custom is to recite "Next Year in Jerusalem!" only once (as per *Siddur HaArizal* and *Yaavetz*).

Rabbi Schneur Zalman's view emphasizes that our power tonight is so great that even without the benefit of a *chazakah* we can bring about that "Next year in Jerusalem" (*The Rebbe*).[359]

❧ POURING BACK THE CUP OF ELIJAH ❧

Our custom is not to drink the fifth cup, since it embodies a sublime Divine energy of the future, one we cannot internalize at this time in history. We can only gaze upon it, and even so we do not truly "see" it.

Instead, in Chabad tradition, we return the wine to the bottle in a ritual that is charged with meaning. Traditionally, the Rebbe would not only pour the wine into the Cup of Elijah but also return the wine to the bottle, instead of leaving this task to a waiter. A special melody, *Keili Attah*, one of the ten songs composed by Rabbi Schneur Zalman, is sung during this ritual.

Pouring the wine *into* the Cup of Elijah and later returning it to the bottle represent two stages in the redemption:

First Stage

We pour the wine into the cup prior to the recitation of "Pour your wrath upon the nations," suggesting a time when the redemption is evidently not complete, since there are nations that have not yet been reformed and still deserve heavenly wrath.

Pouring the wine into the cup represents the idea that, even before the redemption is complete, we will already experience the energy of the future redemption, but we will be unable to internalize this energy.

Second Stage

By contrast, returning the wine to the bottle at the end of the Seder, after reciting "Next year in Jerusalem," represents the time when the redemption is complete: At the culmination of the great "Seder" of history, the infinity of God (embodied by the wine in the Cup of Elijah) will be internalized.

This is symbolized by the fact that we return the wine to the bottle [from which we will subsequently drink], meaning that the lofty energy embodied in the wine is being "contained" and internalized (*The Rebbe*).[360]

APPENDICES

NOTES

קערה
The Seder Plate

1. See *Sefer Hasichot 5704*, p. 86: "All the commentators agree that the Haggadah was composed in a manner of allusion…even the *peshat* of the Haggadah is in the manner of *remez*…."

2. *Torah Or, Vayakhel* 89c. This explains the custom to dip the matzah in water on the eighth day of Pesach (even though there is the remote chance that some flour had not been baked and would thus become *chametz*). This is because on the eighth day we have already experienced one week of transformation, and are therefore capable of engaging with something that is not actual *chametz* but is remotely associated with it (*The Rebbe's Haggadah*).

3. Several reasons have been given for this custom, among them: 1) Having the *chametz* reminds us to fulfill the mitzvah of nullifying and burning the *chametz* the next day. 2) Finding *chametz* from time to time encourages us to keep searching (*Chok Yaakov; The Rebbe's Haggadah*).

4. The Rebbe often discussed this theme. See, for example, *Torat Menachem—Hitvaaduyot*, vol. 31, p. 44.

5. See, for example, the Mishnah, *Bikkurim* 1:4; see, however, commentary of Rambam ad loc.

6. This may explain why we continue to recline today—even though reclining no longer seems to be a royal custom—since we are not seeking only to adopt royal customs but rather to reenact what we experienced during the Exodus.

7. Reclining is not done to the right, since the right hand has to be free for eating. Furthermore, eating while reclining to the right creates a choking hazard (*Pesachim* 108a, as explained by *Rashbam*). Therefore, a left-handed person should also lean to the left (*Shulchan Aruch HaRav* 472:9).

8. *The Rebbe's Haggadah; Torat Menachem—Reshimat Hayoman*, p. 419.

9. Cf. *Rosh Hashanah* 11a.

10. It is forbidden to offer sacrifices anywhere outside the Temple in Jerusalem. It is therefore important to emphasize that the *zeroa* merely *commemorates* the Paschal lamb. Hence the custom to use a bone from the neck of a *bird* and not to eat from the *zeroa*, thus eliminating any comparison to the Paschal lamb. In this vein, Rabbi Yosef Yitzchak of Lubavitch would remove nearly all the meat from the bird neck (*The Rebbe's Haggadah*).

11. Rav Sherira Gaon states that some add a third cooked item to the Seder plate: meat, egg, and fish. The meat and egg correspond to Moses and Aaron, the fish to Miriam (*Maaseh Rokeach* 94:17).

12. In the context of the Exodus, the Torah refers to God's *zeroa netuyah*, "outstretched arm" (Exodus 6:6). As we shall see later in the Haggadah (paragraph beginning *With a Strong Hand*), this refers to the plague of the firstborn.

13. This teaching does not appear in current editions of the *Jerusalem Talmud*. Meiri on *Pesachim,* ibid. cites an identical teaching in the name of the *Midrash*.

Regarding our custom to use the neck of a bird instead of a shank bone, see footnote 10 above and *Minhag Yisrael Torah*, vol. 2, p. 279.

Some suggest that the egg is taken as a symbol of mourning for the destruction of the Temple. This explanation, however, begs further consideration. For it is clear from the Mishnah (*Pesachim* 114a) and the Jerusalem Talmud (*Pesachim* 10:3) that even *while* the Temple stood, those who were outside Jerusalem, and therefore could not offer the two offerings, had two dishes to remember the offerings. [See *Berachot* 19a and *Rashi* ad loc. as well as *Yoma* 19b for other examples of a "remembrance" for the Temple during Temple days.] Certainly in that era they would have no need to mourn the destruction which had not yet occurred. One would be forced to say that for hundreds of years they used some other dish to commemorate the Chagigah offering and after the destruction of the Temple the custom was changed (*The Rebbe's Haggadah*).

14. See Proverbs 5:3-4: "Honey drips from the lips of the temptress...but her end is bitter as wormwood...."

15. The names of the letters of the word *karpas* (*kaf, reish, pey, samech*)—allude to giving charity to the poor and encouraging them with soothing words: *Kaf Reish* means [fill] the palm of the poor; *Pey Samech* means, support him with the words of your mouth (*Alshich*). Additionally: Give *KeSePh* (money) to the *Reish*, the poor (*Chida*).

16. Alternatively, when reaching out to others, do so in a pleasant and loving manner: remove (*motzi*) any negative feeling, animosity (*matzah*), or condescension from your words (*Ben Ish Chai*). Like Aaron, work to remove (*motzi*) any conflict (*matzah*) from among people and bring peace between them (*Chatam Sofer*). This will rectify the dissonance you may have sown in the Heavenly spheres through your past misdeeds (*Chida*).

17. When a festival coincides with Shabbat, the Kiddush is a Biblical obligation.

18. From *plag haminchah* and on, which is one hour and a quarter "halachic" hours prior to sunset. (A halachic hour is one twelfth of the daylight hours.)

19. Others say that the custom to refer to the festival as Pesach came about in order to remember the *Beit Hamikdash* in Jerusalem where the Pesach sacrifice was offered (*Ateret Zekenim—The Rebbe's Haggdah*).

20. See *Likkutei Sichot*, vol. 32, p. 68. During a talk on Erev Pesach (*Torat Menachem—Hitvaaduyot 5750*, vol. 3, p. 50), the Rebbe mentioned that if Moshiach were to come that day, we would still be able to offer the Paschal lamb. Although we would not have time to purify ourselves, we would be allowed to offer the sacrifice, thus experiencing the *kadesh* (sanctity) before the *urechatz* (purification). See above, p. 58a.

21. *Torat Menachem—Hitvaaduyot 5750*, vol. 3, p. 50; *Likkutei Sichot*, vol. 32, p. 71.

22. *Torat Menachem—Hitvaaduyot*, ibid., p. 49.

23. Even where children are not present, the ritual is maintained, since when the Sages institute a ritual they do so without qualification (*Shulchan Aruch HaRav, Orach Chaim*, 473:15). Some suggest that we eat the vegetable now so that we should not have to say two blessings over the *maror*—*borei pri ha'adamah* and *al achilat maror*.

Doing so would be considered too much of a "celebration" of the *maror*. We therefore say the *ha'adamah* now and need only say the *al achilat* when eating the *maror* (*Rabbenu Manoach*).

24. See *Rashi* on *Sukkah* 39b, et al.

25. *Responsa, Orach Chaim* §131, end.

26. See *L'Horot Natan*, vol. 3, §24.

27. Originally, the custom was to use onions. But as people became more sensitive, potatoes were introduced. (*Otzar Minhagei Chabad*, citing *Reshimot*.)

28. Jewish law requires us to recite a blessing before and *after* eating any food that is the size of a *kezayit* or larger. But since we will soon be eating a meal and reciting the after-blessing over the meal, some authorities maintain that the latter blessing would cover the eating of the *karpas* as well (*similar* to the way it covers the after-blessing for the Kiddush.) Others maintain that the after-blessing for the meal would not cover the *karpas*. We therefore eat less than a *kezayit* thus avoiding the question altogether, since one is never required to recite an after-blessing after eating less than a *kezayit* (see *Shulchan Aruch* 473:17-18).

29. Even one who ate a *kezayit* of *karpas* and mistakenly recited an after-blessing—thus preventing his blessing over the *karpas* from covering the *maror*—would still not recite *borei pri ha'adamah* over the *maror*, in accordance with the opinion that the blessing over the *matzah* covers the *maror* (*Shulchan Aruch*, ibid.).

30. The Rebbe added that the Talmud (*Berachot* 5b) teaches that one who engages in an act of "stealing," even if justified, acquires the "taste" of stealing.

31. See *Baal Haturim* on Exodus 12:42.

The three matzot correspond to the three Patriarchs. The second matzah, which we break in half, corresponds to Isaac, our second Patriarch. Isaac is particularly associated with both redemptions, to both "halves of the matzah":

First Exodus: God told Abraham that his descendants would be strangers in a foreign land for 400 years. But in fact we remained in Egypt for only 210 years. This was in the merit of Isaac, as seen in the following *gematria*: In Psalms and elsewhere, Isaac is referred to not as Yitzchak but Yischak. Isaac gave up the letter *sin* of his name Yischak for the letter *tzaddik*, to become Yitzchak. The difference between *sin* (300) and *tzaddik* (90) is 210. By giving up the greater letter for the *tzaddik*, Isaac enabled his descendants the merit to leave Egypt after only 210 years.

Final Exodus: The Talmud relates that in the future, Isaac, more than Abraham and Jacob, will successfully advocate for the Jewish people before God, and thereby facilitate the redemption (*Shabbat* 89b). Splitting the middle matzah thus alludes to the two redemptions and Isaac's particular connection to them (*Chida*).

32. *Derashot*, vol. 2, 306b.

33. *Torat Menachem—Hitvaaduyot 5720*, vol. 2, pp. 14-16.

34. *Maharal* strongly objects to the view that we ate matzah as slaves in Egypt, since nowhere in Scripture, Mishnah, or Talmud is there any mention of this. This objection would also apply to the interpretation by *Sforno* as well (see *Under the Whip* and following note).

35. Commenting on Deuteronomy 16:3.

36. *Torat Menachem—Hitvaaduyot 5716*, vol. 2, p. 195.

37. *Torat Menachem—Hitvaaduyot 5717*, vol. 2, pp. 256-258. In Kabbalah, intellect is called a parent, since it generates and "gives birth" to emotion. Normally, the mind, through meditation, is meant to generate holy emotions, which in turn lead to holy actions. But in our state of exile, our intellect has become "consumed" by worries. According to this interpretation, the meaning of the bread of poverty "that our forefathers ate" is switched to mean the bread of affliction "that ate/consumed our fathers/intellect"!

38. *Sefer Hasichot 5705*, p. 83.

39. *Shulchan Aruch HaRav* 473:40.

40. *Likkutei Sichot*, vol. 12, p. 43. The Rebbe finds an allusion to this idea in the common Talmudic expression: "He asked and he answered [his own question]" (*Shabbat* 145a, *et al*).

41. At the Seder of Rabbi Shmuel of Lubavitch, all of his sons—and, according to one report, all of his daughters—would ask the questions (*Torat Menachem—Hitvaaduyot 5743*, vol. 3, p. 1230).

42. Ibid.

43. Their intention was to connect to and remind themselves of how they sat before their fathers during the Seder and asked the questions. And so they would say as they did during the lifetime of their fathers: "Father, I will ask you four questions…."

When the Rebbes spoke to their fathers, their fathers' presence may very well have been there. Though the average person does not seem to have this capability, he still addresses his father in a nostalgic fashion, as if his father were present (*The Rebbe*, ibid.).

44. *Sefer Hasichot 5707*, p. 104.

45. *The Rebbe's Haggadah* from *Sefer Hasichot 5704*, p. 77. The simple meaning of the verse is: "While Israel was yet a youth [in Egypt], I loved him" (*Mefarshim*). Our translation follows the Chasidic interpretation.

46. *Likkutei Sichot*, vol. 21, p. 20. See also the discourse entitled *Ki Naar Yisrael, 5666* (*Yom Tov Shel Rosh Hashanah, 5666*, ed. 1991, p. 575).

47. This interpretation is problematic, since Rambam's version of the questions (*Hilchot Chametz u'Matzah* 8:2) includes a question about reclining and the Paschal lamb, suggesting that even in Temple times they would ask about reclining.

We must say that Rambam's version of the Talmud included a question about reclining—either in the Mishnah or the Talmud. Otherwise, he could not have stated that this question was asked in Temple times without any source to substantiate his claim (*The Rebbe's Haggadah*).

48. See *Tosfot ad loc.*

49. As *Beit Yosef* points out, Rambam seems to maintain differently. Namely, that the true definition of a *teruah* was lost over time because of the length and travails of the exile.

50. It seems that even after mitzvot have been "fixed," there remains room for minor variations in custom among Jewish communities. Thus there are even various customs regarding the order of the questions of the Mah Nishtanah.

51. See *The Torah* (Kehot) on Genesis 41:43.

52. *Torat Menachem—Hitvaaduyot 5712*, vol. 2, pp. 111 ff. & 122 ff.

53. *Likkutei Sichot*, vol. 1, p. 244.

54. *Sefer Hasichot 5697*, p. 224.

55. *Pesachim* 116a.

56. According to Rav Amram Gaon, it was not **Shmuel** but **Rav** who says we should start with "We were slaves." This helps us understand why we begin with "We were slaves" and not with "In the beginning our forefathers served idols":

Shmuel was an expert in monetary law, while Rav was an expert in ritual law. Jewish law therefore follows Rav's opinion in ritual matters and Shmuel's in monetary matters. So although the author of the Haggadah included both "shames" as taught by Rav *and* Shmuel, he *begins* with the passage suggested by Rav even though it speaks of a time long after our idolatrous beginnings (*Avudraham*).

Some versions have Rava as the sage who defines "shame" as our slavery. This would also explain why we begin with slavery, since Jewish law follows Rava (*Maggid Mishneh* on Rambam, *Hilchot Chametz u'Matzah* 7:4; see *Dikdukei Sofrim* on *Pesachim ad loc.*).

57. Like the slave who says: "*I love my master…I do not wish to go free*" (Exodus 21:5).

58. Numbers 11:4-5 and 14:4.

59. *Likkutei Sichot*, vol. 17, p. 88, fn. 74.

60. See *Rashi* on Psalms 34:1.

61. *Avudraham* therefore amends the text to read "we… would have been slaves to *Egypt*" omitting the word "Pharaoh."

62. At the start of creation, God's presence was primarily focused within the physical world. With the sin of the Tree

of Knowledge, God's presence retreated from this world and continued to retreat farther and farther because of the crudeness of the subsequent generations. Then Abraham came and reversed the trend—he began to draw the Divine presence back toward this world (*Shir Hashirim Rabbah* 5:1).

63. *Torah Or, Yitro* 74a.

64. *Likkutei Sichot*, vol. 17, p. 78.

65. See *Shulchan Aruch* 481:2: "One is obligated to discuss the laws of Pesach and the Exodus and to relay the miracles and wonders that G-d did for our ancestors until one is overcome by sleep." See *Ibn Ezra* and *Chizkuni* on Exodus 12:42, who state that one should not sleep on this night.

See, however, *Maharal*, who states that the Sages did not *force* themselves to stay awake, since one must enjoy the holiday. Rather, they were so enthralled with the celebration that they had no desire to sleep.

66. This seems to imply that their students were present during the discussion (unless one will argue that they influenced their students in a spiritual manner, which did not require their immediate presence). See *Chida*, for example, who assumes that the students were elsewhere. Hence, "the students *came* and told them...." *Chida* explains that this was because the discussion included lofty secrets of the Torah that the students were not fit to hear.

Yalkut Menachem explains that this Seder occurred at a time of intense religious persecution. Perhaps the Seder was held in a cave or in a home with covered windows, so they would not be seen, and the students were stationed outside as sentries. The teachers therefore did not see when the sun arose.

67. II:38a.

68. Psalms 139:12. *Yad Eliyahu*, cited by *Chida*, asserts that this is why the Israelites were allowed to circumcise on that night, even though the Torah commands us to circumcise during the day. The Rebbe, however, in his comment on the phrase "*Koso shel Eliyahu*" states that before the giving of the Torah, the latter law did not apply, and so they were allowed to circumcise at night. This interpretation, however, only explains the *legal* justification for their night-time circumcision. The *mystical* reason for it was because spiritually that night was like day (*Sichot Kodesh 5725*, vol. 2, p. 34).

69. This is one of way of explaining why they therefore were oblivious to the arrival of morning, since for them it had been light all night. In this vein, the students were declaring that the teachers had finally succeeded in enlightening their students and bringing them to a higher level of Divine consciousness. The Divine reality was illuminated for them—now, they too saw the "light of morning," which had been apparent to the teachers all night (*Sichot Kodesh 5725*, vol. 2, pp. 32-34).

70. It was Rabbi Akiva who was able to see the future good within the images of the destruction—see *Makkot* 24b.

71. This seems forced, however, since these were all lofty souls, who were naturally in tune with the spiritual changes that occur along with the passage of time and the attendant *halachic* requirements (*Likkutei Sichot*, vol. 2, p. 539). See also *Gevurot Yisrael* (Kozhnitz) who concludes that despite their usual intuition, this case was different since "they were completely overwhelmed by the revelation they experienced, such that they were completely oblivious."

72. *Sefer Hasichot 5704*, p. 88. On another occasion, Rabbi Yosef Yitzchak put it this way: The masters are on the level of *Atzilut* and their students on *Beriah*. The students declared that even on their level, in *Beriah*, the morning Shema, the "higher unity" was shining (*Sefer Hasichot 5703*, p. 71).

73. *Sefer Hasichot 5752*, vol. 1, p. 246.

74. *Likkutei Sichot*, vol. 7, p. 123.

75. See *Tanya*, ch. 47, as to why these two independent *mitzvot* are combined.

76. See *Rashbatz, Abarbanel, Shaloh, Tzelach, et al.; Tosfot Anshei Shem* on *Berachot* 1:5; *Sefer Hasichot 5752*, p. 247, fn. 32.

In this view, according to the Sages, *days of your life* implies both days and nights. No additional word is necessary to include the nights. To Ben Zoma, *days of your life* implies only the days. The word *all* is therefore required to include the nights.

On the other hand, to Ben Zoma, *days of your life* includes both this world and the Messianic age. To the Sages, it implies only this world. They therefore require the word *all* to include the Days of Moshiach.

77. Some commentators maintain that the Sages disagree with Ben Zoma and do not require the mentioning of the Exodus at night (see Mishnah commentators and *Pri Etz Chaim, Shaar Chag Hamatzot,* chapter 6). Likewise, some commentators maintain that Ben Zoma does not require mentioning the Exodus in the days of Moshiach (see *Rashbatz* and others; see also *Torah Shleimah*, vol. 12, *miluim*, #3).

78. See *Chasdei David* on *Tosefta Berachot* 1:5.

79. See *Berachot* 28b. Rabbi Elazar's predecessor, Rabban Gamliel, was the one who kept the questionable students away from the study hall. Rabban Gamliel's unyielding manner and perfectionism was symptomatic of his identification with the perfection of the Messianic age, wherein no evil is countenanced. The same is true of another exacting sage, Shamai, whose opinion will indeed be followed in the Messianic age. See *Pirkei Avot* (Kehot), commentary on 1:15 and 5:17.

80. Indeed Rabban Gamliel, who embodied the spirit of the Messianic age, later agreed with what Rabbi Elazar had done.

81. *Sefer Hasichot 5752*, vol. 1, pp. 245-253. [Presumably, the phrase then means: "I was like seventy years but did not merit, etc.... But today, having *become* "seventy" (as apparent from the white hairs), I have merited, etc."]

82. See *Sefer Ha'arachim, ma'arechet otiot*, p. 289.

83. *Sefer Hasichot*, ibid.

84. *Likkutei Sichot*, vol. 1, p. 248.

85. *Torat Menachem—Hitvaaduyot 5722*, vol. 2, p. 315.

86. *Torat Menachem—Hitvaaduyot 5713*, vol. 2, p. 76.

87. *Likkutei Sichot*, vol. 1, pp. 249-251.

88. Letter dated 11 Nissan 5737 (*Haggadah Shel Pesach* with Commentary, vol. 2, p. 578 ff.).

89. *Tamid* 32a.

90. See *Hayom Yom*, 21 Sivan and 25 Tammuz.

91. *Tanya*, ch. 43.

92. *Likkutei Torah, Shelach* 40a.

93. Even the notion of a "decree"—as the inexplicable laws are called (*chukim*)—is foreign to the *chacham*, since "decree" implies an imposition on the subjects.

94. This is also why there are fifteen steps to the Seder, since fifteen is the *gematria* of the first two letters of God's Name, *Yud* and *Hey*, which represent intellect—*Yud* represents *chochmah* and *Hey, binah* (*Likkutei Sichot*, vol. 2, p. 539).

95. *Likkutei Sichot*, vol. 3, pp. 961-965; *Torat Menachem—Hitvaaduyot 5713*, vol. 2, pp. 76-78.

96. Exodus 12:26. The connotation is a "burdensome service." He says, "What is this burden that you impose upon us every year?" (*Jerusalem Talmud, Pesachim* 10:4).

97. Which is tantamount to denying the very existence of God (*Machzor Vitri*).

98. *Siddur Rashi*. Alternatively, do not allow him to partake of the fragrant and tasty Pesach lamb, which will cause him to grind his teeth in frustration (*Avudraham*). Eating in front of another person who wants to eat but cannot is called "blunting his teeth" in the Talmud. See *Maharsha* on *Sotah* 49a.

99. *Rashi*.

100. Commentators differ on what his fate would have been: He would have died during the plague of Darkness (*Shibolei Haleket*); he would have lived but remained a slave in Egypt (*Chatam Sofer*); he would have left Egypt with the Jews, but without the merit of the *mitzvot* he would never be emotionally redeemed (*Maaseh Nissim*).

101. Cf. *Torah Temimah* on Exodus 12:26.

102. Using the singular (Eloke*cha*), not the plural (Eloke*chem*).

103. In truth, even in Egypt we possessed an innate connection to God, which is why even idolaters were redeemed. Only those who denied that connection, by choosing Egyptian bondage over God, were not redeemed. Sinai effected an even greater connection, one that cannot be permanently denied and must inevitably come to the fore.

104. *Pri Etz Chaim* 21:5.

105. *Likkutei Sichot*, vol. 1, pp. 248-252.

106. *Torat Menachem—Hitvaaduyot 5743*, vol. 3, p. 1280.

107. *Likkutei Sichot*, vol. 13, p. 235.

108. The *kuf* and *resh* are associated with falsehood and negativity—see *Zohar*, Introduction 4b.

109. *Rabbi Yosef Yitzchak of Lubavitch, Igrot Kodesh*, vol. 3, p. 420. See footnote of the Lubavitcher Rebbe in *Likkutei Dibburim*, vol. 3, p. 525a: "*Siddur HaArizal, Haggadah, s.v. Hakheh et shinav; Kehillat Yaakov, s.v. Rasha*; see also *Zohar* I:57a." See also *Bati L'Gani 5710*. This is also why we thank God for preventing us from becoming prey to the *teeth* of the wicked (Psalms 124:6), since it is only because of the spark of holiness that they possess—*shinei'hem*—that they would be able to harm us (*Sichot Kodesh 5726*, p. 279, citing the Tzemach Tzedek).

110. Including individuals that have no share in the World to Come, such as Doeg and Achitophel—see *Sanhedrin* 90a.

111. *Berachot* 10a.

112. *Likkutei Sichot*, vol. 28, p. 156; see *Sefer Hamaamarim 5669* (ed. 2006), p. 285.

113. Both *Avudraham* and *Shibolei Haleket* cite the verse *Opening your mouth on behalf of the mute*. It seems, however, that they cite it with different intentions. The above verse can refer to speaking up on behalf of someone who cannot speak, such as speaking up for someone in court who does not know his rights (*Bava Batra* 41a). This is how the verse is translated by *Ibn Ezra* and would align with *Avudraham's* understanding of our obligation to the child who cannot ask—we do the talking. But in *Shibolei Haleket's* reading, it would seem that the verse is understood to mean that one should open one's mouth for the mute so that *he* speaks and asks questions. See *Haggadat Torat Chaim* (Katznelenbogen), p. 65, fn. 77; p. 65, fn. 96.

114. See *Zohar* II:170b and *Yalkut Reuveni* on Exodus 14:27.

115. *Haggadah Shel Pesach* with Commentary, vol. 1, p. 141.

116. *Sefer Hasichot 5709*, p. 315.

117. Psalms 63:2.

118. *Torat Menachem—Hitvaaduyot 5743*, vol. 3, pp. 1279-1283.

119. *Haggadah Shel Pesach* with Commentary, vol. 1, pp. 139-142.

120. *Sefer Hasichot 5696-5700*, p. 262.

121. *Sefer Hasichot 5703*, p. 54.

122. See *Torat Menachem—Hitvaaduyot 5723*, vol. 2, p. 283; letters of the Rebbe, dated Rosh Chodesh Nissan 5737 and 5740 (*Haggadah Shel Pesach* with Commentary, vol. 2, p. 674 ff.; p. 700 ff.) and others.

123. This question resembles that of the angels to God when they learned that the Torah was to be given to human beings (*Shabbat* 88b): "Torah is Your most precious treasure, and you are giving it to flesh and blood?!" They were implying that Torah should remain a spiritual thing—why must it find expression in the *physical* through the *mitzvot*?

124. *Sefer Hamaamarim 5735*, p. 349 ff.

125. See *The Torah* (Kehot) on Exodus 22:8.

126. The *gematria* of *maror* is identical to that of the word for death, *mavet*.

127. *Likkutei Torah*, *Tzav* 12d ff.

128. *Pirush Maharzu*: Those who believe in dualism maintain that impurity can only produce impurity and vice versa. The emergence of pure from impure demonstrates the oneness of God, that all is from him.

129. See *Torat Menachem—Hitvaaduyot 5744*, vol. 3, p. 1526.

130. *Sefer Hasichot 5704*, p. 90.

131. *Torat Menachem—Hitvaaduyot 5712*, vol. 2, p. 123.

132. This is why the Torah tells us nothing of Abraham's early life—when *he* sought God—and instead begins the tale with "God said to Abraham." The Torah thereby emphasizes that the Abrahamic legacy is defined primarily not by man's efforts to embrace the Infinite but by the Infinite's desire to embrace us. *Likkutei Sichot*, vol. 25, pp. 48-50.

133. See *The Torah* (Kehot) on Genesis 12:1.

134. The level of thought is associated with "river," since just as a river is constantly flowing, thought is constantly active (*Vayomer Yehoshua 5720* (*Torat Menachem—Hitvaaduyot 5720*, vol. 2, p. 3)).

135. "Ever" is also the name of Shem's great-grandson (Genesis 10:24). Our Sages tell us that Jacob studied Torah from Shem and Ever. Chasidut explains that Jacob learned the Written Torah from Shem and the Oral Torah from Ever. The Oral Torah is rooted in *chochmah*, in Ever, which is "beyond the river (of *binah*)" (*Torat Menachem—Hitvaaduyot 5718*, vol. 3, p. 232).

136. Saintly individuals, such as Moses, are conscious of it and are able to awaken it from its dormancy within others. This occurred, for example, at the splitting of the sea, when Moses awakened the "Hebrew" within the Jewish people, which caused the sea to be swept away before them.

The Torah therefore says (Exodus 15:1): *Then Moses and the Jewish people sang…*—using the singular form for sing (*yashir*), although referring to many people. For it was the *unification* of Moses and the Jewish people that caused the sea to split.

The prophet tells us that the future redemption will be similar to that of the first redemption (Micah 7:15). In the Messianic age we will again experience a crossing of water, returning permanently to the state of "the other side of the

river." This is the meaning of the double expression in the *Az Yashir* (Exodus 15:16): *Until Your nation will cross over, O God, until the nation You have acquired will cross over*—referring to the two crossings, that of the first redemption and that of the future and final redemption.

137. *Likkutei Torah*, *Tzav* 15d; *Torat Shmuel—Sefer 5641*, p. 58.

138. The *Midrash* gives two other explanations: 1) He was a descendant of Ever, and 2) he originated from the land on the other side of the Euphrates river and spoke its language.

139. Deuteronomy 7:7.

140. *Torat Menachem—Hitvaaduyot 5712*, vol. 3, p. 63.

141. *Vayomer Yehoshua 5720* (*Torat Menachem—Hitvaaduyot 5720*, vol. 2, p. 9).

142. See *Sefer Hasichot 5699*, p. 323.

143. *Likkutei Sichot*, vol. 17, p. 328.

144. See *Rashi* on Exodus 18:1.

145. We find a similar anomaly regarding the tribe of Asher. The *Sifrei* (on Deuteronomy 33:24) states that "no tribe was blessed with children like Asher." Yet Asher was not an especially fertile tribe, which is presumably why *Rashi*, in citing the above *Sifrei*, states: "I don't know how [this was true]."

One answer is that Asher was not blessed with quantity but quality. The children of the tribe of Asher were blessed with spiritual greatness, as can be seen from the fact that the daughters of Asher were married to the high priests (see *Bereishit Rabbah* 98:16 and *Rashi* on Deuteronomy 33:24; *Likkutei Sichot*, vol. 1, pp. 109-110).

146. *Sefer Hasichot 5699*, p. 323. See *The Torah* (Kehot) on Genesis 41:2-6.

147. Genesis 30:24.

148. See *The Torah* (Kehot) on Genesis 30:24.

149. *Sefer Halikkutim, Mem* (*mitzvot-matanah*), p. 1441.

150. Abraham was concerned that God's promise might occur only in a spiritual sense. He therefore insisted on entering into a covenant made over a physical deed, which would ensure that the fulfillment of the promise would likewise manifest itself physically. See, however, *Nedarim* 32a, *Abarbanel*, et al., where Abraham's request is seen as a lack of faith (*The Torah* (Kehot) on Genesis 15:8).

151. Condensed from *The Torah* (Kehot) on Genesis 15:12.

152. *Pardes*, beg. of *Shaar Hashe'arim*.

The Torah alludes to the "fifty gates of understanding," which were revealed at the Exodus, by whose inspiration the Israelites were able to climb out of the 49 gates of impurity to the gates of purity. See *Torat Menachem—Sefer Hamaamarim Melukat*, vol. 3, p. 148.

R. Moshe Cordovero adds, citing another commentator, that the Exodus is mentioned *in passing* an additional eleven times. For example, the Torah uses the Exodus to describe when an event occurred, such as *In the third month after the Children of Israel left Egypt...* (Exodus 19:1). Such instances, in which the Exodus is mentioned as an aside, are not counted as part of the fifty.

153. *Sefer Hasichot 5707*, p. 106.

154. *Sefer Hasichot 5708*, p. 206.

155. Exodus 15:9.

156. *Torat Menachem—Hitvaaduyot 5743*, vol. 2, p. 1104.

157. See *Sichot Kodesh 5736*, vol. 1, p. 607.

158. See *Midrash Rabbah, Esther* 10:11, et al.

159. Genesis 46:4.

160. *Megillah* 29a.

161. *Torat Menachem—Hitvaaduyot 5713*, vol. 2, p. 80.

162. *Likkutei Sichot*, vol. 1, pp. 19-21.

163. See introduction to Kehot edition of *Megillat Esther; The Torah* (Kehot) on Genesis 40:23.

164. See Isaiah 11:6; 2:4.

165. See *Torat Menachem—Hitvaaduyot 5751*, vol. 3, p. 72.

166. *Kiddushin* 30b.

167. *Torat Menachem—Hitvaaduyot 5717*, vol. 2, p. 261.

168. See *Rashi* on Deut. 26:1.

169. *Likkutei Sichot*, vol. 14, p. 93.

170. See *Rashi*, Exodus 1:16.

171. See Genesis 31:21-29 and *Rashi* on Deut. 26:5.

172. *Sefer Hasichot 5704*, p. 91.

173. *Sefer Hasichot 5706*, p. 33.

174. *Sefer Hasichot 5704*, pp. 91-92. See also *The Torah* (Kehot) on Genesis 31:43.

175. *Or Hatorah, Devarim*, p. 1040.

176. *Torat Menachem—Hitvaaduyot 5750*, vol. 2, p. 285.

177. See *Sichot Kodesh 5734*, vol. 1, pp. 251-252.

178. In the *Sifrei* and *Rambam* this teaching does not appear, perhaps because, in the end, Jacob did go willingly (*The Rebbe's Haggadah*).

179. *Likkutei Sichot*, vol. 2, p. 540 ff.

180. *Bereishit Rabbah* 47:6 and 82:6; *Zohar* III:257b; *Tanya*, ch. 23, et al.

181. *Likkutei Sichot*, vol. 4, p. 1219. See *The Torah* (Kehot) on Genesis 46:2-3.

182. *Pirkei d'Rabbi Eliezer* 26, et al.

183. Genesis 45:18.

184. Deuteronomy 4:20.

185. See *The Torah* (Kehot) on Exodus 1:14.

186. See *Kli Yakar*.

187. See Deuteronomy 32:15; *Berachot* 32a.

188. Based on *The Torah* (Kehot) on Genesis 47:27, from *Likkutei Sichot*, vol. 15, pp. 407-410.

189. *Keter Shem Tov* #318.

190. *Rashi*.

191. *Rashi*.

192. *Radak*.

193. *Shemot Rabbah* 1:35.

194. *Shemot Rabbah* ibid. Hair is at the "end" of the body; hence, your "ending" has grown—the end of your exile has arrived (*Maharzu*). Additionally, the spelling of the word for "hair" (*sei'ar*) is similar to the word for measure (*shi'ur*). Hence: Your "measure" has arrived (*Matnot Kehunah*).

195. *Radak*.

196. *Zohar* II:5b, 16b. See *Rashi* on Genesis 35:11; *Targum Yonatan* and *Rashi* on Deuteronomy 32:8.

197. See *The Torah* (Kehot) on Genesis 46:11.

198. Discourse entitled *Or L'Arbaah Asar, 5666*. See *The Torah* (Kehot) on Exodus 1:12.

199. Hence the emphasis on the blood of the sacrifice, not on the mitzvah of eating it, since it was in slaughtering the lamb that they were cutting themselves from idolatry. This is why it was important for them to set aside the lamb four days prior to its slaughter, giving themselves four days to internalize this severance from idolatry.

200. *Likkutei Sichot*, vol. 16, p. 114 ff. R. Matya ben Charash (the author of the teaching that G-d gave the Israelites two precepts since they were "naked" of *mitzvot*) chose to establish his yeshiva in Rome, a seemingly unlikely place for spiritual worship. R. Matya sought out those far from the Holy Land, those who were "Roman" in outlook and "naked" of Jewish practice, to bring them into a yeshiva, into Jewish learning. See *Pirkei Avot* (Kehot) 4:15.

201. See also *Shir Hashirim Rabbah* 1:12 (3) and 3:6 (4).

202. Leviticus 12:3; *Megillah* 20a; *Rambam, Hilchot Milah* 1:8.

203. See Psalms 139:12; *Zohar* II:38a; *Simchat Haregel* (Chida) on "*Maaseh b'Rabbi Eliezer*," et al.

204. *Likkutei Sichot*, vol. 17, p. 125 ff.

205. As mentioned, this section of the Haggadah is drawn from the *Sifrei*. However, investigating the original *Sifrei* text is not feasible since the early publishers, beginning with the first edition (Venice, 5306 [1546]), omitted from the *Sifrei* (as well as from the *Yalkut Shimoni*) the entire section that is included in the Haggadah. (The *Sifrei* published with commentary of *Malbim* does include the Haggadah text, as well as the verse, *They embittered, etc.*, but it is not known by whose instruction the verse was included.)

206. But what of the other versions, where the second

verse is omitted? One may suggest that it is the result of an innocent error. It is likely that the original transcribers of the Haggadah (and the *Sifrei*) abbreviated the two verses with an "etc.," [which is quite common in Rabbinic literature], and wrote, *And the Egyptians enslaved, etc., with crushing harshness*—meaning to include both verses, since the second verse also concludes with "crushing harshness." At some point, a copyist wrote out the entire first verse and stopped there, thinking that the original "crushing harshness" referred to the end of the first verse (*The Rebbe's Haggadah*).

207. *Siddur Shaar Hashamaim* on *V'hi She'amdah*; *Shelah* p. 162b (*Matzah Shemurah*).

208. *Likkutei Sichot*, vol. 17, p. 89; *Sichot Kodesh 5726*, p. 348.

209. See Daniel 2:29 and *Berachot* 55b.

210. *Rambam, Hilchot Avadim* 1:6 and *Hagahot Maimoniot* ad loc.

211. *Likkutei Sichot*, vol. 3, p. 848 ff.

212. See also commentary of *Daat Zekeinim Mibaalei Hatosfot* on the Torah.

213. According to this view, the death of the king mentioned at the beginning of Exodus and the death of the king mentioned in this verse are one and the same, as is the opinion of *Abarbanel* (*Haggadah Shel Pesach im Pirushei Harishonim*, fn. 174).

214. See also *Abarbanel*, according to whom the verse from Deut., *And we cried out to God* turns out to be an interpretation of the less explicit verse from Exodus (a seeming reversal of the general format of the Haggadah in which the terse verses from Deuteronomy are expanded upon from other sources in the Torah).

The seemingly awkward placement of "*min ha'avodah*"—literally, "from the labor"—at the *end* of the verse is addressed by *Or Hachaim*: The reason their prayers ascended to God was *because* they emerged from their labor and suffering, since such prayer is more effective. Accordingly, the verse would be translated as follows: "... *and their prayers ascended to God [because they were] evoked by their labor.*" See there for another explanation.

215. *Torah Or, Beshalach* 64a.

216. *Igrot Kodesh*, vol. 4, p. 245.

217. *Torat Shmuel—Sefer 5639*, vol. 1, pp. 116-119. See there for how this can be reconciled with the teaching in *Sanhedrin* (beg. of chapter 11) to the effect that the Generation of the Dispersion does not have a share in the World to Come. Rabbi Shmuel explains that they indeed do not have a share in the World to Come, i.e., they will not be resurrected in the Messianic age. The rectification of their souls enabled them to merit the world of the souls.

218. *Shir Hashirim Rabbah* 2:16. See *Torah Menachem— Hitvaaduyot 5717*, vol. 2, pp. 346-349, where the concept of God being "in need" is explained.

219. Laban says to Jacob, "*If you ill-treat (t'aneh) my daughters...*" which the Talmud (*Yoma* 74b and 77b) interprets as refusing them their conjugal rights.

220. Thus: *And G-d saw the "knowing" of the children of Israel* (*Machzor Vitri*).

221. Although some *Midrashim* imply that they had no merit at all—"*you were naked and bare*"—others indicate that they had in fact repented. See *Mechilta*; *Targum Yonatan*; and *Ibn Ezra* on Exodus 2:25, and 3:9.

222. The merit of the Patriarchs is alluded to in the rituals of the Paschal lamb offering, which they were commanded to offer prior to the Exodus. They were told to place the blood on the lintel and on the doorposts. The lintel alludes to Abraham, the doorposts to Isaac and Jacob (*Shemot Rabbah* 1:36, cited by *Ritva*).

223. See also *Jerusalem Talmud, Taanit* 1:1.

224. See *Shemot Rabbah* 17:2-3.

225. According to *Orchot Chaim*, *amal* connotes futile work. Thus God saw the futility of our procreation, since our children were being thrown into the Nile. According to *Rabbi Yeshaya of Trani* the Haggadah means that God saw our suffering, our "toil," caused by the decree against the children.

226. *Pirkei d'Rabbi Eliezer*, ch. 42; *Midrash Rabbah* 23:8; *Sotah* 11b.

227. Cf. above, note 225.

228. The proof text is not meant to prove that *lachatz* means coercion but to demonstrate that God *saw* our oppression (*The Rebbe's Haggadah*).

229. *Likkutei Sichot*, vol. 1, pp. 111-113.

230. *Rashi* on Exodus 12:12.

231. *Rashi*, ibid.

232. *God will pass through to strike Egypt, and He will see the blood [of the Paschal lamb offering] on the lintel and on the two doorposts. And God will mercifully pass over the entrance and not allow the* mashchit *to enter your homes to attack* (Exodus 12:23).

233. The Torah relates in Numbers (20:16): *[God] sent a* malach *(angel/messenger), and He took us out of Egypt.* This does not mean that the *malach* took us out of Egypt. Rather, God sent a *malach*, namely Moses, an angelic messenger, to speak to Pharaoh and to administer the plagues. Then He, God, took us out of Egypt, something which Moses did not have the power to do (*Shibolei Haleket*).

234. Although God had these various messengers at His disposal, He chose to redeem Israel Himself, without any proxy, because of His great love for Israel (*Alshich*).

235. *Likkutei Torah, Tzav* 12c. See also sources cited in *Torat Menachem—Hitvaaduyot 5712*, vol. 2, p. 112, fn. 7.

236. Regarding the terms *Asiyah, Beriah*, and *Yetzirah*— see *Pirkei Avot* (Kehot), end of Chapter Six.

237. *Haggadah Shel Pesach* with Commentary, vol. 1, pp. 154-156.

238. *Shulchan Aruch HaRav, Orach Chaim*, 473:50-51.

239. The *Mechilta* uses this metaphor to describe the logic of the Egyptians, who decided to chase after and recapture the Israelites. They said: "If we had only been struck by the plagues but at least would have kept the Israelites as slaves, that would have been worth it for us. If we had been struck by the plagues and let them free, but at least held on to our possessions, it would have been worth it for us. But what happened? We were beset by plagues, we set them free, and they took our possessions…."

240. Quoted in *Pesikta d'Rav Kahana*, 11, in connection with the above metaphor.

241. *Likkutei Sichot*, vol. 1, pp. 123-124.

242. On Exodus 9:24.

243. *Likkutei Sichot*, vol. 31, pp. 44-45.

244. Rabbi Yehudah arbitrarily included the final plague in the last set, since it had no other "partners." See *Malbim* on Exodus 7:14.

245. See *Akedah* (on *Va'era* §36), *Ritva*; *Maaseh Nissim*; *Abarbanel*; *Kli Yakar*; and *Alshich*.

246. The final plague, represented by the fourth letter in the third mnemonic, came with a warning.

247. The first three plagues were blood, frogs, and lice. The first two afflicted the Nile, the final one afflicted the earth where the lice came from. It was therefore improper for Moses to administer these plagues, since he was "indebted" to the Nile for saving his life as a child and the earth for enabling him to hide the body of the cruel Egyptian taskmaster he had killed (*Tanchuma, Va'era* 14).

248. R. Eliezer and R. Akiva seem to disagree with each other and R. Yosai about the number of plagues. In truth, however, the Sages do not necessarily dispute one another, but merely explicate and add to the preceding statements of their colleagues. [In other words, R. Yosai's primary message is about the correlation between the plagues in Egypt and those at the sea; R. Eliezer adds that in fact each plague had four dimensions; and R. Akiva adds that there was a fifth dimension as well.] Although the expression "Rabbi so-and-so says" often connotes disagreement with a previous statement, it can also be used when the Sages are in agreement—see *Tosfot Yom Tov* on *Bikkurim* 3:6, et al. (*The Rebbe's Haggadah*).

249. *Pesachim* 2:1.

250. *Pesachim* 5b.

251. Commentary of Rabbi Yehudah ben Yakar on the Haggadah.

252. *Pesachim* 23a.

253. *Likkutei Sichot*, vol. 16, p. 87 ff.

254. Jerusalem Talmud, *Berachot* 5:2.

255. *Avot d'Rabbi Nattan* 6:3.

256. *Avot* 2:9.

257. *Shir Hashirim Rabbah* 1:3 (1).

258. *Avot* 2:10.

259. See *Ketuvot* 62b; *Nedarim* 50a; *Avot d'Rabbi Nattan* 6:2; *Rambam*, intro. to *Mishneh Torah*.

260. See *Masechet Kallah* 1 and *Nedarim* 62a.

261. *Berachot* 61b.

262. *Likkutei Sichot*, vol. 16, p. 87 ff.

263. *Mechilta, Beshalach* 15:2.

264. *Maamarei Admur Ha'emtzaee, Vayikra*, vol. 1, p. 386.

265. *Likkutei Sichot*, vol. 3, pp. 1016 ה-ו.

266. *Raavan, Machzor Vitri*, et al.

267. *Likkutei Sichot*, vol. 2, p. 542.

268. *Likkutei Sichot* ibid.

269. See *The Torah* (Kehot) on Genesis 41:48.

270. Letter dated 11 Nissan 5737 (*Haggadah Shel Pesach* with Commentary, vol. 2, p. 679 ff.).

271. In the desert, the Pesach offering was only brought once by a unique Divine command.

272. Exodus 12:21-27 and *Rashi* ad loc.

273. See *Rosh Hashanah* 11a.

274. *Shemot Rabbah* 15:4.

275. *Torat Menachem—Hitvaaduyot 5743*, vol. 3, p. 1275.

276. *Likkutei Torah, Shir Hashirim* 15b.

277. Letters dated Rosh Chodesh Nissan 5736 and Erev Shabbat Hagadol 5739 (*Haggadah Shel Pesach* with Commentary, vol. 2, p. 668 ff.; p. 697 ff.).

278. *Likkutei Sichot*, vol. 36, pp. 50-51. *Sichot Kodesh 5736*, pp. 409-411.

279. The Talmudic sage Rava taught: One should *lift up* the matzah and *maror* [and show them to the participants] but not the meat [used to commemorate the Pesach offering]. For one cannot say "*this* Pesach offering"; and furthermore, it would give the appearance that one has offered a sacrifice outside the *Beit Hamikdash* (*Pesachim* 116b and *Rashbam* ad loc.).

280. Cf. *Ramban* on Exodus 12:39 and *Abarbanel*.

281. *Pesachim*, chapter 10, on *Rif* 25b.

282. The *Mechilta* relates that the Israelites experienced "*kefitzat haderech*" and traveled in a miraculously swift manner. But even so, the time that it takes to prepare a fire and an oven is certainly enough time for the dough to rise.

283. The pre-midnight matzah corresponds to a situation where spiritual *chametz* is a possibility yet one *suppresses* it.

284. *Likkutei Torah*, Tzav 12 b-c.

285. They began enslaving them with labor involving mortar and bricks, then proceeded to add other types of labor in the field, and then added even more enslavements (*Shemot Rabbah* 1:11; see *Sotah* 11b and *Maharsha* ad loc.).

The work with mortar and bricks was not only the first enslavement, it was their *primary* enslavement, even after the others were added. See *Likkutei Sichot*, vol. 6, p. 13.

286. See also *Shemot Rabbah* 1:27.

287. The number 86 is the numeric equivalent of the Divine Name *Elokim*, the Name associated with the attribute of judgment and thus their bitter enslavement of 86 years (*Sefer Halikkutim, Mem*, p. 1444).

288. See *The Torah* (Kehot) on Exodus 15:20.

289. *Sefer Hasichot 5752*, vol. 1, pp. 303-4.

290. *Sefer Hasichot 5752*, vol. 1, p. 303, fn. 63.

291. This is also the deeper meaning of the phrase "*This is the bread of poverty that our forefathers ate*," which can be rendered: "*This is the bread of poverty that consumed our forefathers [our intellect]*." See above, note 37.

292. Genesis 46:4.

293. *Sefer Halikkutim, Mem*, pp. 1442-3.

294. Ibid., pp. 1443-4.

295. See *The Torah* (Kehot) on Exodus 15:25.

296. Psalms 19:11.

297. *Sefer Halikkutim, Mem*, p. 1444 and 1442. We likewise find that God referred to the day the angel of death was created as not just "good" but "*very good*." For it is only through the presence and sublimation of death that sweeter than sweet—"life of life"—can be achieved. Indeed the *numerical value* of the word for "death" (*mavet*) is equal to *maror*.

298. How do we know that this "me" refers to all future generations and not just to the generation that was alive during the Exodus? This verse is also cited in the response to the wicked child, "*God acted for me—but not for him*." This proves that the word "me" in this verse is to be understood as referring to the person saying it now, not just to those who were alive during the Exodus (*Rabbi Yehudah ben Yakar; Ritva*). Additionally, this verse appears in a passage with laws that pertain to all generations. Presumably, then, the instruction to say "*It is because of this that God acted for* **me**..." pertains to all generations as well (*Maharsha*, ibid.).

299. See *Gevurot Hashem* 61 and 52; *Zohar* II:40a; *Torat Menachem—Hitvaaduyot 5746*, vol. 3, pp. 159, 162. The lower four levels of the soul can be enslaved but not the fifth level, the *Yechidah*.

300. *Likkutei Dibburim*, vol. 4, p. 1383.

301. Isaiah 11:3; *Sanhedrin* 93b.

302. *Likkutei Sichot*, vol. 2, pp. 348 ff.; 544 ff.

303. See *Haggadat HaEncyclopedia HaTalmudit*, p. 29, for the various opinions on what is considered "concluding with praise."

304. Omitting *bless* and *elevate* [and presumably not counting *Halleluyah*].

305. Cited in *Haggadah Vehiggadeta*.

306. *From slavery to freedom*—this alludes to the redemption from Egypt, when G-d freed us from the essence of enslavement and imbued us with inner freedom.

From sorrow to joy—this alludes to the redemption from Babylon after the destruction of the *Beit Hamikdash*, regarding which the term "sorrow" is used several times in Lamentations.

From mourning to festivity—this alludes to the redemption from Media/Persia during the miracle of Purim, which is described in the Scroll of Esther as a transformation from mourning to festivity.

From deep darkness to great light—this alludes to the redemption from Greece during Chanukah, when the Greeks sought to separate us from the Torah, the light of our lives.

From bondage to redemption—this alludes to the future and final redemption through the righteous Moshiach (*Maaseh Nissim*; cf. *Abarbanel*).

307. *Abarbanel* cites *Ramban* as saying that during the Exile, God regularly performs miraculous salvations for us. These salvations occur without our knowledge or understanding.

308. The Mishnah asks: How much of *Hallel* do we recite (at this point)? According to the School of Hillel, we recite the first two psalms (*Pesachim* 116b).

309. Although *Hallel* is generally recited standing, tonight one can recite it while seated. This is because all the activities of this night are meant to be done in the [luxurious] manner of the free (*Shulchan Aruch HaRav, Orach Chaim* 473:47-48).

310. He transcends the heavens just as He transcends the earth. The highest angel of heaven and the lowliest physical being are equally as naught before His infiniteness (*Me'am Loez*).

311. *Likkutei Torah, Shir Hashirim* 37b.

312. *Pesikta Rabbati*, chapter 43.

313. The Psalmist further emphasizes God's dominion over nature: Just as He turned water to dry land at the sea, so did He turn a rock into water for Israel in the desert (*Abarbanel*).

314. What is the difference between *har* (mountain) and *givah* (hill)? A *givah* is not as tall as a *har*, nor is its peak narrow like that of the *har* (*Radak*).

315. See *Midrash Rabbah* 21:10 and *Etz Yosef* ad loc.

316. *Sefer Hamamarim 5670*, p. 250.

317. See *Likkutei Torah, Tzav* 16b-d.

318. Micah 7:15; the *Keter* prayer in the *Musaf* liturgy; Isaiah 11:11.

319. Exodus 3:14 and *Rashi* ad loc.

320. Exodus 4:13 and *Pesikta Zutrata* ad loc.

321. In truth, there is a mitzvah to eat bread on the eve of every festival. It would seem then that we would have to eat matzah in any case (since we cannot have *chametz*). But this is not so since one could have theoretically fulfilled this mitzvah with "rich matzah"—i.e., matzah made with fruit juice. The mitzvah of matzah, however, requires us to eat "poor matzah"—made only of flour and water (*Ran* on *Sukkah* 27a).

322. See *Kerem Chabad* (5752), p. 37.

323. See the citation from Rabbi Shmuel of Lubavitch, below, and *Torat Menachem—Hitvaaduyot 5712*, vol. 2, p. 109.

324. *Shulchan Aruch HaRav, Orach Chaim* 475:18.

325. See above on *Yachatz*.

326. *V'kacha, 5637*, chapter 60.

327. *Derech Mitzvotecha* 22b.

328. *Likkutei Torah, Tzav* 13d; *Derech Mitzvotecha* 23a-b.

329. *Sefer Hasichot 5709*, pp. 312-313.

330. *The Rebbe's Haggadah.*

331. *Sefer Hamaamarim 5708*, p. 166.

332. *V'kacha 5637*, chapter 60.

333. *Shulchan Aruch HaRav, Orach Chaim* 453:1-2.

334. Ibid., 453:1.

335. Ibid., 462:1.

336. *Shulchan Aruch HaRav*, ibid., 453:14-17,19.

337. See *Bach* on *Tur* §475 regarding the combination of *matzah* and *charoset*. See *Likkutei Sichot*, vol. 32, p. 48.

338. **Accentuating the Freedom.** The Seder includes two general obligations by which we commemorate our freedom: 1) the obligation of **speech**—telling the story of the Exodus, and 2) the obligations of **deed**—eating the *Pesach* (in *Beit Hamikdash* times), matzah, and *maror*.

When we *relate* the Exodus, we speak not only of our redemption but also of our enslavement, since it is by remembering the bitterness that we can fully appreciate our freedom. Similarly in our commemorative *deeds*, we remember not only our redemption (with the Pesach and the matzah), but our enslavement as well (with the *maror*).

The Accessory

The *maror* is thus an *accessory* to the Pesach (and matzah), since it helps us to appreciate our freedom.

When the *Beit Hamikdash* stood, we had the ability to commemorate our freedom while actively commemorating the bitterness. (Indeed, the matzah was then dipped in *charoset*, according to some opinions, to simultaneously commemorate the freedom through the *matzah* and the enslavement through the clay-like *charoset*).

But in times of exile and displacement, reliving the bitterness by eating *maror* could compromise our ability to experience the freedom we were granted with the Exodus. It is therefore not Biblically required during the exile and is done only as a remembrance of what was done in *Beit Hamikdash* times (see *Likkutei Sichot*, vol. 32, p. 48; *Torat Menachem—Hitvaaduyot 5746*, vol. 3, pp. 158-159).

339. *Hilchot Chametz u'Matzah*, 7:11 and 8:8.

340. *Likkutei Sichot*, vol. 33, p. 45.

341. See Genesis 42:9 and *Rashi* on Leviticus 18:3. See also *Kohelet Rabbah* on Ecclesiastes 1:4.

342. *Likkutei Sichot*, vol. 32, pp. 50-53.

343. Rabbi Yosef Yitzchak of Lubavitch, *Igrot Kodesh*, vol. 9, p. 311; *Sefer Hasichot 5701*, p. 100.

344. *Sefer Hamaamarim 5692*, p. 383.

345. *Sefer Hamamarim 5708*, pp. 166-167.

346. *Sefer Hasichot 5697*, p. 226.

347. *Likkutei Sichot*, vol. 2, p. 610, and vol. 27, p. 55.

348. The second segment is generally seen as beginning after the Blessing after Meals. However, in a sense, the second segment begins as early as *Korech*, in which we mention the *Beit Hamikdash*: "Thus did Hillel do at the time of the *Beit Hamikdash*...." Allusions to the future redemption continue in the Blessing after Meals, during which we mention and ask for the restoration of "the kingdom of David Your anointed one." Thus did the Rebbe explain Rabbi Yosef Yitzchak's custom to at times pour the Cup of Elijah prior to the Blessing after Meals (*Torat Menachem—Hitvaaduyot 5744*, vol. 3, p. 2038).

349. See *Rosh Hashanah* 11b and *Rashi* ad loc.

350. See Malachi 3:23-24; Rambam in *Mishneh Torah*, Laws of Kings 12:4.

351. See *Likkutei Sichot*, vol. 27, p. 55.

352. Cited in *Sefer Hasichot 5749*, p. 391.

353. *Torat Menachem—Hitvaaduyot 5746*, vol. 3, pp. 63-64.

In general, the fate of the nations of the world in the Messianic age is spelled out in the prophets numerous times as living peacefully with Israel and serving the one God.

Rambam in fact rules that it is part of Moshiach's function to "transform the entire world to serve God together, as the prophet states (Zephaniah 3:9): *I will make the nations pure of speech to all call out in the Name of God, to serve Him with one purpose*."

We provide the "groundwork" for this achievement by being a "light onto the nations" during the exile. It is therefore especially important in our time, as we near the end of the exile, that each of us become an ambassador of universal values—known as the Seven Laws of Noah—to those non-Jews in our sphere of influence (see *Likkutei Sichot*, vol. 23, p. 172).

354. *Sefer Hasichot 5707*, p. 108.

355. *Likkutei Sichot*, vol. 4, p. 1298.

356. *Torat Menachem—Hitvaaduyot 5722*, vol. 2, p. 310.

הלל נרצה
Hallel Nirtzah

357. The twenty-six generations from Adam to Moses are: 1) Adam, 2) Seth, 3) Enosh, 4) Keinan, 5) Mahalalel, 6) Yered, 7) Enoch, 8) Methuselah, 9) Lemech, 10) Noah, 11) Shem, 12) Arpachshad, 13) Shelach, 14) Ever, 15) Peleg, 16) Reu, 17) Serug, 18) Nachor, 19) Terach, 20) Abraham, 21) Isaac, 22) Jacob, 23) Levi, 24) Kehot, 25) Amram, 26) Moses.

358. The word *v'ilu* appears in some versions of the prayer, though not in the Chabad version, which has *ilu*.

359. *Torat Menachem—Hitvaaduyot 5713*, vol. 2, pp. 83-84.

360. *Sefer Hasichot 5749*, vol. 1, p. 391.

361. *Otzar Minhagei Chabad.*

362. *Sefer Hasichot 5704*, p. 81.

363. *Torat Menachem—Hitvaaduyot 5713*, vol. 2, pp. 135-137.

364. *Sefer Hasichot 5703*, p. 75.

BIBLIOGRAPHY

An asterisk denotes a cross-reference within the Bibliography

Abarbanel: Don Yitzchak Abarbanel (1437-1508), author of *Zevach Pesach*, a commentary on the Passover Haggadah. Cremona, 1557.

Agur: Halachic commentary on sections of the **Tur* by Rabbi Yaakov Landa. Naples, 1490.

Akedah: Colloquial for *Akedat Yitzchak*, a philosophical commentary on the Torah by Rabbi Yitzchak Aramah (c. 1420-1494). Salonika, 1522.

Alshich: Rabbi Moshe Alshich, or Alshich, was a prominent Jewish rabbi and biblical commentator (Turkey, 1508 - Safed, 1593), and one of a select few who were granted the title "*Hakadosh*" throughout Jewish history. He was a disciple of R. Yosef Karo, author of the **Shulchan Aruch*, and his own disciples included the Kabbalist R. Chaim Vital. Alshich's numerous works include *Torat Moshe* (Commentary on the Torah), first printed in Belvedere, about 1593, and complete, with indexes, Venice, 1601. A commentary of Alshich on the Haggadah appears in the edition of the Haggadah called *Beit Chorim* (Metz, 1767), which is a collection gathered from his other works.

Arizal: Acronym referring to R. Yitzchak Luria (1534-1572). Founder and leader of a Kabbalistic school in Safed that soon became the dominant school in Jewish Mysticism and exerted a profound influence on the whole Jewish world. The intricate system of the Lurianic Kabbalah, which forms the theoretical basis of Chasidic thought, is authoritatively recorded in the multi-voluminous writings of Ari's principal disciple R. Chaim Vital (1543-1620), such as *Etz Chaim*, **Pri Etz Chaim*, *Mevo She'arim*, *Sha'ar Hahakdamot*, *Likkutei Torah*, etc. See also below, *Sefer Halikkutim*; *Siddur HaArizal*; *Siddur Kol Yaakov*; and *Siddur of Rabbi Shabbetai*.

Aruch Hashulchan: Halachic work following the structure of the **Shulchan Aruch* by Rabbi Yechiel Michel Epstein (1829-1908). Warsaw/Piotrkow, 1884-1908.

Aruch L'ner: Glosses on various Talmudic treatises by Rabbi Yaakov Ettlinger (1798-1871), a German rabbi and author. (*Yevamot*—Altona, 1850; *Makkot* and *Keritot*—Altona, 1855; *Sukkah*—Altona, 1858; *Niddah*—Altona, 1864; *Rosh Hashanah* and *Sanhedrin*, Warsaw, 1873.)

Avodah Zarah: Talmudic tractate discussing the prohibition on idolatry.

Avot: "Ethics of the Fathers." Talmudic tractate discussing moral and ethical teachings.

Avot d'Rabbi Nattan: Commentary on *Avot* by the Babylonian sage R. Nattan, printed in all standard editions of the Talmud.

Avudraham: Commentary on the prayers and the laws of blessings, authored by R. David Avudraham (c. 13th century Seville). Lisbon, 1489.

Baal Haturim: See *Tur.*

Bach: Acronym for "*Bayit Chadash*," a commentary on *Arbaah Turim* (see *Tur*) by R. Yoel Sirkish of Cracow (1561-1641).

Ba'er Heitev: Commentary on the **Shulchan Aruch*. On the sections of *Orach Chaim* and *Even Ha'ezer*, the commentary was written by Rabbi Yehudah ben Shimon Ashkenazi of Germany (1730-1770). On the sections of *Yoreh De'ah* and *Choshen Mishpat*, the commentary was written by Rabbi Zechariah Mendel ben Aryeh Leib, a Polish rabbi who lived in the 17th and 18th centuries. Printed in all standard editions of *Shulchan Aruch*.

Bamidbar Rabbah: See *Midrash Rabbah.*

Bati L'gani 5710: Chasidic discourse published by R. Yosef Yitzchak Schneersohn, sixth Lubavitcher Rebbe, in honor of 10 Shevat 5710 (1950).

Bava Batra: Talmudic tractate dealing with the laws of ownership of real property, inheritance, and documents.

Bava Kama: Talmudic tractate addressing tort law.

Beit Yosef: Major commentary on R. Yaakov ben Asher's monumental code of Jewish law—the **Tur*—by R. Yosef Karo, author of the **Shulchan Aruch* and one of the foremost authorities on Jewish law.

Ben Ish Chai: The title used to refer to Rabbi Yosef Chaim of Baghdad (1832-1909), a leading *Chacham* (Sephardic Rabbi), authority on Jewish law and master Kabbalist. His commentaries on the Haggadah appear in *Haggadah Orach Chaim.* Jerusalem, 1978.

Berachot: Talmudic tractate addressing the laws of reading the *Shema*, prayer, and blessings.

Bereishit Rabbah: See *Midrash Rabbah.*

Bikkurim: Mishnaic tractate discussing the laws of the first fruits of the harvest which are to be brought to the *Beit Hamikdash* and given to the *Kohanim.*

Chacham Tzvi: Responsa by R. Tzvi Hirsch Ashkenazi (1656-1718). Amsterdam, 1712.

Chagigah: Talmudic tractate addressing the laws of the festival sacrifices in the *Beit Hamikdash* and ritual purity. It also contains many esoteric stories and concepts.

Chasdei David: Commentary on **Tosefta* by Rabbi David Padro (1719-1792), Leghorn, Part 1—1776; Part 2—1790.

Chatam Sofer: Rabbi Moshe Sofer (1762-1838), chief rabbi of Pressburg (Bratislava), author of numerous works, including *Derashot* (seasonal sermons); *Halachic Responsa*; *Chatam Sofer on the Torah.* His original Torah insights sparked a new style in rabbinic commentary, and some editions of the Talmud contain his emendations and additions.

Chayei Adam: Laws of the **Shulchan Aruch, Orach Chaim*, in concise form by Rabbi Avraham Danzig (1748-1820). Vilna, 1810.

Chida: Acronym for [Rabbi] "Chaim Yosef

Dovid Azulzai" (1724-1807), who authored a commentary on the Passover Haggadah called *Simchat Haregel*, among numerous works. Livorno, 1657.

Chizkuni: Commentary on the Torah by Rabbenu Chizkiah ben Manoach. Cremona, 1559.

Chok Yaakov: Commentary on the laws of Passover by Rabbi Yaakov Risher. Dessau, 1696.

Chullin: Talmudic tractate discussing various laws of kosher and sacrifices.

Daat Zekeinim Mibaalei Hatosfot: Commentary on the Torah by the Tosafists (see *Tosfot*). Livorno, 1783.

Derashot Chatam Sofer: See *Chatam Sofer*.

Derech Mitzvotecha: Chasidic work by R. Menachem Mendel Schneersohn, author of *Tzemach Tzedek*, offering explanations for certain *mitzvot*. Also known as *Taamei Hamitzvot*. Poltava, 1911; Brooklyn, NY, 1953; revised edition, Brooklyn, NY, 1991.

Devarim Rabbah: See *Midrash Rabbah*.

Dikdukei Sofrim: Collection of alternate versions of the Talmud found in manuscripts and early printed editions, by Rabbi Rafael Nattan Natta Rabinowitz. Fifteen vols., Munich, 1868-1886.

Eishel Avraham: See Pri Megadim.

Esther Rabbah: See *Midrash Rabbah*.

Even Hayarchi: See Raavan.

Gaon of Rogachov: Rabbi Yosef Rosen (Rogachov, 1858 - Vienna, 1936) was the Chasidic Rabbi of Dvinsk, and one of the most prominent Talmudic scholars of the early 20th century. He was known as a *Gaon* (genius) because of his photographic memory and

ability to connect seemingly unrelated Torah concepts. His main work, a commentary on Maimonides, was published during his lifetime, as well as five volumes of responsa. The remainder of his surviving writings appeared in the United States many years after his passing; all are titled *Tzafnat Pa'ane'ach*.

Gevurot Hashem: Philosophical, theological and religious work by Rabbi Yehudah Leow, famed Maharal of Prague (1512-1609). Cracow, 1582.

Gevurot Yisrael: Commentary on the Passover Haggadah by R. Yisrael, the Maggid of Kozhnitz. Lemberg, 1869.

Hagahot Maimoniyot: Commentary on Rambam's *Mishneh Torah* by a student of R. Meir of Rotenberg. Constantinople, 1508.

Haggadah Shel Pesach with Commentary: Includes *The Rebbe's Haggadah and a collection of the Rebbe's edited talks and letters relating to the Haggadah and Pesach in general. Two vols., Brooklyn, NY, 2002.

Haggadat HaEncyclopedia HaTalmudit: Passover Haggadah with commentary culled from the *Encyclopedia Talmudit*. Jerusalem, 2005. (This encyclopedia summarizes the halachic topics of the Talmud in alphabetical order. An ongoing project that made its first debut in Jerusalem, 1947, it currently comprises twenty-nine vols.)

Haggadat Torat Chaim: Passover Haggadah with commentaries of selected Rishonim. Compiled by Rabbi Mordechai Leib Katznelenbogen and published by Mossad HaRav Kook, Jerusalem, 1998.

Hayom Yom: Anthology of aphorisms and customs arranged according to the days of the year, collected by the Lubavitcher Rebbe, R. Menachem M. Schneerson, from the talks and writings of his father-in-law, R. Yosef Y. Schneersohn. Brooklyn, NY, 1943.

Ibn Ezra: Commentary on the Torah by R. Avraham ibn Ezra. Naples, 1488; Constantinople, 1522.

Igrot Kodesh: Letters by R. Menachem M. Schneerson, the Lubavitcher Rebbe. Currently thirty vols., Brooklyn, NY, 1987-2009.

Jerusalem Talmud: See *Talmud*.

Kallah: A minor tractate on engagement, marriage and cohabitation. See *Minor Tractates*.

Kallah Rabbati: An elaboration upon the minor tractate *Kallah. See *Minor Tractates*.

Kedushat Levi: Chasidic work on the Torah by Rabbi Levi Yitzchak of Berditchev. Slavita, 1798.

Kehillat Yaakov: Encyclopedia of Kabbalistic terms by R. Yaakov Tzvi Yalish of Dinov, disciple of R. Yaakov Yitzchak Horowitz, the Chozeh of Lublin. Lvov, 1870.

Kerem Chabad: Periodical on Chabad history, edited by Rabbi Yehoshua Mondshine. Four vols., Kfar Chabad, 5747-5752.

Keter Shem Tov: A collection of teachings of R. Yisrael Baal Shem Tov, culled from the writings of his students. Zalkava, 1794; Brooklyn, NY, 1973; revised edition, Brooklyn, NY, 2004.

Ketuvot: Talmudic tractate discussing marriage contracts.

Kiddushin: Talmudic tractate discussing the laws of marriage.

Ki Naar Yisrael, 5666: Chasidic discourse delivered by Rabbi Shalom DovBer Schneersohn, fifth Lubavitcher Rebbe, on Simchat Torah, 5666 (1905).

Kli Yakar: A classic commentary on the Torah by Rabbi Shlomo Ephraim Lunschitz (d. 1619).

A disciple of Maharal, and later the rabbi of Prague.

Kohelet Rabbah: See *Midrash Rabbah*.

Kol Bo: Halachic work by an unknown author. Naples, 1490. An edition including a commentary on the Passover Haggadah was printed in Fürth, 1782.

Levush: Compendium of Jewish law by Rabbi Mordechai Yaffe of Prague (1530-1612).

L'Horot Natan: Halachic responsa by Rabbi Natan Gestetner. Bnei Brak, 1982.

Likkutei Dibburim: Edited talks by R. Yosef Yitzchak Schneersohn, sixth Lubavitcher Rebbe, delivered in Latvia, Poland, and the U.S.A. during the years 1929-1950. Four vols., Brooklyn, NY, 1957-58. An English translation was published in Brooklyn, NY, 1987-2000.

Likkutei Levi Yitzchak: Commentary on Scripture, the *Zohar and the *Tanya by R. Levi Yitzchak Schneerson, father of the Lubavitcher Rebbe, R. Menachem M. Schneerson. Includes his letters of correspondence. Brooklyn, NY, 1971.

Likkutei Sichot: Talks delivered and edited by R. Menachem M. Schneerson, the Lubavitcher Rebbe. 39 vols., Brooklyn, NY, 1962-2001.

Likkutei Torah: Chasidic discourses elucidating major themes of the weekly Torah portion and festivals, by R. Schneur Zalman of Liadi. Published by his grandson, R. Menachem Mendel of Lubavitch, author of *Tzemach Tzedek*. Zhitomir, 1848; Munich, 1948; Brooklyn, NY, 1965; 1999. See *Torah Or*.

Maamarei Admur Ha'emtzaee: Chasidic discourses by R. DovBer, second Lubavitcher Rebbe. Nineteen vols., Brooklyn, NY, 1985-1992.

Maaseh Nissim: Commentary on the Passover Haggadah by Rabbi Yaakov of Lissa. Zalkava, 1807. Printed also in *Siddur Otzar Hatefillot*. Vilna, 1923.

Maaseh Rokeach: Halachic work by Rabbenu Eliezer bar Yehudah of Mainz. Sanok, 1912.

Maasei Hashem: Homiletic explanations of the stories of the Torah by Rabbi Eliezer Ashkenazi. Consisting of four parts, the third part—called *Maasei Mitzrayim*—includes a commentary on the Passover Haggadah. Venice, 1583.

Machatzit Hashekel: Super commentary to the *Magen Avraham* commentary (on *Shulchan Aruch*) by Rabbi Shmuel HaLevi Yellin (1738-1827), appearing in all standard editions of *Shulchan Aruch*.

Machzor Vitri: Halachic work focusing mainly on the daily and Shabbat prayer services, by R. Simcha of Vitri, France (d. 1105). Includes halachic decisions from his teacher Rashi and other early scholars on issues of *kashrut*, family purity, *tefillin*, mezuzah, and ethics. Berlin, 1893.

Magen Avraham: Commentary on *Shulchan Aruch*, *Orach Chaim*, by Rabbi Avraham Abele of Gombin, Poland (c. 1633-c. 1683). First published in 1692.

Maharil: Acronym for "Our Teacher, the Rabbi, Yaakov Levi." Maharil was a Talmudist and authority on Jewish law, best known for his codification of German Jewish customs. He was also known as *Mahari Segal* or *Mahari Moelin*. His *Minhagei Maharil* (Sabbioneta, 1556)—also known as *Sefer HaMaharil* or simply *Minhagim*—contains a detailed description of religious observances and rites, at home and in the synagogue, and thus provides an authoritative outline of the *minhagim* (customs) of the German Jews. It also contains sermons and textual comments. It had a great influence on the Jews of Central Europe and was largely responsible for the importance attached to *minhag* in these communities. This book is frequently quoted in the codes and commentaries—including *Rema* who cites *Maharil* frequently—and has become a valuable source for later scholars.

Maharsha: Acronym for "Morenu HaRav Shmuel Eliezer Eidels" of Poland (1555-1631), who authored a two-part commentary on the Talmud: *Chiddushei Halachot* on the legal sections, and *Chiddushei Aggadot* on the non-legal sections. Printed in all standard editions of the Talmud.

Makkot: Talmudic tractate discussing the rules and regulations of the punishment of the thirty-nine lashes, and the penalty in cases of false testimony and similar crimes.

Malbim: Acronym for "Meir Leib ben Yechiel Michel" (1809-1879), chief rabbi of Romania, author of a commentary on Scripture named *Hatorah VeHamitzvah*. Vilna, 1892.

Masechet Kallah: See *Kallah*.

Mechilta: Halachic Midrash on Exodus by the school of R. Yishmael (c. 120 C.E.), also known as *Mechilta d'Rabbi Yishmael*. Constantinople, 1515.

Megillah: Talmudic tractate addressing the laws and story of Purim, as well as laws of Torah reading and the synagogue.

Megillat Esther (Kehot): Bilingual Hebrew/English edition of the Book of Esther, with selected commentary culled from the Midrash, Talmud, Kabbalah, Chasidus and other Rabbinic writings. Brooklyn, NY, 2001.

Midrash B'Chidush: Passover Haggadah with commentary by Rabbi Eliezer Nachman Puah. Venice, 1641.

Midrash Rabbah: A major collection of

homilies and commentaries on the Torah, attributed to R. Oshaya Rabbah (c. 3rd century). Some place it as a work of the early Gaonic period.

Midrash Tanchuma: Early Midrash on the Torah, attributed to R. Tanchuma bar Abba. Constantinople, 1522.

Minchat Chinuch: Commentary on *Sefer Hachinuch* by Rabbi Yosef Babad, rabbi of Tarnipol. Lemberg, 1889.

Minhag Avoteinu Beyadeinu: Sources and history of certain Jewish customs, compiled by Rabbi Gedalia Oberlander. *Festivals*, two vols., Jerusalem, 2006; *Marriage*, New York, 2009.

Minhag Yisrael Torah: Sources and explanations of Jewish customs by Rabbi Yosef Levy. Four vols., New York, 1993.

Minor Tractates: The minor tractates are essays from the Tannaic period or later dealing with topics about which no formal tractate exists in the Mishnah. They may thus be contrasted to the *Tosefta*, whose tractates parallel those of the Mishnah. The first eight or so contain much original material; the last seven or so are collections of material scattered throughout the Talmud.

Mishnat Chasidim: A summary of the *Arizal's teachings concerning spiritual worlds, souls, and meditations by R. Immanuel Chai Ricci (1688-1743), divided into "tractates." Amsterdam, 1727.

Me'am Loez: An anthology of commentaries on Scripture originally written in Ladino. Initiated by R. Yaakov Culi in 1730, it was continued by a number of other scholars. In 1967, a Hebrew translation, *Yalkut Me'am Loez*, was produced by R. Shmuel Kravitzer. The first English translation which began to appear in 1977 was called *The Torah Anthology*, and was written (primarily) by R. Aryeh Kaplan.

Metzudot: I.e., either *Metzudot David* or *Metzudot Tzion*, commentary on the Prophets and the Writings begun by R. David Altschuler and completed by his son R. Yechiel Hillel (18th century), based in general on the commentaries of *Rashi*, *Radak*, and *Ibn Ezra*.

Moadim Lesimcha: Analysis of laws and customs pertaining to the Jewish festivals by Rabbi Tuvia Freund. Seven vols., Jerusalem, 2002-2008.

Mordechai: Legal commentary on the Talmud by R. Mordechai ben Hillel, a leading halachic authority in Germany during the period after the Tosafists. Printed in standard editions of the Talmud.

Nedarim: Talmudic tractate discussing oaths.

Onkelus: An Aramaic translation of the Torah authored by Onkelus (2nd century C.E.), a proselyte of Roman origin, under the guidance of Rabbi Eliezer and Rabbi Yehoshua. Rashi (*Kiddushin* 49a, s.v. *harei zeh mecharef*) says of him that although his translation contains explanatory comments he "did not add anything to the Torah…because it was all given at Mount Sinai. It was subsequently forgotten and he restated it, as recounted in Tractate *Megillah* (3a)."

Or Hachaim: Commentary on the Torah by R. Chaim ibn Attar (1696-1743). First published in Venice, 1742.

Orach Chaim: See *Shulchan Aruch*.

Or Hatorah: Chasidic discourses on Scripture by R. Menachem Mendel of Lubavitch, author of *Tzemach Tzedek*. Berditchev, 1913; Brooklyn, NY, 1950 and on.

Or L'Arbaah Asar, 5666: Chasidic discourse delivered by Rabbi Shalom DovBer

Schneersohn, fifth Lubavitcher Rebbe, on Shabbat Hagadol, 5666 (1906).

Or Zarua: Halachic work and Talmudic commentary by R. Yitzchak of Vienna (c. 1200-1270). Zhitomir, 1862.

Orchot Chaim: Commentary on the Passover Haggadah by Rabbi Aharon HaLevi of Barcelona, also known by the acronym Ra'ah (1235-c. 1290). His commentary on the Passover Haggadah appears in *Haggadat Torat Chaim*.

Otzar Minhagei Chabad: Compilation of customs and directives of the Chabad Rebbes and Chasidim, by Rabbi Yehoshua Mondshine. Two vols., Jerusalem, 1995-96.

Pardes Eliezer: Sources for customs pertaining to Jewish festivals, researched and compiled by *Kollel Damesek Eliezer*, headed by Rabbi Eliezer Kestenbaum. New York, 2000.

Pesach Me'ubin: Passover Haggadah including the laws of Passover by Rabbi Chaim Benveniste. Venice, 1692.

Pesachim: Talmudic tractate discussing the Passover laws.

Pesikta d'Rav Kahana: Early Midrash on the Torah portions and the *Haftarot* read on special Shabbatot throughout the year. Published by Shlomo Buber in Lyck, 1868.

Pesikta Rabbati: A small book on the Festivals, containing aphorisms of Talmudic Sages arranged in a manner similar to *Midrash Rabbah*. The *Yalkut Shimoni* quotes certain aphorisms from the *Pesikta*.

Pesikta Zutrata: A Midrash on the Torah and the *Megillot* by Rabbenu Tovia bar Eliezer. Vilna, 1880.

Pirkei Avot (Kehot): Bilingual Hebrew/English edition of Ethics of the Fathers, with commentary anthologized from classic commentators and the Chasidic Masters. Brooklyn, NY, 2009.

Pirkei d'Rabbi Eliezer: A Midrash authored by the Mishnaic Sage, R. Eliezer ben Horkenus, also known as R. Eliezer Hagadol. "The earliest of all Tannaic treatises, revealed and famous in the era of our authoritative rabbis and mystical Kabbalists, the Rishonim, who used and benefited from its light" (from the title page).

Pirush Kadmon: Commentary on the Passover Haggadah by an unknown author, published in *Haggadat Torat Chaim*. Many of the early commentators, such as *Rashbam*, draw heavily from this commentary.

Pri Chadash: Halachic commentary on *Shulchan Aruch* by Rabbi Chezkiah de Silva (1659-1698). Amsterdam, 1592. Also printed in all standard editions of *Shulchan Aruch*.

Pri Etz Chaim: A compilation of the *Arizal's* mystical rituals pertaining to prayer, recorded by R. Chaim Vital and arranged in the present order by the Kabbalist R. Meir Popporos (1624-1662).

Pri Megadim: A threefold commentary on the super-commentaries on the *Shulchan Aruch*: the first on *Orach Chaim*, entitled *Mishbetzot Zahav* on *Turei Zahav*; another entitled *Eshel Avraham*, on *Magen Avraham;* and a third, *Siftei Daat*, on *Siftei Kohen*. Authored by Rabbi Yosef ben Meir Teomim (1727-1792), it was published in Berlin, 1771. Later printed in all standard editions of *Shulchan Aruch*.

Raavan: Acronym for "Rabbi Avraham ben Nattan," a Provençal rabbi and scholar born and educated in the second half of the twelfth century, probably at Lunel, Languedoc. It is for this reason that he is sometimes also called

HaYarchi ("of Lunel") since the Hebrew *yare'ach* is the equivalent of the French *lune*. Author of a commentary on the Haggadah, published in *Haggadat Torat Chaim*. Author also of *Sefer HaManhig*, in which he describes details of customs that he witnessed adhered to by the Jews of Europe.

Rabbenu Bachaye: *Dayan* and preacher in Saragossa, Spain (c. 12th century). Author of a commentary on the Torah with many Kabbalistic concepts, first published in Naples, 1492.

Rabbenu Manoach: Rabbenu Manoach ben Yaakov was a French Talmudist, who lived in Lunel in the second half of the thirteenth century, briefly residing in Narbonne. He was a student of the works of *Rambam, and wrote a commentary on the latter's *Mishneh Torah*, which is quoted in *Shaarei Tziyon* under the title *Sefer HaManoach*, and in *Korei HaDorot*, under the title *Sefer HaMenucha*. It was printed at Constantinople in 1518.

Rabbi Dovber of Lubavitch: Second leader of Chabad (1774-1828), son and successor of R. Schneur Zalman of Liadi, founder of the Chabad Movement.

Rabbi Dovber of Mezritch: Disciple of R. Yisrael Baal Shem Tov, and second leader of the Chasidic Movement (d. 1772).

Rabbi Menachem Mendel of Lubavitch: Third leader of Chabad (1789-1866), son-in-law and successor of Rabbi Dovber of Lubavitch; grandson of R. Schneur Zalman of Liadi. Author of numerous works, including the *Tzemach Tzedek* responsa, *Derech Mitzvotecha*, *Or Hatorah* and *Sefer Hachakirah*.

Rabbi Menachem M. Schneerson, the Lubavitcher Rebbe: Seventh leader of Chabad (1902-1994), son-in-law and successor of Rabbi Yosef Yitzchak of Lubavitch. Author of numerous works: See *Haggadah Shel Pesach with Commentary*; *Hayom Yom*; *Igrot Kodesh*; *Likkutei Sichot*; *Sefer Hamaamarim*; *Sefer

Hasichot; *Torat Menachem*.

Rabbi Mordechai Ettinger: Rabbi Mordechai Zev Ettinger of Lemberg (d. 1863). Brother-in-law of R. Yosef Shaul Natansohn, with whom he studied assiduously and authored numerous works.

Rabbi Moshe Chagiz: Talmudic scholar, Kabbalist, and author (1671-c. 1750). He was one of the most prominent and influential Jewish leaders in 17th-century Amsterdam. Author of numerous works, including *Lekket Hakemach* commentary on the *Shulchan Aruch (Orach Chaim* and *Yoreh Deah*—Amsterdam, 1697 and 1707; *Even Ha'ezer*—Hamburg, 1711 and 1715).

Rabbi Shalom DovBer of Lubavitch: Fifth leader of Chabad (1861-1920), son and successor of R. Shmuel Schneersohn.

Rabbi Shlomo Alkabetz: Kabbalist and poet (Thessaloniki, c. 1500 - Safed, 1580) perhaps best known for his composition of the song *Lecha Dodi*; although sources differ as to when he wrote it (1529, 1540 and 1571 have all been suggested). His numerous works include *Brit HaLevi*, a Kabbalistic commentary on the Passover Haggadah. Lemberg, 1863.

Rabbi Shlomo Kluger: Rabbi in many communities but primarily at Brody, where he held the offices of head of the rabbinical court and preacher for more than fifty years. A prolific author, he wrote 160 volumes (1783-1869). He authored a commentary on the Passover Haggadah called *Ma'aseh Yedei Yotzer*. Lemberg, 1863.

Rabbi Shmuel of Lubavitch: Fourth leader of Chabad (1834-1882), son and successor of R. Menachem Mendel Schneersohn, author of *Tzemach Tzedek*.

Rabbi Shneur Zalman of Liadi: Founder and leader of Chabad Chasidism, known as the Rav (Rabbi), and among Chasidim as the *Alter

Rebbe (Old Rabbi) (1745-1812). Author of *Likkutei Amarim Tanya*; an authoritative revision of *Shulchan Aruch*; *Torah Or*; and *Likkutei Torah*, among others. A detailed biography in English titled *Rabbi Schneur Zalman of Liadi* was published by Kehot (1969; 2002).

Rabbi Yechiel ben Asher: Elder brother of Rabbi Yaakov, author of the *Tur. R. Yechiel was a rabbi of a community in Spain, as was another brother, R. Yehudah. Their father was Rabbenu Asher ben Yechiel, known as the *Rosh.

Rabbi Yehudah ben Yakar: A Kabbalist (c. 1150-c. 1225) who was active in Spain and influenced many disciples, the most famous of which was *Ramban. Author of a commentary on the prayers and the Passover Haggadah, called *Mayan Ganim* (Jerusalem, 1979).

Rabbi Yosef Yitzchak of Lubavitch: Sixth leader of Chabad (1880-1950), son and successor of R. Shalom DovBer Schneerson.

Radak: Acronym for "R. David Kimchi" of Provence (1157-1236), author of a most important commentary on Scripture, explaining the precise meaning of the verses. Publishing of this work began in Venice, 1517.

Rambam: Acronym for "R. Moshe ben Maimon" (1135-1204), also known as Maimonides. Regarded as one of Judaism's foremost Torah authorities, he authored, among other works, *Mishneh Torah*, a phenomenal redaction of the laws of the Talmud.

Ramban: Acronym for "R. Moshe ben Nachman" (1194–1270), also known as Nachmanides. Kabbalist and author, he composed numerous works, including a commentary on the Five Books of Moses, the Talmud, *Milchamot Hashem*, *Sefer Hagemul*, *Sefer Havikuach*, and *Sefer Hageulah*.

Ran: Acronym for "Rabbenu Nissim" ben Reuven of Gerona (1310–c. 1375). Author of a commentary on R. Yitzchak Alfasi's compendium of the Talmud. Ran also wrote commentaries on eleven Talmudic tractates, including one on *Nedarim*, which appears side by side with *Rashi's in most editions of the Talmud.

Rashbatz: Acronym for "Rabbi Shimon ben Tzemach Duran" (1361-1444), a rabbinical authority, student of philosophy, astronomy, mathematics, and especially of medicine, which he practiced for a number of years in Palma (de Majorca). He wrote commentaries on several tractates of the Mishnah and the *Talmud and on the halachic work by *Rif. One of his works, *Yavin Shemuah*, contains his *Maamar Chametz,* precepts concerning *chametz* and matzah, as well as his commentary on the Passover Haggadah. Livorno, 1744.

Rashbam: Acronym for "R. Shmuel ben Meir" (1085-1174). A grandson of Rashi, he authored a commentary on Scripture and the Talmud. In certain sections of the Talmud where Rashi's commentary is unavailable, Rashbam's is substituted. Author of a commentary on the Passover Haggadah, published in *Haggadat Torat Chaim*.

Rashi: Acronym for "R. Shlomo Yitzchaki" (i.e., son of Yitzchak), who lived in Troyes, France and Worms, Germany (1040-1105). His commentary is printed in practically all editions of the Torah and Talmud, and is the subject of some two hundred commentators. Rashi's commentary on the Passover Haggadah appears in *Haggadat Torat Chaim*.

Rav Hai Gaon: Rabbi Hai ben Sherira (939-1038) was a medieval Jewish theologian, rabbi, and scholar, who served as Gaon of the Talmudic academy of Pumbedita during the early 11th century. He received his Talmudic education from his father, Rav Sherira ben Chaninah, and in his forty-fourth year joined his father's Rabbinical Court, and with him delivered many joint decisions. Rav Hai Gaon is known primarily for his numerous responsa, in which he rules on issues affecting the social and religious life of the Diaspora. His legal works include: *Hamekach VehaMimkar; Sefer Hamashkon; Mishpetei Hatannaim*—all published together (Venice, 1604), and *Mishpetei Shevuot* (Venice, 1602; Altona, 1782).

Rav Saadiah Gaon: Rabbi Saadiah ben Yosef Gaon (Egypt, 882/892 - Baghdad, 942) was a prominent rabbi, Jewish philosopher, and exegete of the Geonic period. A prolific author, his works include *HaEmunot VeHaDeot*, the first systematic attempt to synthesize the Jewish tradition with philosophical teachings (Constantinople, 1562); *Siddur Saadiah Gaon*, the earliest surviving attempt to transcribe the weekly ritual of Jewish prayers for weekdays, Sabbaths, and festivals, first published from manuscripts in Jerusalem, 1941.

Rav Tzemach Gaon: Rabbi Tzemach ben Chaim, Gaon of Sura from 889 to 895, is known especially through the reply which he made to the inquiry of the Kairwanites regarding Eldad Hadani. This responsum, which appeared in part in the first edition of the *Shalshelet Hakabbalah* (Venice, 1480), was republished as completely as possible in *Eldad Hadani* (Pressburg, 1891). The authorship of responsa in *Chemdah Genuzah* (Jerusalem, 1863; Nos. 58-61, 111-131) has also been ascribed to Rav Tzemach Gaon.

Rema: Acronym for "Rabbi Moses Isserles" of Cracow, Poland (1530-1572). Author of many works and recognized as the pre-eminent halachic authority throughout the Ashkenazic community. Most famous are his Ashkenazic annotations to R. Yosef Karo's *Shulchan Aruch*, which transformed this predominantly Sephardic work into a universal Code of Jewish Law. He was well-versed in Jewish philosophy and Kabbalah, and authored a commentary on the *Zohar*.

Responsa Bar Levai: Halachic responsa by Rabbi Meshullam Yissachar Hurwitz. Lemberg, 1861-1872.

Responsa Chatam Sofer: See *Chatam Sofer.*

Responsa of Radvaz: Halachic responsa by R. David ben Zimra (1479-1573).

Responsa of Rashba: With thousands of responsa, Rashba, acronym for "Rabbi Shlomo ben Ideret" (Barcelona, 1235-1310) established his reputation as one of the most, if not the most prolific of the *Poskim* (respondents to questions of Jewish Law). First printed in Rome, 1469-72.

Rif: Acronym for "Rabbenu Yitzchak al-Fasi" (1013-1103), also known as Alfasi, Arabic for "of Fes," the place of his birth and where he spent most of his life. A Talmudist and authority in matters of Jewish law, he is best known for his legal code *Sefer Hahalachot*, which extracts all the pertinent legal decisions from the majority of the Talmudic tractates and considered the first fundamental work in halachic literature. This work is printed in all comprehensive editions of the Talmud.

Ritva: Acronym for "R. Yom Tov ben Avraham Ishbili" (1248-1330), rabbi of Seville, Spain, author of a major commentary on the Talmud. His commentary on the Passover Haggadah is published in *Haggadat Torat Chaim.*

Rosh: Acronym for "Rabbenu Asher" ben Yechiel (1250 or 1259-1327), sometimes called *Asheri*, an eminent rabbi and Talmudist best known for his abstract of Talmudic law, which has been printed with almost every edition of the Talmud since its publication. This work records the final, practical ruling of the law, leaving out the Talmud's lengthy discussions. This work was so important in Jewish law that R. Yosef Karo included it together with *Rambam* and *Rif* as one of the three major decisors in determining the final ruling in his *Shulchan Aruch*. Rabbenu Asher had eight sons, of whom the most prominent are R. Yehudah and R. Yaacov, author of the *Tur.*

Rosh Hashanah: Talmudic tractate

discussing the laws of the Rosh Hashanah festival and the Jewish calendar.

Sanhedrin: Talmudic tractate discussing laws concerning the High Court of old in Jerusalem. Also contains a chapter on the future Messianic era.

Sefer Ha'arachim: Encyclopedia of topics discussed in Chasidus, gathered from the writings of seven generations of Chabad Rebbes (Brooklyn, 1970 and on).

Sefer Hachinuch: Anonymous work on the 613 *mitzvot*, following their order in the Torah, believed to be authored by R. Aharon of Barcelona. Venice, 1523.

Sefer Halikkutim: Collection of concepts explained in Chasidic teachings, culled from the works of R. Menachem Mendel of Lubavitch, author of *Tzemach Tzedek*. Arranged in encyclopedic form according to the *alef-bet*, it also contains references to the works of the other Chabad Rebbes for the respective topics. Twenty-two vols. Brooklyn, NY, 1977-84.

Sefer Halikkutim (Arizal): Kabbalistic commentary on the verses of the Torah; fourth of the eight *She'arim* ("Gates") collectively known as *Eitz Chaim*—a compilation of the *Arizal's Kabbalistic teachings, by his primary disciple and exponent, Rabbi Chaim Vital (1543-1620). Jerusalem, 1863.

Sefer Hamaamarim 5643-5680: Set of Chasidic discourses delivered by R. Shalom DovBer Schneersohn, fifth Lubavitcher Rebbe, between the years 5643 and 5680 (1883-1920), the years of his leadership; twenty-seven vols. Brooklyn, NY, 1970-2003.

Sefer Hamaamarim 5680-5710: Set of Chasidic discourses delivered by R. Yosef Yitzchak Schneersohn, sixth Lubavitcher Rebbe, between the years 5680-5710 (1920-1950), the years of his leadership; seventeen vols. Brooklyn, NY, 1951-2010.

Sefer Hamaamarim 5735: Chasidic discourses delivered by the Lubavitcher Rebbe, R. Menachem M. Schneerson, during the year 5735 (1974-75). Brooklyn, NY, 1989.

Sefer Ha'orah: Halachic work attributed to *Rashi. Published by Shlomo Buber, Lemberg, 1905.

Sefer HaPardes: Halachic rulings, customs, commentary on the prayers and the order of the Torah portions, by R. Shlomo Yitzchaki (see *Rashi*). Venice, 1519.

Sefer Hasichot 5680-5710: Talks delivered by R. Yosef Yitzchak Schneersohn, sixth Lubavitcher Rebbe, between the years 5680 and 5710 (1920-50). Brooklyn, NY, 1947-2001.

Sefer Hasichot 5747-5752: Talks delivered by the Lubavitcher Rebbe, R. Menachem M. Schneerson, between the years 5747 and 5752 (1986-1992). Brooklyn, NY, 1989-2010.

Sforno: Commentary on the Torah by Italian scholar R. Ovadiah Sforno (c. 1470-1550), author of a major commentary on the Chumash.

Shaar Hakollel: Sources and reasons pertaining to the liturgical text and customs found in the Siddur of Rabbi Schneur Zalman of Liadi, by Rabbi Avraham David Lavut. Vilna, 1896.

Shabbat: Talmudic tractate discussing the laws of Shabbat.

Shaloh: Monumental work by R. Yeshaya HaLevi Horowitz (1558-1628), chief rabbi of Prague. An acronym for *Shnei Luchot Habrit*, *Shelah* contains explanations and commentaries on the profound aspects of the Torah, *mitzvot*, the festivals, Jewish customs and the fundamental beliefs of Judaism, including basic instruction in Kabbalah. First published in Amsterdam, 1648.

Shemot Rabbah: See *Midrash Rabbah*.

Shevach Pesach: Commentary on the Passover Haggadah by Rabbi Yishmael HaKohen. Livorno, 1790.

Shibolei Haleket: Commentary on the Passover Haggadah by Rabbenu Tzidkiyahu ben Avraham, including original commentary by the author as well as a review of earlier commentators. Vilna, 1886.

Shir Hashirim Rabbah: See *Midrash Rabbah*.

Shiurei Torah: A Halachic work defining Biblical measurements in contemporary terms, by Rabbi Avraham Chaim Noeh (1890-1954). Jerusalem, 1943.

Shulchan Aruch: Code of Jewish Law by R. Yosef Karo (1488-1575), one of the foremost authorities on Jewish law. Consisting of four parts, *Orach Chaim, Yoreh Deah, Choshen Mishpat,* and *Even Ha'ezer*, it later became the standard work of Jewish law for all Jews. First published in Venice, 1564.

Shulchan Aruch HaRav: Code of Jewish law by R. Schneur Zalman of Liadi, first Rebbe of Chabad, following the structure of the **Tur* and **Shulchan Aruch*, but including reasons for the laws as well as decisions by later halachic authorities. Shklov, 1814; Brooklyn, NY, 1960-68; revised edition, Brooklyn, NY, 1999-2008.

Sichot Kodesh: Unedited talks of the Lubavitcher Rebbe, R. Menachem M. Schneerson, delivered between the years 5725 and 5741 (1964-1981).

Siddur HaArizal: See *Siddur of Rabbi Shabbetai.*

Siddur Kol Bo: Prayer book with a contemporary Hebrew commentary, laws, and customs, by Rabbi Yitzchak Isaac Tirna. Vilna, 1905.

Siddur Kol Yaakov: Prayer book following

the opinion of the **Arizal, as published by Rabbi Yaakov Koppel Lipshitz, with Kabbalistic commentary. Slavita, 1804.

Siddur of Rabbi Shabbetai: Order of prayers for the entire year according to the **Arizal. Includes annotations by Rabbi Shabbetai of Rashkow, and certain sections by Rabbi Yisrael Baal Shem Tov. Koretz, 1794.

Siddur Rav Amram Gaon: The oldest surviving prayer book, by R. Amram Gaon (d. c. 875 C.E.). First published in Warsaw, 1865.

Siddur Shaar Hashamayim: Prayer book with a commentary by R. Isaiah Horowitz, author of *Shnei Luchot Habrit* (see *Shaloh*). Amsterdam, 1717.

Siddur Shaloh: See *Siddur Shaar Hashamayim.*

Siddur Tefillah L'Moshe: Prayer book with Kabbalistic commentary by R. Moshe Cordovero of Safed (1522-1570). Przemyśl, 1892.

Siddur Yaavetz: Comprehensive prayer book with commentary, grammatical notes, ritual laws, and various treatises. Also called *Amudei Shamayim*. Compiled by Rabbi "Yaakov ben Tzvi" (Yaavetz), also known as Rabbi Yaakov of Emden (1697-1776). Altona, 1745-48. [Some later popular editions include additions by the publishers].

Sifrei: Halachic Midrash on Numbers and Deuteronomy, authored by the Talmudic sage Rav. Often quoted in the Talmud.

Simchat Haregel: See *Chida.*

Sotah: Talmudic tractate discussing the law of the suspected adulteress.

Sukkah: Talmudic tractate discussing the festival of Sukkot and its laws.

Taamei Haminhagim: Compilation of

sources and reasons for Jewish customs, by R. Avraham Yitzchak Sperling. Jerusalem, 1957.

Taanit: Talmudic tractate discussing fast days.

Talmud: The embodiment of the Oral Law. Following the codification of the Mishnah by R. Yehudah HaNassi, c. 150 C.E.; later discussions, known as the Talmud, were redacted in two parts. The more popular Babylonian Talmud was compiled by Rav Ashi and Ravina (about the end of the 5th century C.E.). The Jerusalem Talmud was compiled by R. Yochanan bar Nappacha (about the end of the 3rd century C.E.).

Tamid: Mishnaic tractate discussing the rules for the daily service in the Holy Temple.

Tanchuma: See *Midrash Tanchuma.*

Tanya: Philosophical magnum opus by Rabbi Schneur Zalman of Liadi, in which the principles of Chabad are expounded. The name is derived from the initial word of this work. Also called *Likkutei Amarim*, this work was first published in Slavita, 1797, and has seen over 5,000 editions. See *Shulchan Aruch HaRav.*

Targum Yonatan: An Aramaic translation/commentary on the Torah authored by Yonatan ben Uziel (circa 50 C.E.), a disciple of Hillel the Elder. The Talmud (*Megillah* 3b) relates that upon concluding his translation of the Prophets, a storm of criticism arose that rocked the land of Israel. A Heavenly voice rang out: "Who revealed My secrets to mankind?" Whereupon Yonatan ben Uziel arose and proclaimed, "It was I that revealed Your secrets. It is revealed and known before You that I did not do it for my own honor nor for that of my father's house, but for Your honor, in order that disputes should not multiply in Israel!" He wished to continue and translate the Writings too, but a Heavenly voice called out, "Enough!"

Taz: Acronym for "*Turei Zahav*"; major commentary on *Shulchan Aruch* by R. David HaLevi Segal of Cracow (1586-1667).

Teshuvot HaGeonim: *Responsa* of the Geonim of Babylonia. Examples of responsa collections are: *Halachot Pesukot min HaGeonim*—Constantinople, 1516; *Sheelot UTeshuvot MehaGeonim*—Constantinople, 1575; *Shaarei Tzedek*—Salonica, 1792; *Teshuvot HaGeonim*—Lyck, 1864; *Teshuvot HaGeonim*—Livorno, 1869; *Shaarei Teshuvah HaShalem*—New York, 1946; *Teshuvot Geonei Mizrach UMaarav*—Berlin, 1888; *Otzar HaGeonim*—Haifa, 1928; *Teshuvot HaGeonim*—Jerusalem, 1927 (second volume 1942).

Tikkunei Zohar: A work of seventy chapters on the first word of the Torah, by the school of Rabbi Shimon bar Yochai (c. 120 C.E.). First printed in Mantua, 1558, *Tikkunei Zohar* contains some of the most important discussions in Kabbalah, and is essential for understanding the **Zohar.*

The Rebbe's Haggadah: Commentary on the Passover Haggadah by the Lubavitcher Rebbe, Rabbi Menachem M. Schneerson. Officially entitled *Haggadah shel Pesach im Likkutei Taamim u'Minhagim*, it is culled from the full array of our classical sources—ranging from Bible, Talmud, Midrashim and the legal codes to more recent writings, covering legal and exegetical texts, Kabbalah and Chasidic works—complemented with original insights and analytic comments by the Rebbe himself. The commentary focuses primarily on explicating the essential meaning of the Haggadah's contents, and to clarify such passages, procedures or customs which may appear somehow problematic. The Rebbe's Haggadah is a critically acclaimed classic, and continues to enlighten and inspire countless students with greater understanding and appreciation of Pesach. First published in Brooklyn, NY, in 1946, a newly-set, revised edition appeared in 2009.

The Torah (Kehot): Translation/commentary of the Torah, which weaves Rashi's commentary—as explained according to the elucidations of the Lubavitcher Rebbe, Rabbi Menachem M. Schneerson—together with the translation of the Torah text. Also contains Chasidic commentary from the works of Chabad Chasidus. *Bereishit*, 2008; *Shemot*, 2006; *Bemidbar*, 2004; Brooklyn, NY.

Tola'at Yaakov: Kabbalistic commentary on the prayers by Rabbi Meir ibn Gabbai. Constantinople, 1560.

Toldot Esther: Commentary on the *Sefer Haminhagim* of Rabbi Yitzchak Isaac Tirna, by Rabbi Shlomo Tzvi Schick. Munkatch, 1888.

Torah Or: Chasidic discourses elucidating major themes of the weekly Torah portion and festivals, by R. Schneur Zalman of Liadi. Published by his grandson, R. Menachem Mendel of Lubavitch, author of *Tzemach Tzedek*. Kopust, 1836; Munich, 1948; Brooklyn, NY, 1955; 1991. See *Likkutei Torah*.

Torah Shleimah: Extensive commentary on the Written Law culled from all major sources of the Oral Law, by Rabbi Menachem Kasher. Jerusalem / New York, 1927-1978.

Torah Temimah: Compilation of Talmudic and Midrashic sayings on the Torah, with commentary, by Rabbi Boruch Epstein. Vilna, 1901.

Torat Menachem—Hitvaaduyot: Unedited talks of the Lubavitcher Rebbe, R. Menachem M. Schneerson, delivered between the years 5710-5724 and 5742-5752; eighty-four vols.

Torat Menachem—Reshimat Hayoman: Handwritten diary by the Lubavitcher Rebbe, R. Menachem M. Schneerson, published posthumously by Kehot Publication Society, Brooklyn, NY, 2006.

Torat Menachem—Sefer Hamaamarim Melukat: Chasidic discourses delivered and edited by the Lubavitcher Rebbe, Rabbi

Menachem M. Schneerson, during the course of his leadership 5711-5752 (1951-1992). Four vols., Brooklyn, NY, 2002.

Torat Shmuel 5626-5641: Set of Chasidic discourses delivered by R. Shmuel Schneersohn, fourth Lubavitcher Rebbe, between 5626-5641 (1866-1881), the years of his leadership [5626-5643 (1866-1882)]; twenty-three vols.

Tosefta: Lit., "supplement." Second compilation of Oral Law from the period of the Mishnah, as a supplement to the Mishnah, by R. Chiya and R. Oshaya (c. 230 C.E.).

Tosfot: A dialectic commentary on the Talmud, generally printed opposite the commentary of Rashi, largely the product of Rashi's students and grandsons (c. 1100-1171).

Tosfot Anshei Shem: Compilation from numerous classic commentaries on the Mishnaic Orders of *Zeraim* and *Taharot* by Rabbi Yehudah Leib Friedland, printed in the standard *"Yachin U'Boaz" Mishnayot*.

Tosfot Yom Tov: Important commentary on the Mishnah by R. Yom Tov Lipmann Heller. Prague, 1614-17.

Tur: Two works were authored by R. Yaakov ben Asher. One, a code of Jewish law—called *Arbaah Turim*—was first published in Piove di Sacco, 1475. The other, a commentary on the Torah called *Baal Haturim*, first appeared in Constantinople, 1514.

Vayikra Rabbah: See *Midrash Rabbah*.

Vayomer Yehoshua 5720: Chasidic discourse delivered by the Lubavitcher Rebbe, Rabbi Menachem M. Schneerson, on the second night of Pesach, 5720 (1960).

Vilna Gaon: Colloquial for R. Eliyahu ben Shlomo Zalman of Vilna (1720-1797), commonly known by the initials of the Hebrew words "HaGaon Reb Eliyahu"—HaGRA. Foremost leader of non-Chasidic world Jewry, and also referred to in Hebrew as *Hagaon Hachasid MiVilna*, "the saintly genius from Vilna."

V'kacha 5637: Series of discourses delivered by Rabbi Shmuel Schneersohn, fourth Lubavitcher Rebbe, during the year 5637 (1877), named for its opening word.

Yaavetz: See *Siddur Yaavetz*.

Yalkut Reuveni: A compilation culled from discourses, Midrashim and Kabbalistic works on the Torah, by R. Avraham Reuven Katz. Prague, 5420 (1660).

Yalkut Menachem: Commentary on the Passover Haggadah by Rabbi Menachem Tzvi Taksin. Piotrkow, 1909.

Yalkut Shimoni: One of the most popular early collections of Midrashic material, compiled by R. Shimon Ashkenazi HaDarshan, a preacher in Frankfurt (c. 1260). Many Midrashim are known only because they are cited in this work, first published in Salonika, 1521-27.

Yehudah Yaaleh: Halachic responsa by Rabbi Yehudah Assad. Lemberg, 1873; Pressburg, 1880.

Yevamot: Talmudic tractate discussing levirate marriage.

Yoma: Talmudic tractate discussing the laws of Yom Kippur and the Yom Kippur service in the *Beit Hamikdash*.

Yom Tov Shel Rosh Hashanah, 5666: Series of discourses delivered by Rabbi Shalom DovBer Schneersohn, fifth Lubavitcher Rebbe, during the years 5666-7 (1905-7), named for its opening words.

Zohar: Basic work of Kabbalah compiled by the Mishnaic sage, R. Shimon Bar Yochai, in Hebrew and Aramaic as a commentary on the Torah.

Zohar Chadash: Additions to the *Zohar*, *Midrash Hane'elam* and *Tikkunei Zohar*. Includes *Zohar* on Song of Songs, Lamentations and Midrash Rut.

INDEX

COLOPHON

Fonts: English Haggadah: **Stone Informal**
Hebrew Haggadah: **Vilna SO** (custom typeface by Schmul Osher Begun)
Titles: **Trajan**; Main Commentary: **Minion**; Notes & Insights: **Verlag Light**
Paper stock: 100gsm IKPP woodfree. Color: PMS 207 U
Printed in China

Cover design, book layout and original artwork by **Spotlight Design**

מוקדש ע"י

ר' **חנן אהרן** וזוגתו מרת **אסתר חייקא**

לזכות בני משפחתם

מרת **רחל חוה** ובעלה **בנימין דוד שלום**

באבינס

בנימין עזרא, טובי' שמואל וירדנה ציפי

ה' עליהם יחיו

גלובינסקי

טאראנטא, קאנאדא

～ つ ℃ ～

Dedicated by
Claire & Howard Glowinsky
in honor of their children
Rachel Hailey & Benjamin David Shalom
Babins
Benjamin Ezra, Samuel Trevor and **Jordana Zoe**
Glowinsky

Toronto, Canada

～ つ ℃ ～

This work was originally dedicated
on the occasion of Sam's Bar Mitzvah,
Shabbat Chazon, 6 Menachem-Av 5771

הוצאת ספרים
קרני הוד תורה
ליובאוויטש